NOTHING SEEMED
IMPOSSIBLE

NOTHING SEEMED IMPOSSIBLE

William C. Ralston and Early San Francisco

By David Lavender

Foreword by J. E. Wallace Sterling

WESTERN BIOGRAPHY SERIES

AMERICAN WEST PUBLISHING COMPANY
PALO ALTO—CALIFORNIA

OTHER BOOKS IN
THE WESTERN BIOGRAPHY SERIES

No Tears for the General
(A biography of General Alfred Sully by Langdon Sully)

Hippocrates in a Red Vest
(A biography of Dr. Michael Beshoar by Barron B. Beshoar)

My Dear Wister: The Frederic Remington—Owen Wister Letters
(A study of a literary friendship by Ben M. Vorpahl)

Journeys to the Far North
(An account of half a century's travels to the Arctic by naturalist Olaus J. Murie)

Library of Congress Cataloging in Publication Data

Lavender, David Sievert, 1910–
   Nothing seemed impossible.

   (Western biography series)
   Bibliography: p.
   Includes index.
   1. Ralston, William Chapman, 1826–1875.
2. Bankers—San Francisco. I. Title.
HG2463.R34L38   332.1'092'4 [B]   75-6321
ISBN 0-910118-64-7

FIRST EDITION

Table of Contents

Foreword

It was the personal interest that Charles de Bretteville, board chairman of The Bank of California, took in the Ralston letters, which led first to an evaluation of their historical value and second to their use in the preparation and publication of this volume. A salute, therefore, to Mr. de Bretteville and the bank!

The letters and correspondence of William C. Ralston cover a period of approximately twenty-five years (1850–1875) with most of them belonging to the last fifteen years of that period. There are four or five times as many letters to Mr. Ralston as there are from him to others. Chronologically they are distributed unevenly through those years with more than a few time gaps. But they provide valuable information about Mr. Ralston himself and his many-faceted business transactions; they have also provided for the author important leads to other relevant historical sources.

After early experience as a shipping clerk for commerce along the Mississippi River, and involvement in enterprises for shortcut routes to the Pacific across Panama and Nicaragua, Mr. Ralston heard and responded to the call of the West and settled in San Francisco. For that city, as well as for the state of California, he became a wholehearted booster. He had pride in their development and faith in their future—a pride and faith which seldom winced and never failed, despite more than a few disappointments and adversities. This pride and faith were reflected in his entertaining of visitors—which he himself greatly enjoyed —and in his sending gifts of California produce to friends, acquaintances, and business associates in the United States and overseas.

The reader will discover for himself the extraordinary range, variety, and complexity of Mr. Ralston's entrepreneurial ventures—shipping, railways, insurance, mining, manufacturing, real estate, viticulture, the theater, and more—particularly the founding of The Bank of California in 1864. Need for financing of his enterprises led to an overseas association with The Oriental Bank of London (and indeed with the House of Rothschild, an association which the bank still maintains!), and through that bank to association with Japan, following that country's new westward orientation after 1867.

Mr. Ralston's business career was begun and lived out during venturesome, hurly-burly days when confidence in the potential resources of the country's Pacific slope went far beyond mere optimism. It was an era when bold men were not averse to taking giant business risks and on occasion the law and some legislators into their own hands for their own purposes; the names of such men—some well known, others less familiar—pepper the pages of this volume. Mr. Ralston, himself competitive, experienced the competition which such men could and did provide. He experienced the recession which struck San Francisco in 1869, a recession partially induced by the shifts in trade routes which followed the completion of the transcontinental railroad in May of that year; and toward the end of his life he felt the impact of the national economic slump of 1873.

Through that wheeling and dealing era, with its successes and failures, he seemed never to lose his ebullience. He loved life and lived it fully, not only in business but also in community endeavors and in a round of social affairs, typified in generous measure by his "mansion" near Belmont and the lavish entertainment it provided for his guests. His story, as recounted in this volume, reminds one of pioneer days and doings of more than a century ago, the beginnings of what is now a great city, and the early developments of what is now the most populous state in the Union. It is a story well told, and one to be remembered.

J. E. WALLACE STERLING

CONCERNING VALUES

Of necessity this book deals with figures—population, distances, the size of ships, mines, and factories, good round sums of money, and so on. These figures were, in their time, far larger than the dilutions of modern technology, exponential growth, and monetary inflation let them appear today.

The bulldozer, for instance, did not exist in the 1860s. The first railroad across the Sierra Nevada was constructed largely by Chinese coolies chipping rock away by hand and removing the excavated material with two-wheeled carts pulled either by themselves or by horses. Under such circumstances, what does a ton amount to?

Inanimate energy for propelling ships and mine machinery came primarily from steam. Steel was rare and expensive. As a result, machines were ponderous and inefficient, except in comparison to handpower. Thus a mill that could reduce one hundred tons of gold ore a day was a monster in 1870. Today it would be negligible.

In Ralston's day, people reached California only with difficulty. Even after the railroad had been opened in 1869, a transcontinental train trip consumed an uncomfortable week. Those factors considered, it was phenomenal for San Francisco's population to have soared from a few hundred in 1848 to 250,000 in 1875. Businessmen were dazzled accordingly and made their calculations with reckless optimism. Beguiled by today's figures, we look on their fever as being somewhat bland and childish, which it most definitely was not.

Equally startling changes have occurred in the value of the dollar. During the 1860s the skilled miners of the Comstock Lode, Nevada, were the highest-paid laborers in the world; they received $4.00 for a ten-hour day, six days a week. Many skilled workers today earn well over $4.00 an hour, plus time and a half for any excess above eight hours a day or forty hours a week. Dollars a hundred years ago of course bought much more than they do today. Moreover, taxes were light; the personal income tax did not exist except for a brief time during the Civil War. Thus to say merely that Ralston died owing $9.5 million in no way suggests the enormity of the sum.

A loose method of converting early California dollars into modern equivalents is to multiply by ten. This is not exact by any means; too many variables are involved. But it comes closer to conveying values than does the mere look of the figures on the printed page.

DAVID LAVENDER

ACKNOWLEDGMENTS

Chief among the many people at The Bank of California who made this book possible are Charles de Bretteville, chairman of the board and chief executive officer; Barbara Barton, librarian; and Hal F. Marks, curator of the Museum of Money of the American West.

Historical societies and libraries as usual lent aid without stint: the Bancroft Library, University of California at Berkeley, James Hart, director, and John Barr Tompkins and staff; the California State Library, California Section, Sacramento, Kenneth Pettitt, librarian, and staff; the Henry E. Huntington Library, San Marino, James Thorpe, director, Carey Bliss, Mary Isabel Fry, Janet Hawkins, and staff; the California Historical Society, San Francisco, J. S. Holliday, director, former librarian Peter Evans, Maude Swingle, and Jay Willar; the Oregon Historical Society, Thomas Vaughan, director, librarian Louis Flannery, and staff.

Historic photographs and illustrations were provided through the assistance of more archivists and librarians than could possibly be listed here. Some of those deserving special mention, however, are Alma Compton, Suzanne H. Gallup, and Peter Hanff of the Bancroft Library, Berkeley; Lee Burtis and Catherine Hoover of the California Historical Society, San Francisco; John L. Lochhead and John O. Sands of the Mariners Museum, Newport News; Matilda Dring of the San Francisco Maritime Museum; Irene Lichens of the Society of California Pioneers, San Francisco; and Merrilee A. Dowty of the Wells Fargo Bank History Room, San Francisco.

Individuals who gave generously of their time and knowledge include Ralston's granddaughter, Dorothy Page Buckingham of Los Angeles; Mrs. Homer D. Crotty of San Marino; W. N. Davis, Jr., chief of archives, California State Archives; Theo Dierks of Fairfax, California; Richard Dillon of the Sutro Library, San Francisco; Rita Hill and Janaloo Hill of Lordsburg, New Mexico, who provided information about vanished Ralston, New Mexico; Lowell Hilpert, geologist, U.S. Department of the Interior, Salt Lake City; Professor W. H. Hutchinson of California State College, Chico; Professor Doyce B. Nunis, Jr., who gave timely help in the matter of pictures; Jack D. Rittenhouse of Albuquerque, New Mexico; and Owen Sheffield of River Edge, New Jersey. Albert Shumati of San Francisco was notably generous in sharing his knowledge of the early days of his beloved city.

My wife, Mildred, not only helped with the research but also typed the manuscript—inestimable boons in both instances.

PROLOGUE

An End to Innocence

During the unseasonably hot weather that marred the last days of August, 1875, William C. Ralston, president of The Bank of California, died and was buried under extraordinary circumstances. He was forty-nine years old.

The sequence began on Thursday, August 26. That morning, stock jobbers deliberately forced down the market value of the Nevada mining shares that were the principal item of trade on the San Francisco Stock Exchange. Worry inside the exchange ballooned into panic outside. Soon frightened depositors were converging on The Bank of California, whose president had for some days been under sharp attack from certain sections of the San Francisco press.

Depositors' demands for gold coin—San Franciscans disdained paper money—soon exceeded the amounts that the beset organization could obtain from largely unsympathetic outside sources. Abruptly, at 2:35 P.M., twenty-five minutes before normal closing time, the leading financial institution west of the Mississippi River closed its doors. Except perhaps for certain manipulators who may have hoped for such an outcome, all San Francisco was stunned.

The next day Ralston confessed to his board of directors that he was $9.5 million in debt, much of it owed to The Bank of California. His assets were roughly $4.5 million. He stated passionately that, if he were given time, he could put his affairs and those of the bank back into order. The directors replied by demanding his resignation.

Leaving the bank, Ralston walked to a familiar swimming spot at North Beach. There, perspiring freely, he donned a bathing suit and struck out toward Alcatraz Island into icy currents, where the waters of San Francisco Bay funnel toward the Golden Gate and the Pacific. Men

11

aboard a nearby schooner soon saw that he was in trouble. Lowering a small boat, they laid hold of his unconscious body and pulled it ashore between the sites now occupied by Fisherman's Wharf and the Maritime Museum. While someone ran for a doctor, others tried clumsily to revive the banker with artificial respiration. The efforts failed. The doctor who appeared pronounced Ralston dead, and his body was taken by wagon to his town house on Pine Street.

The news spread swiftly. Unbelieving men, many of them Ralston's friends and business associates, hurried to his home. As they were milling about the sumptuous drawing room, various officials arrived, including the coroner, who selected a jury on the spot to inquire into the nature of the death. This jury, composed almost entirely of Ralston's intimate associates, heard such evidence as was presented, deliberated for ten minutes, and then returned a verdict of death by drowning. The insurance company that held a $68,000 policy on Ralston's life accepted the decision and paid his widow the sum due her. Many San Franciscans of the time, however—and some later historians—were convinced that the distraught banker, stripped of pride, position, and property, had committed suicide.

While the question was still on everyone's lips, an amazing crystallization of sentiment took place. Viewing the phenomenon with the detachment of a hundred miles' distance, an editorial writer for the Sacramento *Union* remarked that, if William Chapman Ralston had lived, he would have been execrated for the losses that the bank's closure threatened to bring to his depositors and to the city. Instead, his death transformed him overnight into a folk hero.

Funeral services were scheduled for eleven o'clock in the morning, August 30, at the Calvary Presbyterian Church near Union Square. Police made arrangements with care, for they expected that when the casket was moved from the church to the cemetery it would be followed by about eighteen hundred people—units of the National Guard, members of the Odd Fellows lodge of which Ralston had been a member, family friends, and employees of the various firms in which the banker had held a majority interest. Seldom have estimates been more awry.

Long before eleven o'clock Union Square was packed so densely with people that several fainted from the heat and the crowding. When the cortège left for the burying ground, the mourners in the square and others waiting in adjoining streets fell in behind. They formed a line that filled the avenue from curb to curb and reached for three miles. One reporter noted that it took the procession forty-two minutes to tread past a given point. Another estimated that fifty thousand people joined the march. If the figure is accurate, at least half of San Francisco's adult population was involved. Neither before nor since has an American municipality paid comparable homage to a businessman who throughout his career never held either a military or an elective political office.

The following Sunday the ministers of the city's leading churches devoted all or part of their sermons to eulogies of the departed. On the evening of September 8, twelve thousand people assembled in mass meetings to roar approval of resolutions condemning Ralston's detractors and expressing the city's sense of loss at his passing, even though it was evident by then that, had he lived, he might well have been the subject of criminal proceedings.

How does one account for emotionalism of such apparent perversity?

Controversy provided one element. Shortly before his death Ralston had been libelously besmirched by two of the city's newspapers. His fellow San Franciscans no doubt felt that through their demonstrations they were restoring perspective. The good that the banker had done, they were saying in effect, far outweighed his derelictions.

All true—and yet, from the hindsight of a hundred years, the explanation seems incomplete. Fifty thousand people marching spontaneously to a graveyard just for a sentimental redressing of the scales of justice? Surely something more was involved.

Context provides part of the answer. William Ralston and his fellows had just passed through a unique quarter of a century. During that period everything that a man desired had appeared attainable. One might have to work and scheme and fight, but that was excitement only, and in the end all would turn out well. For proof, consider the record. The United States had scarcely won the Southwest from Mexico when the gold that the Mexicans might have found was unearthed instead by Americans. Clearly the favor of providence was involved. Thinking so, tens of thousands of people flocked to this latest Golconda. Scores of millions of dollars in raw gold poured out of the Sierra, stimulating commerce and industry to such an extent that within a decade San Francisco had been transformed from a handful of huts called Yerba Buena into the nation's fourteenth city in population.

It was no will-o'-the-wisp. When California's own output of gold diminished, even richer strikes of precious metal were made across the mountains at the fabled Comstock Lode in what became Nevada. Prosperity surged back, faltered during the late 1860s, and then heated again with new discoveries of rich ore at unprecedented depths.

Beguiled by so lavish a background, men dreamed hugely. Why not connect the Pacific Coast to the rest of the United States by digging giant canals across the narrow waist of Central America and, additionally, by thrusting railroads over the western deserts and mountains? Why not create, in California's fertile central valleys, wheatfields, irrigation canals, and livestock ranches such as the world had never seen? As capital accumulated, men could build factories capable of exporting many goods, and with their ships they could seize the trade of the Orient.

Above all—and this thought intrigued Ralston particularly—why not use these ambitious plans for turning San Francisco into one of history's greatest cities?

There were no limits to possibility, only to boldness. It was California's age of naiveté.

Ralston's career mirrored the state's. Interruptions never lasted long. During the early rush to the West, he suffered disaster as a young owner of ships and as a shipping agent, but soon bounced back as a banker financing young industries, experimental vineyards, and troubled mines. As his, and California's, prosperity increased, he helped put together railroad, telegraph, and steamship companies, woolen mills, sugar refineries, cigar and furniture factories. He erected the West Coast's finest theater, played a significant part in revitalizing Japan's currency, and served as one of the first regents of the University of California. In his lavish city and country homes, he entertained up to a hundred guests at a time with the flair of a Medici prince—indeed, he was often compared to princes.

When the flow of Comstock ore slowed during the late 1860s, he and his bank teetered precariously. But the new discoveries of metal that saved San Francisco saved him, too. Instead of being sobered by the closeness of calamity, he plunged ahead more recklessly than ever. For the sake of his and San Francisco's material gain, he laid plans for removing Rincon Hill from land he owned south of Market Street—technology, it should be remembered, was more limited then than it is now—and thus add a prosperous new commercial zone to the metropolis. To his surprise he met stubborn resistance. Needing funds to combat the opposition, he sought a new fortune by developing supposed diamond mines in the western deserts, and in his zest fell victim to one of the most notorious swindles in American history. The experience left him undismayed. His next plan was to use a fine hotel as a magnet for drawing fashionable retail shops and brisk mercantile enterprises to his land beyond Market Street. To that end he poured millions of dollars into erecting one of the world's most lavish hostelries, the Palace. The city could not support it then. But tomorrow. . . .

He should have known by then that his kind of tomorrow was not coming. The failure of Jay Cooke's mighty New York banking empire in September, 1873, had inaugurated one of the longest depressions in the nation's history. Distance, however, was slowing the spread of its poisons to the Pacific Coast. The Comstock mines were still pouring out treasure; opportunities for cleverness still abounded. Surely, Ralston told himself, there was no real reason for fear.

But he did have to find quick funds somewhere. Bidding desperately, he gained control of the private company that supplied San Francisco with water. His hope was to sell his new monopoly to the city for $15 million, but again he met fierce opposition. Meanwhile powerful and jealous competitors appeared in the California banking field. The stock market gyrated wildly, men who he had supposed would remain friendly no matter what emergencies he brought to them turned their backs, and suddenly, with the closing of The Bank of California, it became evident that boldness alone no longer sufficed.

The Bank of California would recover. Later the state would know other booms, other hopes, other flamboyant entrepreneurs. But the atmosphere would be different. Adolescent San Francisco had finally touched the limits of possibility.

Ralston's death coincided with the ending of the exuberant innocence born of the gold rush. The people of San Francisco sensed the pattern. Hence the outpouring at his funeral. It was a spontaneous farewell not only to Ralston but also to the hopes that he had symbolized. A closer look at the details involved, at the flamboyant times in which he lived, and at the uneasy course of his personal life as well is the primary concern of the book that follows.

CHAPTER 1

Mississippi Seedbed

At some point during the humid summer of 1832, Robert Ralston reversed, at least partly for love, the westward trend of his Scotch-Irish forebears. Packing up his wife, Mary Chapman Ralston, and his two sons, William, aged six and a half, and Samuel, only three or four months old, he abandoned his farm near Plymouth in north-central Ohio and drove his wagon east a hundred miles. His goal was little Wellsville on the banks of the Ohio River, opposite the thin splinter of Virginia (now West Virginia) that thrusts northward between the states of Ohio and Pennsylvania.

This was an almost exact retracing of familiar trails. Robert had been born on August 18, 1797, near Canonsburg in western Pennsylvania. In 1814 his family had moved on into Ohio, at a time when the rough edges of the wilderness still lay on the land. There Robert had cut loose on his own, trying his hand, frontier-fashion, at a variety of trades—farming, tavern-keeping, carpentry, and even schoolteaching for a short period when he was nineteen.

Between jobs he occasionally visited relatives back in Canonsburg. During his travels he crossed the Ohio River on a ferry run by farmer William Chapman of New Cumberland, Virginia, a hamlet across the river from and about eight miles south of Wellsville. Chapman had a redheaded daughter named Mary. Robert Ralston noticed her as she began to fill out, wooed her successfully, and married her on December 14, 1824. He was twenty-seven years old then; Mary was a month short of eighteen.[1]

The new husband took his bride to his farm outside Plymouth, close to his family's home. Their first son was born there on January 12, 1826, and named William Chapman Ralston after his maternal grandfather.

*The Ohio farm where Billy Ralston spent his first six years
had been cleared of trees in much this manner.*

As the naming suggests Mary was homesick. She stayed homesick,
even after a second son, Samuel, finally came along on March 24, 1832,
to help fill her days. Finally she persuaded Robert to go back east.

She had help in convincing him. New opportunities, mostly con-
nected with steamboats, were burgeoning along the riverbanks. When
William Ralston was born, seventy-five steamboats were plying the
Mississippi and its tributaries. Within a decade that number would double.
In addition, hundreds of keelboats, flatboats, and rafts, built fresh each
year, floated produce and Yankee gimcracks to the goods-hungry plan-

tations farther downstream. Few people who saw the growing flood of traffic paid much attention to the little railroads that were pushing across the mountains with the full intent of chaining the agricultural Midwest to the new industrial economy of the Northeast. Steam was king, to be sure—but river steam. Each year the towering craft of the western waters moved more passengers and far greater tonnages of freight to and from the port of New Orleans than went by rail to either Philadelphia, Boston, or New York. The axis of the future was the natural north-south line of the Mississippi Valley, not the fabricated east-west tracks of the railroads. Or so the water prophets argued.

Every settlement beside navigable water dreamed of becoming the great inland port of the Mississippi drainage. Such was Wellsville, the nearest town of consequence to Mary's former home. It had a sawmill and a boatyard. As Robert Ralston's in-laws no doubt let him know, a man skilled in carpentry—Robert had done a considerable amount of bridge-building around Plymouth—could do well there. Moreover, Mary beseeched him. And so it happened that young William Ralston, like Sam Clemens a few years later, grew up with thick forests on one side of him and bright water on the other. He heard the echo of steam whistles, with all their suggestions, as boats from far places nosed toward the landing. He listened to the chant of stevedores; he watched the fine passengers as they leaned on the railings and glanced indifferently at the town that had occasioned a small interruption on their journey to places whose very names meant excitement then—Pittsburgh, St. Louis, Memphis, New Orleans.

Mary's joy at being near her parents again did not last long. She bore two more sons in Wellsville, Andrew Jackson on April 25, 1833, and James Alpheus on March 7, 1835. She never recovered from James's advent. On April 25, 1835 (by coincidence it was Andrew Jackson's second birthday), she died. Overwhelmed by the prospect of raising a family of four small boys, Robert Ralston ten months later married Harriet Herford, daughter of a Wellsville judge who bore him three more children, two girls and a boy.

There may have been frictions. At least Andrew Jackson Ralston remembered many years later that Chap, as the oldest boy was then called, felt very protective about his three full brothers and assumed, as best he could, some of the responsibility for bringing them up. (Eventually all of Mary's children followed William to California; none of Harriet's did.) Be that as it may, Chap led no blighted life. He was husky and athletic. He had the boatyards to clamber through, the river to swim in, the forest for hunting, and, on his grandparents' farm, fine horses to ride, the last a joy he never lost. He received at least as much education as the average smalltown lad of the times. He could figure sharply—his "head for business" quickly impressed his associates—and could spell and write with commendable efficiency. When he quit school in 1840, aged fourteen, to work in a grocery store, it may not have been because the family income needed supplementing, as Andrew Jackson recalled, but because young Chap had already grown beyond the limited challenges offered by the neighborhood teachers.

Storekeeping was no challenge, either. Two years later, aged sixteen, young Ralston took a job on a little steamboat plying between Wheeling and Cincinnati. Unlike Mark Twain, he was not caught up by the glamor of piloting. Instead he became an assistant clerk.

The word "clerk" no longer carries the connotations it held in pre-Civil War America. A clerk then was not a counter-tender. He made things go. On riverboats he and his staff handled the bills of lading, saw to stowage and unloading and delivery, took care of provisions, made arrangements with woodlots along the riverbanks for fuel. Clerks kept the records. They learned the mysteries of cost accounting. They were much more likely than pilots to become captains and owners of boats in their own right.

While Chap Ralston was serving his apprenticeship as a clerk, his father continued building boats. A major effort was the *Dominion*, a craft big enough to ply the Mississippi. Chap transferred his activities

The Cincinnati river front looked like this when Ralston first saw it as an apprentice clerk on a steamboat.

20

to her, probably as an assistant clerk. It was a short-lived position, but it brought him his first major adventure as well as the first of many abiding friendships formed along the Mississippi—friendships that would do much to influence his later career.

The *Dominion,* Captain Tyler in charge, undertook to ferry through certain rapids near the Iowa–Missouri border a consignment of merchandise that had been entrusted to a young man named John Commingers Ainsworth. Ainsworth and his uncle owned a small steamboat that they used for picking up freight along the upper Mississippi and delivering it to centers farther downstream. On this particular trip high water made the rapids look unusually risky, and so they made arrangements to switch their freight to the *Dominion,* which by chance had stopped nearby at Keokuk, Iowa.

It proved to be an unlucky change. As the *Dominion* was nosing downstream, an unexpected reflex wave smashed her against a rock. She split and although Captain Tyler tried to beach her she sank near shore. According to legend, which supplies no details, Ralston performed well during the emergency. Evidently he and his fellows salvaged part of the cargo; at least Ainsworth years later recalled that there was "some" loss only.

In order to work out terms for meeting that loss, the principals held several meetings. During the talks Ainsworth, who also had been born in Ohio, and Ralston, who was four years his junior, became firm friends.[2] Later Ralston would persuade Ainsworth to try his luck on the Pacific Coast and in 1860, when Ainsworth set about creating a steamboat empire of his own on the Columbia River, banker Ralston of San Francisco would provide part of the necessary capital, in spite of vehement opposition from his associates.

Meanwhile, however, the sinking of the *Dominion* had left the young clerk both boatless and jobless. Uneasily, one imagines, he carried the bad news back to his father. Somehow they scratched together more funds, found a few resilient associates, and built yet another craft, the *Constitution,* in which they all took an interest as part of their pay.[3] Ralston was then about twenty years old.

After the ship was running, he clerked aboard her for a brief time. Then abruptly, and despite his interest in her, he left the *Constitution* to join the new 750-ton *Convoy,* built, partly owned, and captained by Cornelius Kingsland Garrison of St. Louis. The shift probably would not have occurred so quickly if Garrison had not been impressed enough by the young man to offer liberal inducements, perhaps a position as first clerk. Although the decision proved to be a turning point in the young man's life, its date remains unknown; evidence suggests late 1846.

Garrison was seventeen years older than Ralston. Contemporary drawings show a receding hairline above a handsome, clean-shaven face. He had wide set eyes and a long nose; curly hair puffed out over his ears. He was imaginative, persuasive, vigorous, and ruthless, qualities that frequently seemed to go hand in hand during those freewheeling times.

Born on March 1, 1809, near West Point, New York, he was the second child of a family of seven. At the age of thirteen he had gone to work on a Hudson River sloop. During off hours he studied so diligently that at sixteen he was able to travel to New York City for courses in architecture and construction. He took the degrees he earned to the Canadian side of the lower Great Lakes, where he became involved, along with his other construction work, in the building of four steamboats. About 1833 he shifted to St. Louis. There he and his brothers Oliver and Daniel became jacks of many trades, selling boat supplies, making steel pipe, and manufacturing land and marine steam engines. Part of their earnings they invested in building two big river steamers, one of them the *Convoy*.[4]

In view of the eminence later attained by both Ralston and Garrison, it is remarkable that nothing specific is known about their years together on the Mississippi River. There must have been other episodes as dramatic as the sinking of the *Dominion*. Steamboating in the late 1840s was fiercely competitive, marked by desperate races and exploding boilers. In spite of its dangers, however, it attracted throngs of gay, cosmopolitan, debonair passengers. But mostly it must have been, for the new associates, urgently busy. The war with Mexico was under way and supplies were pouring down the river for two armies—Zachary Taylor's in northern Mexico and Winfield Scott's, marching from Veracruz to Mexico City. Once the peace treaty was signed, a new rush into Texas began. Among its leaders was a hard-driving seafarer whom Garrison and Ralston would soon know well—Charles Morgan, spinning steamship lines out of New Orleans to the burgeoning Gulf ports of the Southwest.

New Orleans reflected in dazzling radiance the energy and prosperity of the period. It was a vibrant, exotic, pleasure-loving city, bright with color and Old South crinoline, more French in its ways than American. How Ralston, still in his early twenties, reacted to its allurements is unknown. Biographers are tempted to fill the gap in his story by describing the city instead. The implication is that he too shared the gaiety—and indeed the lavishness he later displayed in San Francisco may have had its roots in New Orleans.

It is possible, however, to draw a different picture. William Ralston came from a religious family. His brothers Andrew Jackson and James Alpheus were almost oppressively devout. His sobersided, black-suited, long-time friend Stephen Franklin, whom he first met in New Orleans, was an elder in the Crescent City's leading Presbyterian

The energy of New Orleans was part of the vitality of young America
that Ralston absorbed during his years on the Mississippi.

Church. After migrating to California in 1849, Franklin helped found
San Francisco's Calvary Presbyterian Church, of which Ralston became a member as soon as he settled in the Golden State.[5] Throughout
the rest of his career he maintained that membership. During the years
1857–1858, he served on Calvary's board of trustees, so his stays in
New Orleans may have been less titillating than descriptions of the
city's wickedness suggest—with emphasis on *may*. The truth is that
we do not know.

Far more significant than the flings he had, if any, were the friends
he made. John Ainsworth, Cornelius Garrison, Charles Morgan, and
Stephen Franklin have already been mentioned. To the list can be added
three more—Jacob Kamm, William Norris, and Ralph Stover Fretz.
Kamm was the Swiss-born engineer of Garrison's *Convoy*. Norris was
the captain of a rival boat. A decade later both men would be powerful
figures on the western rivers—and both would serve as charter sub-
scribers to, and long-time directors of, Ralston's Bank of California.

Fretz's influence was still greater—greater, possibly, than Garrison's although there is no real way to measure such imponderables. Like Garrison, Fretz was seventeen years older than Ralston. Quiet and something of a loner, he has left few traces behind. About all we know is that he was born in Pennsylvania in 1809, was educated at a small college at Canonsburg (Robert Ralston's hometown), and owned a steamboat, of which he was also the captain. Unlike Norris and Garrison, Fretz used that boat not for public conveyance but for conducting his own private trade among the hamlets bordering the lower river. Meanwhile his younger brothers, John and Christian Augustus Fretz, attended to the family's stores and warehouse operations in New Orleans. Fretz was, if the term is permissible, a conservative plunger. He took bold chances, but first he liked to have all the factors in mind. Unquestionably his steadying hand often served as a counterbalance to Ralston's native impetuosity during their eighteen years together.

It is remarkable that one obscure young man could gain so many potent associates during no more than five or six of his formative years. It also seems equally remarkable, at least on the face of things, that all those river men (except Charles Morgan), plus scores more like them, simultaneously gave up their jobs and migrated to the Pacific Coast. There were, however, compelling reasons behind the shift. The number of competing boats on the Mississippi and its tributaries jumped from 187 in 1840 to 740 in 1849.[6] In time those figures would climb again but for a dismaying period during 1848–49 there was a falling off in freight occasioned by the signing of peace with Mexico. Westward, meanwhile, the Columbia River in the Northwest and the combined Sacramento–San Joaquin system in California offered new fields for exploitation.

As soon as American settlements appeared on those distant riverbanks, pioneer traders began sketching plans for steamboats. Hulls could easily be built from local materials, but engines had to be imported. The nearest source was the Garrison brothers' foundry at St. Louis, and it is probable that boatmen from the Pacific were sounding out the builders even before the settlement of the Oregon question with Britain and the ending of the war with Mexico.

At first the Garrisons hesitated. Overland transport did not exist. Their ponderous engines would have to be shipped around Cape Horn, a tedious and expensive process. Moreover, the Far West was isolated and undeveloped. What assurance existed that the hopeful boatmen of the Pacific could really find enough business to pay their bills?

Then the explosion came. By the fall of 1848 word of the California gold discoveries had reached the Mississippi Valley. In December the rush by water began. In February, 1849, while the gold fever was mounting ever higher, the *Convoy* caught fire at Natchez and burned with twelve hundred tons of cotton on board. That ended hesitations

Ralston was jobless and footloose when news of the California gold strikes swept eastward, filling the nation with wonder.

as far as Cornelius Garrison was concerned. Why not seek rehabilitation in the West rather than on the crowded river?

He prevailed on his firm to accept orders for engines to activate small steamboats projected for the Sacramento and Willamette rivers, plus another for running a sawmill. These engines the brothers placed in charge of Jacob Kamm, who shepherded them around the Horn to San Francisco Bay.

Garrison hurried ahead to the Isthmus of Panama. In company with some of the earliest goldseekers, he threaded the jungles to the Pacific side and was lucky enough to catch prompt passage northward. After surveying the situation in California, he continued to Oregon. One tale adds that he ventured on into Puget Sound and paddled past the site of future Seattle in a dugout canoe manned by Indians. Oddly enough, whatever he saw failed to impress him as much as chaotic Panama had. Well before 1849 was over, he was back at the Isthmus with plans for furnishing banking services, provisions, and transportation to the frantic throngs flooding back and forth between the oceans.[7]

Ralston was still on the Mississippi, stranded by the burning of the *Convoy*. Although he was widely known by then as an able and ambitious clerk, the slump in business evidently kept him from finding the kind of position that he wanted. At least two acquaintances claimed, on separate occasions years later, to have loaned him money to help him through that dry period.[8] And still no jobs appeared. Finally, in July 1849, five months after Garrison's departure from New Orleans, he sought to leave discouragement behind by boarding a little sailing bark, the *Madonna*, for Panama.

Today there is no way of knowing exactly what he intended. Like thousands of other uninformed young hopefuls, he may have dreamed of repairing his fortunes by continuing across the Isthmus and picking up free gold in the California mountains. Or Garrison may have sent for him to come to Panama and join the new enterprise that the older man had in mind. Or perhaps Ralph Fretz, who was already in contact with Garrison, was the one who suggested that the young man plunge with them into an unfamiliar business in one of the world's most lethal areas.

In any event, whether by design or accident, Ralston did meet Garrison and Fretz in Panama and decided to stay there with them. Later he would have cause to look back on that radical step with some wonder. Because of it he came into close contact with one of the richest men in America, Cornelius Vanderbilt, Sr. It brought him a love affair whose tragic ending marked the rest of his days. Eventually it led to storybook connivings, dark plots, and bitter betrayals, the whole played out against as appalling a physical background as can be imagined.

CHAPTER 2

The Panama Morass

The miseries of the Isthmus crossing began far out in the shallow bay fronting the dockless port of Chagres. Ships had to drop anchor two miles or more from the town and then, by rope ladder and sling, transfer freight and jostling gold seekers into a heterogeneous collection of lighters for transport ashore. By the time of Ralston's arrival in mid-July, 1849, a wheezing 250-ton paddlewheel steamer, the *Orus,* was serving as a ferry—if it wasn't busy somewhere else. During its absences, skiffs and dugout canoes acted as unstable substitutes.[1]

The town, population 700, stood on the right bank of the Chagres River. It consisted of a sprawl of single-room, grass-and-bamboo huts, whose conical tops, thatched with dried palmetto leaves, made the village look like a stand of oversized beehives. Long-necked vultures perched grotesquely on the roof peaks. Dogs, pigs, naked children, barefooted men in soiled white trousers, and cigar-smoking women moved indolently around the piles of offal that littered the streets. Above them on a small bluff brooded the abandoned castle of San Lorenzo, its moldering stones and tarnished brass cannons all but smothered under vines. Beyond the broad stream, on the left bank, stood raw, new American "hotels," their wooden maws filled with rows of cots separated here and there by thin partitions advertised as providing privacy for women and married couples.

The surrounding land was low and marshy. During the rainy season, which lasted from May to November, the ground was a quagmire of blue mud. Insects swarmed; though roundly damned they were indifferently resisted, for the connection between mosquitoes and yellow fever, often called Panama fever, had not yet been established.

After each argonaut had dug his baggage out of the piles dumped on

The landing at Chagres was the beginning of a miserable "shortcut" from the Atlantic to the Pacific by way of Panama.

the beach by the lighters, he began searching for a way to move up the Chagres River to the mule trails that led over the continental divide to Panama City. During high water the *Orus* occasionally packed aboard as many passengers and as much luggage as she could hold, took a festoon of log canoes in tow, and churned against the current as far as a trailhead village called Gorgona. Ralston, traveling in July, may have been able to arrange steamboat passage. If not, he had to join other wayfarers in bargaining for a *bongo*, a dugout canoe hollowed from a huge log. A big bongo could hold a dozen persons, including the crew, who propelled the craft by poling, by towing from the riverbank, or even by jumping overboard, seizing the gunwales and dragging it ahead. The passengers meanwhile were protected from alternate rains and blazing tropical sun by ragged awnings of leaves.

Traveling by bongo could be an acrimonious procedure. The Creole entrepreneurs who owned the craft and provided the Negro crews overcharged whenever they could and then arrived at the assigned meeting place as late as they chose—if they arrived at all, for they felt free to vanish entirely if they were able to make better bargains elsewhere. Their shiftless crews mishandled baggage, were hard to pry out of the local taverns they visited on the way upstream, and in general declined to be impressed by the argonauts' need to make ship connections for California on the far side of the Isthmus. Impatient Americans responded by being overbearing, loud, and inconsiderate. Many drank too much—bad water and the prevention of fever were excuses—and, heated to the point of belligerence, brandished fists and revolvers in noisy efforts to get from their hirelings more speed than circumstances allowed.

The trip to the head of navigation devoured anywhere from two days to a week, depending on the stage of the current and the cooperation of the crews. During that time, relaxed travelers found much to interest them—the emerald jungle, the exotic flowers (including a rare white orchid with spikes six feet tall, which bloomed during the wet summers), the chattering monkeys, screeching parrots, and torpid alligators. Sugar, rice, corn, and cattle plantations occasionally interrupted the monotonous greenery, and every half a dozen miles or so it was possible to land at a hamlet of bamboo huts, buy tropical fruit, and perhaps rent a hammock covered by mosquito netting in which to pass the night.

Adaptable stampeders were a minority, however. Most found the trip an ordeal. The bongos were uncomfortable, the heat oppressive, and the rattling awnings an inadequate protection against the sun. Accommodations in the riverside towns were limited and often verminous, the food suspect, the prices outrageous. Accordingly many stampeders camped along the way, eating cheerless rations, which they carried with them. If they failed to reach a suitable landing place before dark, they had to spend the night hunched in their canoes, drenched by violent downpours. For those who were feverish or afflicted with stomach cramps and diarrhea, as many were, the experience could be disastrous. An indeterminate but appreciable number of the thousands who made the crossing suffered permanent injury to their health—or, in extreme cases, died along the way.

During the dry season the bongos halted at Gorgona. The trail from there to the Pacific was impassable during wet weather, however. Accordingly Ralston and those who traveled to Gorgona with him, whether by canoe or steamer, had to continue seven miles farther upstream to Cruces. There they found the terminus of an ancient trail that still retained much of the cobblestone paving laid originally by the Spanish muleskinners who once had transported incalculable treasures of oriental spice and New World bullion from the Pacific landings to the Atlantic Coast.

Renting mules on which to cover that trail was as tumultuous a process as obtaining bongos. Saddle animals commanded $10 to $40 each for the trip, depending on the demand. The charge for pack stock varied according to the weight of the load. The animals were small, nimble, cantankerous, and dreadfully overworked. There were seldom enough on hand at either Gorgona or Cruces to meet the demands of the California-bound argonauts, and so many travelers ended up walking the last miles to the Pacific.

"Incident on the Chagres" by Charles Nahl, premier artist of early California, suggests the dangers of the Panama crossing.

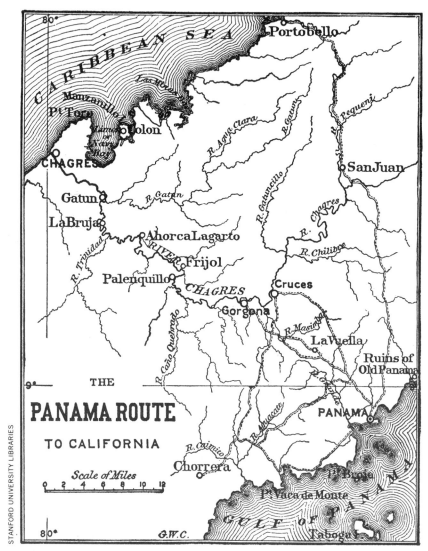

After a steaming trip by bongo to Gorgona or Cruces, depending on the level of water in the river, the argonauts switched to mules.

The trail was fearful. After crossing the continental divide, it dropped precipitously between deeply eroded walls. In summer the narrow channel was thick with mud and slashed across by flooded ravines. Encounters with pack trains bound in the opposite direction produced blasphemous jams. Many mules died en route, and their loads had to be tossed aside until new transport could be found. The carcasses were disposed of by the numerous buzzards that hovered overhead, waiting.

Five days or more out of Chagres the exhausted travelers rode onto the open plains bordering the city of Panama, its gray walls pierced by the arched, bell-hung Gorgona gate. Founded in 1519, the port had grown during the heyday of the Spanish Empire into a rich and busy metropolis. But as Spain's power had crumbled, so had Panama's physical glory. Many of the churches, their towers still glinting with oyster shells embedded in the plaster coatings, had been abandoned to vines and bats. The cracked bells of the others clanged discordantly night and day. The narrow streets were rough with cobblestones. The buildings lining them were decrepit but, if occupied by Americans, brightened with the Stars and Stripes hung from the balconies and with garish signs advertising rooms, meals, and supplies. At the intersection of the two main streets was a plaza of bare earth, ringed with tethered and quarrelsome mules. The only cart in town had just been built by a stranded Yankee carpenter. The population was about six thousand.

The main streets were like caverns, lined solidly by whitewashed stone structures two to six stories high. Their ground floors were occupied by shops, bars, billiard parlors, servant quarters, and, quite often, by stables. Offices and living quarters were above. In the evening, when sea breezes stirred the humid air, the residents repaired to their balconies. Guarded by flimsy railings, these thrust out so far above the streets as almost to touch their counterparts on the opposite side. By twilight, if verandahs existed beneath the balconies, as at hotels, they were filled with men playing dominoes.

As soon as the newcomers had found their baggage—it generally arrived late, wet, and battered—they began haunting the town's numerous ticket offices in hope of learning something about ship schedules and available space to California. During most of 1849 the answers that greeted them were discouraging.

Only one through service operated on a timetable. It was composed of two allied firms—the United States Mail Company, which linked New York and New Orleans with Chagres, and the Pacific Mail Steamship Company, which joined Panama City to San Francisco and Astoria, Oregon, at the mouth of the Columbia River. Both companies had come into being as a result of America's acquisition of Oregon and California. As their names indicate, their primary function was to carry mail and for this service both received subsidies from the government.

When bidding for the mail contracts, both firms had agreed to use ships capable of transporting passengers or, if need be, troops. Panama of course interrupted the flow. Mail was lifted across the barrier by native contractors. Passengers had to take care of themselves, at their own expense, even though they had purchased tickets that read as if good for the entire journey.

Before either company had finished building its liners—the Pacific Mail Steamship Company intended to send three steamers around Cape Horn to the West Coast—they were overwhelmed by the gold stampede. Demand was so frenzied and available space so limited that opportunistic

Hundreds of wayfarers endured Panama as best they could
while waiting for the welcome call, "A steamer is in!"

ship captains on both sides of the North Atlantic crowded bunks into
any vessel that would float, even river ferries, and rushed the gold
hunters to Chagres. No comparable swarm of ships existed on the West
Coast, however, with the result that thousands of wayfarers ended up
stranded in Panama City.

Desperate men camped for weeks in dreadful hovels outside the
crowded town, waiting for escape. Frantic quarrels over tickets erupted
each time a vessel bound for California appeared in the bay. Speculators
who managed to obtain space were often able to sell a single ticket for as
much as $1,000.

By the time Ralston arrived some of the fury was diminishing. The
Pacific Mail Steamship Company had finally managed to get its three
ships around the Horn, and by midsummer all were shuttling on fairly
regular schedules between Panama and California. Unattached vessels,
attracted by tales of the extraordinary demand, were beginning to appear.
At the same time the flow of traffic was thinning as potential travelers in
the United States, frightened by reports of hardship on the Isthmus,
chose to go west by some other route.

"Thinning" was a relative term, however, as Ralston discovered
when watching what happened to his erstwhile companions on the trail.
Each day those who had not purchased through tickets and were travel-

ing catch-as-catch-can wandered restlessly out to the great seawall that lined the tip of the little peninsula on which the city stood. From its wide, rough top they peered yearningly at the broad bay. Generally there was little to see in the mists, for at Panama, as at Chagres, the roadstead was so shallow at low tide that ships were forced to anchor two or three miles from shore.

Wearied at last, the watchers turned back into town. Half sick or half drunk, confused, bored, and often wishing that they had never left home, they tramped endlessly back and forth across the cobbles, looking for rooms, food, entertainment, or supplies to replace the things they had lost, broken, or consumed during their journey. If they chanced to find what they wanted, they were dismayed by the price and the mélange of coins that accompanied even the simplest transactions.

Wrathful questions arose. Why didn't "they"—that is, anyone connected with travel or supply arrangements—do something to improve the intolerable conditions? Since much of Ralston's youthful energy would be spent in helping Cornelius Garrison and Ralph Fretz work out profitable solutions, it is well to pause here for a look at the tangled context that greeted him and then did much to shape his own attitudes and methods of attacking opposition.

When he appeared in Panama, grandiose schemes were afoot, each bearing the seeds of competitive warfare. Already surveyors were in the jungles, marking out the route for a trans-Isthmus railroad. This staggering project was the brainchild of William H. Aspinwall, who was also head of the Pacific Mail Steamship Company. Aspinwall's plans included abandoning Chagres as a docking site in favor of swampy Manzanillo Island, four miles away at the entrance to Limón Bay, sometimes called Navy Bay, where Columbus had ridden out a storm in 1502. Manzanillo was steamy and pestilential. Mountains of earth would have to be hauled in to create foundations for docking facilities, railroad tracks, switching yards, warehouses, machine shops, office buildings, and all the other paraphernalia of a port. There would have to be a causeway to the mainland, and beyond that lay miles of fever-ridden mangrove bogs.

There was, however, one great allure. The ocean front at Manzanillo was deep. As soon as facilities had been completed, the liners of the United States Mail Company (and its rivals) could nose easily into waiting slips. Passengers and freight could be transferred painlessly to railroad cars, whisked across the Isthmus in a matter of hours, and transferred without delay into launches that would carry them to the steamers of the Pacific Mail Steamship Company. Those ships would ply not just to California but also, if Aspinwall's plans matured, along the entire west coast of South America and on beyond to Hawaii and the Orient—a heady vision, which would take time to realize.

Cornelius Vanderbilt, an even bolder man than Aspinwall, also glimpsed that dream. Panama, however, was closed to Vanderbilt by the monopolistic franchise which Aspinwall held from the government of New Granada. (Panama in those days was a province of New Granada, the early name of the republic of Colombia.) Vanderbilt accordingly shifted his attentions to Nicaragua—as would Garrison in time.[2]

The isthmus at Nicaragua was more than three times as wide as at Panama. Very little land travel was involved, however. As Vanderbilt's studies revealed, shallow-draft steamers could enter the mouth of the San Juan River at Greytown, bull westward a hundred miles (there were five troublesome rapids along the way), and thus gain broad Lake Nicaragua. Sixty miles of lake travel would bring the ships to lovely Virgin Bay. The Pacific was only sixteen miles farther west, across a line of hills much lower than those in Panama—so low, indeed, that for centuries men had been proposing a series of canals around the rapids in the river and on through the hills to the western ocean.

Prior to the gold rush the proposals had been shrugged aside as hopelessly nonremunerative. Vanderbilt, however, had watched the frenzied throngs pouring into the eastern ports of the United States during the early months of 1849. He had noted the amounts of gold that were already beginning to move back from California. Inevitably the thought occurred to him: why not produce an alternate crossing of Central America so attractive that it would pull the rug out from underneath Aspinwall's monopoly? Then the whole Pacific would be his to conquer.

In 1849, Cornelius Vanderbilt was fifty-five years old, more than six feet tall, ruddy, rough-hewn, and awesomely self-confident. He had risen from nowhere. His father had eked out a living by growing vegetables on Staten Island and then carrying them in a tiny sloop to the produce markets in New York City. Cornelius hated that vegetable farm but he liked the water. By working relentlessly he managed to acquire a ragged little schooner of his own. He ferried passengers and produce into New York City, then obtained another boat and peddled notions along the Jersey coast and up the Hudson River.

From sail he progressed to steam—big riverboats at first and then fast coastal vessels that he sent in and out of every major port between Philadelphia and Boston. Competition, led by such figures as Liveoak George Law, later an incorporator of the United States Mail Company, was remorseless. By being a little sharper, a little tougher, and on occasion a little more lawless than the others, Vanderbilt pulled ahead of them. Soon he owned more steamships than any other man in the United States—and most of them were built to his own design. His associates called him Commodore, very deferentially.

He launched his Nicaragua project early in 1849, incorporating what he called the American Atlantic and Pacific Ship Canal Company. By

Ralston worked for piratical old Cornelius Vanderbilt (above), fought against him—and was engaged to marry his granddaughter.

promising liberal payments to the government of Nicaragua, he obtained an exclusive franchise to do the work and collect tolls from those who used the canals.

As he must have anticipated, his actions produced international repercussions. Costa Rica insisted on being consulted—that is, paid—on the grounds that she had as much jurisdiction as Nicaragua over the San Juan River, which flowed along the border between the two countries. Costa Rica, however, was weak; both Vanderbilt and the United States ignored the protest. Great Britain was another matter. That empire, holder of a protectorate over eastern Nicaragua (the so-called Mosquito Coast), bristled at the prospect of Americans invading the area with a canal. Swords rattled until diplomats, deciding that the issue was not worth a war, sat down to draft a treaty that would define the international status of any canal built anywhere in Central America.

Without waiting to learn the outcome, Vanderbilt sent engineers into Nicaragua to produce working plans for the canal, just as Aspinwall had sent railroad surveyors into Panama before the details of his franchise had been settled with the government of New Granada.

Garrison—and Ralston with him—must have realized that no one could make long-range plans involving Panama without taking that gigantic rivalry into account. On the other hand, fruition of those daring plans lay years ahead. Meanwhile a host of disorders on the Isthmus were crying out for solution. The reward for success would be immediate profits. So why worry too much about distant railroads, distant canals?

Acting on that premise, scores of petty entrepreneurs were already trying, at the time of Ralston's arrival, to meet the more pressing needs. Inasmuch as most of the workers were Americans, they instinctively ignored the Spanish prototypes that surrounded them and imitated instead the patterns of the free-enterprise system that was currently gathering headway in the United States. As was true in the United States, their chief handicaps were self-contained. Neither distance nor the restrictive laws emanating from New Granada hampered them as much as did their excessive competition with each other, their inadequate sources of supply, and their lack of imagination. Anyone whose inner and outer resources were broad enough to transcend those limitations was almost certain to soar high.

Cornelius Garrison, who was also called Commodore by his associates, was one of the first of that caliber to appear on the Isthmus. It was the good fortune of his protégé, William Ralston, to be able to work at his side as he applied his many talents to the rapidly evolving situations that he faced—the kind of fluid situations that Ralston himself would repeatedly encounter, years later, in California. But it was young Ralston's misfortune to see as well, when crises threatened, how often Garrison used glibness and recklessness as acceptable tools rather than relying on more traditional methods.

CHAPTER 3

Slippery Footholds

By Garrison's own account, the first field to attract him in Panama was banking.[1] Frontiersman Isaac Wistar, who crossed Panama in 1849 on his way from California to the East, has a different tale. He says that Garrison and Fretz began their business operations as proprietors of a gambling house.

It was a rough-and-ready place, according to Wistar, who admits to losing all his money there. The story goes that Garrison one night fell into a drunken quarrel with a certain notorious Vicissimus Turner. They staggered by moonlight onto the seawall to settle their dispute with pistols. There they agreed that whoever won the toss of a coin would yell "Fire!" At that they would grasp each other's coat lapels and shoot. Turner won and yelled. Their spasmodically rising pistols collided and both bullets missed. As they were preparing to try again, they discovered that Turner needed a percussion cap for his derringer. Garrison held one out for him to use. Turner dropped it. As they fumbled for it in the dark, they got to laughing and called off the encounter.[2]

Conceivably neither Garrison nor Wistar was lying about the nature of the establishment. No bank in Panama could progress far without lining up reputable correspondents in the United States. That took time, even though both Garrison and Ralph Fretz had impeccable connections to help them along the way—the first through the Garrison brothers' foundry and boat works in St. Louis, the second through the Fretz brothers' mercantile establishment in New Orleans. Filing the necessary papers in distant Bogotá, capital of New Granada, consumed more days. During the lag the partners may have sought to fill their tills by running the gambling hall that Wistar described when writing his memoirs years later.

An artist for **Harper's Magazine** *saw Panama City as looking like this at about the time Ralston was living and working there.*

Ralston must have arrived in Panama City at about the time that the gaming house (if it actually existed) was being transformed into the bank that gave him his initial training in finance. It was a very different sort of bank from those we know today. It was not a corporation existing under government charter and regulated within strict legal frameworks by a self-perpetuating board of governors. Rather, it was a simple partnership between two men. Its only restraints were local economics and such loose guidelines as were laid down in Bogotá. Of necessity its policy evolved not from custom—local customs derived from ancient Spanish models—but from spur-of-the-moment decisions that the partners reached while meeting the unfamiliar problems that each day flowed across their counters.

How much money the two men invested in the partnership is unknown. It had to be enough for them to buy dribbles of gold dust from returning miners who had carried it to Panama in the expectation, generally realized, of receiving from $1.00 to $1.50 an ounce more for it there than was offered in San Francisco. They needed to be able to trade, on request, American dollars for foreign coins, charging as high a premium for the service as local competition allowed. They made loans—"advances on liberal terms," in the words of their advertisements in the Panama *Star*. More importantly, they provided local businessmen with bills of exchange on various banks in leading cities in the United States. The merchants who purchased those bills, again at a premium, used them for their own transactions in the cities involved.

This cartoon by F. Marryat shows the conditions that the firm of Garrison, Fretz & Ralston sought to improve with their mule trains.

The contacts that enabled Garrison & Fretz to develop this exchange business soon led them to additional responsibilities as commission merchants supplying ships and retail outlets. Odds and ends of the merchandise they needed came to them from many sources, including tramp freighters. Their main reliance was the Fretz brothers' house in New Orleans. Soon one of Ralph's younger brothers, Major John Fretz, came to Panama to help with the growing piles of paper work.

Physically the greatest clog to the flow of specie for the bank and supplies for the wholesale operations was Panama's archaic transportation system. Central depots for receiving and forwarding freight and express was one crying need. Another was the organization of boat service and mule trains capable of carrying merchandise, steamer trunks, and passengers over the Isthmus on dependable timetables.

For some reason—perhaps the competition of shallow-draft steamers during the times of high water on the Chagres—the bongos eluded the pioneer organizers. Land travel proved more amenable. Early in 1850 Garrison & Fretz announced, in advertisements published as far away as San Francisco, that they were offering themselves to public consideration as "Commission Shippers, Forwarding & Transportation Merchants." They were building, they said, a large warehouse in Panama City and were prepared to supply rental horses to trans-Isthmian travelers. In a short time they would add to those operations, so they promised, a hundred carefully chosen Kentucky mules for moving the travelers' baggage.[3]

Presumably William Ralston—by then generally called Billy or, on occasion, Toppie by his intimates—was involved in all the operations. He was twenty-four years old and as healthy, strong, and energetic as a yearling bull, no small consideration in Panama. His experience as a riverboat clerk had made him familiar with bills of lading and with the commercial paper that was often associated with them. He got along as easily with stevedores as with bookkeepers and shippers. Because he was quick-witted and cheery, he drew business as well as expedited it. Such talents were too valuable to be confined for long to mule corrals or even to a teller's cage. Soon he was traveling frequently on company business between the Isthmus and the United States—more trips, probably, than can now be reconstructed.[4]

At an indeterminate date in 1850, he was on the Mississippi River, probably to procure the Kentucky mules that his firm had promised to add to their packing operations. There he encountered John Ainsworth and encouraged that young man in his desire to try his fortunes on the West Coast. Ainsworth traveled as far as Panama City with Ralston and afterwards remembered his friend as being occupied primarily as an agent for a line of ocean steamships.[5] It is a casual reference but it indicates how early Ralston also became involved in ocean transportation, Panama's most cutthroat trade and one that eventually would split the firm of Garrison & Fretz apart.

As 1850 opened, the Pacific Mail Steamship Company was still the only line offering scheduled service between Panama City and San Francisco. Though traffic jams were not as frantic as those of a year before, the company ships had more business than they could handle. Meanwhile, news of the pressures in Panama had at last attracted a superabundance of unscheduled vessels to scramble for what the Pacific Mail vessels could not handle. Many of those Johnny-come-latelies arrived in Panama Bay in acute need of fresh food and equipment.

Because the details of selling tickets, shepherding baggage, and procuring supplies were onerous, most captains of the unscheduled ships preferred to assign the tasks to agents. There was a plethora of them, too, competing fiercely. Each endeavored to attach himself to some wholesale firm that catered to ships. Each cornered travelers in need of passage, sold them tickets, and then endeavored to make the contracts good by placing their clients on the next vessel that appeared. The processes involved considerable hanky-panky with greedy captains and there were times when a vessel that had oversold its space fled the repercussions by slipping out of the shallow bay in the dark of the night.[6]

The situation called for another scheduled line, preferably one already operating in the Atlantic and hence able to sell through tickets from New York to San Francisco. The new competitor would have to

THE MARINERS MUSEUM

The Brother Jonathan was typical of the steamships that plied the Atlantic Coast between New York and Chagres.

43

be well enough established to withstand the chilly reception that Pacific Mail undoubtedly would give it. And the new line would need the services of a reputable agency in Panama City.

Two lines offered themselves. One was headed by Liveoak George Law, a director of the United States Mail Company. That company held its subsidy from the government under a proviso that it confine its operations to the Atlantic side of Central America. There was nothing in the contract, however, that said a director of the company could not move into the Pacific on his own initiative. Early in 1850, Liveoak George did just that. The name of the Panama agency that helped implement his move has not survived.

The other candidate was J. H. Howard & Sons, a small, aggressive firm engaged in the West Indies trade. The rush of 1849 had led the Howards to extend the services of their Empire Line, as they called it, to Chagres. The expansion proved so profitable that within a year the company was ready to move on into the Pacific. Needing an agency, Howard approached Garrison. The men may have met years earlier when Garrison was transferring cargo from his Mississippi steamboats to Howard's ocean freighters; or they may have been introduced by Garrison's good friend, Charles Morgan, who was financially involved in the Howards' Empire Line and chartered ships to it. In any event, Garrison & Fretz accepted the Panama assignment.

Howard sent three steamers around the Horn—the slow but luxurious *Sarah Sands,* the *Northerner,* and the *New Orleans.*[7] The last-named, a key ship to this story, was not owned by Howard & Sons, but was operated on charter.

Meeting the demands of the new client soon absorbed most of Billy Ralston's time. It was profitable work: big volume and high prices. One of an agent's responsibilities, for instance, was importing coal over long distances (very little coal was available on the Pacific Coast) and storing it at stations on Taboga Island in Panama Bay, at Acapulco, Mexico, and at San Francisco. Garrison once remarked that his firm on one occasion furnished $50,000 worth of coal to a steamer for a single run from Panama to San Francisco and back.[8] The standard commission for such services was 2½ percent of the coal's value. From that bottom level, remuneration ranged up to 20 percent of the price of passenger tickets sold in Panama.

Understandably eager to retain such lucrative business, both Law's unnamed agent and Garrison & Fretz worked diligently to further the interests of their clients. The gains they achieved came in large part at the expense of the Pacific Mail Steamship Company.

That company had just declared a 50 percent dividend and wished to maintain the rate. As a warning to the newcomers that they were entering dangerous waters, it increased its capitalization to $2 million—

the stock offering was immediately oversubscribed—and used part of the money to enlarge and improve facilities. It also slashed freight and passenger rates.

Defiantly the competition matched the cuts.

Northward, meanwhile, Cornelius Vanderbilt was accelerating his own approach to the Pacific. English bankers whom he had approached about financing the canal he hoped to build across Nicaragua had been cautious. They wanted more exact engineering studies so that they could make accurate estimates about costs. They also wanted dependable prognostications of traffic flow. Partly out of impatience—the Commodore hated to be balked—and partly to start impressive amounts of travel moving through Nicaragua, Vanderbilt modified his plans.

His charter from the Nicaraguan government allowed him the right, if the canal proved impossible, to substitute rail, water, and carriage transport across the isthmus. Ignoring the word "rail," he ordered for immediate delivery several small steamers capable of thrusting from the Atlantic up the San Juan River into Lake Nicaragua, and a galaxy of blue-and-white stagecoaches for dashing from the lake to the Pacific over a road that was to be paved with wooden planks. The management of these varied operations was assigned to a new organization called the Accessory Transit Company, duly chartered by Nicaragua in return for a promise of an annual payment to that government of $10,000 or 10 percent of the Accessory Company's gross profits, whichever was the greater. The stock of the new company was placed on the open market, but Vanderbilt and a few handpicked cronies retained just enough so that they would be able to control voting at the meetings of the board of directors.

To prove the feasibility of the route to doubting Thomases in England, the crusty old Commodore traveled it in person during the closing days of 1850. Boarding his fine new 1,500-ton steamer *Prometheus* and taking a tough little riverboat, the *Director,* in tow he steamed to Greytown at the mouth of the San Juan. There he shifted to the *Director*. Water was low—it was the dry season—and at one of the rapids the captain of the boat gave up. They could go no farther, he said.

Vanderbilt responded by ordering out some winches the boat carried, had them fastened to riverside trees, and hired enough Nicaraguan workers to haul the *Director* through the white water by brute strength. The travelers then steamed across the sparkling lake to Virgin Bay, switched to mules, and rode down a jungle trail to a bamboo hamlet called San Juan del Sur (or, as it was often spelled in those days, San Juan del Sud). At San Juan, Vanderbilt decreed, the Accessory Transit Company would place its western terminus.[9]

The journalists who had accompanied the expedition were then given a long discourse on the advantages of the new scheme. The company

This 1851 map shows Vanderbilt's challenge to the Panama Route—up the Rio San Juan, across Lake Nicaragua, and by stage to the Pacific.

THE MARINERS MUSEUM

The old fort of San Carlos guarded the strategic outlet from Lake Nicaragua to the San Juan River.

would station shallow-draft steamboats in relays along the San Juan River and let passengers walk around the rapids during times of low water. Even counting the hikes, the trip would be easier than the dreadful, disease-infested crossing of Panama. Furthermore, travel distance from New York to San Francisco would be shortened by nearly five hundred miles. Let the opposition try bucking those advantages!

Recognizing the threat, the Pacific Mail Steamship Company decided to free its hands for the struggle by ridding itself of its local opposition. It arranged through a complaisant ally to put chartered vessels on the New York–Chagres run in competition to the United States Mail Company. The intent was clear: to frighten Law's fellow directors in that company so badly that they would pull their errant associate back into his own pasture. Simultaneously the Aspinwall group purchased, probably at exorbitant prices, all but one of the ships that carried the colors of J. H. Howard & Sons' Empire Line. The sole exception was the chartered *New Orleans*. That forlorn vessel was so plastered with liens and tangled in litigation that Aspinwall let her alone and, since a single ship isolated in the Pacific was of no use to Howard & Sons, they dropped her charter. The *New Orleans'* part owner and agent in San Francisco, J. W. Raymond, thereupon withdrew the vessel from the Panama run and put her on the Sacramento River.[10]

The strategy was only partially successful. George Law did withdraw from the Pacific, leaving that much of the field open. Promptly J. H.

Howard & Sons acquired new vessels to replace those sold to Pacific Mail and hurried a new Empire Line fleet to the Pacific to resume the competition that Aspinwall had supposed he was eliminating.[11]

Why the canny Aspinwall should have left himself vulnerable to so crass a maneuver is a mystery. Either he neglected to stipulate in the original purchase agreements that Howard was to remain out of contention for a given time, or else Howard found some way of violating the agreement. How much Garrison & Fretz—and Billy Ralston—knew in advance of their client's slyness, which must have seemed to Aspinwall like a double cross, cannot now be determined. In any event, Garrison & Fretz regained their lucrative agency business. The development may even have had something to do with their purchasing, during this period, a tiny 309-ton vessel called the *General Warren*. Such a ship was too small to count in the Panama plans, however, and so Garrison & Fretz sent her north to compete on the San Francisco–Portland run with the Pacific Mail Company's equally small *Columbia*.[12]

The new Howard fleet represented by Garrison & Fretz was mediocre in quality. Its largest ship was the ill-tended *New Orleans,* rechartered from J. W. Raymond. A vessel comparable in size but in better repair was the *Union.* Supplementary transportation was furnished by two dwarfs scarcely larger than the *Warren*—the paradoxically named *Monumental City* and the meager 436-ton *Commodore Stockton.*[13]

William H. Aspinwall, of the Pacific Mail Steamship Company and the Panama Railroad, was a key figure in the battle of the routes.

Someone—Howard? Garrison?—also worked out an accommodation with Vanderbilt. His new 1,100-ton *Pacific* was scheduled to circle Cape Horn and reach San Juan del Sur in June, 1851, there to inaugurate Vanderbilt's Nicaragua–San Francisco run. No one knew how many passengers the *Pacific* might pick up along the way or how many more, disembarked on the Atlantic side of Nicaragua by the *Prometheus,* might be waiting at San Juan. To be on the safe side, Vanderbilt arranged with Howard & Sons for the *Commodore Stockton* to pause at San Juan on her own maiden journey north and pick up any excess stranded there.[14]

Clearly the bluff old commodore was not worried by the prospect of competition from Howard & Sons' Panama-based Pacific ships. He could crush that company, and its agents, whenever he chose. But for the time being they helped further his purposes. In so doing they also annoyed the Pacific Mail Steamship Company, Vanderbilt's chief adversary. And so Vanderbilt and Howard, firms that on the face of things should have been opponents, began working together, an arrangement not without significance for Billy Ralston.

Ralston was in New York that spring of 1851.[15] Presumably he was involved in details connected with supplying Howard & Sons' new fleet as it moved up the West Coast, back into contention with Pacific Mail. Quite possibly it was during this period that he first met Cornelius Vanderbilt—and, more to the point, Billy's age considered, one of Vanderbilt's many granddaughters, Louisa Thorne.

There was little time right then for romance. Howards' ships were nearing Panama City, and their success in the renewed struggle would depend largely on the efforts of the agency staff on the Isthmus. Bidding farewell to Garrison, who remained in New York to complete arrangements connected with other phases of the firm's interrelated activities, Ralston returned to the tropics. With him he took the eldest of his full brothers, Samuel.[16] Sam was nineteen at the time, amiable, levelheaded, and eager to stretch his wings. In Panama, under his brother's direction, he would soon find ample opportunity.

CHAPTER 4

Scrambling High

The next several months provided William Ralston with a long educa-tion in the art of meeting emergencies. The problems began in Panama in July, 1851. Certain suppliers, to whom the owners of the *New Orleans* were heavily indebted, announced that they were going to attach the ship (which was then somewhere between San Francisco and the Isthmus) and sell her at public auction in order to recover their money.

Loss of the chartered steamer, the largest in the Empire Line's new fleet, could be painful, yet there was no time to warn Howard & Sons in New York of the impending threat. Accordingly Garrison & Fretz determined to bid on the vessel themselves.

Who actually made the decision is unknown. Garrison was in New York; Fretz's whereabouts, as usual, were not recorded. In any event, it was Billy Ralston who on July 12 attended the auction in the base-ment of Panama's city hall, ran the bidding up to $50,000 payable in American gold coin, and so obtained for his firm a big brother to the little *General Warren*.[1] As soon as the *New Orleans* was in their hands, Garrison & Fretz rechartered it to J. H. Howard & Sons.

Keeping steamers free of legal entanglements was only part of the problem of keeping them afloat. A few days later the long overdue *Commodore Stockton* returned from her first trip to San Francisco badly in need of repairs.[2] Hard on her heels came the *New Orleans*, limping from previous neglect. Almost simultaneously word arrived that a drunken crew had let the pride of the fleet, the *Union,* run aground off Baja California. The steamer's 250 passengers and $270,000 in gold bullion en route to New York were removed without loss, but the ship itself was soon battered apart by heavy waves.[3] Meanwhile

Catastrophes like the one suffered by the steamship **Union** *off Lower California in 1851 were frequent on the Panama run.*

travelers from the East who had been guaranteed through service to San Francisco by Empire Line agencies in New York and New Orleans were piling up in Panama and clamoring for passage. Unless it were provided soon, they would demand refunds and switch to one of the vessels of the Pacific Mail Steamship Company, a sore blow not only to the Empire Line's profits, but to its prestige as well.

After worried discussions in which Ralston must have participated, the firm decided to take a chance. First it gave perfunctory attention to the most obvious of the *Stockton*'s ailments, then loaded aboard a hundred or more passengers, and on July 30, 1851, dispatched the ship northward once more. The *New Orleans* meanwhile was hurried to Taboga Island, ten miles out in the bay, where repair facilities were located, and there subjected to a thorough overhauling.

The decision proved ill-judged. Two days after weighing anchor, the *Commodore Stockton* reappeared at the Taboga Island yards, leaking badly. Drained of cash by the purchase of the *New Orleans* and by other pressing demands, Garrison & Fretz were not able to meet the demands of the enraged passengers for ticket refunds. But, the company said, the stranded wayfarers could live aboard the *Stockton* free of charge until the vessel was able to sail again, or until fresh funds had arrived from the East.

The passengers thereupon rioted. They ejected the ship's captain and agents, Ralston probably among them, seized the vessel, and declared that they were going to sell her in order to recover the money due them. At that Garrison and Fretz called for troops from the government's little fort in Panama City.[4] Gradually the turmoil calmed, the leak was patched, and in due time the *Commodore Stockton* resumed her journey.

On August 25, Garrison returned from New York. Immediately he was greeted with another crisis. More than two hundred passengers, fuming at being delayed in Panama, were scheduled to sail north aboard the *New Orleans* on September 1. Unhappily the captain of the vessel contracted cholera and died the night before the promised departure. No trustworthy substitute was available on such short notice; and evidently neither of the firm's two experienced ship commanders, Garrison and Fretz, felt free to leave their company's tangled affairs for the six weeks or more that the journey would consume. Consequently the assignment fell to Ralston.

Though he had never before commanded a ship, he knew his way around one. Trained mates, charts of the West Coast, and competent steersmen who had recently made the run were available to him. If unexpected storms or breakdowns occurred, they would tax his inexperience, but the *New Orleans* had just gone through an extensive overhauling and the season was not one when severe weather was likely. Off he went, probably with the serene confidence that he brought to all his tasks. His brother Sam traveled with him.

Even when accidents did not occur, travel to California by ship could be uncomfortable, as this sketch, "A Crowded Steamer," shows.

Nothing in the sparse records indicates that the trip was other than routine. Almost surely the *New Orleans* replenished her coal at Acapulco. Farther north, at night, the glow of the volcano of Colima furnished brief distraction. Although the terrible crowding of earlier days did not afflict the passengers, there were still dismaying rushes for the dining saloon at mealtime. Table linen, soon stained, was infrequently changed; food was not only monotonous but half-spoiled; ventilation, especially in the steerage and above the boilers, was conspicuously absent. Reading, card-playing, illegal gambling, impromptu musicales, and amateur plays helped to pass the time. After the ship had passed Cape San Lucas at the tip of Baja California, the rough mountains of the coast were generally in sight, and that, too, provided a bit of variety. The trip was no luxury cruise, however, even for first-class passengers, and the bored travelers of the *New Orleans* undoubtedly responded to their first glimpse of the Golden Gate, on September 19, with huzzas of relief—followed, possibly, by pangs of disappointment.

The vast, gleaming, island-dotted bay into which the ship was steaming was obviously one of the superlative natural harbors of the world. Still, to anyone used to the lushness of Panama and the lower Mississippi River, as Ralston was, the surroundings were hardly prepossessing. Summer's drought gripped the land. The barren hills, dotted with a few dwarf trees and clumps of brush, were the color of old straw. Against that desolation San Francisco looked shrunken and unimpressive.

As yet the city occupied only a small, hill-constricted swale on the northeastern side of the peninsula's tip. Telegraph Hill climbed steeply to the north, its top crowned by a semaphore signal tower that announced the approach of ships. California Hill (today called Nob Hill) interfered with expansion to the west. To the south, beyond oblique Market Street, was the blockading bulk of Rincon Hill, since removed to make way for approaches to the San Francisco–Oakland Bay Bridge.

Once a shallow cove had curved like the blade of a scimitar into the hollow between these uplifts. That sparkling recess was disappearing, however. Turned energetic by the high prices commanded by waterfront lots, real estate speculators were slicing away the flanks of the hills and dumping the earth onto the tidal flats, so as to bring the city closer to the ship anchorages. Other speculators were extending private wharves like hungry fingers into the water from the bay end of each east-west street. Abandoned ships had been winched up between the wharves and lodged against the advancing shoreline, where they were converted into warehouses, tawdry shops, even hotels. A wind that rose each afternoon filled the streets and even the air above the docks with the dry season's maddening clouds of dust.

The past months had been violent. A widespread reaction against the excesses of the gold stampede had produced, during the spring of

1851, an acute economic downswing. Steamboat tickets to Sacramento had dropped from $50 each to $2. Merchants who had imported more goods than could be absorbed and who lacked warehouses for storing the material, sold it at such sacrifices that canny buyers had been able to ship quantities of tea back to China and bales of manufactured articles back to New York at a handsome profit.[5] The gloom had been heightened in May when a ferocious fire, climax of many blazes, wiped out 22 blocks of the business district.

Slowly, signs of improvement appeared. During the summer a Committee of Vigilance usurped control of the city's corrupt law enforcement agencies. Though the group paid little attention to rampant fraud within the bankrupt city government, it did frighten San Francisco's more brazen criminals into hiding, and that helped restore confidence. In the interior many disappointed miners were seeking new beginnings by exploiting California's rich agricultural potentials. More determined prospectors, joining hands for the sake of economy, developed new mining techniques that would almost double gold production—from $41 million in 1850 to $76 million in 1851.[6] The bulk of that metal was just then moving toward San Francisco, passing through many hands along the way and stimulating each in turn.

Whether or not Ralston detected those signs of recovery is impossible to say. The *New Orleans* was his main concern. He calmed down agent Raymond, who, as part owner of the ship, objected to the way the forced sale in Panama had been handled. As a publicity device he passed on to the newspapers information that he had gleaned from Garrison about American filibustering in Cuba. He then capitalized on the mild excitement that followed by giving free passage as far as Panama to a George White, who wanted to join the insurgents. The newspapers printed his and White's exchange of letters, and thus Ralston was able to imprint on the minds of potential travelers a brief awareness of the name *New Orleans*. On September 27, leaving behind no indication that he had been in any way impressed by the brawling town, he turned south again. Like the trip north, the journey was uneventful.[7]

He returned the following March, 1852, not as a captain (so far as is known Ralston never again commanded a vessel) but as a passenger aboard the *New Orleans,* charged with certain investigations. One, which may not have confronted him until he stepped off the ship, was connected with the disastrous wreck of his firm's little ship, the *General Warren*. Late in January the vessel had left Portland loaded with grain and passengers destined for California. Just outside the mouth of the Columbia River a gale tore her apart. Eleven persons escaped. Forty-one others, and the ship, were never seen again.[8] Although no record exists concerning the aftermath, there must have been repercussions:

The first photograph ever taken of San Francisco shows the crowded harbor in 1850, one year before Ralston stepped ashore in the city.

the claims of shippers and passengers against Garrison & Fretz, and the claims of Garrison & Fretz against whatever marine insurance company carried their account. As a key member of the firm arriving on the scene at a critical time, Ralston could not have escaped involvement.

His other investigation was being undertaken at the behest of Cornelius Vanderbilt and involved a projected railroad between San Francisco and San Jose, the latter a hamlet located near the southern tip of San Francisco Bay. For some time agitation had been sounding in Congress for a transcontinental railway to be built with the aid of government money or land grants. If the road actually materialized, it might well pass through San Jose on its way up the peninsula to a logical terminus at San Francisco. One method of fortifying that possibility, so the promoters in San Jose argued, was to anticipate the transcontinental with a railroad already operating between the two towns—one that in the meantime would give a boost to San Jose's own economy.

Buoyed by the vision, the promoters incorporated the Pacific & Atlantic Railroad Company. At an enthusiastic public meeting in San Jose on January 26, 1851, they obtained subscriptions to $100,000 worth of stock—although only 10 percent of the sum was actually paid in cash at the time. Using those subscriptions as evidence that they really had a viable enterprise in the making, the promoters sent emissaries to New York and London in the hope of raising the $2 million that the road to San Francisco would cost.

Vanderbilt was one of the financiers they approached. Needing a more objective analysis than he could get from his visitors, he asked Garrison to find someone capable of investigating the proposal for him. And so it came about that on March 5, 1852, Billy Ralston made his second visit to San Francisco. Once again no record survives concerning either his survey or his conclusions. On March 20, however, three days after his departure, the San Francisco *Alta California* stated that the directors of the railroad company were expecting to receive commitments of at least $1 million in outside capital.[9]

Ralston almost certainly carried his report to New York in person.[10] Nothing more was heard of the matter. A spate of troubles had concentrated Vanderbilt's attention on his Nicaragua adventure.

The Commodore was thrusting an ever-expanding fleet into the Pacific. At its head was the 2,500-ton *North America,* huge for the time and place. The great ship had rounded the Horn during the winter and at the new port of San Juan del Sur had picked up 400 persons that Vanderbilt's Atlantic liner, *Prometheus,* had recently deposited on Nicaragua's eastern shore. Thanks to catching the *North America* without delay, the travelers reached San Francisco on January 19, 1852 —a mere 26 days from New York. The record was clear warning to all competitors that difficult times lay ahead.

Hard on the heels of the triumph, however, came disaster. On February 27, 1852, the *North America,* loaded with 900 passengers, crashed ashore fifty miles from Acapulco. No lives were lost—the passengers made their way to Acapulco "in starving condition, having lost all their money, clothes, &c"[11]—but the wounded ship could not be salvaged.

Needing stopgap transportation until the rest of his Pacific fleet could arrive on the scene, Vanderbilt turned to his friend Charles Morgan, the primary backer of Howard & Sons' Empire Line. The upshot, whatever the Howards' own feelings may have been, was the removal of their line from the overcrowded West Coast. Vanderbilt bought the *Monumental City.* Garrison & Fretz, the owners of the *New Orleans,* shifted that vessel's charter from Howard & Sons to Vanderbilt's Nicaragua Steamship Company.[12]

Taking a flier on their own, Ralph Fretz and William Ralston joined a friend, William Nelson, in purchasing the hard-used *Commodore Stockton.* They then chartered the vessel to Vanderbilt. For the purchasers it was a poor investment. On one of her first runs north under the new flag, the *Stockton* put into Acapulco so battered by storms that the port authorities decreed that the ship would have to undergo extensive repairs before resuming her journey. Apparently extortion was involved on behalf of favored contractors, and the owners refused to meet the exorbitant demands. The ship was thereupon condemned and

The building of a railroad across Panama sped travel, facilitated commerce, and gave a new twist to Ralston's activities.

sold to a company from Chile. Seventeen years later Nelson, Fretz, and Billy Ralston were trying, without success, to gain restitution.[13]

The demise of the Empire Line brought no hardship to its erstwhile agents. Quite the contrary. With a speed that suggests prior discussions, Garrison & Fretz formed a new alliance with the powerful New York shipping firm of Davis, Brooks & Company, which only recently had decided to jump headlong into the Pacific scramble. As a means to that end the company formed a subsidiary organization, the New York and San Francisco Steamship Company, and in January started the first of two luxury liners, the *Winfield Scott,* around the Horn. A second vessel, the plush *Cortes,* was scheduled to arrive in Panama in October.[14] These ships, which Garrison & Fretz undertook to manage on the Pacific, were far superior to anything Howard & Sons had possessed.

Ralston, who was engrossed in all these swirls, surely sensed the ambiguities involved. With one hand, Garrison, Fretz, and he were helping further Vanderbilt's Nicaragua route. With the other hand, they were forming an association with a firm whose profits (and theirs) would depend on taking as much traffic as possible away from both Vanderbilt and the Pacific Mail Steamship Company.

Such tangles—they were commonplace along the slippery reefs of the shipping business—did not interfere with Ralston's social life. Among the events that he attended while in the East during the spring of 1852 was a glittering ball at the home of Charles Morgan. According to legend, that swish occasion formed the backdrop for his first meeting with Louisa Thorne, daughter of W. K. Thorne, one of Vanderbilt's seven sons-in-law.[15] Or perhaps they simply attended the function together, having met a year earlier, as could easily have been the case. In any event, they were soon deeply in love, quite regardless of the fact that here was another ambiguity: as a representative of the New York and San Francisco Steamship Company, Billy Ralston would soon be working diligently in Panama against the girl's own grandfather. But perhaps Vanderbilt did not mind. He had worked enough with Ralston to know his abilities and quite possibly approved of the developing romance, insofar as he considered it at all.

No wedding date was set. Agency affairs in Panama—banking, trans-Isthmian transportation, and wholesaling as well as shipping—cried for attention. Back Ralston went, taking with him still another younger brother, Andrew Jackson, aged eighteen. Because of their firm's new association with Davis, Brooks & Company, the two young men found themselves precipitated into living conditions that at times must have been pure misery.

The Panama Railroad was creeping slowly toward its crossing of the continental divide. During the closing months of 1851, passenger ships had begun landing their fares at the deep-water docks on Manzanillo

THE MARINERS MUSEUM

Among other duties, Ralston supervised his firm's branch office in Colón (shown above), Atlantic terminus of the Panama Railroad.

Island. From there trains carried the travelers—some 30,000 moved along the rails in both directions in 1852—sixteen miles into the Chagres Valley. Mule trains, including those operated by Garrison & Fretz, then decided to compete with the bongos and hacked out trails through the jungle from Cruces and Gorgona in order to contact the slowly advancing railheads.

These activities roused considerable stir in Aspinwall (later Colón), the town that the railroad had created amidst the swamps of Manzanillo Island. It was a fungus-blotched collection of warehouses, train sheds, soiled restaurants, claptrap hotels, and dispirited office buildings used by local businessmen. Cholera and yellow fever ravaged the countryside. Fearful residents started each new day with what was widely regarded as the ultimate bulwark against disease—champagne laced with bitters and chilled with expensive ice imported in sawdust from New England. On meeting, friends proffered quinine pills as courteously as Frenchmen held out snuffboxes.[16]

Davis, Brooks & Company wanted their new agents to open a branch office in Aspinwall. The chore fell to Billy Ralston.[17] Probably it was his job also to supervise the erection of new facilities for the expanded mule trains. The trips he made back and forth along the line were so speedy that they became a local legend.[18]

The mule trains had to be efficiently run. Huge quantities of gold were moving out of California to the eastern United States. A single Panama vessel might carry bullion worth $1.5 million or more, and as soon as that treasure was transferred to muleback it became a powerful temptation. Government troops provided an escort service of sorts, but transportation companies wanted insurance protection as well. It was difficult to get. One measure of the new potency that Garrison & Fretz gained through their association with Davis, Brooks & Company was an announcement, issued during the fall of 1852, that nine American underwriters, dividing the risks among themselves, were according to specie transported by Garrison & Fretz the same preferential rates formerly granted only to carriers for the Pacific Mail Steamship Company.[19]

For the sake of both its banking and agency activities, the company also established a trans-Isthmian express service. Trained messengers met incoming ships at Aspinwall, gathered information about arriving passengers and their baggage, and also about the world money market, and then sped the news to Panama City. Along with that intelligence the messengers carried the latest newspapers from New York and London. After combing the journals for useful data, Garrison & Fretz turned the papers over to the news-hungry Panamanian dailies.[20]

In other ways, too, the partners sought to help themselves by softening the rigors of the Panama crossing. Nearly two years earlier Garrison had led a drive, in which he remained interested, to improve the city's "burying ground." Fretz and he joined other American businessmen in raising funds to build and staff a hospital. The Masons and the Odd Fellows—Ralston was an active Odd Fellow—established aid stations to help sick and indigent associates along their way.[21]

Outward expansion signified inner prosperity. During the last months of 1852 the *Winfield Scott* carried more treasure out of California than any of its competitors. The *Cortes* set, on its first trip from Panama to San Francisco, a new speed record of 13 days and 12 hours. A grand ship! Garrison & Fretz advertised the *Cortes* as "the best ventilated vessel on the Pacific"—a winning point in the tropics. Even the steerage was made comfortable by "square ports of enormous size, which, when open, cause a current of air to rush in, causing it to be almost as cool as the deck." When the captain of this paragon, William H. Hudson, received a particularly glowing tribute from one group of passengers, Ralston made sure that the laudatory words appeared not only in the Panama newspapers but in the New York *Herald* as well.[22] Indeed, the firm succeeded to its own hurt. Despite extensive overhauling the *New Orleans,* which they owned, proved unable to compete with the new vessels for which they were agents. Accordingly Garrison & Fretz sent her to Australia to be sold.[23]

Ralston, not yet twenty-seven, shared in the acclaim brought by his firm's business triumphs. When the merchants of Panama City held a testimonial banquet for the province's representative to the national congress at Bogotá, Ralston occupied a seat of honor next to the governor. As was customary in those days, the meal concluded with a series of toasts—to the guest of honor, to the governor, to Commerce, to Prosperity, and so on. Ralston was called on for the final tribute— to the ladies, conspicuously absent.

Surely this was intended as a reference to his romance with Louisa Thorne, and he understood it to be such, for when he arose he protested too much. Everyone else in the room, he said, was a husband. Many were fathers. Why call on him? With that, and to the accompaniment of indulgent smiles, he launched into what reads like a prepared text, heavily larded with the sentimentalities popular at the time.[24]

> TO THE LADIES—With them the gay and thoughtless are tempered in their merriment; the toil-worn are helped on with their labors; the despondent are cheered . . . and when the last of earth comes to Man in his dying hour, he is consoled upon entering on his long journey through the shadow of the valley of Death, by the softly murmured but nevertheless devout, earnest, and heartfelt prayers . . . from the fair being who sits beside him, sorrowfully watching each flickering of the decaying light.
> Mr. Chairman, I propose "Sweethearts and Wives."

Of course he was pleased. The new tax lists, published in the Panama *Star* on January 15, 1853, showed that Garrison & Fretz had become one of the three biggest taxpayers in the province of Panama. Davis, Brooks & Company, the shipping firm they represented, had profited so handsomely that it was planning to reorganize its Panama subsidiary as the New York and California Line, increase capitalization to $1.5 million, buy new ships, and intensify efforts to lay hold of a still greater share of the traffic moving across Central America.[25] As Ralston considered the proliferating activities, he probably began to wonder about asking for a transfer to some site, either New York or San Francisco, that might provide a more suitable home than Panama for a new bride.

Alas for plans! In making his calculations he failed to take into account the volatile temperament of his fiercely ambitious friend and mentor, Cornelius Garrison.

CHAPTER 5

Desolation

One day in February, 1853, the Garrison & Fretz express messenger from Aspinwall brought information to Panama City that must have filled the company office with a buzz of speculation. Cornelius Garrison, who was then on his way back from New York, had recently agreed to serve, at a salary of $60,000 a year, as manager of Vanderbilt's West Coast affairs. His headquarters would be in San Francisco.

Repercussions in Panama were immediate. The first problem revolved around the *Uncle Sam,* an Atlantic liner built by wealthy Edward Mills, who was inaugurating a new service from New York to Aspinwall. As yet Mills had no ships in the Pacific. Therefore he prevailed on Vanderbilt to transport the California-bound passengers that used the *Uncle Sam,* on this first trip only, from Panama City to San Francisco. The Vanderbilt vessel assigned to the duty was the steamer *Sierra Nevada,* which had just rounded Cape Horn on its way to join the Commodore's Pacific fleet.

The message from Aspinwall instructed the Garrison & Fretz office to hold the *Sierra Nevada* at Panama City until the *Uncle Sam*'s passengers had straggled across the Isthmus. (Garrison would be among them.) During the wait, Fretz and Ralston were to attract still more business to the *Sierra Nevada* by launching a vigorous advertising campaign in the Panama newspapers.

Here were ambivalences indeed! The message said nothing about ending relations with Davis, Brooks & Company, whose plans for expansion were already under way. The new line (the New York and California Steamship Company) would be an opponent not only of the Pacific Mail Steamship Company but of Vanderbilt's Nicaragua route as well. Did Garrison expect to serve two masters simultaneously?

Apparently he did. And so, in the absence of other instructions, the Panama agency continued advertising in glowing terms the advantages of Davis, Brooks & Company's *Winfield Scott* and *Cortes*. Alongside those panegyrics, and also above the name Garrison & Fretz, they placed equally glowing copy extolling a competitive ship, the *Sierra Nevada*.[1] As Billy Ralston helped prepare the rival claims he must have wondered what had been happening in New York—and what effect it would have on his coming marriage.

The tale he pieced together was complex and surprising. In the summer of 1852 the English investors whom Vanderbilt had been trying to interest in financing a canal across Nicaragua finally rejected the project. Stock in the canal company plummeted. Stock in Vanderbilt's Nicaragua Steamship Company and in Accessory Transit Company, which moved both freight and passengers across Nicaragua, tumbled in its wake.

By this time the Commodore had invested millions of dollars in his drive to dominate the flow of traffic between the eastern and western coasts of the United States. With characteristic doggedness he determined to keep the project going and at the same time halt the declining stock values in his various enterprises. Bulking large among those enterprises was a separate agency that he had created earlier for handling supplies and maintenance work for his steamship and transit companies. Vanderbilt had never assigned that agency business to outsiders, as most steamboat owners did, because by operating the firm himself he could divert into his own coffers every dollar that was produced by the Nicaragua adventure.

Complicating his troubles was the rebellious mood of his fellow directors and shareholders in the Accessory Transit Company, of which Vanderbilt was president. Mismanagement, inefficiency, and sagging morale were undermining operations within Central America. Concurrently the government of Nicaragua was charging that Accessory Transit had violated the terms of its franchise by failing to remit, as specified, 10 percent of its annual profits. The complaint was justified so far as gross profits were concerned. Vanderbilt, however, talked in terms of net. The Accessory Transit Company was pouring money, often wastefully, into new facilities along the crossing; hence there were no profits; therefore the company's obligations to the government ceased with its annual remittance of $10,000. To Vanderbilt's fellow directors this seemed penny-pinching. What would happen if the government cancelled the Accessory Company's exclusive franchise?

The core of the problem, the disgruntled shareholders told each other, was this: Vanderbilt was not really interested in the transit company. It was simply a device for feeding traffic, through Vanderbilt's agency, into Vanderbilt's steamship company. *He* profited. *They,* as

Cornelius Vanderbilt constructed the steam yacht **North Star** *for taking his family, including Ralston's fiancée, on a trip to Europe.*

shareholders in the orphan unit, received only the paltry leavings.

Abruptly Vanderbilt resigned as president and director of the transit company. He was a thick-skinned old curmudgeon, and it is unlikely that the bickering of his fellows was more than an incidental factor in his decision. His main motives lay elsewhere. He was building, at a cost of $285,400, a palatial, 270-foot, 1,900-ton steam yacht, *North Star,* on which to take twenty-five members of his family, Louisa Thorne among them, on a dazzling tour of Europe. He did not want business worries oppressing him during the journey, yet he wanted to recoup his recent losses. He thought he knew how to manage both desires at once.

He sold his Nicaragua Steamship Company, and the steamers it operated in both the Atlantic and Pacific, to Accessory Transit for $1.35 million. The bulk of the sum was raised by placing on the market a new issue of 40,000 shares of Transit Company stock. It was agreed that his agency would retain the business of the enlarged company, thereafter known officially as the Nicaragua Transit Company, but popularly as Nicaragua Steamship Company.

The amalgamation of the steamship and transit operations suggested to Wall Street that an efficient, comprehensive through service between coasts would follow. Stock in Nicaragua Transit soared. One suspects that Vanderbilt, anticipating just that outcome, had acquired quantities of Accessory Transit Company stock when it was depressed and then unloaded when the amalgamation brought about the rise. At least he was not suffering for money in 1853. He had recently invested $11 million in such a way, he told a reporter, that it was currently yielding him 25 percent a year.[2] In selling so much of his stock, however, he left himself vulnerable, as Ralston, among others, would soon learn.

In spite of selling the ships and resigning as president of Accessory Transit, Vanderbilt had no intention of letting control of affairs in Nicaragua slip from his grasp. He could still exert considerable pressure through his agency, if that company were properly managed. As yet he was not satisfied with the men (one of them a son-in-law, J. M. Cross) whom he had placed in charge of his offices in New York and San Francisco. Searching for new talent, he turned to Charles Morgan and Cornelius Garrison.

He knew both men well. His namesake, Cornelius Garrison, who was also called Commodore, intrigued him particularly. After a fumbling start with Howard & Sons, the Garrison & Fretz agency had moved ahead spectacularly with Davis, Brooks & Company. Garrison, in addition, was familiar with the sweaty details connected with any isthmus crossing—riverboats, mule trains, express services. As a banker, he understood finance. Would he consider transferring those talents to Vanderbilt's San Francisco office?

Garrison would—at a price. He probably figured what the agency would be worth if he owned it himself and set his sights accordingly—$60,000. Vanderbilt gulped and agreed. And then Garrison ranged out still farther. Because he was now in a position to place insurance contracts on Vanderbilt's West Coast ships and Nicaragua treasure trains, he was able to pressure two eastern insurance companies into appointing him as their California representative for another $25,000 a year.[3] The combined sum—$85,000 annually—probably made him the highest salaried man in the United States at the time. Nor did his income end with his salary. He insisted on and was granted the right to retain his interest in Garrison & Fretz, even though a conflict in interests was certain to exist between that firm's established shipping commitments and Garrison's new job.

The San Francisco appointment meant that Garrison would have to withdraw from active management of affairs in Panama. In order that the void could be satisfactorily filled, William Ralston was elevated to a full partnership in the company. The announcement came March 10, 1853, the day Garrison boarded the *Sierra Nevada* for San Francisco. It consisted of a small change in the standing advertisement that the company ran in each issue of the Panama *Star*. The firm name was changed from Garrison & Fretz to Garrison, Fretz & Company, and Ralston's name appeared for the first time alongside those of C. K.

Garrison and R. S. Fretz. His salary was $4,000 a year. He was six weeks past his twenty-seventh birthday, and he had been on the Isthmus three and a half years.

Immediately after his promotion he was given a task worthy of his new position. From somewhere Garrison, Fretz & Company had learned that Pacific Mail, alarmed by the plans of Davis, Brooks & Company to expand its Panama service, was trying to forestall the step by buying out its potential rival. If that happened, the agency in which Ralston had just become a partner would be without ships to represent. At an agitated meeting in Panama it was decided that someone should go to New York to keep abreast of the situation there. Ralston was chosen, partly so that he could say good-bye to Louisa before she sailed with her grandfather for Europe.[4]

Both missions were rewarding. The girl's parents agreed that Louisa and he could be married as soon as possible after the *North Star* returned in September from its cruise.[5] If anything was agreed about the location of the newlyweds' first home—Panama, for a granddaughter of Cornelius Vanderbilt?—the records have been lost.

While the romance was blossoming, Davis, Brooks & Company sold out to Pacific Mail. In order to replace the business lost through the transaction, Ralston turned to Edward Mills. As Billy undoubtedly knew, Mills was constructing a new steamer, the *Yankee Blade,* to serve as the Pacific counterpart of his *Uncle Sam,* which was then plying between New York and Aspinwall. If work went according to schedule, the *Yankee Blade* would reach the Pacific side of Panama during the early months of 1854. And, yes, Mills would be glad to have Garrison, Fretz & Company represent her.[6] Until then the agency was to find space as best it could for California-bound passengers who traveled as far as Aspinwall aboard the *Uncle Sam.* Although at the start this business would fall short of being an adequate replacement for the vanished Davis, Brooks account, it could be built up by diligent effort and by the acquisition of more ships. Well content with what the future seemed to hold, Ralston went to the docks to see Louisa off and then returned to Panama.

There he learned that Garrison, as Vanderbilt's new representative in San Francisco, was vigorously promoting the Nicaragua route. Vanderbilt's steamers, he proclaimed in California's leading newspapers, would carry mail to the East Coast free of charge and get it there ahead of letters traveling the longer Panama route subsidized by the government. The target of the attack was, of course, the Pacific Mail Steamship Company. But the other companies were not spared. Acting under Garrison's direction, the purser of the *Sierra Nevada* told the San Francisco press that the Isthmus was a vast charnel house, afflicted with "black vomit of the most malignant type. . . . The resi-

*Vanderbilt paid Cornelius Garrison $60,000 a year for operating
the Nicaragua Steamship agency in San Francisco.*

dents of the city meet each other with suspicious, inquiring looks, and
nights are spent in small, silent processions of friends hurrying to the
tombs with the remains of those that a few hours since had been with
them in the vigor of life."[7]

Next time try Nicaragua—even though it meant avoiding ships
represented by Garrison, Fretz & Company.

But before the rivalry between the routes grew really heated, circumstances cooled it. A week after Garrison opened his office, word
reached San Francisco that the *Independence,* one of the four Nicaragua Transit Company steamers that he supervised in the Pacific, had
burned with a loss of at least 125 lives.[8] Before that shock had been
absorbed, another Nicaragua Transit Company ship, the S.S. *Lewis,*
overshot the Golden Gate in the fog and at 5 A.M. on April 9, 1853,
wrecked on a reef near Bolinas. All 385 of her passengers, including 49
women and 24 children, reached shore, but the ship went to pieces.

All told, Vanderbilt and his successor company had sent six ships
into the Pacific between February, 1852, and April, 1853—and had lost
four of them.[9] As partial replacement, Nicaragua Transit paid the

69

Pacific Mail Steamship Company $225,000 for the *Cortes,* an erstwhile vessel of Davis, Brooks & Company.[10]

The Pacific disasters left Vanderbilt vulnerable to attack from his own subordinates. During the earlier manipulations that had given birth to the Nicaragua Transit Company, successor to the business of both the original Accessory Transit Company and the old Nicaragua Steamship Company, the Commodore had let go of more stock than he had perhaps realized. He was lulled, too, by what appeared to be the lucky timing of the sales, for as soon as the news of the burning of the *Independence* and the wreck of the S.S. *Lewis* reached the East, the price of Transit Company stock dropped again. He had unloaded at exactly the right moment—it seemed.

The collapse in price, however, gave Garrison and Morgan an opening to attack their employer. Working swiftly and probably in collusion with some of Vanderbilt's disgruntled fellow directors in the old accessory company, they bought enough shares to dominate Nicaragua Transit. They then fired Vanderbilt as the company's agent and gave the business to a new firm created by and for themselves. The president of this new agency was Charles Morgan.[11]

Ralston was waiting in New York on September 23, 1853, wh the Vanderbilts returned from their four months' cruise.[12] He saw the iced fury that led his prospective grandfather-in-law to write his betrayers: "Gentlemen, You have undertaken to cheat me. I won't sue you, for the law is too slow. I will ruin you. Yours truly, Cornelius Vanderbilt."[13]

The carrying out of that threat was certain to affect Ralston's future, yet at the time he gave the gathering conflict no heed. When the *North Star* docked, Louisa was desperately ill. He hovered beside her bed for several days, mostly in company with the girl's mother, Emily— ever afterwards he felt a profound attachment for Mrs. Thorne—and then, at approximately the date proposed for the wedding, he watched her die. The bereaved parents gave him a miniature of her that had been painted on ivory during the cruise, and with that as a memento he returned to Panama.[14]

WITHIN WEEKS VANDERBILT HAD DEVISED a plan to regain his agency. He would depress the stock of the Nicaragua Transit Company, and then, when prices were low enough to ruin his adversaries, would buy control. He would then eject them from their agency, just as they had ejected him.

To do this he formed what he called the Independent Opposition Steamship Company. He ordered the *North Star* to be converted into a passenger ship to cover the Atlantic end of the run. From Edward Mills he bought the *Uncle Sam* and the *Yankee Blade*, which was almost ready to sail, and ordered both steamers to the Pacific.[15] Because Nicaragua Transit held an exclusive franchise to any crossing of that country, he had to make connections by way of Panama. Needing dependable representatives on the Isthmus and in San Francisco, he turned to Fretz and Ralston. Would they undertake to supervise the West Coast operations of his new Independent Opposition Line?

It was a remarkable proposal. In the first place, Cornelius Garrison would be a redoubtable foe. He had reorganized Nicaragua Transit Company with exemplary speed and efficiency. He had put new machinery in the *Cortes,* had spent $126,000 building a fine plank road from San Juan del Sur to Virgin Bay on Lake Nicaragua, and had polished up all the other facilities under his jurisdiction. Favorable conditions assured, he demanded that his ship captains and stagecoach drivers adhere without excuses to swift new schedules.

The result had been an immediate swing in public favor to the Nicaragua line. On December 1, 1853, for example, the *Sierra Nevada* sailed from San Francisco with twice as much treasure ($1,635,000 as compared to $800,000) and twice as many passengers aboard as the Pacific Mail's recently purchased *Winfield Scott.* Such gains were quickly reflected in the company's balance sheet. Profits for the last six months of 1853 reached $533,410.[16]

To top matters, Garrison had been elected mayor of San Francisco after six months' residence in the city. Obviously he could exert political as well as economic pressure. Yet Vanderbilt seemed to think that Fretz and Ralston could attack Garrison and Morgan successfully enough to help the Commodore force down the value of Nicaragua Transit stock on the New York exchange.

There was more. Vanderbilt had just been betrayed by his agency managers. Nevertheless he expected Fretz and Ralston to resist whatever blandishments might be offered them by their long-time friend, Cornelius Garrison. Unless Vanderbilt had been very sure that the two men would abide steadfastly by any promises they made, he would scarcely have asked them to expose themselves to such strains. To what extent he counted on the memory of his dead granddaughter to influence Ralston's deportment can only be surmised.

On their part, Fretz and Ralston had reason to listen favorably to the proposal. Garrison had not hesitated to undercut their shipping business for the sake of his new Nicaragua project. Now that business was gone, purchased by Vanderbilt. Opportunities to form new connections with a company strong enough to buck both Vanderbilt's Independent Opposition Line and the Pacific Mail Steamship Company simply did not exist. They either joined the Commodore or abandoned agency work.

In the end they accepted—but retained, eerily enough, their banking and merchandising partnership with Garrison in Panama. That business would be managed by Ralston's two brothers, Sam and Andrew Jackson, and by Major John Fretz. Billy Ralston and Ralph Fretz would move to San Francisco to supervise the agency there.

The final details of the agreement were worked out in New York City during early February, 1854, by Ralston and John Fretz. On the afternoon of February 20, they boarded the *North Star* for Aspinwall. That night high waves and a slashing snowstorm forced the ship to heave to behind Staten Island. (As Ralston moved through the converted passageways, he must have imagined Louisa there, only months before.) Three days later, a man was swept overboard. Delayed by searching fruitlessly for him in the tumbling seas, the *North Star* did not reach Aspinwall until shortly after noon, March 2.

Two other crowded ships had docked just ahead of them. Fifteen hundred bewildered travelers milled around the train depot, trying to buy tickets as far as the railhead at Obispo. Ralston, whose way had been prepared in advance, circled the mob to the coaches and was in his seat when the locomotive jerked forward at 3:10. At 4:35 he disembarked at Obispo, swung onto a saddled mule, and spurred ahead into winter's twilight. At 7:15 he clattered over the cobbles in the plaza.[17] The Panama *Daily Star* for March 3 was agog over the speed.

FASTEST TIME—THE QUICKEST YET
Trip Across the Isthmus in 4 h. 5 m.!!

"Old Toppy [the account concluded] always was a 'fast 'un,' but this feat not only breaks all others by more than *two* hours, but every thing yet that *he* has attempted on time!" In another column, the reporter announced sadly, "We understand that Mr. Ralston goes immediately to San Francisco as agent of Vanderbilt's Independent Lines."

On March 20, one month after leaving New York, he and Ralph Fretz were there. Their next days were busy. They had to claim Vanderbilt's West Coast records from his discharged agents, G.B. Post & Company (for whom Post Street had been named), then rent office space, hire clerks, and set up whatever mode of business suited them best.[18] They contacted suppliers, local banking houses, the express agencies that brought gold dust in from the mountains, and newspapers, whose publicity was vital. They found bachelor living quarters and began learning their way around the city's social as well as its economic circles.

San Francisco had grown remarkably since Ralston's last visit two years before. Population, the *Alta California* estimated, had reached 55,000.[19] A United States mint opened on April 1, 1854, ending private coinage by private bankers, some of whom had profiteered unduly by putting less gold than was required in the slugs they manufactured. More and longer wharves extended into the bay. Fire-resistant buildings of dressed granite imported from China were replacing frame buildings throughout the center of the city. Streets were paved with asphalt blocks quarried from tar seeps in Southern California, or with planks sawed from the redwood forests that still blanketed the peninsula's hills to the south. One of Ralston's first public utterances was a protest to the board of supervisors against the number of thoroughfares that had been paved by private contractors in return for the privilege of collecting tolls.[20] He felt that the city should do its own street work, a somewhat naive suggestion in view of the notorious corruption that riddled San Francisco's contracting system.

Presiding over this crass and energetic city was Mayor C. K. Garrison. From this distance a satisfactory evaluation of his single year in office is difficult to make. His virtues certainly shone. Though not a church member himself, he headed the committee that raised enough money for the new Calvary Presbyterian Church to erect a building near Union Square and to import as minister one of his friends from New Orleans, William Anderson Scott.[21] He ended the gouging that hack drivers inflicted on unsuspecting fares. He pushed hard for better schools, including one for Negroes. He divided his small salary as mayor among various charities, and he attacked the city's more earthy crimes—gambling, prostitution, illegal saloons, and even Sunday theatricals—with a crusader's zeal. After his retirement from office, 150 leading citizens invited him to a testimonial dinner, presented him with a gold dinner service valued at $12,000, and ended the evening with "three hearty and vociferous cheers and a tremendous 'tiger.'"[22]

But Garrison was also suspected of dealing in the more sophisticated crimes of fraud and embezzlement. Twenty years after his term was over, the San Francisco *Daily Bulletin* charged that he and other moneyed men of the city spent $30,000 buying his election so that they could manipulate the prices of waterfront lots then being reclaimed along the bay shore. When he ran for reelection on September 6, 1854 (he lost in spite of allegedly spending $50,000), his supporters in the Second Ward were charged with gross ballot irregularities. In February, 1855, the Grand Jury indicted him and one of his aldermen (also defeated for reelection) for converting to their own use $75,000 in city property. It was during Garrison's incumbency that another alderman, "Honest Henry" Meiggs, forged $800,000 in city warrants, then chartered a ship and fled to South America. No charge of wrongdoing ever stuck to Garrison himself, however. (The indictment for embezzlement was dropped when the prosecuting attorney entered a *nolle prosequi*.)[23] Either Garrison was so innocent that he did not notice what went on around him—or he was nimble.

CALIFORNIA HISTORICAL SOCIETY

Cornelius Garrison was Ralston's ingenious,
hard-driving, and untrustworthy mentor.

Ralston was too busy to pay much heed to the political eddies. Travel
to and from California was beginning to slack off, after booming almost
unbelievably throughout 1853 and the early months of 1854. Fearful of
the response that declining receipts would elicit from Vanderbilt, his
new agents sought to reverse trends by advertising stridently, slashing
fares, and pressing their steamer captains for more and more speed.
Naturally the opposition—the Pacific Mail Steamship Company and the
Nicaragua Transit Company—replied in kind.

The war grew ruthless—just how ruthless Ralston soon learned first-hand. On July 20, 1854, he boarded the new *Yankee Blade*, with Henry Randall as captain, for a run to Panama to settle problems that had arisen there. The *Sonora* of the Pacific Mail Steamship Company left San Francisco at the same time. A race developed. For several days the *Yankee Blade* held a small lead. Then, when the ship was about a hundred miles short of entering the broad Gulf of Panama, the firemen reported that the long run under forced draft had depleted the coal supply, and not enough remained in the bunkers to take the steamer on to Panama.

That night, while the officers were wondering what to do, they saw the lights of the *Sonora*. Hopefully, they sent up rockets as a signal of distress. The captain of the *Sonora* fired answering rockets but did not stop to learn the seriousness of the situation. The *Yankee Blade* could sink for all he cared.

Furious, Randall and Ralston turned the ship into a bay on nearby Coiba Island. There they led the crew and a volunteer group of passengers into the jungle and cut and loaded enough wood to carry them to their destination.[24] They arrived at Panama City just in time to halt a ship that John Fretz, acting on advice from the *Sonora*, had chartered to go to their rescue.

The return trip to San Francisco developed into another race. The ships ran neck and neck even with their tragedies. During the journey eight passengers aboard the *Sonora* died of cholera contracted in Panama, while six of the *Yankee Blade's* passengers succumbed to the same disease.[25] Ralston, who was again on the *Blade,* undoubtedly participated in the hurried sea burials.

Garrison's advertising man took occasion to boast once more that Nicaragua offered the only healthful crossing. He also composed a long ballad, "The Humbug Steamship Company," of which one verse is sample enough.[26]

> You are driven round the steerage
>   like a drove of hungry swine
> And kicked ashore at Panama
>   by the Independent Line;
> Your baggage is thrown overboard,
>   the like you never saw.
> A trip or two will sicken you
>   of going via Panama.

Against this background of intense animosity ships of all three lines prepared to sail simultaneously in mid-September—the Pacific Mail's *Sonora*, the Nicaragua Company's *Cortes*, and the *Yankee Blade*. The last named carried $462,770.31 in gold and more than 800 passengers. After making sure that there was ample coal in the hold, Ralston ordered Captain Randall not to be outdistanced anywhere along the way.

A few days later that order would not have been given. Economic indicators in the East had convinced Vanderbilt that the slump in California travel was not as temporary as his new agents hoped. In his opinion a major recession was on the way, and soon there would not be business enough to support all three of the competing trans-Isthmus steamship companies. He decided to get out of the field before he was hurt and then let the decline in the stock market finish depreciating Nicaragua Transit Company securities without further effort on his part.

First, however, he wanted to recoup his expenses. Accordingly he sought out the eastern officers of the rival firms, United States Mail, Pacific Mail, and Nicaragua Transit. Would they like to be rid of his competition, now that traffic was dwindling? Very well. He would sell them, jointly, his Atlantic and Pacific ships for $800,000. He also demanded another $100,000 a year in exchange for his promise not to reinvade the field.[27]

Fearful of what he might do if he stayed—after all, Cornelius Vanderbilt was America's mightiest shipping magnate—his competitors agreed. In return for the share of the $800,000 that Garrison and Morgan advanced, the Nicaragua Transit Company received the *Yankee Blade* and the *Uncle Sam*—good ships but expensive, as matters developed.

The news of the transaction reached Ralston and Ralph Fretz late in September. They must have been bitter. Little more than half a year had passed since Vanderbilt had persuaded them to upset their established business in Panama and move to San Francisco. Then, without warning, he had sold out from under them.

As they were wondering what to do next, the coastal steamer *Goliah* arrived in the bay—the date was October 9, 1854—with 200 hysterical passengers from the *Yankee Blade*. They told a tale of horror.

Captain Randall, driving southward under full steam, had tried to gain on his rivals by shaving Point Arguello, west of Santa Barbara, as closely as he dared. In broad daylight on a sunny afternoon, he struck a reef with such force that the ship's bow splintered and stuck immovably. Lifeboats were swung out, but the pandemonium was such that one of them sank, drowning seventeen of the twenty-one people who had scrambled into it. By dark only 200 or so of the 800 persons aboard the ship had gained the shore. Captain Randall and several crew members were among them.

A dreadful night followed—how dreadful cannot be said with assurance because of the exaggerations that crept into subsequent accounts of the disaster. Evidently, however, some of the crew who reached land had guns with them. Defying Randall, they appropriated the few tents and provisions that had been brought from the ship, set up camp apart from the others, and, it was whispered, passed the time plundering the corpses that washed ashore.

Matters aboard the ship were still more shocking. During the night clouds rolled in and the seas rose. Terrified passengers took turns tolling the bell in the hope that help might hear. Meanwhile the crewmen still aboard raided the liquor stores and became howling drunk. Worst of all, a band of criminals was reputedly on board, fleeing in disguise from indictments in San Francisco. They stalked passengers of known wealth, robbed and murdered them, and tossed their bodies overboard. Or so the reports that reached San Francisco said. In any event, and from

The wreck of the **Yankee Blade**—*recorded in this sketch by a passenger— brought trouble to the ship's managers, Fretz and Ralston.*

CALIFORNIA HISTORICAL SOCIETY

whatever cause, thirty persons, including seventeen in the swamped lifeboat, died during the ordeal.

By chance the *Goliah,* southbound for San Diego, came into sight the next morning. In spite of heavy seas, her crew removed the 600 persons still aboard the stricken *Yankee Blade* and, grossly overcrowded, carried them to San Diego. Turning northward again, the rescue ship then retrieved the 200 people stranded on the beach and brought them to San Francisco. Shortly thereafter the *Yankee Blade* disappeared.

With whom did responsibility for the sufferers lie? The ship had sailed as part of Vanderbilt's Independent Opposition Line. Before it struck the reef, ownership had passed to Garrison and Morgan's Nicaragua Transit Company. How would Vanderbilt react to the ambiguity?

Without waiting to learn, Fretz and Ralston advanced $10,000 of their own funds to the owners of the *Goliah* as recompense for the troubles and delays the ship had incurred in transporting 800 persons to safety. They also chartered, from Pacific Mail, the steamer *Brother Jonathan* and sent her to San Diego for the persons deposited there. In time Vanderbilt seems to have reimbursed his agents for the expenses; at least no hints to the contrary have survived.

The wayfarers stranded in San Diego expected the *Brother Jonathan* to carry them to Panama. That was no part of the charter arrangement, however. Pacific Mail needed the steamer in San Francisco. Back she went, arriving October 15. In order to continue their journey, the travelers would have to buy new tickets to New York. Faced with that, they naturally demanded that the price of their original tickets be refunded. Fretz and Ralston refused. Refunds on that many tickets would cost $125,000 or so. They hadn't enough cash on hand. Anyway, their agency was now defunct. Further discussions should be conducted with Cornelius Garrison, part owner of the firm that had taken over the *Yankee Blade* just before she crashed.

To the passengers this seemed like a brazen runaround. They held an indignation meeting in the plaza and in noisy confusion passed resolutions condemning Fretz and Ralston for ordering the speed that had indirectly caused the catastrophe; for bringing them back to San Francisco and dumping them on the charity of the town; and for not refunding their passage money. Separate resolutions denounced Randall's lack of seamanship in running the *Yankee Blade* onto the reef, and then failing to stay with his ship, with the result that discipline there had collapsed and half a score of murders had been perpetrated.

A committee of five, followed by a large crowd, strode to Fretz and Ralston's office to serve the papers. Policemen summoned by the agitated partners blocked the doorway. After milling indecisively, the passengers shifted their attention to the offices of the Nicaragua Steamship Company, where at length Garrison passed out partial refunds totalling $30,000. Undoubtedly he tried to recover the sum from Vanderbilt, though whether or not he succeeded remains unknown. Divers later managed to recover part of the ship's cargo of gold.[28]

During the hullabaloo Garrison proposed that his former associates close the office they still owned together in Panama and join him in San Francisco.

The offer could hardly have been alluring. By then—1854 had almost run its course—it was evident that San Francisco's economy was sagging even lower than pessimists had predicted. A full third of the overbuilt city's warehouses, shops, and office buildings stood empty. Immigration had almost ceased; as time would show, the state's population gain for 1855 would amount to a meager 6,000 persons. Bankruptcies were multiplying. Worst of all, gold production had dropped for the first time since the discoveries of 1848, even though 80,000 or more miners still roamed the mountains.[29]

The conduct of government did nothing to restore confidence. Henry Meiggs' forging of city warrants (page 73) had led San Francisco's lax officials to reexamine the city's accounts. With clucks of outrage they discovered a deficit of $2 million, a significant part of it stemming from Garrison's administration. Since fraud was apparently involved in much of the debt, the city fathers, all at once righteous, threatened to repudiate the debt, a recourse that would not hurt the guilty but would bring anguish to those who held the disowned paper. Meantime spurious land claims, purportedly based on old Spanish and Mexican grants, were clouding real estate titles. And in Sacramento the legislature (charged, like all state legislatures of the period, with electing United States senators) was so torn by conflicting claims and so whipsawed by sensational charges of bribery that it reached no decision. For nearly two years California was without one of its senators in Washington, a condition hardly conducive to stability.[30]

No, the picture was not encouraging. Yet where else could Fretz and Ralston turn? There was nothing for them in Panama. The railroad across the Isthmus had at last been completed. Inasmuch as the same set of directors controlled both it and the Pacific Mail Steamship Company, the existence of independent rivals would be more precarious than ever.

By contrast, Garrison was partner in a vigorous transportation company that he would work hard to keep abreast of Pacific Mail—and out of Vanderbilt's hands. Despite the taint of corruption that clung to him, he was a figure of consequence in San Francisco, involved in politics, insurance, real estate, and incipient railroads as well as in shipping. Even civic leaders who did not like him—notably that chill, asthmatic banker on leave from the army, William Tecumseh Sherman—consulted him regularly.[31] Finally, he was a friend and mentor, closer to Ralston than Billy's own father was. Now he was holding out his hand at a time when Ralston needed help, and the younger man took it gladly, as he had on the Mississippi years before.

They closed what was left of the old Garrison, Fretz & Company offices in Aspinwall and Panama City. Although records on the point are silent, Ralston may well have gone to the Isthmus to help with the chore. His younger brother, Andrew Jackson Ralston, returned to the Midwest, to merchandising first in Keokuk, Iowa, and later to St. Louis. John Fretz and Sam Ralston joined the Garrison firm in San Francisco. The two California Ralstons, both bachelors, took rooms at 280 Stockton Street. They were a gregarious, outgoing pair and liked to live well. It is improbable that they indulged in many luxuries during this time of transition, however. The challenges that faced them and their firm were too serious to allow for anything less than unremitting attention to their work.

CHAPTER 6

Lessons in Elasticity

Cornelius Garrison spent the year 1855 in such deep trouble that one of his associates, William T. Sherman, manager of the banking house of Lucas, Turner & Company, predicted that he was a "gone coon."[1] It is doubtful, however, that Garrison himself felt any such worry. Men like him were the source of John H. Hittell's declaration in *The Resources of California* that "hazardous speculation is the body of our commercial system. . . . We came to enjoy an exciting life and to make money rapidly. . . . When men fail [in California] they do not despair."

Garrison certainly did not. Strategems bubbled from him without pause. Now that the partners were together again, he proposed, why not revitalize the moribund banking firm of Garrison, Fretz & Company? The organization had developed valuable contacts while operating in Panama. Surely those associations could be transferred to San Francisco and become the foundation of a vigorous new company. As had been true in Panama, this new house would be closely associated with shipping enterprises, particularly the Accessory Transit Company. To be sure, the transit company was being threatened by Vanderbilt's desire for revenge and by competition from the newly completed Panama railroad. But aggressive action would carry them through—or so Garrison argued.

In pursuit of money for developing both Accessory Transit Company and the bank, he sailed for New York on December 9, 1854, to consult with Charles Morgan.[2] Two months later—a lightning trip for the times —Garrison was back triumphant.

First Morgan and he had reduced, at least for the time being, the danger of unbridled competition with their Panamanian rivals by working out rate schedules with the Pacific Mail Steamship Company.[3] Word

Charles Morgan, New York transportation magnate, joined Garrison in a reckless effort to break Vanderbilt in Nicaragua.

of that agreement stabilized the price of Transit Company stock, so that Vanderbilt would be less likely (Garrison hoped) to strike at them by purchasing shares in the open market. Quiet thus assured, Morgan and he had then made plans for improving facilities in Nicaragua to counteract sufficiently the lure of the Panama railroad.

In spite of the expenses that the building program would involve, Morgan also agreed to participate in the banking venture. He promised to provide half a million dollars in fresh capital if Garrison, Fretz, and Ralston supplied another $200,000 plus their old firm's experience, goodwill, and connections.[4] Morgan would also establish an associated bank, Charles Morgan & Company, in New York, the interlocked houses acting as each other's representatives on the two coasts.

The name of the San Francisco firm was to be Garrison, Morgan, Fretz, & Ralston. Ralston, just turned twenty-nine, must have been pleased. For the first time he was not "& Co." but was publicly recognized as a full-fledged partner of enormously influential men.

Unhappily, both his euphoria and Garrison's optimism proved premature. On Saturday, February 17, 1855, the Pacific Mail steamer *Oregon* came through the Golden Gate with news that spread panic among the San Francisco financial community. The potent St. Louis banking firm of Page, Bacon & Company had failed.

Page, Bacon & Company's San Francisco branch was one of California's largest and most respected firms. Legally it was not liable for the debts of the parent company. Hysteria, however, paid no heed to those factors. As news of the St. Louis failure spread during the waning hours of the day, a run developed. By closing time nervous depositors had removed $300,000 from the bank's vaults.[5]

The next day, Sunday, several prominent citizens gathered in the bank's offices to discuss means of defending the beleaguered firm. After long discussion the group published a stoutly worded expression of confidence in the company and its officers.

A digression concerning the peculiar nature of early California banking is needed here in order to explain the episode. Gold-rush California did not and could not possess banks in the modern sense of the term. To most of the men who had drawn up the state's constitution at Monterey in 1849, a bank was a corporation, and a corporation was the epitome of evil. Corporations were created by special acts of a state's legislature. Frequently the passage of the acts was obtained by improper means, and the corporations that resulted (so ran a widespread belief) were devoted to improper practices, notably monopoly.

A common privilege accorded to state chartered banks was the right to issue paper money. Often this right was not accompanied by adequate legal restraints. The result, especially in the Midwest during the 1830s, had been such a wholesale production of bank notes that they had declined in value, to the dismay of those who found themselves paid for their work or produce in depreciated paper. If the bank issuing the notes failed, as hundreds did during the nationwide panic that began in 1837 and lasted well into the 1840s, the loss was total.

Early banking involved collecting massive heaps of raw dust and bullion, which were then loaned out at astronomical rates.

California's constitution makers, none of whom had had banking experience except as customers, had been determined to avoid the danger.[6] The embryo state, they had argued, was in a fortunate position; gold dust was so abundant that there was no need to authorize paper substitutes in order to provide a circulation medium. So they had contented themselves with writing into the constitution a provision allowing the formation of "associations" for the receiving of gold and silver on deposit, but had hedged this right with a clause forbidding such associations from issuing any kind of certificate of deposit that might circulate as money. To clinch matters they had then added yet another restraint that declared, "The Legislature shall have no power to pass any act granting any charter for banking purposes."

The initial receivers of gold and silver were mining camp merchants whose stores possessed burglar-proof safes, or express companies that were willing to transport the treasure to San Francisco, where it could be loaded aboard a steamer for remittance to the East. But in a land where loans at times commanded interest of 60 percent a year, bullion did not rest for long in its iron boxes. The owners and holders began using it, and thus, as naturally as breathing, one form of banking appeared on the California scene. Other functions—the discounting of notes, the sale of exchange, and so on—soon followed.[7]

The state took no notice. The constitution had declared that there were to be no banks, and the legislature acted as if there were none. It laid down no safeguards whatsoever, even for "associations" (i.e., partnerships) formed for receiving gold and silver. Their operations were governed only by the demands of competition, the consciences of the partners, and the amounts of capital they had available at any given moment.

Liquid capital was a constant problem. Heavy fluctuations marked the movement of gold. A dry winter, and 1854–1855 was unusually dry, meant that placer and hydraulic miners could not operate and hence were unable to pay their bills. By contrast widespread rain released gushes of bullion. Most found its way to San Francisco. There it was either refined and molded into bars by private assayers or was stamped at the new mint into twenty-dollar gold pieces, which were called double eagles.

Businessmen with claims on this bullion were invariably in debt to eastern supply houses. They settled their accounts in gold, most of which was sent east through the agency of their San Francisco bankers. The ships that carried this bullion sailed on regular schedules—"steamer day," in San Francisco jargon. The twenty-four hours preceding each sailing were marked by heavy withdrawals of gold dust, gold bars, and gold coin from each bank. This was followed, for the banks, by painful periods of drought while new deposits accumulated.

No rules existed concerning the reserves that an "association" should keep on hand to tide it over those dry periods when bullion was not moving down from the mountains or when currency supplies were depleted by steamer-day withdrawals. Customers' deposits were safeguarded only by general laws against misappropriation and by the business morality of each bank's partners. Reputation thus came to be an association's chief recommendation to the public. Thus, on that troubled February day in 1855, Page, Bacon & Company had to rely on appeals for confidence.

Confidence, however, did not fill empty tills, and the California bank had let its tills become very empty indeed. The fault lay in the East. The parent house in St. Louis, heavily overcommitted to midwestern railroad contractors, had found itself tottering and had urged the Californians to rush as much gold as possible to the firm's New York agents. Promptly the San Francisco branch dispatched more than a million dollars. Communications were slow and the money reached its destination too late to prevent the closure of the St. Louis house. When news of the failure reached San Francisco, a run inevitably developed. Meanwhile a million dollars were out yonder somewhere, impounded, doing no one any good.

In prosperous times expressions of confidence might have forestalled panic long enough for tills to fill again. In February, 1855, however, when business was stagnating and local government was demoralized, talk was not enough. Pressures on Page, Bacon & Company continued throughout the week, spreading meantime to all of the city's financial institutions.

On Friday, February 22, the doors of Page, Bacon & Company stayed closed, ostensibly so that its employees and customers could enjoy Washington's Birthday parade. Unhappily, Henry Haight, one of the four partners of the branch, issued at that same time another proclamation urging patience on the people of San Francisco. If Page, Bacon & Company went under, he added, so would every financial institution in the city.

A fresh wave of hysteria followed. Was *every* bank that near ruin? On Saturday the runs grew out of hand. Nine of the city's sixteen banks and the majority of its insurance companies failed utterly. The debacle spread to the interior, dragging down most of the state's smaller banks and causing, directly or indirectly, the failure of scores of business enterprises.

Under the circumstances, it seemed best to Garrison, Fretz, and Ralston to delay the opening of their new bank. Besides, Garrison was suddenly snarled in acute troubles of his own.

That same February, as has been noted, he was indicted for illegally selling, while mayor, certain waterfront lots belonging to the city, and benefiting from the transactions. Although the criminal charges were dropped, the administration that succeeded Garrison's repudiated the sales on the ground of gross irregularity. The purchasers of the lots thereupon sued Garrison, arguing that it was up to him to make good their losses.[8]

The suits engulfed him at a time when he was already beset by other real estate difficulties arising from his slippery connection with a proposed railroad between San Francisco and San Jose—the same railroad that Vanderbilt had declined to support in 1851. For two years after that rejection, the idea had lain quiescent. Then, in October, 1853, Garrison, John M. Horner, E. L. Beard, and Joseph Palmer of the banking house of Palmer, Cook & Company had reorganized the company in the hope of using the line as a tool for increasing the value of real estate they owned in south San Francisco, in the vicinity of the proposed tracks.[9]

The depression brought on by the bank failures doomed the plan. Despairing finally of raising enough money to start laying rail, Garrison pulled out of the company, burdened with real estate that in the opinion of William T. Sherman was "utterably unsaleable; taxes are heavy and street assessments worse." San Francisco's flamboyant ex-mayor was, the banker concluded, "in a devil of a way."[10]

Sherman had personal reasons for worrying over Garrison's affairs. The two of them were involved in yet another railroad—the first one, as matters developed, to go into operation west of the Missouri River. This was the Sacramento Valley Railroad. As originally projected, it was to run eastward from the city of Sacramento to an old mining camp called Negro Bar, where the American River broke out of the Sierra foothills. From Negro Bar the tracks were to turn north to Marysville.[11]

The depression played havoc with those plans, too. In the end Negro Bar, twenty-two miles from Sacramento, and not Marysville, sixty miles away, became the goal of the grading, which began February 12, 1855. During the agonies of readjustment, the founder and president of the company, Charles L. Wilson, was replaced by Joseph Folsom, a retired army officer and wealthy property holder. (Negro Bar promptly changed its name to Folsom.) Folsom died July 19, 1855, and was succeeded as president by Cornelius Garrison, who had been a director of the company since its inception. His vice-president was William Tecumseh Sherman.

They made an ill-matched pair. Sherman, plagued with asthma and despising San Francisco's excesses, was icily correct, cautious, and militarily precise. Garrison, magnificently healthy and boisterously gregarious, was ready to plunge headlong into almost any kind of enterprise that promised quick returns. On April 8, Sherman had written to a St. Louis correspondent who was curious about Garrison, "I unquestionably state that he is a very, very *unsafe* man. He is vigorous,

*Garrison and Ralston were both deeply involved in California's
first rail company, the Sacramento Valley Railroad.*

violent but unscrupulous. No criterion but Number One! If I were
associated with him in business I could not sleep."[12]

Now, four months later, they were associated, guiding the affairs of
the pioneer railroad of the West.

The situation they inherited was so bad that in October, 1855, the
contractors who were building the line attached the company's assets
and had the court appoint a trustee, J. Mora Moss, to watch over the
stockholders' interests. In spite of the tangles that resulted, Sherman
and Garrison continued in office—one of the railroad's first locomotives
was named the *C. K. Garrison*—and by the end of the year the line had
reached its shrunken goal at Folsom. There it stopped.[13]

All this was not without its import for Billy Ralston. Beset by pro-
liferating troubles, Garrison was not able to devote adequate time to
either the Accessory Transit Company or to the still dormant bank of
Garrison, Morgan, Fretz & Ralston. Both enterprises required attention. Work on the Nicaragua facilities was being disrupted by an out-
break of cholera and by the filibustering activities of that "Gray-eyed
Man of Destiny," William Walker. Concurrently the agreement between Accessory Transit Company and the Pacific Mail Steamship
Company concerning passenger and freight fares between San Francisco and New York City was breaking down and needed renegotiating.

Meanwhile the proposed bank, the project closest to Ralston's heart,
was in danger of being caught asleep. The failure in February of so many

87

financial institutions had left San Francisco undersupplied with banks, and by August potent competitors were preparing to step into the gap. If the partnership of Garrison, Morgan, Fretz & Ralston was ever to take shape, now was the time, in spite of the continuing depression. But could Morgan be persuaded that affairs in California merited the risk?

Ralston was chosen as envoy to go to New York and persuade him. Another emissary, Charles Macdonald, who had been with Garrison since their days in Panama, was ordered to Nicaragua. Macdonald's unenviable task was to bolster morale in the fever-ridden jungles, speed construction work, and quicken the delivery of vital coal to the vessels that carried passengers across Lake Nicaragua and down the San Juan River to the Atlantic.

Ralston left first, aboard the company steamer *Uncle Sam*. Although the bank was his primary concern, he undoubtedly was ordered to keep his eyes open during the crossing of Nicaragua so that he could present Morgan with up-to-the-minute information about conditions, and especially about Walker's filibuster.

Walker, a native of Tennessee, was two years older than Ralston. He weighed 130 pounds, stood five and a half feet tall, was sandy-haired and freckled. He was a wanderer. He had studied medicine in Nashville, had floated around Europe, then had settled as a newspaperman in New Orleans, where he studied law on the side. In 1850 he came to San Francisco, worked there as a journalist for a time, and then opened a law office in Marysville.[14]

California at that time was a recruiting ground for soldiers of fortune who hoped to seize territory from weak governments in different parts of the Western Hemisphere and set up new countries, with themselves in power. In 1853, Walker left his law office long enough to try liberating Baja California and Sonora from Mexico, with the intent, evidently, of attaching them as new slave territories to the South. Although the filibuster soon collapsed, its leader earned, during his arduous marchings, a reputation as an inspiring commander and bold strategist. Because of that, he was approached early in 1855 by a certain Byron Cole, who had plans for obtaining imperial land concessions in Nicaragua.

Two factions struggled for supremacy in the Central American republic. One, currently in power, was the "Legitimist Party" with headquarters at Granada on Lake Nicaragua. The other was the "Liberal Democratic Party," based at León. Byron Cole proposed to recruit American riflemen, disguised as colonists, to aid the Liberal Democrats. After the Democrats had taken power, the colonists would be rewarded with generous grants of land.

Cole asked Walker to head the army. Agreeing, Walker rounded up fifty-six adventurers and a small brig, the *Vesta*. He then asked Cornelius Garrison, whom he may have known in New Orleans, for help in

BANCROFT LIBRARY, UNIVERSITY OF CALIFORNIA, BERKELEY

Among the men Ralston knew well
in early San Francisco
was banker William T. Sherman,
later famed as a Civil War general.

Another early associate was
"the Gray-Eyed Man of Destiny,"
William Walker, who attempted
to seize Nicaragua.

SOCIETY OF CALIFORNIA PIONEERS

financing the expedition, but was rejected. Undeterred, he sailed south in May, 1855.[15]

Garrison, Fretz, and Ralston kept as close track of events as communications allowed. For one thing, Garrison's relations with the Legitimist government were strained. Vanderbilt, it will be recalled, had refused to pay Nicaragua, as required by charter, 10 percent of the Accessory Transit Company's annual profits, arguing that he had plowed his gains back into improvements and hence there were no net gains. After Garrison and Morgan had seized control of the transit company, they continued the stand, paying an annual $10,000 to the Legitimists and nothing more.

Largely because of the government's weakness, they had gotten away with the contention. The immunity might end, however, if the Legitimists beat off their challenger and became more solidly established. So the Americans watched Walker carefully, wondering whether to aid him: he might be grateful if he won. But if he didn't win. . . . They held fire.

At first Walker's adventure had gone badly. In early September, however, just before Ralston landed in Nicaragua, luck changed and his red-shirted filibusters won a skirmish near the western shore of the huge lake. Hoping to exploit his advantage, Walker feverishly called for fresh equipment from his Pacific depot. To speed its delivery he commandeered every mule belonging to the Accessory Transit Company.

This high-handedness created an emergency for Ralston. Recent outbreaks of cholera in Nicaragua had turned nervous travelers to the Panama route. In an effort to draw attention back to Accessory Transit, Billy had bet $5,000 in San Francisco that passengers sailing with him aboard the *Uncle Sam* would reach New York at least two days ahead of those going via Panama.[16] But when the passengers landed, there were no riding mules available to carry them twelve miles along the plank road to Virgin Bay, embarkation point for their journey across Lake Nicaragua. In spite of their protests, Billy prevailed on the nearly three hundred male travelers to hike the distance. The handful of women passengers were not deemed capable of the effort, however, and were transported to Virgin Bay in two or three wagons that company agents managed to locate for them.

Baggage was the next problem. The only way to bring it up was to send the wagons back to the Pacific for it. That activity would consume two or three days, however, and cost Ralston not only his bet but also the favorable publicity he had hoped to gain for the Nicaragua route. Accordingly he lured the grumbling passengers aboard the lake steamer waiting at Virgin Bay, perhaps by having the steward ring the dinner gong. He then ordered the captain to cast off and head for the Atlantic. The luggage, he told his irate fellow travelers, would be for-

*Walker's storming of Rivas created problems in diplomacy
for Garrison, Morgan, and Ralston.*

warded to New York by the next ship. And so three hundred wayfarers, Billy Ralston among them, journeyed another ten days or so, much of it through humid tropical heat, without being able to change even their underclothing.[17]

Whether the stratagem saved his $5,000 is not a matter of record. Also missing, unfortunately, is the report he gave Morgan about conditions in Nicaragua. The chaos being what it was, the outlook could hardly have been reassuring. Investors, moreover, knew of Walker and of the cholera epidemic. On reaching New York, Billy found that the value of Transit Company stock was sagging on the exchange—"sick transit," Wall Streeters jibed. To bolster prices and keep Vanderbilt at bay, Morgan was buying, in his name and Garrison's (and possibly Ralston's) whatever shares appeared on the market. This drain, coming on top of the expenses of the construction work and of fending off Vanderbilt's lawsuits, was onerous, and at times Morgan thought it might be best to let the vengeful Commodore take over.[18]

At least there was one bright spot. Discussions with representatives of Pacific Mail—Ralston almost surely participated in the final stages —resulted in new rate schedules and traffic-sharing agreements that were advantageous to Accessory Transit Company.[19] Aided perhaps by that break in the gloom, Ralston was able to persuade Morgan to go ahead with the opening of the new bank in San Francisco.

His assignment completed, the young man boarded the *Northern Light* for Nicaragua, where he arrived November 1, 1855. Immediately he found himself in a witches' brew of trouble, much of it stirred up by Garrison's other emissary, Charles Macdonald.

Ostensibly Macdonald had been sent to Nicaragua to improve the company's operations there. He was not tactful, and the employees he crossed resented his interference. ("For what purpose Mr. Garrison sent him here I do not know," sniffed agent George Fitzgerald at Virgin Bay in a letter to another official, "as he could be of no service to the company."[20]) Small jealousies were by no means the sum of the trouble, however. After having knocked the heads of a few underlings together, Macdonald attached himself to Walker's camp to check on matters there. It was then that the cauldron began to boil.

Later Walker admitted that he told Macdonald that when the proper time came he would help those who helped him.[21] Whether the words were uttered as a threat, a plea, or a bribe does not appear. In any event Macdonald decided to help. He did not protest when Walker commandeered one of the transit company's lake steamers, *La Virgen*, for moving troops against the Legitimists' capital at Granada. An undetected landing, a forced march over sodden trails, a quick charge against the city's flank—on October 13, Granada capitulated.

It was not the end of the killing. Legitimist forces still held Fort San Carlos, which controlled the outlet from Lake Nicaragua into the San Juan River, the boat route to the Atlantic. Sixty or so of Walker's volunteers again commandeered *La Virgen*, with no protest from Macdonald, and steamed toward San Carlos in the hope of repeating their leader's success at Granada. They were repulsed. Later, when another company steamer came up the river loaded with passengers destined for the west coast, the government artillerymen at San Carlos opened fire, convinced by the actions of *La Virgen* that the transit company was on the side of the rebels. Their bombardment splintered the superstructure of the ship and killed a widow and her small son. Another child was injured.

An even more terrifying experience awaited noncombatants gathered in the transit company depot at Virgin Bay, awaiting transportation to the Atlantic. A detachment of government cavalry floating through the jungle sought to retaliate for Macdonald's interference in the war by firing on the undefended buildings. They killed five of the terrified travelers and wounded more in what became known as the "massacre of Virgin Bay." When the man in charge of the depot rushed out to stop the shooting, he was carried away as a captive. Macdonald ransomed him for $2,000, but the people at the depot were not mollified.[22] If he had not overstepped his authority to meddle where he had no business being, they told Ralston, the disaster would never have occurred.

Macdonald meanwhile had rejoined Walker at Granada. He was present when Walker signed a peace treaty that put the rebel Democrats in power in Nicaragua. Although the Man of Destiny was offered the presidency of the new government, he chose for the time to act as commander in chief of the army instead. Needing money to operate, he demanded a loan of $20,000 in gold from Macdonald—or perhaps Macdonald offered the money. Testimony on the point varies.[23]

In any event Macdonald stood quietly watching as Walker's agents abstracted a thousand double eagles from iron boxes of gold coin being shipped to New York by Palmer, Cook & Company. The amount was made good, so far as Palmer, Cook & Company was concerned, by a $20,000 draft in their favor drawn on Charles Morgan. The "loan" itself was secured by being set against the annual 10 percent of net profits that Accessory Transit Company owed the government of Nicaragua under the terms of its original franchise—sums that until then the company had been protesting vigorously.[24]

All in all, the situation that faced Ralston on his arrival at Virgin Bay could hardly have been murkier. The company employees, who until recently had been accustomed to working with the Legitimist government, were enraged at Macdonald and Walker as the source of their troubles. But that was the least of the problems. Macdonald had committed the company to the rebels, yet Walker's position was still highly precarious. His small, ill-disciplined army was ravaged by cholera; his government's resources consisted of only $20,000 in dubiously acquired gold coin. Grave doubts existed in Ralston's mind that either the United States or Great Britain, the latter country prickly still over its difficulties on the so-called Mosquito Coast, would recognize the new government. If Walker collapsed, then what? Meanwhile Vanderbilt was watching eagerly, more than ready to turn the turmoil to his own advantage. And what would Morgan do when that unauthorized draft for $20,000 reached his desk?

An emergency council with Garrison was clearly in order. Ralston directed Macdonald, resentful now in his turn, to sail with him back to San Francisco.[25] On hearing what had happened, Garrison exploded and fired Macdonald on the spot.[26] But a night or two later a most curious thing happened. He rehired Macdonald and sent him with two other envoys back to Nicaragua, there to draw up with Walker a new contract designed to stabilize the company and at the same time eliminate Vanderbilt's threat.

It was an involved plot, as will appear, and it is difficult to believe that Ralston did not have a hand in concocting it. He had been associated with Accessory Transit throughout its turbulent life and understood the stakes. He had just been in New York, where he had talked to Morgan about the dangers Vanderbilt was posing in the stock market.

He knew better than anyone else in San Francisco, except for Macdonald, the ins and outs of the situation in Nicaragua. Walker might not endure, true. But in Billy's estimation the company had better hope that he did, because if a Legitimist counterattack succeeded, the victors would almost surely cancel the transit company's franchise in retaliation for Macdonald's activity. So why not make the best of the situation by using it to strike at Vanderbilt?

The scheme went as follows. Garrison, Morgan (and Ralston?) together held more than 20,000 shares of Transit Company stock. Why not let their brokers dribble these out, short, to Vanderbilt without letting the Commodore know the source? Then, after he had regained control of the transit company, they would persuade Walker, who was now indebted to Garrison and Morgan, to cancel the transit company's charter and expropriate its holdings on the ground that the firm had failed to meet the annual 10 percent payments specified in the original pact. As soon as word of the cancellation reached Wall Street, Transit Company stock would crash. The plotters would reap handsomely from the stock they had sold short. They would then form a new transit company to which Walker would issue a new franchise. They would buy the expropriated holdings of the old company, and Vanderbilt would be left with the husk of an enterprise that suddenly had become almost valueless.

The scheme worked. Morgan, warned perhaps by a message from Ralston in Nicaragua, covered the $20,000 draft. Macdonald and his fellow emissaries, Edmund Randolph and Garrison's son William, prevailed on Walker to cancel, in strict secrecy, the franchise of the old transit company and issue another to a new firm headed by Garrison and Morgan. He also sold the "new" company, in a book transaction, the riverboats, lake steamers, warehouses, work stock, and so on taken from the "old" one. Operations in Nicaragua of course continued exactly as they had before the transfer.

Walker's price for all this was the cancellation of his debt to Morgan and Garrison. The total included cash loans of $30,000 (the main part was the $20,000 advanced by Macdonald) and another $70,000 in passenger and freight charges for volunteers and equipment that Garrison and Morgan began transporting to Nicaragua. For this $100,000 the plotters received property valued on the company books at $500,000.[27] Meantime the "old" company, owned now by Vanderbilt, was held responsible for the disputed 10 percent of annual profits allegedly due the government!

The switch caught Vanderbilt by surprise. During the closing days of 1855 he had contracted for the dribbled stock as fast as it was offered. His buying bolstered prices more than Morgan's earlier purchases had; in fact, quotations rose during January when it was known that Vanderbilt was in the saddle once again. Then on March 12, 1856, Walker released the news that the company's franchise had been rescinded. Prices plunged. Morgan covered his and Garrison's (and Ralston's?) short positions with stock they had been holding. They cleared, rumor buzzed, a million dollars.[28] It was probably only a quarter of that.

Vanderbilt reacted by ordering his ocean liners, the Pacific-based *Cortes* and *Uncle Sam* included, off the Nicaragua runs. His hope, of course, was to break the new transit company by keeping Nicaragua traffic out of its hands. The attack was porous, however. Morgan had a fleet in the Gulf of Mexico, and Garrison had the *Sierra Nevada* in the Pacific. Soon they had a new shuttle service operating to the Central American republic. Early returns were gratifying, especially after the cholera epidemic abated.

Although documentation is lacking, it seems probable that Billy Ralston benefited materially from the scheme.[29] Beyond the question of money, however, is a more important one. What impression did the events of the past year leave on his young, still flexible, and keenly observant mind?

During those twelve months his mentor, Cornelius Garrison, had extricated himself from a criminal indictment and from a series of painful lawsuits, apparently by compromising the latter out of court. He had consolidated his real estate holdings, had helped revive a moribund bank, and had been largely instrumental in pushing the Sacramento Valley Railroad ahead to its diminished goal at Folsom. By outmaneuvering one of America's great tycoons, Morgan and he, with Ralston's help, had turned apparent defeat into dazzling triumph.

Altogether it had been an amazing display of resilience. Regardless of the means that Garrison had used to reach his ends, regardless even of the ultimate outcome of events in still turbulent Nicaragua, the

The new bank of Garrison, Morgan, Fretz & Ralston, one of whose checks appears above, interested Billy more than filibustering did.

95

adventure was not likely to be forgotten by anyone who loved excitement and adventure as much as Ralston did.

Yet—and this too is significant—Billy showed no indication of wanting to follow Garrison any farther into Nicaragua. His commitment was to the new bank of Garrison, Morgan, Fretz & Ralston. It had opened for business on January 2, 1856, in rented quarters at a corner of Clay and Montgomery streets. The staff consisted of only four men: Sam Ralston, cashier; R. C. Lawler, accountant; T. H. Morrison, receiving teller; and John Goddard Clark, a clerk Ralston had first worked with in Panama. Considerations other than size were involved, however, most importantly the matter of responsibility. Although Ralston was not yet thirty and was listed last among the partners, his was the voice that counted most within the small quarters. Garrison was involved in other activities. Fretz's health was poor. Morgan was far away. Thus the burden rested chiefly on Ralston's shoulders.

He liked it. He had vitality to spare, and yet he was weary with foreign adventures. During the past two or three years, Billy had developed a deep affection for San Francisco, wayward though the city was. He was convinced that as California grew, the town beside the bay would mature into one of the great metropolitan centers of the nation. Even in the face of the political and economic storms that swept through the city during the spring months of the new year, he clung stubbornly to that faith.

CHAPTER 7

The Cleansing

Believing in San Francisco's future during the dreadful year of 1856 took an act of supreme faith. The kind of security that business wants—and that banking especially needs—did not exist. Fraudulent land claims, trumpeted as stemming from old Mexican grants, kept shaking the real estate titles that often were used as collateral for loans. The financial downswing, born of the excesses of the early 1850s and intensified by the bank failures of 1855, showed no sign of ending. Yet, and this was a great bitterness to honest men, there were shady roads to wealth if one chose to follow them. Devious arrangements linked city hall politicians to opportunistic contractors on one hand and to criminals on the other. Into this bottomless swamp poured most of the staggering tax revenues derived from San Francisco businessmen. Meanwhile, civic improvements stayed negligible and governmental functions were conducted with gross negligence.

What could be done? The United States government was remote and distracted by the agonies of bleeding Kansas. The capitol in Sacramento was afflicted with its own scandals and with the pangs of adjusting to an administration headed by a twenty-eight-year-old governor, J. Neely Johnson of the new nativist American Party. (Members of this semi-secret organization were often called Know-Nothings from their habit of denying all knowledge of the party.) Thus if San Francisco's political stables were to be cleansed, the citizens would have to do the job. By "citizens" those who discussed the problem generally meant businessmen, for businessmen were, in their own minds, the ones who most needed relief. What they seldom mentioned was the part they had played in the speculative excesses and the attendant neglect of civic responsibilities that had brought on much of the trouble.[1]

The result of the exasperation was armed revolt aimed at the Democratic machine that controlled the city hall. Because the masters of the machine, notably David Broderick, were powerful not only in San Francisco but also in the state and even in Washington, the rebels did not attack them directly. Instead they struck hard at lesser fry, hoping that vigorous action would carry their message to its real destination.[2]

The revolt flouted normal democratic procedures. (It had to, the rebels insisted, for the machine controlled the ballot boxes.) Because of that flouting, not every businessman subscribed to the uprising. Friend lined up against friend, partner against partner—Ralston against Garrison, for instance.

Deeper motives were also involved. One was the fierce rivalry that existed between the Southern and Northern wings of the Democratic Party in California. Broderick was a Northerner. Most of San Francisco's top businessmen, Ralston among them, leaned toward the party's Southern faction—the Chivalry wing, it was called. On top of that were class antagonisms. Broderick's machine, manned in large part by Irish ward heelers, drew much of its strength from semiliterate, easily manipulated Catholic newcomers from the Emerald Isle.[3] The city's respectable, educated, rich, and middle class Protestants regarded the Irish invasion with a distaste that swelled to alarm in 1855 when the nativist American Party swept to victory in most of the state but failed in San Francisco. There, in that failure, was proof—the machine could not be toppled by normal means!

From such seeds sprang the famed (or notorious, depending on one's view) Vigilance Committee of 1856. Ralston worked with the vigilantes from the beginning. Unfortunately for this account he left no records. Except for occasional glints here and there, we know nothing of his revolutionary activities during that wild period. Yet the episode was important enough to his chosen city that a summary of it becomes essential in shedding light on the milieu through which he moved and hence on Ralston himself.

THE CATALYST OF THE UPRISING was a one-time banker named James King of William. Presumably Ralston knew him well.

King had been born in Georgetown, D.C., on January 20, 1822. His father was named William and consequently, so the story goes, James added "of William" to his own name in order to distinguish himself from other James Kings in the vicinity. Although he was among the first of the argonauts to reach California, he did not prosper until he switched to banking, first in Sacramento and then in San Francisco. The success did not last. He lived extravagantly, made injudicious loans, and suddenly found his bank faced with ruin. To save his customers, and himself, he sold the firm to Adams & Company, one of San Francisco's largest banks, and then went to work for the purchasers at a salary of $1,000 a month.

Adams closed its doors during the financial panic of February, 1855. A fierce struggle to control the firm's remaining assets ensued. Eventually they wound up in the hands of Palmer, Cook & Company, whose senior partner, Joseph Palmer, was a business associate and close friend of Cornelius Garrison.

James King emerged from the economic vendetta stripped clean. After months of humiliation he obtained from somewhere enough money to start a small newspaper, the *Evening Bulletin*. He used its columns for venting his rancor on the city's Irish officeholders, their friends in the underworld, and Palmer, Cook & Company, which served as the chief depository for state and city funds and as a principal factor, rumor said, in keeping the local Democrats in power.

Even in that era of free-swinging journalism, King's lack of restraint was remarkable. When Charles Cora, a gambler and consort of a notorious prostitute, Arabella Ryan, was being tried for the murder of a United States marshal, the *Bulletin* blared from its front page, "If the jury which tries Cora is packed, either *hang the sheriff* or drive him out of town. If Billy Mulligan [the warden of the jail] lets his friend Cora escape, *hang Billy Mulligan* or drive him into banishment." When the trial ended in a deadlocked jury, King cried furiously, though there was no evidence of packing, "Rejoice, ye thieves and harlots! Rejoice with exceeding gladness! . . . The money of the gambler and prostitute has succeeded and Cora has another respite."

The recipients of this attention grew annoyed and began looking, it was charged later, for a way to silence the editor. They found it when King turned his vitriol on James P. Casey, who had been fraudulently elected in September, 1855, as Supervisor of San Francisco's Twelfth District. Some years earlier Casey had served time in New York's Sing Sing prison. Though the tale was fairly well known in San Francisco, Casey took umbrage—either real or pretended—when King repeated it in the *Bulletin*. He demanded an apology. When contrition was not forthcoming, he accosted the editor on a street corner at 5:00 P.M., May 14, 1856, and mortally wounded him with a pistol. Promptly then Casey surrendered to the county sheriff, David Scannel, who he had reason to suppose would protect him from any mob that gathered.[4]

A mob did assemble, in response to the tolling of the great bell atop the building of the Monumental Fire Company beside the plaza. The mayor, backed by hastily summoned militiamen, held it at bay for the evening. During the confused pause, a handful of businessmen decided that the time had come for open insurrection.

Leadership was placed in the hands of an executive group known as the Committee of Vigilance. Its model was an earlier body of the same name that in 1851 had sought to purge San Francisco of its worst criminals. The head of the committee, both in 1851 and in 1856, was an able wholesale merchant named William T. Coleman. The swiftness with which Coleman and his fellows went to work in 1856 suggests not only that they had learned the modes of insurrection from their earlier experience, but also that they were following a plan of operations prepared beforehand.

They faced formidable problems. They had to impose almost instant organization and discipline on an excited and unruly citizenry. They needed money. Above all, they had to brace for counterattacks. If such attacks succeeded, then the committeemen would probably suffer harsh retaliation. Accordingly Coleman insisted that his committee be allowed to work in absolute secrecy. This proviso entailed a most undemocratic corollary: unquestioning obedience by the rank and file. Both requests were immediately granted.

Volunteer troops poured into vigilante headquarters. Many were militiamen and brought with them rifles, bayonets, and ammunition filched from state armories. As fast as the volunteers appeared, drillmasters—how were so many sergeants found in so short of time?—organized them into companies and regiments and began putting them

The street slaying of James King of William, ex-banker and crusading journalist, precipitated the vigilante uprising of 1856.

SOCIETY OF CALIFORNIA PIONEERS

through their paces. At the same time fund raisers moved through the downtown areas soliciting donations from wealthy businessmen.

William Ralston, who knew Coleman well and conceivably had held prior discussions with him about the uses of vigilantism, was one of the earliest contributors.[5] He acted covertly. He had no more idea than the executive committee (of which he seems not to have been a member) what the outcome of the insurrection might be, and he wished to avoid retaliation. He may also have been trying to skirt a confrontation with his partner, Cornelius Garrison, who promptly and vigorously supported the city administration.

The opponents of the vigilantes called themselves the Law and Order Party. Predictably San Francisco's frightened ward heelers flocked to its banners. So did a majority of the state's political leaders. (Garrison, it is worth remembering, had been mayor of San Francisco less than three years before.) Most lawyers supported the Law and Order group, as did a few maverick businessmen. Among the latter was banker William Tecumseh Sherman. Sherman's motives were twofold. He despised vigilantism as a matter of principle. And he had just been appointed a major general of the state militia, charged in part with maintaining legally constituted authority.

As tensions mounted, Mayor Van Ness called on the governor of the state, young J. Neely Johnson, for help. Both Garrison and Sherman

Leader of the vigilantes and a business friend of Ralston's was merchant William T. Coleman.

WELLS FARGO BANK HISTORY ROOM

attended the midnight conference that Johnson held with Coleman.[6] Nothing was resolved. On Sunday, May 19, four days after King's wounding, 2,500 vigilantes marched against the city jail.

Ralston probably shouldered a gun and stepped out with the rest, as he is known to have done a few weeks later.[7] In crises of this sort he seemed to feel a compulsion to mingle with the rank and file, a characteristic that would manifest itself again during the Civil War. The camaraderie that springs from united effort under pressure stimulated him. He liked pomp, parades, and any feeling of power. So he may have decided, as early as this soft spring morning in May, that the time had come to stand up and be counted, even by Cornelius Garrison.

There was no resistance. Sherman had not been able to rally his disobedient militiamen to the support of the 150-man posse assembled by Sheriff Scannel. Offering only verbal protest, Scannel surrendered both Casey and the gambler Cora to the executive committee of the vigilantes. Two days later, the very day on which James King of William died of his gunshot wound, the pair were tried and found guilty. On the day that King was buried they were hanged from gallows hastily erected in the street in front of vigilante headquarters.

Persons who decried vigilante justice hoped that the bloodshed would satisfy the reformers and that they would disband. They did not. They meant to conduct a thorough housecleaning, using the threat of more hangings as a guarantee of effectiveness. Governor Johnson thereupon issued a proclamation placing San Francisco under martial law. He ordered Sherman to use the militia to force compliance. The militia were undependable, however, and when the commanding officer of the federal arsenal at Benicia capped the hopelessness by refusing to replace the arms taken by men deserting to the vigilantes, Sherman resigned.

Johnson appointed a new militia general, Volney Howard, who began forming cadres of loyal men and searching for weapons. The vigilantes retorted by building a sandbag barricade ten feet tall and six feet thick around their headquarters building, thereafter called Fort Gunnybags. Cannons were placed in the corners of the barricade, loopholes were provided for rifles, and an alarm bell was mounted on the roof. On June 14, the committee summoned the people to a mass meeting. About 15,000 responded and were worked into a fury by speeches that equated opposing the vigilante program with permitting civic corruption.

At about that time Cornelius Garrison sailed for New York. It is possible that he wished to avoid being hauled before an inquisitorial body of vigilantes and grilled, as others were, about misdeeds that had occurred during his own term as mayor. More probably, however, he had been planning the trip for some time in order to carry on consultations with Charles Morgan about the new Nicaragua Transit Company. In any event, he departed. It was now up to Ralph Fretz and Billy Ralston

Vigilantes show their strength by parading through the downtown streets. Ralston occasionally marched with such groups.

to carry the infant banking house of Garrison, Morgan, Fretz & Ralston as best they could through the city's turmoils and uncertainties.

Events moved from bad to worse. A justice of the state supreme court, David Terry, unearthed an obscure law that compelled the commander of the federal arsenal at Benicia to release a quantity of rifles for General Howard's loyal militiamen. The weapons were loaded aboard a small sailing craft captained by one Reuben Maloney and started across the bay to San Francisco. Learning of the move from informers, vigilantes manned an attack vessel, stopped Maloney's ship, and appropriated the guns. Thoughtlessly, however, they turned Maloney and his crew loose.

Realizing the danger, Coleman ordered Maloney arrested on trumped-up charges of ballot-box stuffing. The intent, of course, was to keep him from testifying about the piracy to state or federal officials. The Law and Order people moved faster, however. When Sterling Hopkins, head of the vigilante police, found Maloney, he was already surrounded by a group of Law and Order people headed by Justice Terry himself.

During the scuffle that ensued, Terry stabbed Hopkins in the neck

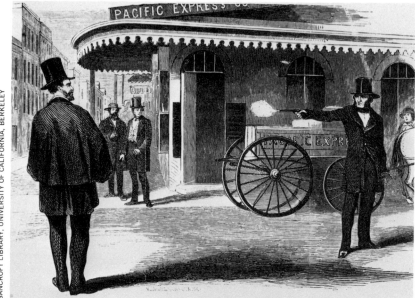

King's assassination is given imaginary reconstruction by an artist for **Frank Leslie's Illustrated Newspaper.**

with a bowie knife, a deep and potentially fatal wound. The judge then sought refuge in a militia armory but was overwhelmed by a squad of vigilantes and incarcerated in Fort Gunnybags.

Intense excitement swept the city. Hotheads demanded Terry's immediate execution. But one did not treat a justice of the supreme court quite so peremptorily. Temporizing, Coleman and his associates announced that they would keep Terry under arrest until Hopkins either died or recovered. When this failed to stem criticism, they placed the justice on trial for assault and then let the case drag out for 25 agonizing days. Their great fear was of an attack by federal troops responding to a call from Governor Johnson. What would happen if such a confrontation occurred, no one, the committee included, dared predict. Certainly it was a quandary that must have presented Ralston, along with other leading supporters of the movement, with fundamental questions about the nature of governmental proceedings.

Fortunately Hopkins did not die. After bitter wrangling among themselves, Terry's jailers turned him loose on July 24. Although they did it secretly, the word spread and a thousand angry vigilantes paraded in front of Fort Gunnybags in protest against their own leaders.

Economic shocks added to the ugly mood. Earlier, on July 1, the state's disbursing agent, Palmer, Cook & Company, had omitted paying

State supreme court justice David Terry, pictured stabbing a vigilante,
became a prisoner the committee dared neither free nor hang.

$90,000 interest due on certain state bonds. The legislature launched an investigation, and on July 29, amid growing cries about corruption, the bank collapsed. The reverberations, which must have alarmed Ralston and Fretz, reached into every part of California. Radicals among the vigilantes grew sterner than ever. Evil was still abroad, they said in effect, and this was no time for softness.

The internal discord was paralleled by a swelling chorus of criticism from the outside. Strongest of the new voices was that of William Anderson Scott, pastor of the ornate new Calvary Presbyterian Church, of which Billy Ralston was a member.

Throughout the summer, while the rest of San Francisco's Protestant preachers were delivering fiery sermons in support of the vigilantes, Scott stayed silent. This exasperated his church officers—nine of the eleven men on the board approved of the committee—and they put intolerable pressure on him to speak out. On July 27 he did—to their fury. In a blistering sermon that Ralston almost surely heard, the aroused minister blamed all San Franciscans and not just a few ward heelers for the disorders afflicting their city. The whole atmosphere, he thundered, was redolent of "the corrupting influences of gold and of riches suddenly accumulated, often by dishonest means." Summary punishment was no solution. "The stream of blood will not end while men take the law into

*Billy Ralston's friend,
the Reverend W. A. Scott of
Calvary Presbyterian Church,
was hanged in effigy
for opposing the vigilantes.*

SOCIETY OF CALIFORNIA PIONEERS

their own hands. . . . There is a constitutional way to amend our laws and to remove unfaithful officers."[8]

The response of the Committee of Vigilance to dissent from both inside and outside the organization was to show how resolute it could be, at least with lesser victims. It tried two hoodlums for murder, found them guilty, and on August 2 held another public hanging in front of Fort Gunnybags. Coleman then announced that the group's major ends had been attained. Dozens of wrongdoers had either been deported or had fled in terror, and therefore the army of the vigilantes was to disband following a grand farewell parade on Monday, August 18. The men should keep their guns, however (many of the weapons had been pilfered from state armories) just in case the executive committee decided that alarm bells should ring again.

Merchants, professional men, and bankers prepared for the parade by swathing their stores and the adjacent streets with brightly colored bunting. Four companies of artillery, fifteen cannon abreast, led the parade. The executive committee followed on horseback. Behind them rode a regiment of dragoons. Then came the infantry, bands interspersed between the different regiments. About 6,000 men participated. All but lost in the multitude, yet marching smartly, was Billy Ralston.[9]

Afterwards the committee announced that it had spent, between May 14 and August 18, a total of $31,326.00, all raised by contributions.[10] What Ralston's donations amounted to is unknown. Evidently they were substantial, as were those of the other bankers in the city, excepting always Sherman and Garrison.

Because the committee still existed and quantities of guns taken from the armories remained in the hands of the people, Governor Johnson refused to rescind the proclamation that had placed San Francisco under martial law. Quiet returned to the streets, however, and men began catching up with long-delayed projects. For Fretz and Ralston this involved, among other things, making arrangements to move their bank to a new location at the southwest corner of Washington and Battery streets, where they would be closer to the mint, the customs house, and the docks. The decision was wise, and two other banks—Drexel, Sather & Church and Lucas, Turner & Company—promptly made plans to follow.[11] They in turn pulled other businesses in their wake. To Ralston the unexpected development was suggestive. It was possible, if circumstances were right, to control the direction of a city's growth. For anyone interested in real estate values the implications were profound, a fact that Ralston would remember later on, during other critical times.

Before the physical move to the new location occurred (it took place in October) fresh alarms showed that vigilantism was not over. The cause of the excitement this time was the arrest by federal authorities, on charges of piracy, of the men who had led the raid on the vessel transporting weapons from Benicia to San Francisco. When they were refused bail, the tocsin sounded again and the supposedly disbanded army of vigilantes was ordered to place itself on the alert.

The Reverend William Scott resumed his denunciations from the pulpit. Irked by the criticism, unknown persons late on Saturday night, October 4, hanged him in effigy from a lamppost in front of his church's Roman Corinthian portico. Obviously they wanted the congregation to see the grotesquerie the next morning and ponder its message.

The episode shocked Ralston. Although most of the deliberations of the Executive Committee of the Vigilantes had been conducted in secrecy, their decisions had been enforced openly. This hanging in the dark had been furtive, like obscene writing on a wall, and showed the levels to which irresponsible terrorism could sink. Hotly he and forty-nine other members of a congregation that once had been almost solid in its support of the vigilantes composed, signed, and sent to the city's newspapers a strong letter of protest.[12]

The letter was symptomatic of a widespread shift in moods. Not long before the hanging, the Executive Committee of the Vigilantes had formed a political organization called the People's Party and had drawn up a list of candidates for municipal office that it urged voters to support during the elections scheduled for November 4. But, many citizens were beginning to ask, how free would those elections be if masses of citizens still held guns wrongfully taken from the state armories?

Irascible vigilantes retorted that they needed the guns for defending the polls against the kind of ruffians who had dominated earlier elections.

The contention brought forth a sharp rebuttal: suppose the vigilantes' defense of the polls turned into duress on behalf of candidates endorsed by the People's Party?

The debate caused the executive committee to waver. Moving promptly, William Sherman and others formed a compromise group that worked out a method whereby all arms belonging to the state were surrendered without penalty to the holders.[13] Although Ralston's stand in the dispute is unknown, his anger over the effigy, an event that seems to have signalled the turn in popular opinion, probably supplies a clue.

As soon as the weapons had been collected, Johnson ended martial law, and the relieved citizens entered the polls with no more than routine supervision. All went quietly, and the city hall was swept clean in as orderly a fashion as even the Reverend Mr. Scott could have wished.

Since that day controversy about the vigilantes has never ended. The acts that produced success were violent, terrifying to those in opposition and utterly outside the bounds of constitutional law. But those who seized power during the insurrection relinquished it when their self-assigned task was finished, an outcome not common to all revolutionary coups. Most importantly, the savage shortcut worked. To impatient, hurry-up, materialistic San Francisco—and to Billy Ralston—that was the criterion that counted.

WHILE THE CITY WAS ADAPTING to its new regime, Cornelius Garrison brought to Ralston's personal affairs an equally profound change. While in New York, the senior partner of the firm had successfully fended off a lawsuit with which Vanderbilt had beset him, and with Morgan had worked out ways to expand and improve their Nicaragua steamship service. They sent a fine, new 1,900-ton vessel, the *Orizaba*, around the Horn into the Pacific to join the *Sierra Nevada*. They hired James Burch, creator of the million-dollar California Stage Company, to study means of moving travelers across Nicaragua rapidly enough to offset the charms of the trans-Panama railroad.[14] But while doing all this, they underrated the wily Vanderbilt.

As the Commodore knew, the government of Costa Rica had been aroused by Walker's incursion into neighboring Nicaragua and was massing its forces to drive the filibusters out—while at the same time asserting Costa Rica's claim to jurisdiction over parts of the San Juan River. Vanderbilt's agents supported the attack with arms and money. Although Garrison and Morgan rushed help to Walker, the effort came too late. On May 1, 1857, Walker surrendered to an American naval unit that happened to be stationed, not entirely by chance, near Nicaragua's Atlantic Coast.[15]

The way was now open for Vanderbilt to resume operations. He chose not to do so in return for a subsidy of $40,000 a month paid him by the Panamanian lines. The decision effectively closed Nicaragua to all California travel.

Grimly, Garrison and Morgan resolved to ask Costa Rica for a new franchise and continue the fight. To do this they needed to retrench. Garrison resigned as president of the Sacramento Valley Railroad and then took a jaundiced look at the California economic scene. He did not like what he saw. Depression still clung to California. During 1855 and 1856 bankruptcies in San Francisco had wiped out $9 million in debts, a grievous blow to the mercantile community. Real estate values had shrunk by $10 million. Gold production had dwindled from 1852's dazzling $81.3 million to $57.5 million in 1856.[16]

State and municipal treasuries were bare. Several schools had closed for lack of funds, and rumor said that the inmates of the state prison were literally starving. Legislative investigations revealed that embezzlement by the state treasurer had triggered the disastrous collapse of Palmer, Cook & Company. Concurrently the supreme court had declared, on a technicality, that $3 million in state bonds were unconstitutional. Unless the legislature passed a special act guaranteeing redemption, the holders would be left with worthless paper.

The bank of Garrison, Morgan, Fretz & Ralston occupied the southwest corner of Washington and Battery streets (an empty lot in this 1856 picture).

The balance sheets at Garrison, Morgan, Fretz & Ralston reflected the grayness of the times. Deposits were down; profits from exchange were nonexistent. Gloomily the partners freed some of their money by reducing the firm's capital from $700,000 to $500,000. The relief was short-lived, and it was no surprise when Garrison and Morgan jointly proposed that they leave the field altogether—a step already taken by W. T. Sherman of Lucas, Turner & Company.[17]

Reject banking for a renewed fight against Vanderbilt? Ralston shook his head. He had just gone through the ordeal of vigilantism by which San Francisco's businessmen had sought to bring stability back to their city. He saw—or thought he saw—evidence of improvement. The legislature was about to institute measures that would honor the unconstitutional bonds. The city's new administration was working diligently to overhaul the municipal machinery, cut expenses, and thus reduce the outrageously high taxes. New techniques of gold recovery were being developed, and bankers willing to finance the experiments might reap well in spite of the overall decline in gold production. California's agricultural and industrial potentials had scarcely been touched. San Francisco's magnificent harbor, opening into a vast hinterland accessible by river transport, gave the city advantages superior to those available anywhere else on the coast. Such a town, he reasoned, would inevitably continue to grow. If so, then there was a future for banking.

Ralph Fretz agreed with him, and again the tumultuous partnership split. The firm of Garrison, Morgan, Fretz & Ralston was formally dissolved and its assets divided. The next day, July 15, 1857, the new bank of Fretz & Ralston opened in the same headquarters at Washington and Battery streets. Its capital, according to surviving tax lists, was $50,000, a drastic shrinkage from the $700,000 with which Garrison, Morgan, Fretz & Ralston had started business a year and a half before. But though money was short, commitment to the city and state were far stronger than they had been in the days when steamboating had commanded the major attention of the senior partners in the original firm.

CHAPTER 8

On the Move

Between 1850 and 1859, young Edgar Mills, a banker in the foothills mining camp of Columbia, California, handled more raw gold, probably, than did any other individual in the United States—some $55 million worth according to sober financial histories.[1] Not by chance, Ed Mills was one of Billy Ralston's closest friends.

Mills had been born in upper New York State in October, 1827. Thus he was twenty-one months younger than Ralston. For a time he had worked as a civil engineer for local railroads. Dissatisfied, he responded to the first rumors of the California gold rush. With a brother, James, he bought merchandise they hoped to sell to miners, rented space in a sailing vessel, and set out on the long voyage around Cape Horn.

Their departure helped persuade an older brother, Darius Ogden Mills, to follow. (Darius was 23 then, two years older than Edgar.) Giving up his job at a bank in Buffalo, he joined the stampede to Panama. There, at the opening of 1849, he found himself stranded on the beach with thousands of other frustrated gold seekers for whom no transportation existed.

Instead of fighting for space on the few ships bound for California, Darius persuaded a hundred or so stranded travelers to catch an almost empty vessel bound in the opposite direction, to Callao, Peru. In Callao the adventurers chartered a small bark for $10,000, and then spent sixty miserable days, often becalmed in tropical heat, traveling to San Francisco.

Discouraged by reports from the diggings about the average miner's slim profits, Darius decided to try merchandising instead. A trial venture in Stockton proved unproductive, but when he switched to Sacramento his fortunes leaped. He was soundly established and prospering when

Darius Ogden Mills, Sacramento financier who became head of The Bank of California, poses for a visiting-card picture in 1861.

James and Edgar finally landed from their slow circuit around the Horn.

By fall Darius had accumulated through trade and purchase $40,000 in gold dust, which he took east, where it could be sold to advantage. Again he invested in merchandise for sale in California. Profits were laggard this time—by then Sacramento was glutted with storekeepers— and so he shifted to banking, where his first training had lain. The bank he opened in Sacramento boomed so fabulously that "the luck of D. O. Mills" became a local proverb. He hired his brothers as his chief assistants and in the summer of 1850 he sent Edgar to Columbia, in Tuolumne County, to open a branch.

It was an inspired decision. During the next several years Columbia and its satellite camps produced $87 million in gold. Cool, green trees shaded the hot, red dust of the streets where 15,000 people lived. After being swept twice by fire, the core of the town was rebuilt out of dusky brick fortified by black iron doors and iron shutters. The Mills bank ended up looking as blocky and solid as a prison. Now and then violence erupted around it. On one occasion, in 1855, a mob wrested a reputed murderer from the jail and hanged him from a tall flume recently erected by the Tuolumne County Water Company, a creation of D. O. Mills. There were even times when the miners talked of doing violence to Mills himself. Convinced that he was overcharging them for water, they undertook to build a rival ditch of their own. The would-be competition made Mills even richer: in the end he acquired the mismanaged canal for about one-tenth of its original cost.[2]

Although the point cannot be documented, it seems probable Ralston's business every now and then took him to this rich and interesting area. Competition among San Francisco bankers to obtain gold bullion was keen. One reason lay in the nature of the transcontinental money flow. A western bank that had raw gold could send it east in settlement of accounts, meantime keeping gold coin in California where it could be loaned at interest rates of 2 percent or more a month. In addition, when San Francisco bankers accepted gold dust from the mountains in payment of bills, they discounted its gross value by one-quarter to one-half of 1 percent in compensation for possible impurities —an accepted custom that generally amounted to additional profit for the handlers.[3]

Certain San Francisco bankers, Ralston among them, were very aggressive in their efforts to keep as much gold dust as possible moving toward their vaults. Their agents in the mountains advanced gold coin to the miners in return for a promise of bullion at cleanup time—if there was any bullion. As mining techniques grew more risky, complex, and costly, the advances in coin grew correspondingly heavy. More and more frequently, then, the bankers visited the mining camps to check on their agents and on the uses being made of their money.[4]

As in many business dealings, personal friendships played an important part in the process—and Ralston, as several reminiscences testify, had a genius for friendship. He was well and favorably known to many miners and to the men who dealt with miners. Many of these cordial relationships must have developed in the mountains rather than on the streets of San Francisco. Almost surely the intimacy with Edgar Mills ripened there also.

The association with Edgar's brother Darius was likewise of long standing, at least if the reminiscences of Gertrude Atherton, once California's most famous woman writer, are accepted as accurate. Gertrude's grandfather was dour Stephen Franklin, whom Ralston had first known as a prosperous merchant in New Orleans. After being ruined financially by a peculating partner, Franklin had moved his family to California to begin life anew. By then there wasn't much steam left in him. He accepted an ill-paid job as a newspaper editor, helped found the Calvary Presbyterian Church, of which Ralston became a member, and withdrew into gloomy solitude with his books.

Meanwhile his pretty, wayward daughter, Gertrude's mother-to-be, ran wild. Since Franklin could not control her, William Ralston and Darius Ogden Mills undertook to do so. After several stormy sessions they pressured her, in 1856, into marrying Tom Horn, whom they considered her most eligible suitor. It was an injudicious bit of meddling. Four years later (three years after Gertrude's birth), the bickering, drink-sodden marriage ended in a sensational divorce.[5] The point here is not the mistaken judgment, however, but the fact that Ralston must have become closely associated with one of California's most successful bankers, D. O. Mills, not long after arriving in San Francisco from Panama.

It may well be that gold dust trickling from Columbia to San Francisco saved the new bank of Fretz & Ralston during the uncertain months that followed its opening. It was experiencing hard sledding because of twin blows suffered by California's financiers during the fall of 1857.

First the ship *Panama* arrived with word that the steamer *Central America* had sunk off Cape Hatteras in September with a loss of 420 lives and $1.6 million in newly mined California gold. Runs followed on banks whose shipments were involved, and within days three of the city's most respected institutions—Strather & Church, Wells Fargo, and Pioche & Bayerque—were forced into temporary suspension. That shock was followed almost immediately by word of a financial panic in the East touched off by the collapse of the supposedly impregnable Ohio Life Insurance and Trust Company.[6]

Sympathetic shivers ran through the San Francisco business community. Caution turned into stagnation. When W. T. Sherman returned

A panic that shook Wall Street in 1857 (pictured above) sent sympathetic shivers through San Francisco's business community.

to California on business early in 1858 he found a pall of gloom. "The whole town is for sale," he wrote a friend, "and there are no buyers. Tallant & Wilde, Fretz & Ralston, and Wells Fargo & Company have nothing worth having. Their rooms are silent and deserted."[7] But, it should be noted, none of them failed, though for some it was a close thing.

Ralston, in addition, had private reasons for dejection. His brother Sam had developed a persistent cough and was losing weight. As autumn dragged out, it was obvious that he was not up to facing another of San Francisco's raw winters.

The two had been next to inseparable ever since Billy had taken Sam to Panama with him. In San Francisco they shared rented rooms on Stockton Street, and whenever Ralston wanted to explore, in talk, some complex and worrisome problem, he turned to Sam.[8] Sending him away would create a gap in both their lives, and yet something had to be done. After long discussion they decided that Sam should try to recuperate in the sunny climate of southern Europe.

The emotional loose ends that resulted did not suit Ralston's temperament. His short, stocky body pulsed with energy. He was warm-hearted and impulsive. When his bank teller, T. H. Morrison, admired

A mutton-chopped Billy Ralston as he looked during his early days in San Francisco.

CALIFORNIA HISTORICAL SOCIETY

a fine horse that Ralston had let him ride, Billy promptly gave the animal to him for a New Year's present.[9] Such a man needed people around him—people he could lead. "At a dinner he carved," one friend recalled. "If a member of a driving party, he always held the reins"[10] —no mean feat when the reins led, as in Ralston's case they generally did, to four straining, powerful, black horses.

The rooms on Stockton Street were oppressive after Sam had left. Seeking distraction, Ralston moved his quarters to the prestigious Union Club, and then plunged into a sequence of parties and dinners. At one of the affairs he met a pretty newcomer to town, Elizabeth Fry, niece and ward of a bumptious, self-important but kindhearted midwesterner named John D. Fry.

The Frys were a prominent family in Illinois. Old Jacob Fry, John's uncle, was a general of the militia and a state senator. John, too, had been a member of the legislature and also sheriff of Green County. He had not been solidly enough rooted, however, to resist the lure of gold. In 1849 he had helped a friend, shrewd, cold, calculating William Sharon, to form a wagon company for crossing the plains and mountains to the promised land.

Like many others who found shoveling disagreeable, the pair decided

Until his death in 1859, Sam Ralston was his brother's closest friend and confidant.

117

to live off the miners rather than off mining. They bought suitable goods in Sacramento, followed a group of prospectors into the hills of Placer County, set up a ramshackle store in the middle of a handful of rough cabins, and christened the settlement Frytown.[11] After prospering somewhat, they moved to Sacramento and then to San Francisco. There Sharon speculated successfully in real estate. Ralston knew him slightly—with no premonition, of course, of what that casual acquaintanceship would grow into.

Fry meanwhile had become a special agent of the Post Office Department, a job that frequently took him to Washington. On one of his trips he learned that a family tragedy had left a niece, Elizabeth Red, alone in the wide, wide world. He assumed responsibility for her, and she took his name, becoming Elizabeth Fry. A few weeks after her twentieth birthday, which occurred on September 9, 1857, they traveled by way of Panama to California. Presumably she intended to live there. Short, dark-haired, and energetic, she looked more fragile than she really was. One imagines that she must also have felt terribly insecure.

Lonely Ralston rushed her so breathlessly that her uncle grew concerned and, family lore attests, demanded to know what the banker's intentions were. Ralston said that they were honorable. With a burst of candor he added, so the story goes, that his love for her was not the soaring love of youth. That passion had gone to Vanderbilt's granddaughter, Louisa Thorne, whose miniature he always carried and whose memory would never fade. But if Lizzie, as she was called, would accept him in spite of his devotion to a dead predecessor, he would, with complete awareness of the honor accorded him, make her his wife.[12]

She agreed and rushed into preparations for a wedding to be held early in the afternoon of Friday, May 21, 1858, at the Calvary Presbyterian Church with William Anderson Scott officiating. At that point Liz had been in California only a few months. The conjecture that she, like Ralston, was fleeing emptiness rather than putting a seal on happiness is unavoidable.

Billy—or Toppie, as Liz and his close friends called him—meanwhile laid plans for what is surely one of the strangest honeymoons on record. He and his wife would visit the Calaveras grove of giant sequoia trees and from there go to Yosemite. Furthermore he would take with him on his bridal trip, at his own expense, several members of the wedding party—and a newspaper reporter.

He could have cruised anywhere, so why pick the Calaveras trees? Why Yosemite? The two spots had been discovered, separately, only half a dozen years before. There were rough accommodations at the big trees, but none as yet at Yosemite. The honeymooners would have to go to the valley by packtrain and then camp out. Ralston was familiar with the outdoors, but there is no indication that Lizzie was. Yet this

Elizabeth Fry, generally called Lizzie, married
Ralston after a whirlwind courtship.

was the wedding trip to which she agreed. Why did Ralston decree it?

For one thing, he always responded wholeheartedly to California scenery, especially in its unique and monumental aspects. He liked to share his enthusiasms. During the coming years he would repeatedly take important visitors on buggy tours of the rugged coast beyond the Golden Gate, to the geysers of Sonoma County, to Yosemite. If he could not go himself, he delegated the guiding to a competent employee, but go the visitor must. And so, evidently, must Liz.

It is quite probable that Ralston had already seen the wonders that he wanted to show her. If not, he had listened enviously to those who had. Edgar Mills had told him about the Calaveras grove, which was only a day's horseback trip from Columbia. The Reverend William Scott had written a stirring account of his visit to Yosemite in 1855, a year when only forty-two people entered the valley. Such accounts, or even his own memories, were certain to stir Ralston.

On top of that, he liked to be spectacular. Both the places he proposed to visit were, right then, very much in the public eye. Exploiters had recently stripped hundreds of feet of bark from two of the larger Calaveras trees and had shipped it east to be reassembled at international fairs. A literary man, James M. Hutchings, and an artist, Thomas Ayres, had done a less harmful but no less effective job in turning attention, by means of print and paint, to Yosemite's vast waterfalls and towering cliffs. A honeymoon there, covered by a reporter, was bound to attract notice.

Finally, the trip was psychologically safe. He could show the marvels to his bride, watch her face . . . and, surrounded by chattering friends, still not commit too much of himself during those first days of intimacy when neither of them, it would seem, really wanted intimacy.

Be all that as it may, the wedding went off as scheduled. It was, predictably, one of the social events of San Francisco's spring season. The church was crowded and, a reporter noted dutifully, lighted brilliantly with new-fangled gas distilled from coal. A sprig of white syringa glowed in the bride's dark hair. There was just enough "of rose tint upon her cheek to relieve the whiteness of her dress," wrote bridesmaid Sarah Haight, who kept a convenient but not very revealing diary of the trip.[13]

Afterwards, with a great flutter of crinoline, the party hurried to the home of Mr. and Mrs. Darling on Lombard Street for a reception. The formalities attended to, a score or more chosen friends slipped home, changed clothes, and joined the newlyweds aboard the California Steam Navigation Company's four o'clock riverboat for Benicia. Among them were three of the groom's attendants: a wealthy young merchant named Joseph Donohoe, T. H. Morrison, an officer in the bank of Fretz & Ralston, and Ed Mills.

Garrison was not there but had a tribute ready. As the riverboat pulled away from the dock, the Nicaragua steamers, *Orizaba* and *Sierra Nevada,* dipped their colors and fired a salute with the cannon that had been placed aboard as defense against the unpredictable Nicaraguans.

The recognition was pleasing. Yet Ralston must have been thankful that he no longer had any corporate connection with the ships. Despite expensive and feverish efforts, Garrison and Morgan had not been able to obtain a new franchise from Costa Rica. Accordingly, in one of the abrupt about-faces that came so easily to those flexible men, they had cuddled up to their old enemy, Cornelius Vanderbilt. In return for an unknown consideration he ceased competing with Morgan in the Gulf of Mexico and also purchased a half interest in the *Orizaba* and *Sierra Nevada.* Garrison then began advertising that the two steamers would soon resume service to Nicaragua, where connections would be made with Vanderbilt's Atlantic ships. The San Francisco newspapers rejoiced, for vigorous competition with the Pacific Mail Company's Panama route would drive down fares. Travel would increase and the resultant flood of newcomers would help lift California's economy out of its doldrums.[14] Or so the argument ran.

Immediately thereafter the announced sailings were cancelled. Vanderbilt had been using the new ships as ammunition for forcing the Pacific Mail Steamship line into increasing his subsidy for idleness from $40,000 to $56,000 a month. Although the principals tried to keep the maneuver a secret, the traveling public jumped to accurate and angry conclusions. A protest meeting was held in Portsmouth Square, and the *Bulletin* railed, on April 1, 1858, that the whole community was resounding with "bitter . . . curses at the treachery and base avarice of Vanderbilt and Garrison, in colluding to break down healthy competition."

Ralston was well out of it. Yet that was not the sum of his thoughts as the riverboat churned northward through the bay. Half of the powder expended on that tribute to his and Liz's marriage belonged to Vanderbilt. And the miniature that he always kept near him was of Vanderbilt's dead granddaughter. How moody was he as his new wife joined him to watch the saluting ships fade from sight? There is no way of knowing.

At Benicia, just west of where the Sacramento and San Joaquin rivers twine together, the celebrants debarked to enjoy a noisy banquet. Afterwards some of them caught the night boat back to San Francisco. The rest, a dozen or so, boarded a smaller vessel bound for Stockton. It was a short night—late to bed and an early rising for an arduous day —the first day of the well-populated honeymoon.

Without giving his heavy-eyed companions time for breakfast, Ralston pushed them into waiting carriages and led the way out of Stockton across a flat, monotonous, mosquito-ridden countryside to a tiny hamlet called Mugginsville. They ate there and then drove on east, climbing slowly into spring-green hills bright with poppies. As oak groves mixed with evergreens appeared, so did signs of placer mining. Sarah was dismayed. "How unsightly it makes the country appear," she told her diary: "how few flowers or how little vegetation there is where there is gold . . . how often its blighting effects are on the human heart"—conventional wisdom that she probably did not voice aloud to either Ralston or Edgar Mills.

In the afternoon they passed through Angel's Camp, where Mark Twain a few years later would propel himself toward fame with a short story called "The Celebrated Jumping Frog of Calaveras County. " At sunset they reached Murphy's and fell ravenously on the huge supper that Ralston provided. A long day. Even so a curious compulsion was on them—or at least on Ralston. They decided to go on to the big trees that night. After renting fresh buggies and horses, they plunged into the darkness. Much of the way lay beside a stream whose rush filled the night with tumult. Wind gusted. An unexpected rain crashed. In the confusion the party became separated. After agitated shouting back and forth they finally pulled together again. At midnight, having traveled 87 miles by horse and buggy since dawn, they reached the Calaveras grove.

Sarah was up early to walk among the towering redwoods, smelling the new dogwood blossoms and enjoying the rain-sweetened stillness. The rest of the party had less time to enjoy the sights they had come so far to see. Ralston routed them out of their beds, back into the buggies, back to Murphy's. Another rain took the stiffness from the men's hats and made the ladies' sunbonnets cling to their faces. There was a great deal of laughing, Sarah wrote, but perhaps there was a tiff between the newlyweds as well. When the group changed from buggies to open coaches at Murphy's, Liz chose to go with Sarah, Joe Donohoe, and Ed Mills in one vehicle, while Ralston traveled in another with old Judge McRae.

The road stayed rough. The jouncing, said Sarah, threw her and Liz and the two young men together in a promiscuous manner. In the afternoon the sky cleared and sundown was glorious. They trotted through Columbia, Ed Mills' hometown, by moonlight and did not stop until they reached Sonora.

The next morning the group split again, some returning to San Francisco. Only eight remained together to continue the honeymoon to Yosemite: Liz and Billy Ralston, a Mr. and Mrs. Kincaid; Sarah Haight and three bachelors, Donohoe, Mills, and Judge McRae.

The last part of the journey was by packtrain, two days along a wild mountain trail. They had guides, cooks, roustabouts. Toppie, as Sarah called Ralston in her diary, labored diligently to make sure that all went well. He never tired, she wrote. "He travels the fastest, works the hardest, and has one of the biggest hearts in existence." His "little *girl*"—so he called Liz, according to Sarah—looked very pretty in black-and-white checked bloomers, with her hair falling in long braids down her back. A merry time. They explored a cave in a rowboat, galloped through stately woods, splashed through crystal streams. The first view of the valley turned them briefly silent, and then they rode in between the giant cliffs, "the branches of the trees and the fragrance of the wild honeysuckle a pleasant exchange for the reflection of the sun's rays from the great white rocks."

They camped near the bank of the Merced River, at the foot of El Capitan, out of sight of the falls but within plain hearing. "A large fire was burning. All the party were tired and stretched themselves out in various postures. . . . Gradually the moonlight advanced and covered the whole camp and shone on the beautiful river."

The bridesmaid at least was enjoying the wedding trip.

THE NEW COUPLE HAD MARRIED in such haste that they had not yet found a house in which to live. On returning to San Francisco, they settled for a time at Tehama House, a hotel built in 1850 at the northwest corner of California and Sansome streets, four blocks from the Fretz & Ralston bank building. Then, when it became evident that Liz was pregnant, they began househunting more assiduously.

In those days the cream of San Francisco lived on the south side of Market Street. The premier area, the only one, Gertrude Atherton later remarked, in which a person could be born respectably, was South Park. There, out of sight of the city on the far side of a ridge that shut out the wind, a landowner named George Gordon had laid out a long, narrow park modeled after Berkeley Square in London, and had surrounded it with a London-style iron fence. He then divided the land around the park into narrow lots and gave a key to the park to each purchaser. As a further inducement he paved the street leading over the ridge to the city with planks and ran a horse-drawn omnibus along it every ten minutes.[15] The stateliest San Franciscans flocked there to live, creating an ambience that struck observers as Deep South.

South Park's rival as a residential area was the ridge itself, Rincon Hill. A hundred or so feet high (it has since been leveled to make way for the abutments of the bridge to Oakland) Rincon Hill commanded on clear days a spectacular view of the bay, the city, and the long wharves that reached out into roadsteads crowded with the masts of clipper ships and the smoky, black funnels of steamboats. Characteristically, Ralston chose to live on the hilltop, at the corner of Harrison and Fremont streets.[16]

A camping trip to Yosemite climaxed the Ralstons' well-attended honeymoon (this view from Glacier Point was painted sixteen years after their visit).

GIFT OF THE COWELL FOUNDATION, OAKLAND MUSEUM

South Park and Rincon Hill, in 1855 San Francisco's plushest residential areas.
The Ralstons moved onto the hill in 1858.

Before the move was completed he received shocking news. His brother Sam, his health apparently restored, had started back to California from Europe. On the way he paused in St. Louis to visit his younger brothers, Andrew Jackson, generally known as Jack, and James Alpheus.

Jack and Jim Ralston were running a store in St. Louis. Whenever Billy wrote them, which wasn't very often, he filled his letters with advice: the younger men should make a point of always acting with firmness and decision, of finishing whatever they promised to do, of pressing on as if the word "can't" did not exist. But there are times when "can't" does exist. In December, at Jackson's home, Samuel Ralston fell ill and died.

The loss made the naming of Billy's first son, born March 4, 1859, inevitable: Samuel Fry Ralston. The father sent Jack a piece of California marble to put on the first Sam's grave as a memento of the state in which the deceased had hoped to live. In order that baby Sam would know the source of his name, Billy commissioned a life-sized portrait painted from a daguerreotype. When he received from St. Louis a trunk filled with Sam's effects, he wrote emotionally that they were "precious & *above* price"; they would not be used, but kept for the baby.[17]

126

*Samuel Fry Ralston,
Billy's first son,
was named for
Billy's dead brother.*

About this same time he suffered another loss. In 1859, the government contracts with the United States Mail and Pacific Mail Steamship companies for carrying mail between the east and west coasts expired. The first-named company decided not to seek a renewal, and Pacific Mail began laying plans to move into the Atlantic. At that point Vanderbilt announced that he would compete for the field unless Pacific Mail increased his subsidy to $100,000 a month. The company refused. Vanderbilt thereupon formed the aggressively competitive Atlantic and Pacific Steamship Company. Garrison went east to become one of its principal officers. Although he soon broke with Vanderbilt over lack of freedom in his new position, he never returned to California to live.[18]

Ralston's two closest confidants, Sam and Cornelius Garrison, were gone now. Ralph Fretz, to be sure, was still at the bank, solid, dependable, and quiet. His conservatism furnished a necessary counter to Ralston's quick judgments and soaring imagination, but Fretz was not a man to turn to for the sort of stimulation that accompanied the birth of new and radical concepts. To that extent, William Ralston was now on his own for the first time in his life.

He worked hard. Banking in California during the years preceding the Civil War was exacting. In spite of the still-depressed economy, speculation and chance-taking remained widespread. A banker needed to study his customers carefully in order to have at his fingertips the infinite number of details necessary for making decisions about loans and investments. Paradoxically enough, given his own penchant for plunging, Ralston reputedly knew more about the San Francisco mercantile community than any other banker in the city—and knew it because, like his cautious partner Fretz, he went out of his way to learn who was solid and who was not.[19]

Meantime he had to supervise the bank's arduous daily routine. Each morning the express companies delivered to the firm's doors the boxes of gold dust, gold ingots, and crude amalgam collected by its agents and correspondents in the interior. These had to be weighed and classified. Some was sent on to private refiners; some went directly to the mint for coinage. At the same time gold and silver coins were clinking across the counters, either for deposit or for the repayment of loans. Except for drafts, bills of exchange, and discounted notes, there was no paper. By nightfall hundreds of pounds of money were on hand to be stacked and counted. Some was put into the vaults; some was boxed, as was part of the bullion, for shipment to New York. Notes and drafts had to be filed, and letters written.

On steamer day the pace quickened, for this was when bills were collected and remittances sent east. Long after the doors had swung shut for the day, the clerks were still at work, pursuing errors as they struck their balances. Yet the bank's atmosphere was never strained. Although Ralston could be brusque when his concentration was interrupted, he was basically friendly and considerate. On busy days he moved quietly among the staff, encouraging those who were harried and often taking a weary teller's place while the man caught a breath of air.[20]

His outside interests were comparable to those of many small-city bankers. He was a member of the Chamber of Commerce, and in 1858 served on its Committee of Appeals to hear disputes that had not been resolved by attempted arbitration.[21] In December, 1857, he became a director of the Sacramento Valley Railroad, whose twenty-two miles of track still carried the only steam trains in California.[22] He worked with other bankers on ways to speed coinage at the mint and to establish uniform methods of valuing and handling the annoying mélange of foreign coins that still circulated through the city.[23]

He was gregarious. He liked to saunter through the financial district, stopping on street corners to chat with other businessmen. At his office he was approachable by the smallest depositor. He went to church regularly—for two years he was a trustee of Calvary Presbyterian— and with Lizzie he attended the many dances, masked balls, and theater parties that filled the San Francisco social calendar. Although surviving photographs show him with a stern visage—possibly he thought bankers should look that way—we are assured that normally he was smiling and animated.[24]

Both Lizzie and he liked to have people continually about them. At times, indeed, it seemed that they dreaded being alone together, just as they had apparently dreaded intimacy on their honeymoon. Characteristically, when they learned that the sweetheart of one of the bank tellers was hesitant about making the long trip to the coast to learn whether or not to marry her fiancé, they rushed letters to her, offering to open their home to her for as long as she wished to stay. She came, settled in, succumbed finally, and was married there.[25]

In politics Ralston was aligned with the so-called Chivalry, or South-leaning, wing of the Democratic Party. His closest ties were with Milton S. Latham, an Ohioan who had moved to Alabama as a young man and then had emigrated to Sacramento in discouragement after losing an election by three votes. On the coast he was more successful and was sent to Congress at the youngest permissible age, twenty-five. After being defeated for reelection by Broderick's wing of Northern Democrats, he served for a time as Collector of the Port of San Francisco.

He was tall, slender, bearded, and suave. He had a handsome, brilliant, socially ambitious wife. They were often with the Ralstons, and when Latham ran for the governorship in 1859, the banker supported him vigorously. Latham was elected, but held his office only five days. Shortly after his victory at the polls, David Terry, one-time justice of the state supreme court, killed Senator Broderick in a sensational pistol duel. Picking a replacement for Broderick was the duty

Milton S. Latham,
future governor, was
a Rincon Hill neighbor.

of the state legislature, which assembled in Sacramento in January, 1860. It selected Latham, who was replaced by his lieutenant governor, John C. Downey of Los Angeles.[26] Ralston now had, if he wished to use it, a direct pipeline to Washington.

It hardly seemed that he would use it, except for such routine requests as any businessman might make. His interests were primarily local. He had aligned himself with the Southern faction of the Democratic Party not out of conviction but out of habits acquired in New Orleans and through later business and social relationships in San Francisco. The tremors shaking the eastern part of the nation over slavery and its related issues scarcely touched him. What he wanted, for the bank of Fretz & Ralston and for himself, was a resurgence of California's long-stagnant economy.

Just possibly a revival might be in the making. As 1859 ran its course, rumors began leaping the Sierra about fabulous new mineral strikes in what was then the western edge of Utah Territory, now Nevada.

At first many Californians were skeptical. Earlier booms had collapsed as quickly as they had begun, notably 1858's feverish rush to the Fraser River in British Columbia. Ralston, though, could not help being excited. A stampede of any proportion would benefit his holdings in the California Steam Navigation Company and the Sacramento Valley Railroad, for their combined efforts would be necessary to move freight to the end of the wagonway leading across the mountains. And if the strikes did amount to half of what rumor suggested, the bank would be in a position to reap richly, for Billy Ralston's contacts with miners and with the men who dealt with miners were probably better than those of any other banker on the coast.

Under the circumstances, it behooved him to be ready.

CHAPTER 9

Reaching Out

Because it was Ralston's business to know about mineral resources, he was probably aware that the desert mountains immediately east of the Sierra Nevada had been the scene of placer mining ever since 1850. It was a desolate area, brightened only by the Carson River. Winding beside the river was the immigrant trail to California. Stockmen ran cattle and grew hay in neighboring swales, and hamlets appeared here and there to meet the needs of travelers.

The mountains north and west of the river were drab—coarse soil, gnarled sagebrush, scattered juniper trees. The high point of the range was called Sun Mountain. Rough little gullies seamed its eastern flank. The largest ones, Gold Canyon and Six-Mile Canyon, headed within two miles of each other but drew apart as they snaked down to the Carson River.

From 1850 through 1858 the two gullies turned out an estimated $600,000 in placer gold. It was no bonanza, but it kept ever-shifting groups of miners laboring over their sluice boxes whenever the weather allowed. As spring warmed the land early in 1859, two such parties, each unaware of the other, started for the upper reaches of both canyons. By extraordinary coincidence—after all, the gulches were too familiar to seem capable of surprises—both groups made dazzling strikes: more dazzling, indeed, than the prospectors realized at first.[1]

The discoverers were used to free gold. The term means that the metal is not locked in chemical combination with other elements but can be removed from the ore by simple crushing and washing. Profitable amounts of such gold existed in the initial strikes. Associated with it, however, were unfamiliar ores. Obviously complex, these compounds were not susceptible to ordinary treatment. Worse, they interfered with

This painting is artist Joseph Harrington's conception of the discovery of the Comstock Lode in 1859.

routine procedures, and the impatient discoverers cast the stuff aside.

Visitors to the mines, which had stirred up considerable local excitement, were more curious. Among them were B. F. Harrison, a Carson Valley rancher, and J. F. Stone, a miner from Grass Valley, California, who had recently taken over a stage station beside the immigrant trail. In July, 1859, the two men, apparently traveling separately (surviving accounts are ambiguous), carried samples of the mysterious ore across the mountains to the twin mining towns of Nevada City and Grass Valley, and gave them to assayers there.

Astonishment resulted. Melville Atwood, the assayer who worked with the samples from the claim at the head of Six-Mile Canyon, declared that a full ton of such rock would yield $3,876 in precious metal. Only a quarter of that value was gold. The rest was silver, a metal all but unknown in California mines.

Although an assayer's report is supposed to be as private as a doctor's diagnosis, this news was too sensational to keep bottled. Several men from Grass Valley immediately started on horseback across the Sierra Nevada. Others fell in behind them, and soon a swarm of

prospectors was spread out across the eastern face of Sun Mountain. Our concern now, however, is the claim at Six-Mile Canyon.

By the time the Californians arrived, the shallow, rust-colored pit had been given a name, Ophir. Six men owned it. Two, Peter O'Riley and Patrick McLaughlin, had made the original discovery. Two more, Henry Comstock and Emanuel Penrod, had muscled in on the strength of Comstock's loud assertion that he and Penrod held prior rights to a 160-acre agricultural claim to the ground. The remaining pair, John D. Winters, Jr., and J. A. Osborne, had been given interests in return for building, near the mouth of the projected shaft, crude arrastras in which the ore could be crushed.

The Californians immediately began trying to purchase the interests of the six claimants. The bargaining was not done in concert. A would-be buyer cornered one of the sextet as best he could and began dickering with might and main, hoping to conclude his deal before the prospective sellers realized that they might do better by acting together.

Penrod, Osborne, and McLaughlin succumbed quickly, receiving from $3,000 to $3,500 each for their interests, far more money than any of them had ever before seen in a single sum. (The buyer of McLaughlin's share, at $3,000, was George Hearst of Grass Valley; later he would father William Randolph Hearst.) Comstock tried to be slier. He struck a tentative agreement with Judge James Walsh, also of Grass Valley, to sell his interest for $11,000, provided that a representative amount of ore yielded, under normal smelting conditions, values comparable to those Atwood had obtained through chemical analysis.

The two men selected 3,151 pounds. During the last week of August they carried it on mules over the mountains to Folsom, transferred it to the Sacramento Valley Railroad, and at the river loaded it aboard a California Steam Navigation ship for the rest of the journey to Joseph Mosheimer's reduction works in San Francisco. The mineralized rock yielded $1.50 a pound.[2] Though William Ralston may not have heard of the earlier assay in Grass Valley, he certainly learned of that sale. Promptly, like every other financier in San Francisco, he began considering its implications for himself and for the city.

Soon Washoe, the name for the entire region surrounding Sun Mountain, was on every California tongue. Although winter was near, the flow of treasure hunters quickened. Center of their activities was a pair of settlements constructed mostly of raw boards and tattered canvas. The southernmost, at the head of Gold Canyon, was called Gold Hill. Approximately two miles north, near the Ophir Mine, was Virginia City. Between the towns and extending a short distance beyond each one was a series of parallel, erratically mineralized veins. Or perhaps those many, apparently discrete veins were really offshoots of a single parent vein buried far beneath the gravelly surface of the hillside. Legal determination of that geologic dispute could make a difference of millions of dollars to the worth of a mine, as Billy Ralston would learn soon enough.

By fall the fissure was known as the Comstock Lode, simply because Henry Comstock, who had made no discoveries, had trumpeted himself into prominence as part owner of both original claims. As for Sun Mountain, it was rechristened Mount Davidson, for Donald Davidson, one of the California purchasers of a sixth interest in the Ophir. The reason for singling him out is uncertain.

Mining at the Ophir was pushed vigorously, even while ownership was changing hands. Some of the ore was ground to a powder in the arrastras and washed for the sake of the free gold it contained. Blackish chunks that looked rich in silver sulphides were put aside for reduction in San Francisco. In October, fearful that snow might soon close the Sierra passes, the partners selected and sacked for shipment 38 tons of the likeliest looking ore. Henry Comstock, James Walsh, and George Hearst then escorted the mass by pack mule, wagon, train, and riverboat to Mosheimer's smelter.

Freight cost $140 a ton. Smelting charges came to $412 a ton. Even so the shipment netted $91,000. When the gleaming ingots were taken from the smelter to Alsop's bank for display, crowds of unemployed miners followed excitedly. Should they too head for the Comstock? A new fillip came almost immediately from Sacramento. According to newspapers there, 21 tons of ore from the Central Mine, just south of the Ophir, had grossed $50,000.[3] Why, this was better than the golden days of '49—or so the hopeful assured themselves.

Actually, as financiers quickly realized, the Washoe strikes were nothing like the California diggings of 1848 and 1849. Those gold pockets had been shallow and widely distributed, needing nothing more for exploitation than a strong back and a few simple tools. Mining in Washoe would be different. The minerals there were concentrated in a small area. Only a few men could find good claims, and the purchase price of those would climb steeply as bidding grew competitive. Sinking deep shafts and milling the complex ores would be costly. A backlog of funds would thus become as essential as hoisting machinery—and as expensive. The money would have to be accumulated from a wide variety of sources, funneled like other supplies across a difficult mountain chain, and then, under the supervision of experts, put to work solving the region's many severe problems.

Partly through his association with Darius and Edgar Mills, Ralston had already mastered the procedures involved in assembling funds for complex placer operations—building dams for turning rivers out of their beds, importing water in giant flumes so that hydraulic hoses could batter down gold-bearing cliffs, and so on. Consequently he was ready to act when calls for money began coming out of Washoe during the winter of 1859–60.

The Ophir was the mine that attracted his attention. It had become expensive. Thanks to the returns received from that epochal 38 tons of ore shipped in October, discoverer Peter O'Riley demanded and received from John O. Earl, a San Francisco capitalist, $45,000 for his share in the claim—as contrasted to the $3,000 that his original partner, Patrick McLaughlin, had received from George Hearst. Of the original six owners, only John D. Winters still retained his interest.

The situation was classic. Poor, untrained prospectors had discovered a claim whose potential riches they were incapable of exploiting. Realizing this, they had sold out for prices that seemed to them very generous. The new owners were chance takers, but something more as well. They understood the ins and outs of mining, including the problems of finance. They had bought quickly in order to obtain control before prices soared. Then, relaxing, they surveyed the alternate courses open to them. Throughout their thinking ran the uneasy awareness that no one, given the state of the profession in 1860, could estimate accurately how much profitable mineral existed at depth, beneath those first dazzling surface indications.

Under the circumstances, should they develop the mine slowly, using its own production for meeting costs? Or should they hurry things along by inviting outside capital to participate? If the latter course were chosen, should they try to get along with high-interest loans? Or should they yield control to a stock corporation composed of men capable of attracting capital through a sale of securities to the general public?

The purchasers of the Ophir decided on the stock-company approach. They probably could not have done anything else. By then they knew that although selected samples of their ore were very rich, the great bulk was of lower grade and could not meet the cost of shipment to and reduction in San Francisco. It would have to be excavated at great depth and milled nearby, either by themselves or by some custom mill hired to do the job. The price of borrowing money for such enterprises was prohibitive—as high as 60 percent a year. The only way to solve the financial problem while reducing individual risks was to broaden the ownership of the mine. The purchasers could do that by exchanging their interests for shares of stock in a company formed to operate the property. They would lose control, but balancing that loss were the speculative possibilities inherent in their new stock. If the mine developed well, they could sell the certificates for . . . well, there was no possible way to guess how much.

Talks began during the winter, Ralston in the thick of them. The catalyst was John Earl. It is probable that Earl had first gone to Virginia City as advance agent for a syndicate that had begun discussing the possibility of purchase immediately after verifying the reports about that first 38 tons of ore.

Just how the principals were brought together is unknown, but by April they had come to terms. On April 12 the Ophir Silver Mining Company was incorporated in San Francisco. Capital was set at $5,042,000. The shares—16,800 of them—had a nominal value of $300 each.[4] (During the early days of the Comstock, shares represented the number of feet, or portions of feet, that the company concerned owned along the lode. The Ophir covered 1,400 feet. For the sake of bringing stock prices within reach of investors, each "foot" was divided into 12 shares for a total of 16,800—inches, one might say.) How much of this stock the company granted to each of the original purchasers is not a matter of record.

A man named William Blanding was elected president of the company. William Ralston became treasurer. Records fail to reveal how many shares he owned. Inasmuch as the development of the mine would be paid for in part by assessments levied against each owner in proportion to his holdings, he may have preferred not to plunge too deeply.

Did he go to the Comstock to see what he had bought? No record exists to say that he did. Yet given the excitement of the times, together with his own restless energy, curiosity, and penchant for moving about, his staying at home would be harder to explain than his traveling.

If the trip occurred, it was probably made in the spring of 1860, after the worst of the winter's snow had left the high country. From its start Ralston would have seen much to ponder—matters of both private and statewide concern that were being thrown into sharp perspective by this new mining rush. That being so, a digression about the problems is not irrelevant.

First there was the crisis of the harbor. Ever since the founding of the American city beside Yerba Buena cove, that priceless asset had been brutally mishandled. Waterfront lots were profitable and hence a tempting source of revenue for the chronically bankrupt city. In 1847, well before the signing of the treaty that ended the war between the United States and Mexico, the military governor of California, General Stephen W. Kearny, had authorized the sale, at public auction, of land between high and low tide, "the proceeds of such sale to be used for the benefit of the town of San Francisco."[5]

Later military governors followed suit. Speculators rushed to buy, filled in the purchases with earth, erected buildings in the fill, and ran long wharves out toward deep water. Unwilling to give up so lucrative a source of revenue, the new civil administrators of the growing town had continued selling off the advancing waterfront, even though California's constitution placed ownership of all coastal lands in the hands of the state.

Worried by the uncertainties that resulted, owners of waterfront land prevailed on the legislature (corruptly, it was charged) to pass a special act confirming their titles. At the same time the lawmakers sought to settle jurisdictional disputes by delineating a boundary, the so-called "red line," between state and municipal control. The effect was next to nil. Yielding to bribery, San Francisco's early officials continued to breach the line. The waterfront inched farther into the bay; private wharves, most of them built without authorization, multiplied until they were almost as thick as the teeth of a giant comb.

To give these structures a semblance of protection against state interference, and also to raise revenue, the commission charged with funding San Francisco's municipal debt executed, in 1853, ten-year leases to docks already built or building. The result was a mess. Companies holding property on short-term leases of questionable validity were not going to spend money on improvements. Undredged, the harbor grew shoal from mud sloughing off the filled land. Abandoned hulks obstructed some of the roadsteads. Teredos, a kind of sea borer, honeycombed the pilings that supported the busy docks. Something had to be done, but whose responsibility was it?

Into the impasse stepped an extraordinary promoter named Levi Parsons. He proposed that the lessors of the docks and other interested capitalists form a giant corporation called the San Francisco Wharf and Dock Company. This company would dredge the harbor and construct a seawall, or bulkhead, to prevent further shoaling. In return the firm would receive from the state a fifty-year franchise granting it the exclusive right to build docks and adjoining warehouses and collect tolls for their use. In lieu of taxes the company would pay 10 percent of its gross revenues to the state. Profits were assured because, although San Francisco's Board of Supervisors would have the right to set rates, these could not be so low that the dock company would not earn at least 10 percent on its investment.

The San Francisco Wharf and Dock Company was chartered in December, 1858. Among its constituents were the lessors of seven of the city's principal wharf and warehouse complexes. Included was the Broadway Wharf, operated by the California Steam Navigation Company, of which Billy Ralston then was or soon would be a director.

A word about the California Steam Navigation Company. During the early days of the gold rush, boat traffic across San Francisco Bay and

Levi ("Bulkhead") Parsons hoped to control the city's harbor by means of the San Francisco Wharf and Dock Company.

The Broadway Wharf, shown here with the steamer **Yosemite** *alongside, was slated for inclusion in the harbor monopoly.*

along the San Joaquin and Sacramento rivers had been fiercely competitive, to no one's lasting gain. Wearying of the warfare, the leading boatmen had agreed in 1854 to consolidate resources. The result was the formation of the powerful California Steam Navigation Company, whose secretary and chief executive officer was William Norris. Ralston and Norris had been friends years before on the Mississippi.

The new company built fine ships and conducted its service with a flair. It ended the wild steamboat races that too often had led to explosions and groundings. But it was a monopoly. When would-be competitors appeared, the Navigation Company either bought them out or crushed them by cutting fares and unleashing the superior power of its boats. Rates then went back up, to the inevitable complaint that the soulless monopoly was wringing its fat dividends from helpless travelers and browbeaten shippers of merchandise essential to the interior.

As the stampede to Washoe swelled the number of passengers and tonnages of freight using the Broadway wharves, the California Steam Navigation Company grew concerned over their deterioration. Something had to be done, and so the directors decided to join Levi Parsons' questionable new corporation.

A bill granting the San Francisco Wharf and Dock Company the franchise it wanted was introduced in the legislature in February, 1859.

Opposition was immediate and strident. Merchants in the interior objected to exclusive control of the harbor by a tight-knit coterie of San Franciscans. Shippers in San Francisco who were not members of the new corporation feared that they would be the victims of discrimination. Theoreticians argued that a monopoly of any kind would cripple trade; only a "free" port operated by either the city or the state would allow San Francisco to realize her potentials.

The People's Party, child of the vigilantes of 1856, opposed the franchise bill. The Chamber of Commerce (Ralston was a member of both it and the People's Party) passed resolutions condemning it. Pamphlets and newspaper articles, pro and con, poured from the press.

After acrimonious debate, the legislators rejected the measure. The margin was so narrow, however, that Levi Parsons—ever afterwards called Bulkhead Parsons—promised to reintroduce the bill in 1860. The battle of words resumed, with both sides heaping arguments on the five-man legislative committee that came to San Francisco to investigate the harbor problem in detail. In due time that committee reported in favor of the measure by a vote of three to two.[6]

Ralston's good friend Milton Latham inherited the problem on being elected governor. Eager not to stir controversy that might hurt his chances of being sent to the United States Senate by the legislature as a replacement for the slain Broderick, Latham avoided commitment. In his inaugural address on January 9, 1860, he urged only that the lawmakers study the matter carefully before acting. His wife was more outspoken and freely condemned the measure in public conversations. A belief swept through Sacramento that if the legislature approved the bulkhead bill, Latham would veto it. After he had been elected senator, rumor declared that the voting had been manipulated by supporters of the bulkhead measure in order to get him out of the way. His successor, Lieutenant Governor John Downey, might be more amenable.[7]

This time the bill passed. Fifteen years later, during the course of a slashing front-page attack on Ralston, the San Francisco *Daily Evening Bulletin* charged that victory came because Ralston and the California Steam Navigation Company brazenly bought the necessary votes.[8] The accusation lacked firm documentation, perhaps with reason; venality seldom leaves clear tracks. Still, in the absence of proof, it is permissible to do a little wondering.

The *Bulletin's* attack was prepared at a time (1875) when Ralston was enormously powerful, a natural target for what the *Bulletin* considered to be its crusading zeal. But the misdeeds imputed to him came in 1860, when he was just beginning his rise. Other men and other organizations involved in the bulkhead controversy had more at stake and were far stronger. For instance, tax lists indicate that the resources of Fretz & Ralston were $50,000; those of Pioche, Bayerque & Company, the only San Francisco bank that openly supported the bulkhead bill, were $500,000. The California Steam Navigation Company was, to be sure, very strong; but it was only one of many corporations, including the even mightier Pacific Mail Steamship Company, that were involved in the controversy. And so the question arises: granting that corruption accompanied the passage of the bill—and corruption was a political staple of the times—why single out in this battle of titans one relatively obscure man for blame?[9] But that's just guesswork, too.

The bill went to Governor Downey on April 2, 1860. He studied it for fourteen days and then vetoed it. The legislature sustained him—but only just—and San Francisco exploded with joy. When Downey visited the city shortly afterwards, he was met at the docks by brass bands, mounted police, smartly aligned militia units, and masses of marching stevedores carrying banners inscribed with such legends as "What is the proper number of toes? V-toes!" The president of the Chamber of Commerce delivered a stentorian speech declaring that all California was indebted to Downey for staving off "one of the most odious and oppressive monopolies ever attempted to be fastened upon the commerce of any country in any age."[10]

So the spider was dead. But what of the harbor? It was still crippled by rot, and no surgeon, whether state, municipal, or private, was in sight. Leases on the docks, without which San Francisco would perish, were due to expire within three years. What about that? No one concerned with the port and with the companies that depended on it, as Ralston most certainly was, could view such questions with equanimity.

Other considerations about the future met him at Sacramento, where he changed from riverboat to one of the crowded cars of the Sacramento Valley Railroad. He was a director of that firm, too. Its principal backer was the bank of Pioche, Bayerque & Company, chief financial proponents of the dead bulkhead bill.

The railroad's situation—it was still the only line in California—was frustrating. Its purpose, which it was fulfilling, was to tie the mining business of the northern foothills to the manufacturers and commission merchants of San Francisco. Profits were elusive, however. Too much money and railroad stock had been allowed to dribble into the pockets of the contractors, Lester L. and John P. Robinson. For the railroad the result was an excessive burden of debt, much of it bearing interest charges of 3 percent a month.

If interest were disregarded, the line was in good shape. The slow decline in mining in the area it served had been offset by a rise in agricultural production, so that net profits (before interest) had stayed at about $90,000 a year—not bad for twenty-two miles of track in a region still sparsely settled. Obviously the rush to Washoe would help boost revenues—as matters developed net profits (before interest)

*The levees of Sacramento connected steamboats from San Francisco
with the new little railroads pushing toward the mining country.*

jumped 11.3 percent in the year 1860 alone[11]—but the improvement was
not likely to overcome the load of debt and make dividends possible.

Still, there might be a way to escape the burden. Towns deeper in
the interior, notably Auburn and Nevada City, wanted the railroad to
push on to their depots from its current terminus at Folsom. In pursuit
of that goal, businessmen in the two villages had paid for surveys, had
obtained cost analyses, and had won from the legislature permission to
hold an election which, if results were affirmative, would authorize the
payment of $150,000 in county bonds to whatever company constructed
the railroad they wanted.

Believing that the bond issue would pass, Ralston and the other
directors of the Sacramento Valley Railroad chartered a new corporation, the Sacramento, Placer & Nevada Railroad Company.* As a
separate entity, the new concern would not be responsible for the debts
of the Sacramento Valley Railroad, yet could save a great deal of
money by using Sacramento Valley rolling stock on its tracks instead
of buying its own. The debt-ridden old firm, in other words, would feed
business to the new company, whose burdens, lightened by county
subsidies, would not be so great as to preclude dividends.[12]

---

*Nevada in this connection means Nevada County, just as Placer means Placer
County. It has no reference to Nevada Territory, site of the Comstock Lode. That
Nevada was not carved out of the western part of Utah Territory until 1861.

So far, so good. But then the Comstock introduced a new element. After reaching Folsom, most trans-Sierra traffic swung off to the right through Placerville in order to cross Johnson Pass south of Lake Tahoe. Placerville businessmen began agitating for a railroad from Folsom to *their* town. Preliminary surveys, financed probably by Pioche, Bayerque & Company, indicated that such a shortline was feasible both physically and financially. But to lay that cost on top of the expense of building to Auburn—the directors hesitated.

Then reports began to come in, one of them perhaps from Ralston, of endless traffic toiling upward through the spring mud to Johnson Pass. If the fantastic boom lasted . . . why not control *all* its traffic? Build the already incorporated Sacramento, Placer & Nevada to Auburn as feeder for a new wagon road that would cross the Sierra north of Lake Tahoe. Create another line to Placerville as feeder for the existing wagonway over Johnson Pass south of Tahoe. Let both shortlines meet the Sacramento Valley Railroad at Folsom. Each branch of the stubby Y would be legally separate, yet by means of interlocking directorates the men in charge of the debt-laden Sacramento Valley company would end up in full control of every passenger and pound of freight moving between the bay area and the new mines.

It was too heady a prospect to resist. A few months later the Sacramento & Placerville Railroad Company was formally incorporated.[13] Thus the seeds were planted for a monopoly which, if it flourished, was bound to involve the waterborne carriers of the California Steam Navigation Company, plying between San Francisco's rotted docks and the sounder ones at Sacramento. Bill Ralston was still only a minor cog in the enmeshing wheels. But as he moved toward the Comstock that spring, he began to see with new clarity some of the ways by which alert men could wrap up a state.

CHAPTER 10

No Time for Caution

In spite of high assay reports from the mines, Virginia "City" almost ceased functioning during the winter of 1859–60. Of the three thousand or so people who had hurried to the scene on the wings of the first rumors, most turned back as soon as blizzards began howling down the slopes of Mount Davidson. Of the three hundred who stayed, perhaps thirty found regular employment in the Ophir and the Central, the only two mines that operated throughout the snowy months.

Whether employed or not, the inhabitants lived in smoky caves gouged into the hillside or in squat huts insulated by earth heaped against the walls. Stocks of whisky were exhausted before the trails were opened in the spring; after that the only amusements were gambling, storytelling, and the continual swapping of "feet" in claims that no one had yet investigated.

The spring melt opened the way to new hordes. Perhaps as many as ten thousand people, most of them male, trudged up the two canyons, only to discover that if they wanted a piece of the lode, they would have to buy it. The majority thereupon either left in disgust, hired out as laborers to the lucky, or scratched together grubstakes for prospecting the neighboring ranges. Quarreling, roistering, frenzied promotion, and the confusions of a brief Indian war kept surface conditions in a continual flux. Underneath the spume, however, a great deal of hard work went steadily on.

Technical difficulties were multiplying. One concerned water. Although surface quantities were meager and foul tasting, the amount increased at depth, flooding the shafts and stopping work. To get rid of it, the Ophir installed the first of the hundreds of pumps whose rhythmic chugging would soon be part of the heartbeat of the Comstock. The company also began driving a drainage tunnel designed to tap the vein a short distance beneath the underground lakes. That, too, would set a precedent for later projects of enormous scale.

Then there was timbering. As the shaft deepened, the vein widened until conventional methods of underground support no longer sufficed. Again work stopped while Philip Deidesheimer, a German-born engineer lured from a California quartz mine, worked out a solution during the fall of 1860. Soon every mine on the Comstock was following the technique of squareset timbering that Deidesheimer introduced first in the Ophir.[1]

Problems continued after the complex ore had been hoisted to the surface. Most of the claim holders, digging in shallow pits near the surface, had neither the funds nor the knowledge of chemistry and mechanical engineering that were needed to cope with the difficulty. Fortunately the slack was taken up by another California engineer, Almarin B. Paul. During the winter of 1859–60 he worked out a process of sorts (later it would need revision), and on the strength of his flow sheets won milling contracts from several small producers. He then ordered machinery from San Francisco and by laboring without ceasing was able to start operations a few hours ahead of his nearest rival.[2] Soon several competitors were erecting custom mills wherever trickles of water were available.

The Ophir decided not to patronize the outsiders but to mill its own ore. Ralston's vote was not decisive, of course, but the plans that emerged were grandiose enough to suit even his flair for magnificence. First the company found and purchased 2,000 well-wooded, well-

Virginia City, 1861. The Nevada town grew rapidly as Californians raced across the Sierra to exploit the region's silver.

watered acres in the Washoe Valley, twelve miles from the mine. It hacked a wagonway through the mountains to the site—the road crossed the lower end of Washoe Lake on a long bridge supported by massive pilings—and set scores of builders to work dressing granite stone not just for the mill building but also for machine shops, stables, and living quarters for the laborers. Costs were estimated at $500,000, a staggering sum for the time and place.[3]

Engineers meanwhile delved into accounts of silver reduction processes used in Germany and Mexico. After deciding on paper what would work best, they ordered the necessary machinery without first running tests in a pilot plant. The procedure was risky, but quick. Besides, the era was one that valued daring and showiness. If nothing else, ostentation bespoke confidence, and confidence would sustain stock prices when and if the owners decided to market their shares.

Involvement in the Ophir was so expensive that most of the first stockholders had no desire to add to their risks. A few, however, decided to reach out still farther, on the theory that the bonanza ore being opened in the Ophir would extend south into other claims. Because their nearest neighbor, the Central, was making a good showing, at least near the surface, they could not afford to buy it. On beyond the Central and its adjoining claims, however, was the Gould and Curry, named for its original holders, Alva Gould and Abe Curry. The claim covered 1,200 feet of the lode. George Hearst had been attracted to it during his stay on the Comstock in 1859, and had picked up a piece for $450.00. William Blanding, president of the Ophir, and John O. Earl had also acquired interests.

This trio put together a syndicate that purchased the mine and then, on June 25, 1860, incorporated a company to operate it. Earl was elected president, Ralston treasurer. Among the directors were some of San Francisco's shrewdest speculators: Lloyd Tevis, Alpheus Bull, and Thomas Bell, all of them business associates of Ralston's. Lacking at the outset the kind of ore that gilded the Ophir, they worked slowly. First they borrowed $10,000 at 3 percent a month. After that was gone they levied assessments against the stock to the amount of $166,068. That money produced during the next eighteen months ore that yielded $65,000 worth of bullion. A losing game. But the thin lead of mineral that the workers were following tantalized them.[4] It might pinch out. Or it might widen, as the Ophir's vein had, into a bonanza.

No MATTER HOW OFTEN RALSTON did (or did not) travel to Virginia City that year, he was surely home on August 2 for the birth of his second child, a girl. The father, legend says, chose her name: Edna

Louisa. The source of Edna is unknown. Louisa, gossips whispered, was for Billy's first and enduring love, Louisa Thorne, Cornelius Vanderbilt's dead granddaughter. However understanding the mother may have been—and we are assured that she acquiesced graciously[5]— it is impossible not to wonder how she really felt at the christening.

The father was expansive. A growing family in a growing city! Years of economic stagnation were ending. Although some of the upward push was supplied by the embryo mines of the Comstock, even more was the result of adaptation. Frustrated placer miners who had turned from California's overworked mountain streams to agriculture in the valleys were at last solving the problems created by a climate and a topography quite different from those they had known in the East. As a result exports of wheat, flour, leather, and wool were increasing significantly. Immigration swelled as word of these triumphs trickled toward the Atlantic Coast.

As the great entrepôt for all the state except the south, San Francisco benefited hugely from the upswing. Women, to be sure, often were repelled by the crudeness of the city's energy. More than 700 establishments, they sniffed, sold liquor to a population still predominantly male. Prostitution flourished. Sand-laden winds played havoc with housekeeping, clothing, and complexions.

Men saw different aspects. The census of 1860 revealed that San Francisco had become the fourteenth city in population in the United States. It could boast of three brick buildings five stories in height and

By 1860, San Francisco was the nation's fourteenth city in population —rough but exciting with promise for the future.

sixty-eight of four stories. Water, purchased until 1858 from street vendors, was being delivered through mains, as was illuminating gas made from coal imported, at times, from as far away as Australia. The fringes of the metropolis had spread so far from the plaza that horse-drawn omnibuses were needed for transportation along streets newly paved with blocks of wood or asphaltum. The theater flourished; fine eating was a tradition; ice brought south from the glaciers of Alaska was a commonplace. Sunday picnics, band concerts, and frequent parades lent to the city an air of what boosters described as Parisian gaiety.

The East no longer seemed so far away. Since September, 1858, regular stagecoach service had been linking St. Louis with San Francisco by way of the southwestern deserts and Los Angeles, a 2,700-mile trip that outsped the Panama steamers, under favorable circumstances, by as much as a week. A pony express, inaugurated in April, 1860, carried important letters and news over the shorter central route between Sacramento and St. Joseph, Missouri, in an almost unbelievable eight days.

Even more dazzling, so far as Ralston's prospects were concerned, was a bill passed by Congress in July, 1860, authorizing a subsidy of $40,000 a year for ten years to whatever company won and then ful-filled a contract to construct a telegraph line from Missouri to San Francisco. The award went to Western Union. At once its officers realized that they would have to deal with one or all of four contentious California telegraph companies that were clamoring for recognition as the builders of the line's western section—a plum whose sweetness had been increased by the legislature's promise of a subsidy of $6,000 a year for ten years to the first California company that connected with an eastern transcontinental wire.

The emissary chosen by Western Union to deal with the contenders was Jeptha A. Wade, who reached San Francisco via Panama in December, 1860. Hoping to calm the troubled waters, Wade suggested that the rivals pool their resources and form a new company for build-ing eastward to meet Western Union somewhere in Utah. Each refused, tempestuously. At the meetings Wade arranged, pistols were bran-dished in lieu of sounder arguments. In the end, however, lawsuits accomplished what neither threats nor negotiations could. Out of a welter of conflicting claims concerning charter rights and patents, the California State Telegraph Company, headed by Horace Carpentier, emerged triumphant. It absorbed the other firms, and Ralston was named one of the directors of the enlarged company that resulted, a strong indication that his services had played a significant part in Carpentier's victory.

The officers of the powerful new California State Telegraph Com-pany then joined with several of San Francisco's leading financiers to create a subsidiary, the Overland Telegraph Company, capitalized at $1.25 million, for building from Carson City (wires had reached that Nevada hamlet in 1859) eastward to Salt Lake City. The fantastic job, a long step forward in ending California's isolation, was completed between July and October of 1861.[6] Ralston was a member of Overland's board of directors, too, and helped generate the vigor that pushed the work to completion.

The saga of the telegraph companies was indicative of the economic resurgence occurring throughout California. Opportunities were appearing almost magically, but their demands for funds were such that a bank that hoped to participate needed greater reservoirs of capital than were possessed by the limited partnership of Fretz & Ralston. Searching for money (the Comstock mines had not yet begun to pay), Ralston turned to Joseph A. Donohoe, one of the young·men who had traveled to Yosemite with the bridal party of 1858.

Donohoe had prospered in California. With Eugene Kelly of St. Louis he had founded Eugene Kelly & Company, San Francisco's most successful wholesale dry goods store. About 1856, Kelly had moved to New York to look after interests there, leaving Donohoe in charge on the coast. Not long after Ralston's wedding the firm dissolved, and Donohoe joined Edgar Mills and other acquaintances on a leisurely trip around the world by sailing vessel. On his return he was ready for some new enterprise, as was Eugene Kelly in New York.

Discussions during the fall of 1860 resulted in a decision to found a new bank. The partnership on the coast would be known as Donohoe,

Needing capital for expanding his banking activities, Ralston turned to Joseph Donohoe, a flinty dry goods merchant.

Ralston & Company, with Kelly and Fretz as the "& Company." The firm's representative in New York would be Eugene Kelly & Company, a new bank that Kelly proposed to establish in the East.[7]

But if new opportunities for a bank were great, so were the risks. In November, 1860, at about the time that surveys of the financial field were beginning, a Pony Express rider raced up to the terminus of the telegraph line at Carson City, Nevada. A news editor maintained there by the joint resources of the Sacramento *Union,* the San Francisco *Daily Bulletin,* and the *Alta California* read the dispatches the rider carried and reached in excitement for the electric key that connected him with the communities on the far side of the mountain. Abraham Lincoln had been elected president of the United States, and the secession of at least part of the South appeared inevitable. That in turn might mean war.

How would California react? Even on the coast no one was sure. The majority of the inhabitants disparaged any move that might upset the Union, but they lacked effectiveness because their political loyalties were divided between the new Republican Party and the Northern wing of the Democrats. By contrast the Southern wing of the Democratic Party, though numerically a minority group in California, was united, aggressive and ably led. Over the years it had elected a majority of its candidates to important offices, and it was supported by many of the state's leading industrialists and by such respected civic leaders as William Anderson Scott of the Calvary Presbyterian Church.

Occupying an ambiguous position between these antagonistic groups were isolationists who wanted California to remain aloof from any struggle that developed. The state, they argued, was too far removed from the rest of the nation to let itself be upset by sectional differences between North and South. If war did erupt, then the entire West Coast should also withdraw from the Union and establish an independent Republic of the Pacific, whose vast stores of precious metals and whose burgeoning agriculture and industry would enable it to take at once a respected place in the family of nations.

To some Southerners, this talk of western separation offered intriguing possibilities. They might not be able to swing California to the side of the South in the event of conflict, but by fomenting a Pacific Republic they could at least prevent the state from aiding the North.[8]

William Ralston mirrored the uncertainties. His years in New Orleans had given him a sympathetic understanding of the Southern viewpoint. Because of his friendships with San Francisco's so-called Chivalry Democrats, he had tended to vote their ticket at election time, and yet his closest political associate, Milton Latham, was talking in Congress as though he favored the idea of a Pacific Republic.[9] Emotionally, however, Ralston remained an Ohioan from well north of the

Mason and Dixon line, and he was deeply disturbed by the thought of what might happen to the country and the state if they were sundered by open conflict.

Amidst such civic and personal tensions, prophets of doom found much at which to point in alarm. If war came, the traditional links with the East would be in jeopardy. The Southern stagecoach route would certainly be cut. Harbor blockades would chill the recent upswing in trade. Southern privateers would prowl the shipping lanes, eager to seize the gold bullion on whose safe transit so much of California's economy depended. If Southern plotters attempted to seize either California or Nevada by force, guerrilla warfare would inevitably follow. Nor was isolation a realistic escape, for a Pacific Republic, divorced from the rest of the nation, would find familiar patterns of commerce and finance totally upset.

Under the circumstances, cautious men might well have postponed founding a new bank until the future was clearer. Caution, however, was not a characteristic of either Donohoe or Ralston. In their opinion the production of ore in the Comstock mines was bound to accelerate. This would brighten still more the other opportunities building around them. Thus, they insisted, it was no time to sit back while bolder men moved in ahead of them.

Their view prevailed. On the last working day of 1860, the quartet announced that the new bank of Donohoe, Ralston & Company would open for business the following June, no matter what turmoils gripped San Francisco at the time.

CHAPTER 11

Spume from the War

Billy Ralston was, quite literally, restless. He needed to be moving, planning, changing. He was easily dissatisfied. The formation of the new bank of Donohoe, Ralston & Company during the approach of rebellion was one manifestation of that overflowing energy. Another was his mania for building houses.

The Rincon Hill home into which he had moved with Lizzie shortly after their honeymoon suited him for less than three years. Early in 1861, he bought another lot nearby at 324 Fremont Street where the views seemed better, and hired architects to prepare a grander dwelling. He then bundled Liz and babies Sam and Louise into cramped rooms in his old bachelor quarters, the Union Club above the Wells Fargo Bank. The arrangement did not work well and soon they were packing again to move to a rented house on Mission Street.[1]

To men endowed with such drives, additional demands often serve as additional stimulants. So it was with Ralston. Instead of flagging under the shock waves of the Civil War, his activity accelerated.

On April 24, 1861, San Francisco learned that Confederate cannon had fired on Fort Sumter and that President Lincoln had responded by calling for 75,000 troops. Immediately a fear swept through California loyalists that Southern sympathizers might attempt some kind of coup designed to tie their state to the Confederacy. One wildfire (and baseless) rumor said that General Albert Sidney Johnston, a Texan and commander of the Military Department of the Pacific, planned to enlist Southern-born Californians, disgruntled Mexicans, and Irish and French adventurers to seize every federal installation in the bay area.

Ralston reacted without hesitation. To the surprise of many of his Rincon Hill and South Park neighbors, he shed his veneer of Southern culture and came out strongly for the Union. Nor were words enough. Searching for action that would have immediate impact, he joined other civic leaders in planning a citywide demonstration of loyalty. Their hope was to make the show massive enough so that it would give second thoughts to would-be rebels while winning over to the Union cause men who were either uncommitted or who leaned toward an independent Republic of the Pacific.

The affair was scheduled for Saturday morning, May 11. The place was a strategic downtown gore where Montgomery, Market, and Post streets came together. Like so many public events in San Francisco, this one began with a parade. Military and naval units, firemen, employee groups, and the loyalist members of the city's fraternal orders formed ranks in the plaza and marched through streets draped with bunting to the meeting place. There 25,000 cheering spectators met them, and they all jammed together around the speakers' stand. Ralston introduced the orators of the day. After emotions had been sated by shouting and applause, a Committee of Thirty-Four was appointed "to

Word of the Civil War brought Northern sympathizers to this mass meeting on Market Street. Ralston was among the organizers.

detect and suppress treasonable activities against the Union in California." Its chairman was Billy Ralston.[2]

The committee straightaway organized subgroups to work for the election of Republican Leland Stanford as governor of California, to foster enlistments in the regular army and the state militia, and to check the parallel efforts of Confederate recruiters. Another goal, and the one that absorbed Ralston's energies, was the creation of a home guard of civilians.

Ostensibly the guard was a back-up organization for the militia and the regular army. Actually it was designed to unearth and deal with unrest in swifter ways than were available to the more orthodox units. The organization and spirit of the guards stemmed directly from the vigilante army of 1856. Its volunteers were formed into companies of sixty, each with a captain and two lieutenants elected by the men they commanded. The credentials of all citizens came under scrutiny. A register was drawn up of all available, privately owned guns. Ralston, as a matter of parenthetical information, offered a Sharp's rifle to the cause.[3] It was a heavy hunting weapon and suggests that in calmer days its owner may have occasionally sought relaxation in stalking some of the big game animals that were still common in California.

With his Sharp's, the banker drilled night after night in a pavilion in Union Square—he liked that sort of thing—and then spent endless other hours on procedural, financial, and organizational problems. The guard that he helped shape was tight, devoted, and efficient. How much psychological effect it achieved in stimulating loyalty and discouraging subversion during those early days is, of course, impossible to say. At the time, however, its impact seemed so tremendous to Andrew Forbes, who drilled with Ralston, that he proclaimed flatly, "Ralston saved California for the Union!"[4] Hyperbole. Several other men were accorded that accolade for their efforts. What really saved the state was the preponderance of Northern sympathizers within its borders. But helping rally them, through the guard and various other ways, filled an emotional need and hence served some purpose in forestalling rebel scheming and in ending talk of a Pacific Republic.

Another cause that enlisted his support was the Sanitary Commission. That group had been founded in the East in June, 1861, to care for wounded soldiers. Some 500 Sanitary Commission agents visited the battlefields to render first aid and distribute food, clothing, bandages, and medicines sent them by 7,000 local aid societies. The work needed money as well, and that proved more difficult to raise. In 1862, in the wake of several Union defeats and growing pessimism about the outcome of the war, contributions dwindled almost to vanishing point.

The dearth shocked a California preacher, Thomas Starr King, into action. King was an extraordinary person. He had educated himself for

The Reverend Thomas Starr King, ardently supported by Ralston, pleaded for donations to help Northern hospital casualties.

the ministry while clerking in a Massachusetts navy yard to support five younger brothers and sisters. At the age of twenty-one he had been ordained a Unitarian pastor, but found that his lack of college degrees kept him from rising in the East. Accordingly he had accepted a call from a small, debt-ridden Unitarian church in San Francisco, where he arrived in April, 1860.

He was homely, dark-eyed, and intense. Though weighing only 120 pounds and standing a mere five feet tall, he delivered his impassioned sermons with a powerful and singularly resonant voice. An ardent Republican, he stumped the state tirelessly for Lincoln in 1860 and for Stanford in 1861. After those victories had been won—because of them he, too, was credited with saving California for the Union—he centered his war efforts on the Sanitary Commission.

The campaign began in Platt's Music Hall on Sunday, September 14, 1862. Eighty "officers of the meeting," Ralston among them, occupied the platform with King. According to an awed estimate by a reporter from the *Daily Alta California,* 6,000 persons jammed the auditorium and were lifted to frenzies of cheering by King's eloquence. Afterwards Ralston and a dozen other businessmen were formed into an "Executive Committee on Collections for the Patriotic Fund" and sent throughout the commercial district soliciting donations. Four days later they were able to wire east, through the bank of Donohoe, Ralston & Company, $100,000 in gold.[5] All told, California gave the Sanitary Fund, during the course of the war, $1.23 million, or more than 25 percent of all contributions raised throughout the North.

As in any civil war, there were wrenches. At the Calvary Presbyterian Church, William Anderson Scott, the Southern minister who had officiated at Ralston's wedding, took to asking God's blessing on both Abraham Lincoln and Jefferson Davis. Ralston and other friends urged him to desist. Outsiders were more truculent. On September 22, 1861, they hanged Scott in effigy, the second time he had been so treated for unpopular stands. On the first occasion Ralston had joined others in writing a letter of protest to the newspapers. This time, he chose to remain silent while the trustees of the church (Ralston was no longer a member of the board) asked for Scott's resignation—a disgrace they softened somewhat by giving him $8,000 when he decided to leave the city.[6]

Milton Latham also brought unhappiness to Ralston. While campaigning for reelection during the summer of 1862, the senator condemned Lincoln's voidance of certain civil rights, especially his suspension of the writ of habeas corpus. On August 25, Ralston wrote Latham a vigorous protest, underscoring his words, as he often did, with heavy slashes of his pen, and even misspelling one of them in his agitation. "I am in favor of the *powers that be wright or wrong,* I *beg* of you to think." Unless Latham changed tunes, the voters "will kill you dead as a mackerel—*boiled down.*"[7] It was an accurate prophecy, Thomas Starr King took the campaign trail against the senator, and Latham was thoroughly trounced by John Conness, candidate of a coalition of Republicans and Union Democrats.[8]

No MILITARY CLASHES OF CONSEQUENCE occurred in California during the war. Of the many plots dreamed up by imaginative rebels, only one approached success. Although Ralston had nothing to do with its foiling, his later career became so curiously entangled with the affairs of the principal schemers that a sketch of the adventure is pertinent here.

The leader of the desperadoes was a young Kentuckian named Asbury Harpending.[9] In 1857, aged sixteen, Harpending ran away to California via Panama. According to his own account, which nowhere suffers from understatement, he journeyed immediately to the overworked goldfields, leased a discredited hydraulic mine, and within a few months "cleaned up" (Harpending's term) $60,000. Next he went to Mexico, where he won the confidence of a certain Don Miguel

Paredis, who owned a choice mine in the interior. There they made money "at a rate sufficient to burn one's brain."

In the fall of 1860, before he was quite twenty, Harpending, now worth $250,000 cash and with another million in sight in Mexico, went to San Francisco on a brief vacation. Lincoln's election changed his mind about mining, and he joined a secret society of Confederates who were fomenting the sort of plot chronically dreaded by Unionists—a strike aimed at capturing key military installations throughout the San Francisco Bay area. Although Harpending poured $100,000 into the venture, the lure of the Comstock Lode coupled with a chill warning from General Albert Sidney Johnston led to its collapse.

His next idea was to arm a ship for preying on the sidewheel steamers that carried gold from San Francisco to Panama on the first leg of its eastern journey. He did not want to be a mere pirate, however, and so he traveled to the Confederate capital at Richmond, Virginia, and legalized the adventure by obtaining letters of marque from Jefferson Davis. As he was returning to California through Panama, he met and enlisted the help of another Kentuckian, Ridgeley Greathouse, who was later described by a newspaper reporter as "a square-headed, handsome fellow, with yellow hair, blue eyes, a pretty mustache, and a wide-awake business look."[10]

Conceivably Ralston knew Greathouse. The Kentuckian was one of four brothers who ran a bank and stageline centered in the northern California town of Yreka. He was also the cousin of still another native of Kentucky, Lloyd Tevis, an associate of Ralston's in the Gould and Curry mine and other investment ventures. The connection naturally heightened Ralston's interest in the conspirators when the story broke.

In San Francisco the would-be privateers fell in with a swashbuckling, twenty-year-old Englishman named Alfred Rubery. (Harpending later remembered Rubery as being a nephew of the famous British orator and statesman, John Bright. More probably, Rubery was the son of a wealthy widow who was able to put pressure on Bright.) After a long search, the trio located a ship they could afford to buy, the *J. M. Chapman*. "We" purchased her, Harpending wrote in his reminiscences, letting readers assume that his mining income was the source of the funds. Actually it was Greathouse who provided the $6,500 asked by the ship's owners, plus additional sums for buying stores and munitions and for hiring a crew of fifteen, who supposed that their job was to carry guns to Mexican insurgents.

Learning from tipsters what was afoot, local and federal authorities seized the *Chapman* as she was preparing to slip away from her dock during the dark morning hours of March 14, 1863. After sharp questioning the crew were freed as being dupes of the leaders. The schemers were incarcerated on Alcatraz Island to await trial. Lloyd Tevis furnished bail for his cousin Greathouse, as Ralston certainly knew, but Harpending and Rubery languished in confinement.

The episode reawoke frenzied fears of a Confederate attack on San Francisco harbor. "A bombardment of an hour," moaned the *Daily Alta California* on March 17, "would set the town, as it is for the most part built of wood, on fire in fifty places. If a high wind—not at all improbable in summer—should be added, there is no power that we possess that would be sufficient to save San Francisco from destruction." Surveys were rushed for additional fortifications on Rincon Hill as well as on several islands in the bay. Ralston joined the mayor, the collector of the port, and leading merchants in wiring Senator Conness and President Lincoln an urgent request for two more ships to patrol the Golden Gate, one inside and one out.[11]

The plea was denied. One reason was that the state was already the beneficiary of a half-million dollar contract for building a flat-decked, ironclad monitor modeled after the famed challenger of the Confederates' *Merrimac*. Holders of the contract were James Ryan, Francis Secor, and Peter Donahue—no relative of Joseph Donohoe, who spelled his name differently. A one-time shipbuilder in New Jersey, Peter Donahue was prospering in California as a majority stockholder in the Union Iron Works and the revived San Francisco & San Jose Railroad Company. He and Ralston had been friends ever since Donahue's original foundry had done repair work on the first ship Ralston had taken from Panama to San Francisco, the *New Orleans*. In the 1860s both the Union Iron Works and the railroad were clients of Donohoe, Ralston & Company, and so it is likely that the bank also helped put together the special company formed for building the monitor, named *Camanche*.

The parts for the *Camanche* were fabricated in New Jersey. Shortly after the arrest of Harpending's privateers, the materials were loaded aboard a sailing vessel, the *Aquila,* for transport around Cape Horn to San Francisco. But what defense was a disassembled vessel on the high seas? The question gained bitterness with the arrival of word that two Confederate raiders, the *Sumter* and the *Alabama*, were prowling the Pacific. What force existed in the bay to check them? Nervous workers sped the strengthening of San Francisco's shore installations, but calm was not restored until the appearance, at intervals during late October and early November, 1863, of several warships of the Russian fleet. They were commanded by an admiral whose name really was A. Popoff.

Washington granted the fleet permission to put into San Francisco on a visit of amity. Uneasy city officials asked Popoff what he would do if the *Sumter* and *Alabama* struck at the city while his ships were anchored in the bay. The admiral replied that if the Southerners attacked only the harbor fortifications, he would stay neutral, but if they bombarded the city, he would intervene in the name of humanity.

San Francisco rejoiced. Spirits climbed still higher on November 10, when the *Aquila* sailed into port laden with the knocked-down *Camanche*. But alas for complacency. On November 16 a gale sank the *Aquila* at her dock, the parts of the *Camanche* plummeted to the harbor bottom, and defenses once again rested largely on the goodwill of the Russians. To show their gratitude, Governor Stanford, Mayor Coon, and leading citizens entertained the foreign officers at a sumptuous banquet in Union Hall on Howard Street. After three hours devoted to consuming oysters, boned turkey, ham in champagne, assorted waterfowl, five flavors of ice

The half-sunken **Aquila,** *loaded with an unassembled monitor designed to defend the bay, was salvaged with Bank of California money.*

159

cream, and sixteen varieties of cake, the celebrants, Liz and Billy Ralston among them, danced until dawn.[12]

It is difficult to believe that Ralston did not notice the irony in all this. At the very time that the majority of Californians were intent on protecting their harbor against rebels, they were squabbling among themselves over the question of who should control the port—the city or the state.

As noted earlier, Governor Downey's veto of Levi Parsons' bulkhead bill had blocked efforts by private interests to take charge of the harbor, but had left unsolved the problem of how best to bring stability to its disgracefully managed facilities. San Francisco reformers, fearing the venality of the state legislature, wanted control vested in the city. Voters across the bay and along the navigable rivers of the interior valley, however, were as fearful of a San Francisco civic monopoly as they were of a private one. They preferred state control. By and large the operators of the docks and warehouses believed that the state would be less likely than the city to interfere with their interests, and therefore they opposed a municipal take-over, even though most of them lived within the city boundaries.

As time passed urgency increased, for the great majority of the waterfront leases were due to expire during 1863. Unless the issue was resolved by the new legislature that began its sittings in January of that year, damaging confusion would result. Thus the point became the dominant political controversy of the 1862 election, one of the most exciting ever held in the city.

A count of the ballots after the polls closed showed that reform-minded proponents of municipal control had swept the slate in San Francisco. Elsewhere pluralities favored a state take-over. Even so the *Daily Alta California* exulted that if the assemblymen and state senators elected in the city stood firm, it might yet be possible "to free commerce from the shackles of the politicians and to render our city a cheap port."

Advocates of state control beat the San Franciscans to the punch by introducing into the legislature an act—the Oulton Bill—that would place the "wharves, docks, and water fronts of the City and County of San Francisco" in the hands of a state harbor commission. An amendment was then accepted that would automatically extend, on the passage of the bill, all waterfront leases by ten years. Lobbyists for the bill thereupon held wide open houses in Sacramento, offering (it was alleged) the most unsubtle of bribes to wavering legislators. According to charges printed twelve years later by the San Francisco *Daily Evening Bulletin* (August 30, 1875), William Ralston was in the thick of the activity, though no concrete evidence of his passing money or exerting other forms of undue pressure was offered in the story.[13]

If as much tainted money was used as the *Bulletin* implied, it was wasted. The proponents of state control could not push the Oulton Bill as amended through the legislature—but neither could the San Franciscans pass the act they wanted. As adjournment neared after four months of acrimonious debate, weariness brought about a compromise. The amendment extending the leases was struck from the bill and a three-man state commission charged with operating the harbor was constituted in such a way as to give each major interest group a voice. One commissioner was to be elected by the voters of San Francisco, one by the voters of the rest of the state, and one by the members of the legislature.

The elections were held September 3, 1863, at about the time Ralston and other civic leaders were learning that the federal government would not provide the harbor with the protective warships they had requested. Two months later, November 4, while the last of the visiting ships from Russia were looking for suitable anchorage, the newly elected commissioners held their first meeting. Their first official act was to order a survey of the harbor. The report was discouraging. Vessels in a hurry to load or unload often could not reach empty berths because of heavy silting. All the streets leading to the waterfront were in ill-repair. "The wharves, too, are settling and tumbling all along the City front."[14] The sinking of the *Aquila* with its load of monitor components was at least partially due to inadequate means of anchoring.

Shortly after the sinking, the new harbor commission demanded that the occupants of all city waterfront property surrender to the state the facilities they had been using. About half of them did so. The rest, including the California Steam Navigation Company, refused and compounded their defiance by continuing to collect tolls from vessels and shippers using their facilities. Their intent, of course, was to force lawsuits in which they could challenge the constitutionality of the commission's existence.

The legal actions were protracted. The California supreme court did not rule against the wharf holders and in favor of the state until the closing days of 1866. The commission next demanded the tolls that the occupants had been collecting during the progress of the suits. Again they refused. This time the commission was reluctant to go to law. Its limited budget could not stand the expense.* It did not want the tolls hanging in abeyance, for it needed the money in order to push the dredging of the harbor and the building of a seawall. Therefore, in 1868, it sought a compromise.

According to the hostile *Bulletin* of August 30, 1875, Ralston arranged the compromise—and saw to it that it was highly favorable to the holdouts. During the years of the suit, they had collected, the paper charged, $500,000. Ralston persuaded the commission to settle for $50,000.[15] He

---

*The commission's counsel, incidentally, was Edward Tompkins who had married Sarah Haight, one of Lizzie Ralston's bridesmaids, who had gone on the honeymoon trip to Yosemite.

was able to bilk the state by that much, it was charged, because he had managed the election of the commissioners so adroitly that two of them were subservient to him.

Although antics of that sort were common in California during that era, firm proof of malfeasance on Ralston's part is lacking. The most one can say with assurance is that William Ralston, as representative of one of the state's most powerful financial entities, the California Steam Navigation Company, acted as a vigorous defender of private property against government encroachment. Arguments that private facilities, when used to meet public needs, should be subject to public supervision, struck him as an outrage to individual freedom, and he reacted with skill and energy, but not necessarily with illegal devices.

The tale of the harbor has two small sequels. One concerns the privateers, Harpending, Greathouse, and Rubery. In October, 1863, at about the time the first Russian ships were sailing past Alcatraz, they were found guilty of aiding the enemy, were fined $10,000 each, and sentenced to ten years in prison. In December, Greathouse and Harpending were released under terms of a general amnesty declared by Lincoln. Alfred Rubery, the Englishman, was pardoned by the president at the request of John Bright.

The freeing of the city's only known Confederate agents was so unpopular in San Francisco that Harpending feared he would be rearrested on trumped-up charges if he stayed in the city. He fled south—not to Mexico, where his million-dollar mine had been abandoned during the invasion by Maximilian's French troops, but to the Kern River diggings

Ralston's second son, William Chapman Ralston, Jr., was born April 25, 1863.

BOTH PAGES: COLLECTION OF DOROTHY PAGE BUCKINGHAM

near the southern tip of the Sierra. He was impoverished, but no matter. He located the mining district of Havilah and "cleaned up," he says, $800,000 which he sent to San Francisco to be banked.[16] He does not name the bank, but evidently it had nothing to do with Ralston.

As for the sunken *Camanche*, its parts were finally lifted from the harbor bottom by divers brought from the East. In November, 1864, a year after the sinking, the ungainly ship, its flat deck topped by a squat round turret, was launched at elaborate ceremonies. On January 22, 1865, her officers loaded aboard two hundred guests and took them on a trial run past a band playing patriotic airs at the end of the Market Street wharf (not yet surrendered to the commission), past the booming guns of saluting ships, and on to the naval yard at Mare Island. After a banquet there, the guests returned to San Francisco aboard the revenue cutter *Shubrick*. Because the outbound trip aboard the low-riding, wave-washed deck of the *Camanche* had been deemed risky, only fifteen women had accepted invitations to join the excursion. Lizzie Ralston was one of them.[17]

THE YEARS HAD NOT BEEN ALTOGETHER GOOD to Lizzie. Shortly after she and her husband had moved into the new Rincon Hill house at 324 Fremont Street, their daughter, Edna Louisa, had sickened and in March, 1862, at the age of 20 months, had died. To the parents' grief was added that of William's brother, Andrew Jackson Ralston. Jack had married in

Emelita Ralston, born July 26, 1865, was named for the mother of Ralston's dead sweetheart.

St. Louis in 1861 and within less than a year his bride had died, almost simultaneously with little Louisa. His business was failing, too, and he was so distraught that Billy urged him to come west and live in the Fremont Street house until he regained his bearings—a visit that extended to four years. The youngest brother, James Alpheus Ralston, also moved west, but seems not to have added himself to the heavy-hearted ménage.

On April 25, 1863, thirteen months after little Louisa's death, another baby was born to the Ralstons—a boy, William Chapman, Jr. Still another child, a girl this time, arrived on July 26, 1865. The father promptly called her Emma Thorne Ralston, for Cornelius Vanderbilt's daughter Emma, mother of the first Louisa. Billy had kept in touch with the Thornes throughout the years, and when he needed a name for the child that replaced both vanished Louisas, he once more turned impulsively toward them. Saying that she disliked Emma as a name, Lizzie managed to alter it to Emelita,[18] but that was as far from the shadow of her predecessor as she could get.

CHAPTER 12

The Bank of California

Wealth inundated William Ralston during most of the 1860s. Much came from currency speculation unleashed by the wartime fiscal maneuvers of the government in Washington. Some was made possible by the rapid acceleration of California's agricultural and industrial output. But the initial thrust—and the one that at times must have made Ralston believe that luck really was riding on his shoulder—arose from his participation in the two bonanza mines of the Comstock's early period, the Ophir and the Gould and Curry.

The Ophir yielded its treasures first. While its mill was being built in the Washoe Valley, miners on the slopes of Mount Davidson excavated and stockpiled some 21,000 tons of ore. The 3,000 tons of that dull-looking rock that assayed highest were set aside for prior treatment when the plant began operations. Results were astounding. Although the mill was so inefficient that it lost between one-third and one-half of the gold and silver in the ore, the net yield of those 3,000 tons was just short of one million dollars. Thus the company was able to pay off, within a few weeks, the cost of the mill, the expenses of mining the ore, and the fees of batteries of lawyers hired to prosecute or defend suits concerning ownership of alleged offshoots of the bonanza vein. All that done, there still remained $100,800 to disburse to the stockholders as dividends. Moreover, enough ore was in sight underground and on the surface to yield another $1.5 million during 1863.[1]

For speculators dividends were merely a gloss. They wanted to ride high on a soaring stock market—and did. In April, 1862, shares in the Ophir were selling at $1,225 each. Six months later, in October, the price reached $3,800. That was the peak. In January, 1863, a gush of water flooded part of the mine. At about the same time a formidable

*Buying and selling stock in mines like the fabulous Ophir
could be more profitable than dividends from the ore.*

contender, the Burning Moscow Mining Company, instituted a series
of lawsuits that would eventually cost the two firms upward of $1 million.
When news of the travails reached San Francisco, prices broke. By
June, 1863, shares in the Ophir had dropped by $1,000 each; at year's
end they were being traded for $1,650.[2]

No official in a Comstock mine needed to be caught by such a decline. Insiders knew, or could learn, the milling figures that might justify
a rise in stock prices. They were the first to be aware of adverse circumstances that might cause a drop.[3] Although specific figures about Ralston's purchases and sales have not survived, one imagines that as
treasurer of the Ophir Silver Mining Company he did not suffer for
want of information.

The fortunes of the Gould and Curry, of which Ralston was also
treasurer, followed a comparable pattern. As soon as its managers

The expensive Gould and Curry mill near Virginia City was designed to awe potential stockholders as well as to reduce ore.

were convinced that they had broken into an extensive vein of high-grade ore, they spent $900,000 building a mill of cut stone beside an artificial lake surrounded by emerald lawns. Like the Ophir mill, this one was shockingly inefficient and in 1864 had to be rebuilt at a cost of more than half a million dollars. All told, mining and milling expenses reached $6 million by the end of 1864. Another million was lost to inefficiency. And still the mine paid its stockholders, during those years, $3 million in dividends.[4]

Stock prices rocketed from $500 a foot in April, 1862, to $6,300 on July 1, 1863. By that time insiders suspected the Gould and Curry bonanza, like the Ophir's, was dwindling away into borasca (barren ground). Although enough ore was in reserve to keep the mill operating and dividend checks rolling through 1865, the end was in sight, for those privileged enough to see it.[5] Quietly they all began to unload, Ralston among them.

During those years the only other Comstock mines that consistently paid dividends were the Savage, which adjoined the Gould and Curry, and the shallow workings near Gold Hill, the town at the south end of the Lode. All the rest expected success, however—or at least their promoters knew how to prey on expectations. A speculative mania seized even the humble miners, dishwashers, timber cutters, and hotelkeepers of Virginia City, and then rolled on across the mountains to unsettle a large part of the population of California.

The excitement was fueled by a sudden fad for the incorporation of business firms. For reasons not pertinent here, most commercial ventures in California prior to the 1860s were conducted by partnerships. But as the scale of operations increased and expenses mounted, the advantages of establishing corporations that could accumulate capital through the sale of stock to the public became more apparent.

Mining companies led the way. At first shares were traded through street brokers who operated, quite literally, on the sidewalks of San Francisco's financial district. A full sales contract was drawn up to accompany each transaction. As the tempo increased, that method proved cumbersome. To speed affairs by standardizing procedures within a central agency, the San Francisco Stock Exchange was founded in September, 1862. It was followed the next year by two more exchanges in San Francisco and one in Sacramento.

A fantastic proliferation of incorporations followed—more than 4,000 in 1863 alone. Of these, 2,933 were mining companies.[6] Obviously hundreds of these firms were less interested in producing mineral than in draining funds from gullible purchasers of stock. A great many, however, did produce ore that needed milling. Because mill building was expensive, those companies chose to patronize custom mills. The result was another craze of building. Stamps and grinders and amalgamating pans were erected beside every trickle of water within sight of Mount Davidson: 54 in the vicinity of the Lode itself, 12 beside the more distant Carson River, and 9 in the Washoe Valley.[7] Many were also corporations, financed largely through the sale of stock.

Each year from 1860 through 1863 saw the production of Comstock mineral doubled. In 1864 the rate slowed, but even so the yield of the mines approximated $16 million.* The hope of limitless increases intoxicated everyone but a handful of cautious insiders. Virginia City's population jumped from 4,000 in the fall of 1862 to 15,000 in the summer of 1863. Multistoried buildings arose in the center of the town; theaters and churches proliferated almost as rapidly as saloons. A constant stream of freight wagons and stagecoaches brought in not only coal, timber, and blasting powder, but also all the luxuries that San Francisco could provide.

Preacher Thomas Starr King, visiting Virginia City in 1863 on behalf of the Sanitary Fund, was repelled. To him the community was "a city

---

*To keep the figures in perspective: California's production of gold in 1864 was $24 million.[8] California's output was declining, however (from $44 million in 1860), whereas Nevada's was rising. California's mines were scattered along scores of miles of foothills; the Comstock mines were concentrated atop a two-mile fissure.

of Ophir holes, gopher holes, and loafer holes.'' A more accurate if less euphonious description came from Eliot Lord, geologist and early historian: ''Men walked the streets of Virginia City as if pacing the roof of a fabulous treasure house. . . . All prudent considerations were laughed to scorn. . . . To insist upon rigid economy in accounts and to stop tight each petty leak was thought unbecoming.'' Extravagant display in mine and mill buildings was a sign of faith in the Lode—and a useful way of impressing stockholders.[9]

The excitement was not an unmitigated blessing to California. The diversion of mining energies and experienced miners to the far side of the Sierra Nevada was one reason for the sharp decline in California's gold production during the early 1860s. The pouring of money into Nevada's sagebrush in the hope of quick returns retarded long-range developments closer to the coast. A feverish dependence on luck and a desire to speculate rather than to build, two troublesome characteristics of many Californians, became still more noticeable.

Even granting the demerits, however, the benefits that flowed from the Nevada discoveries were greater. The solving of many technical problems at Virginia City and Gold Hill stimulated quartz mining throughout the West. Mining law was stabilized. The flow of currency quickened. California ranchers who raised freight horses and mules and the barley to feed the animals; the fabricators of machinery and of work clothing; entertainers and stockbrokers—all those and the thousands who depended on them throve because of the rush.

Banks in particular felt the upsurge of prosperity. Donohoe, Ralston & Company reputedly handled more bullion on its way from Nevada to the East than did any other financial institution.[10] Like the rest of San Francisco's banks, the firm sold increasing numbers of bills of exchange, acted in various capacities during incorporation procedures, and made possible the voluminous transactions of the new stock exchanges. Ralston thus occupied an enviable position. As a stockholder he was part owner of rich mines. As a banker he was a necessary medium in the complex web of financing that enabled those mines and many others on the Lode to function.

THE GOVERNMENT OF THE UNITED STATES provided him and other San Francisco financiers with an additional bonanza—an opportunity for using the gold they handled to speculate profitably in a fiat paper money called greenbacks because of its color. The demands of the Civil War for money had swiftly exceeded the supply of specie in the country. In February, 1862, accordingly, Congress passed a revenue bill that paved the way for issuing $450 million in paper money. This money was

THE BANK OF CALIFORNIA

Although the government designated its Civil War "greenbacks" as legal tender, most Californians refused to accept them.

declared by law to be "legal tender in payment of all debts, public and private, within the United States, except duties on imports and interest on the public debt."

By July greenbacks were appearing in California in considerable numbers. Some of the bills were brought by travelers; more were shipped in for paying federal employees and workers on federal projects. Californians who were owed money refused to accept these bills. No other support than the word of the government lay behind them, and inevitably their value soon depreciated in terms of gold—a decline that confirmed California's traditional suspicions about paper money. The *Alta California* spoke for most of the populace when it described the greenbacks as "dirty, defaced, and counterfeit shinplasters, raked out of the gutters of New York."[11]

Nevertheless they were legal tender. People who held them naturally tried to pass them off in full settlement of obligations. When the bills were either refused outright or heavily discounted in terms of gold, the owners—and various patriots—cried out that creditors who discounted the bills were traitorous Shylocks, battening unfairly on the travail of the nation.

Unaffected by the outcry, Ralston and other leaders of the business community put heavy pressure on the legislature to defy Congress by legalizing the state's preference for hard money.[12] The lawmakers responded in April, 1863, with a specific contract law that allowed persons entering into commercial arrangements to specify the kind of money that should be used in making payments. When a test case was brought before the state's supreme court, the judges reflected the mood of the times by upholding the law.

It was not California's only assertion of fiscal independence. In February, 1864, Congress passed and Lincoln signed a National Bank Act. Designed to provide a market for government bonds, this law allowed banks to issue paper money in proportion to the number of bonds they purchased. Federal emissaries immediately besought Ralston and other San Francisco financiers to recharter their banks as federal institutions. They refused. Paper money, no matter what support it had or by what name it went, was simply not acceptable, even on the grounds of patriotism, to the majority of Californians.

These decisions for independence probably worked to the state's advantage, at least from a short-term view. A stable currency based on gold helped isolate California from the inflationary fevers that shook the rest of the nation. Together with the Comstock mining excitement and the need for new plants to produce goods that had once been imported, the stability attracted venture capital both from the Atlantic states and from England. By the end of 1864, an estimated $4.5 million had migrated westward, looking for investment opportunities.[13]

The gap in value between gold dollars and greenbacks opened easy avenues to quick profits. At one point, for example, $5,877 in California gold would buy $10,000 in greenbacks. In the East these greenbacks could be used for purchasing $10,000 worth of merchandise, an effortless profit even when inflation was rampant along the Atlantic.[14] Afterwards there was another profit when the imports were sold in California, a transaction that produced more gold coin for more greenback purchases in the East—an exchange business that redounded to the gain of the banks that handled it, Donohoe, Ralston & Company among them. Small wonder that a feeling of expansiveness pervaded San Francisco's business houses. As far as they were concerned, this effortless flow of currency advantages into their laps produced surer, though perhaps less exciting, gains than even the fabled treasure troves of the Comstock.

One could speculate in money itself without the need to buy merchandise. Although the trend in greenback values was downward throughout most of the war, daily fluctuations were erratic and influenced overnight by news from the battlefields. As a result little bucket shops for buying and selling paper money appeared throughout the city, adding one more element to San Francisco's penchant for gambling in paper certificates of all kinds.

Presumably Ralston, too, played the money market for the sake of quick gains. In the main, however, he looked farther ahead, to the day when the Union would be victorious and the value of its paper money would rise again. The medium he used for expressing his financial faith was life insurance. In 1863 such policies were unfamiliar and avoided by most Californians. By contrast Ralston plunged deep, beginning with an annuity that he purchased for $14,500 in gold. If he died within ten years, his estate would receive $40,000 in greenbacks. If he lived to the maturity date of the contract, he himself would receive the $40,000 —a fine buy if greenbacks were worth par by then.

Shortly after making that first purchase he added others. Soon the face value of his annuities reached $165,000—more life insurance than was carried by anyone else in San Francisco. Most of the purchases were made when a greenback dollar was worth 38 cents or so. When Ralston cashed in the annuities, the greenback had risen above 90 cents, a return of roughly 250 percent in addition to the normal increment of the policies.[15] Small wonder that he, too, felt expansive.

He listened readily to anyone's bold plans. One man who fascinated him was Agoston Haraszthy, a Hungarian refugee and jack of many trades. Forced to flee from his native land at the age of twenty-eight because of political involvements, Haraszthy had settled in Wisconsin in 1840. There he had founded Sauk City, had built bridges and flour mills, and had run a small steamboat on the upper Mississippi, where, conceivably, he may have first met or at least heard of Billy Ralston. In 1849 he had moved to California, not to the goldfields as most migrants did that year, but to San Diego, in the hope of establishing vineyards like those he had known on his father's estate in Hungary.

In San Diego, Haraszthy served as sheriff, mayor, and finally, in 1852, as state legislator. After completing his term, he settled in San Francisco. From other Hungarians already located there as assayers,

Ralston was an early backer of Agoston Haraszthy's efforts to improve California wine.

he learned how to refine gold bullion. Because he was popular in Democratic circles, he was recommended for and received a position as head refiner for the new San Francisco mint. When shortages appeared in his accounts for 1857, he was charged with embezzlement. He defended himself by saying that the mint's furnaces were faulty and that the missing gold had been sucked off in fine particles through the flue. He lost his job but was acquitted on the charge of embezzlement.

His real love remained grapes. He sent one of his three sons, Arpad, to France to study winemaking. He ordered cuttings from Europe and experimented with them in the hills south of San Francisco. Deciding that the climate there was too foggy, he bought sunnier acres in the Sonoma Valley, on the north side of the bay.

In 1861, the retiring Democratic legislature sent Haraszthy to Europe to investigate winemaking procedures. In Paris he rejoined his son Arpad. Together they traveled far and wide, selecting and bringing back with them more than 100,000 cuttings from choice vines. The Republican legislature turned down the bill that Agoston submitted on the grounds that he had not been specifically authorized to buy cuttings or to travel as far as he did. His being a well-known Democrat with Southern leanings may also have influenced the decision.

Undismayed, Haraszthy distributed the cuttings to friends throughout the region and sent articles on grape culture to any newspaper or magazine that would print them. Meanwhile he employed hundreds of Chinese to make extensive plantings in his vineyard at Sonoma, where he built a legendary mansion that he named Buena Vista. Overextended, he turned to William Ralston for help. The result was the Buena Vista Vinicultural Society, incorporated for $600,000.[16]

Sanguine always, Haraszthy oversold himself to his backers. Paying the mortgages he had incurred and completing the developments he had launched precluded the paying of dividends as promptly as the stockholders demanded. Young Arpad, in charge of champagne making, was accused of disloyalty and was fired. A little later Agoston resigned under pressure applied, it was said, by Ralston. Still optimistic, he went to Nicaragua and bought a sugar plantation. While trying to wriggle across a stream on a tree branch, he fell and was devoured by an alligator. Buena Vista, of which Ralston remained a director at least until 1870, was meanwhile struggling into solvency, a key factor in the development of California wines.

Another enterprise that caught Ralston's attention during those years was fire and marine insurance. Times were opportune. Worried by the drain of premiums to the East and swayed by the lobbyists of home companies, the California legislature in 1862 passed an act requiring out-of-state insurance firms to deposit $75,000 in Sacramento as reserve funds before they could receive a license. This forced thirty-three out-

In the lovely Sonoma Valley spread the vineyards of the Buena Vista Vinicultural Society, of which Ralston was a director.

side companies to retire from the field. Promptly an old insurance hand named Jonathan Hunt proposed to Ralston that they incorporate a California fire and marine insurance firm large enough to dominate business on the coast. After rooting themselves in California, they would spread to Oregon and Nevada. That done, why not move on into the Midwest, the first California concern of any kind to compete outside the state with long-established easterners?

The prospect excited Ralston. On July 14, 1863, the Pacific Insurance Company filed articles of incorporation with the secretary of the state, and the fledgling company opened an office on California Street a little below Montgomery.[17] Hunt was president. There were fifty-eight directors. Among them were Billy Ralston and a casual acquaintance named William Sharon. The treasurer of Pacific Insurance, named at Billy's insistence, was Andrew Jackson Ralston, not long since arrived in San Francisco from his business failure in St. Louis.

As long as Ralston acted on his own, he could plunge as far as available funds allowed. It was otherwise when he acted as one of four banking partners. Two of those partners, Joseph Donohoe and Eugene Kelly, mistrusted his exuberance. They were content with the profits of routine banking. Their firm led all others in the handling of California and Comstock bullion. They had as much business as they wanted in furthering expansion programs of established San Francisco businesses. They

174

limited their risk-taking to a few cautious loans to the more promising Comstock mines, and when Ralston urged them to edge farther afield, frictions developed.

Chief igniter of trouble was Ralston's old friend from Mississippi steamboat days, John C. Ainsworth. Along with Jacob Kamm, another Mississippi friend of Ralston's, Ainsworth was trying to bring order to the chaotic commerce of the Columbia River. Quantities of freight moved up that huge and beautiful stream to inland army posts and to the new goldfields in the eastern part of Washington Territory. No one made much money, however, because too many competing hands were struggling for a share of the traffic.

Geography caused part of the trouble. Swarms of boats plied the lower reaches of the river between the estuary and the Cascade Range. Within the mountains, however, were two formidable blockades, the Cascades rapids at the western end of the gorge and the Dalles at the eastern end. Rival portage operators at the Cascades exacted their tribute before merchandise could be loaded on small boats for the run to the Dalles. Another, longer portage had to be made there before the freight could be reloaded on the steamers that plied the upper Columbia and its chief tributary, the Snake.

In spite of the handicaps, the potentials of the fragmented river were alluring. No other natural highway opened from the Pacific into the interior of the United States. If the conflicting interests of the many operators could be reconciled, the unified transportation system that resulted was bound to be both useful and profitable. Using the California Steam Navigation Company as a model and Ralston as an advisor, Ainsworth, Kamm, and an associate named William Ladd set out to achieve the necessary unity. By the end of 1860 they had knit together a loose organization, which they called the Oregon Steam Navigation Company, or more popularly, the OSN. As recognition of his services in bringing about the amalgamation, Ainsworth was elected president.[18]

Success was instantaneous. Thanks to unexpected gold discoveries in Idaho, the company earned a net profit of 48 percent during its first year of operation. Fortune, however, served also to reheat old jealousies between the rival portage operators at the Cascades. Though both were shareholders in the OSN, they refused to work for the common good but instead sought ways to gain traffic advantages for themselves.

Realizing belatedly that it had been a mistake to let any private property needed by the company remain in private hands, Ainsworth decided that the OSN would have to buy all the portage facilities. That accomplished, the company could then speed traffic by constructing short railroads around each rapid. Unable to raise the necessary money or materials in Oregon, he traveled south to San Francisco and sought out Billy Ralston.

Iron rail for track was a rare commodity on the Pacific Coast in those days. Nevertheless Ralston, as a director of the Sacramento Valley Railroad, knew where to find some. Enough rail to build twenty miles of track had recently been imported from the East by C. L. Wilson, who had been ousted as president of the Sacramento Valley road some years before and who now had notions of running a short line from Folsom along the foothills to Marysville. Unhappily for himself, Wilson owed a large sum of money to wholesaler William T. Coleman, erstwhile head of the vigilantes. Coleman slapped a lien on the iron, and there it sat beside the San Francisco docks, just enough for Ainsworth's purpose.

Ralston introduced Ainsworth to Coleman. They struck a bargain. Wilson fumed but could not raise enough money to free the material. Ainsworth could—through Ralston, who somehow persuaded Fretz and Donohoe to okay a loan to the OSN of $50,000 in gold. Ainsworth took the money and the rail to Oregon, gained control of the portages, built the little railroads he had dreamed of, and achieved for his company an unbreakable monopoly on transportation up the Columbia.[19]

There were double repercussions. When the invigorated OSN began

Old-time friends from the Mississippi sought Ralston's aid in financing a Columbia River monopoly, the Oregon Steam Navigation Company.

Keys to the OSN monopoly were the portage railroads around the Columbia's rapids. Ralston found the necessary rail.

extending its services into the northern Rockies, it interfered with the plans of the expanding California Steam Navigation Company. This in turn brought Ralston into conflict with the friend whose business growth he had made possible. That was for the future, however. Of more immediate concern was the reaction of Eugene Kelly. When news of the OSN loan reached him in New York, he exploded. The money, he said, was poorly secured. He predicted, moreover, that Ainsworth would repay it in greenbacks, to the bank's loss.* This was a sore point, for Ralston and he had already exchanged hot words about the handling of greenbacks, and now the issue produced so voluminous a correspondence that Ralston grew—to borrow Ainsworth's understatement—"provoked."[20]

Related to the dispute was a controversy over where to lend money. Kelly, legend says, wanted his bank in New York to have the right to invest in the East some of the money that Donohoe, Ralston & Company

---

*Actually, Ainsworth repaid the debt in gold.

was making in California, a proposal in which Donohoe concurred.[21] If this is true, Kelly was running counter to the financial tide of the times, for, as was noted earlier, by 1864 eastern money was beginning to flow west for investment. In any event, Ralston did insist that profits earned in California should be utilized in California.

Since Oregon drew most of its economic and industrial sustenance from California, lending money to Ainsworth did not seem to Ralston to involve any contradiction. Kelly, however, found the stand wholly unreasonable. As the dispute waxed, the possibility of compromise grew dim. After long deliberation, Ralston decided to break away from his partners and form a bank whose policies would be in closer accord with what he though fitting both for himself and for the state.[22]

The improvement in West Coast business conditions had outstripped even Ralston's anticipations. Small partnerships—among them Donohoe, Ralston & Co., for which he had once held such high hopes—could no longer provide the permanency and the pools of capital and knowledge demanded by the growing economy. Recognition of that fact, combined with the speculative mania triggered by the Comstock, had led (it will be recalled) to the formation of 4,000 business corporations in 1863 alone. Not one of those corporations was a commercial bank. As was noted earlier, California's constitution, framed in 1849 by men who feared that private concerns would release floods of paper money, had forbidden the issuance of charters to banking corporations.

Could that archaic rule be relaxed without stirring up a political hornet's nest? Financiers had been trying for some time without success until nature came to their help in January, 1862. That month heavy rains sent the Sacramento River flooding through the state capitol. Fleeing from the ravages of the yellow water, the legislature assembled at a temporary meeting place in San Francisco. There Sam Brannan and other bankers laid hold of the lawmakers and persuaded them to pass an act allowing the incorporation of *savings* banks. As soon as the law was passed, Brannan and his associates founded the Pacific Accumulation Society, but its organization proved too cumbersome and its policies too conservative for immediate success in those speculative times.[23]

Ralston did not want his plans limited by the word "savings." In his opinion, California's new economic maturity justified a wholly commercial bank. He was reluctant, however, to spend time and risk political troubles by trying to obtain still another special act from the legislature. Nor was there any need to, in his estimation. The law was a dead letter anyway as was shown by the passage in March, 1864, of amendments liberalizing still further the savings bank act of 1862. A determined group of financiers, he argued, could incorporate a commercial bank under the general incorporation law of 1853 and not draw a whisper of a challenge from the authorities.[24]

In a remarkable feat of salesmanship he convinced twenty-two of the leading businessmen of the state that he was right. What he proposed was that they buy, in gold, enough shares of stock at $100 a share to provide the new bank—he planned from the outset to define its scope by calling it The Bank of California—with capital funds of $2 million.[25] Since a strong New York connection would be essential, he presumably went by ship to the East and sought out James Lees of the house of Lees and Waller, with whom he had done business during his banking days in Panama.[26] He persuaded the New Yorkers to act not only as East Coast agent for the still unformed and possibly illegal Bank of California but also to see about establishing further connections in London. His purpose was twofold. He wanted The Bank of California to handle, through this English connection, some of the foreign money that was moving into the western United States. He also hoped that the same connection would enable The Bank of California to ship silver bullion from the Comstock mines to the Orient.

As fast as subscriptions came in from the men he had first approached, he invested the money in commercial paper so that the new bank would have a sizable amount of business on its books on opening its doors. It is said, too, that the incorporators paid Ralston $50,000 for swinging to the new bank the bulk of Donohoe, Ralston & Company's accounts. All of this was done in the utmost secrecy, to preclude any attempt by either Donohoe or Kelly to upset the plans.[27]

The board of directors of the new institution included James Whitney, Jr., and William Norris, president and secretary respectively of the California Steam Navigation Company; Louis McLane, head of the potent Pioneer Stage Company; John O. Earl, merchant and president of the Gould and Curry mine at Virginia City; A. J. Pope, lumber merchant; and Thomas Bell, deeply involved in quicksilver mining. Among the early stockholders were Alvinza Hayward, a mine owner we will meet frequently later on; H.W. Carpentier, head of the California State Telegraph Company, of which Ralston was still a director; and Jacob Kamm, Portland shipbuilder and a major stockholder in the Oregon Steam Navigation Company. Employed to be secretary of the concern was that epitome of dignity: black-clad, cane-swinging Stephen Franklin, whom Ralston had first met in New Orleans.

Named as president of the new Bank of California was Darius Ogden Mills. In 1862, Mills had sold his bank in Sacramento (his brother Edgar bought half of it), but he was still looked upon as California's premier financier. By 1864 he was losing his heavy head of youthful hair and was growing the fuzzy sideburns that marked his appearance in later years. He was reserved, methodical, careful. One man who had many dealings with him in later years declared that "he transpired icicles and micturated ice water. . . . He had a keen mind, a possessive impulse, and just enough

Issued in May, 1864, this certificate introduced San Francisco to the first wholly commercial bank in California.

Certificate of Incorporation

We the undersigned persons do hereby certify, that we have associated ourselves together, and desire to form a Company for the purpose of engaging in the business of Banking, and that we desire to incorporate the same under the provisions of an Act of the Legislature of the State of California, entitled "An Act to provide for the formation of Corporations for certain purposes," approved April fourteenth, in the year of Our Lord Eighteen hundred and fifty three, and all Acts Amendatory thereof and supplementary thereto. And we certify, First; That the corporate name of the Company shall be "The Bank of California." Second; That the objects for which the Company is formed are to engage in and carry on the business of Banking to such extent, and in all such branches as may legally be done, under the Constitution and laws of the State of California. Third; That the Amount of its Capital Stock shall be two millions of Dollars, with the right to increase the same to five millions of Dollars, and the time of its existence fifty years. Fourth; That the number of shares of which the Stock shall consist shall be Twenty thousand of One hundred dollars each.

gambling instinct to look for sure things before he gambled."[28] His acceptance of the presidency gave an air of rock-bound dependability to the new bank, which was probably the reason (along with his stock-holdings) for his election. Ralston, whose restless imagination had devised the plan and whose persuasiveness had pulled the men together, was named cashier. There were no vice-presidents.

The certificate of incorporation was filed on June 13, 1864. Three days later the San Francisco newspapers carried notices of the dissolution of the partnership of Donohoe, Ralston & Co., to be effective June 30. No one, not even Donohoe or Kelly, questioned the authenticity of the new organization. Quite the contrary. San Franciscans applauded the move as long overdue and predicted that other corporations would soon follow, a feeling verbalized by the *Mercantile Gazette and Prices Current* of June 22, 1864, when it declared, "We have incorporated institutions for savings and accumulation which have done and are still doing very important service in the concentration and utilization of the

The signatures are those of the twenty-three men who subscribed $2 million for opening The Bank of California.

surplus capital of individuals which would otherwise be unemployed. . . . The Bank of California, however, is of a totally different character . . . a new thing—not indeed new elsewhere, but new here; it introduces a new feature into our financial affairs, and if successful, or in other words, profitable, is but the type of others which will follow in due course.''

Others did follow, some two dozen by the end of 1873, in which year the state supreme court finally decided that the incorporation of commercial banks was not unconstitutional after all. At about the same time the commission codifying California's multiplying morass of statutes dismissed the prohibitory section of the constitution as obsolete.[29] Ralston was the first to realize the extent of that obsolescence. On the strength of that conviction, he dared found the first incorporated commercial bank in California and thus prepared the way for all the others.

Donohoe and Kelly moved out of the Washington Street building on schedule and opened their partnership bank of Donohoe, Kelly & Co. a few blocks away. For some reason The Bank of California was not ready to begin operations at once. Such business as needed doing on Friday, July 1, and Saturday, July 2, was performed by the old firm of Fretz & Ralston. The next day was a Sunday, and on Monday, July 4, Ralston was distracted by his duties as grand marshal of noisy patriotic parades, band concerts, and a fireworks display to whose expenses he contributed $150.[30]

The next day, Tuesday, July 5, the bank opened. Its incorporators had been busy. Already they had lined up 506 deposits aggregating $1,641,605.83. Bills receivable amounted to $1,362,457.05. During the next two and a half weeks the bank shipped east nearly a million dollars in gold coin and bullion, more than double the amount forwarded by any other bank during the same period.[31] On July 20, 1864, the assistant treasurer of the United States in San Francisco named The Bank of California as the place of deposit for all funds payable to the Bureau of Internal Revenue. The next day the bank loaned $60,000 to the contractors who were rehabilitating the Civil War monitor, Camanche—a loan whose payment was guaranteed by the Board of Supervisors of the County of San Francisco.[32]

After a start like that, Billy Ralston could be excused for thinking that active times lay ahead.

CHAPTER 13

The First Storms

In spite of the dazzling figures with which The Bank of California began its operations, many people thought that Ralston had picked an unhealthy time for launching the new enterprise. Word that the leading mines of the Comstock could find no more profitable ore at the bottom of their shafts was shaking the stock market. By the fall of 1864 shares in the Ophir had dropped from a high of $3,800 each to $300; in the Gould and Curry, from $6,300 to $900. Inevitably the decline spread to the stock of manufacturing companies that supplied the mines, and from there to the business community in general. The San Francisco Stock Exchange, so recently a pandemonium of eager bidding, was now hushed in gloom.

On top of that the weather was bad. During the winter of 1863–64, California experienced the most severe drought in her history. Cattle and sheep died by the hundreds of thousands. Grain fields withered; an embryo export trade in wheat and flour collapsed. Such placer mines as remained at work in the Sierra foothills ceased operations.

Unemployed men flocked into San Francisco and became angrily involved in politics. Democrats supporting Gen. George B. McClellan as the next president formed armies of "Broom Rangers" that paraded through the streets brandishing brooms and torches. Unionists favoring Lincoln's reelection retorted with more precise marches led by squads of discharged soldiers. Catcalls resounded along the curbs and at mass meetings. Worried by the shoving and threats, timorous observers predicted riots. None came, but the fear depressed business.

Through all this Ralston stayed unruffled. Although the opening of the new bank placed heavy demands on his time, he managed to keep on working with various committees charged with arranging a rapid-fire sequence of patriotic and political demonstrations. After Lincoln's assassination he chaired a committee that purchased and placed in front of San Francisco's new Lincoln School a monumental plaster statue of the slain president, the first piece of Lincoln sculpture erected in the United States. His switch from the Democratic to the Republican party was now complete. Three years later President Grant himself credited Ralston with playing a major part in holding California in the Republican column during the national elections of 1868.[1]

He maintained his equanimity throughout the stock market crash of '64. He realized that it was in part an overreaction to the excessive speculation of 1863 and that it reflected fears about the Comstock's future, not about its present state. The known bodies of ore that still awaited treatment contained many millions of dollars' worth of silver and gold. Turning that treasure into bullion would require time and money. Handling it as it moved to San Francisco and on east was bound to be profitable. Moreover, as long as a mine operator can still see his vein, he never quite believes it has turned barren. That faith was particularly strong in the case of silver mines. The richest properties in Mexico, men told each other confidently, had often had to work their way through borasca (barren ground) before finding new bonanzas at greater depth. The main thing was to keep on searching. As long as the Comstock miners dared do that, they would need the bank's help. Ralston was determined to give it to them, depression or not.

There were short-term considerations as well. On July 4, 1864, the day before The Bank of California opened its doors, its officers had announced through the San Francisco newspapers that they planned to establish branches in Virginia City and Gold Hill. To pull back at the first sign of trouble would not be good publicity. Besides, the branches would find plenty to do beyond just maintaining appearances. First, there would be salvage operations. When Donohoe, Ralston & Company had split, Ralston had walked off with most of the old firm's Nevada business, which had been conducted through a Virginia City bank called Stateler & Arrington. Shortly thereafter Stateler & Arrington had failed, owing $30,000 to the new Bank of California.[2] That was too much to let go by default. If the new agencies were opened as promised, their manager could endeavor to collect the debt while at the same time keeping a hold on a fair share of the Comstock's continuing business.

Legend says that president D. O. Mills and other directors of the bank disagreed violently with that reasoning and that Ralston changed their minds only after intense argument. The tale is questionable. For one thing, several of the bank's stockholders—Mills, Ralston, Joseph and William Barron, Thomas Bell, John Earl, Alpheus Bull, Alvinza Hayward—were deeply involved in the Comstock as officials of various mining companies. The fact that they had unloaded most of their holdings

A photographer, using the standard background props of the time, caught Ralston in this stiff pose about 1865.

to escape the market crash of 1864 did not mean that they were abandoning hope in the lode's future.

Quite the contrary. As the stock sagged, they repurchased much of it at bargain rates. They wanted work to continue. Some would be undertaken for the sake of "bulling" the market—that is, leaking "information" in order to manipulate stock prices. But there was also the hope of further lucky strikes, for surely the $30 million or so that had been skimmed off the top of the lode did not represent the full potential of the giant vein. Certainly risk was involved. But California's history since the days of '49 had disposed men to risk.

The agencies opened on schedule, at Virginia City in September, 1864, and at Gold Hill nine months later. Their manager, reputedly chosen at the insistence of John D. Fry, Ralston's father-in-law, was a small, keen, ice-blooded, silk-hatted poker player, real estate speculator, and money manipulator named William Sharon. Sharon's assistant was another of Billy's younger brothers—James Alpheus Ralston.

Deeply religious, James Ralston liked to spend his Nevada weekends traveling by stagecoach to Carson City. After bathing in the nearby hot springs, he performed missionary work in the Nevada state prison, listened to a brimstone sermon, and then jounced back up Gold Canyon discoursing to his fellow travelers about predestination, original sin, and the true meaning of the Trinity.[3] He seems an odd assistant for William Sharon, whose morals were hardly impeccable, but the two men got on well.

When Sharon and Jim Ralston reached Nevada, loans to mines and mills were made under an agreement among local bankers that held interest at 5 percent a month. With Ralston's and Mills's consent, Sharon cut the figure to 2 percent. He did not do this because, as is sometimes said, his studies of the Comstock gave him special insight. Complex geology, mineralogy, and engineering techniques do not yield that easily to cram courses. But he could judge the quality of the men to whom he talked about loans, and he could sense their faith. Mostly, however, he knew that his principals wanted work at the lode to continue, for they had their faiths too. One way to keep the wheels turning was to reduce the staggering interest rates imposed during the reckless days.

By doing this The Bank of California rendered a real service to Nevada and to the San Francisco firms that supplied the Nevadans. Maintaining a closed mine or, especially, an idle mill is expensive as well as nonproductive. Machinery, hoses, and fittings of all kinds deteriorate quickly; restoring them for fresh operations is slow and expensive. As long as any chance exists that work will be resumed, it is better to keep them operating on a reduced scale. Using the funds that Ralston had entrusted to him, Sharon made this procedure possible. If he had not, Virginia City's depression would have lasted much longer than it did and hardships to workers and stockholders would have been much greater than they were.[4]

In addition, Sharon was lucky. A few months after his arrival in Virginia City, he gained control of the supposedly worthless Yellow Jacket mine. Almost immediately its workers broke unexpectedly into bonanza ore that grossed during the next three years $6 million. Strangely, only $320,000 of the sum were ever distributed in dividends. Worse, $300,000 in assessments were levied on the stockholders in order to make capital improvements requested by management. Conceivably mining expenses were exorbitant. More probably, however, Sharon was bulling the market, declaring a small dividend or imposing an assessment according to how he wanted prices to move.[5] He benefited enormously. Probably Ralston did, too, though evidence is lacking. But most of the investors who bought and sold according to the rigged rise and fall of prices merely filled the pockets of the manipulators. Still, if the Yellow Jacket could stumble onto a plum, then so could any other mine on the lode. Spirits quickened and work kept going.

CONTINUED WORK AT THE COMSTOCK meant a continued flow of passenger, freight, and express traffic back and forth across the Sierra. From the outset, as was noted earlier, two of the concerns with which Billy Ralston was closely associated, the California Steam Navigation Company and the Sacramento Valley Railroad, had hoped to dominate the flow. But the railroad soon found itself faced with a formidable rival, the Central Pacific. Because Ralston was deeply involved in the fortunes of the Sacramento Valley line, that battle, too, caught the attention of men concerned over the future of The Bank of California.

Except for the railroad's own shortsighted arrogance there might never have been a Central Pacific. Ever since the inception of the Sacramento line in 1854, its chief engineer, Theodore Dehone Judah, had envisioned it as the California end of a gigantic rail system reaching westward from the Mississippi. Unhappily for his dream Ralston and the other directors of the company looked in the opposite direction, toward the sea.

Their saltwater orientation was natural enough. Nearly every pound of freight and a majority of the immigrants headed for California came by ship. San Francisco's most lucrative business occupation was the distribution of this influx of seaborne merchandise and people throughout the interior by means of interlocked steamboat, stagecoach, express and wagon freight companies. The Sacramento Valley Railroad, the first steam line in the state, was one more feeder of that commerce—and hence one more strand in the monopolistic transportation net that San

Theodore Judah's plans for the Central Pacific Railroad were rejected by Ralston and other San Francisco businessmen.

Francisco had flung across the interior. Inevitably the directors of the railroad were not inclined to foster anything that would break the pattern, as a transcontinental rail line most certainly would.

When traffic to the Comstock picked up in 1860, the directors of the Sacramento Valley Railroad promptly made plans to add that commerce to their line by means of a pair of extensions mentioned in an earlier chapter. One, the Sacramento, Placer & Nevada, would run from Folsom toward Auburn and Nevada City on the north side of the American River drainage system. The other would spiral from Folsom to Placerville on the south side of the drainage.

Because a rail crossing of the Sierra would be impossibly expensive for private enterprise, the journey over the summit would be made by wagon road. One such road already ran from Placerville across the mountains south of Lake Tahoe. The one in the north stopped at the California mining camp of Dutch Flat, but the residents of the area, hoping to divert Comstock traffic through their hamlets, had offered a subsidy of $25,000 to whatever company built a road in that section. Immediately the directors of the Sacramento Valley Railroad announced their intention to comply.

At that point Judah reappeared from Washington, D.C., where he had been lobbying Congress on his own for federal aid to build a transcontinental railroad. He thought the necessary bill would soon pass, and he urged the Sacramento Valley Railroad people to be in a position to pluck

188

the bounty by having plans and a usable survey ready for presentation to the government ahead of anyone else.[6]

The directors shrugged the proposal aside. Didn't Judah understand the facts of San Francisco's economic life? Besides, like most residents of the bay city, the directors doubted that a railroad could be built across the snow-tormented Sierra for the sums Congress was considering. They told Judah to calm down and then compounded the affront by sending him into the mountains to run surveys for the wagon road they proposed to build.

Instead Judah spent most of his time looking for a workable railroad grade. Finding one, he hurried back to San Francisco late in October, 1860, hoping to persuade the directors of the railroad and their financial agents, the banking house of Pioche, Bayerque & Company to reconsider the transcontinental plan.

Ralston almost certainly was at the meeting. He was a close friend of Lester L. Robinson, the driving force behind the Sacramento Valley Railroad, and of J. Mora Moss, a partner in the banking house of Pioche, Bayerque & Company. Ralston's banks—first Fretz and Ralston, then Donohoe, Ralston & Company, and finally The Bank of California— frequently worked with Pioche, Bayerque & Company on projects that were larger than either firm wished to handle alone. They had no intention of becoming bogged in Judah's scheme, however. Angered by the engineer's cavalier disregard of instructions about the wagon road survey, Lester Robinson fired him. Pioche, Bayerque & Company then rejected his railroad proposal so flatly and publicly that no one else in the city would listen to him.[7]

Furious at the treatment, Judah carried the plan to Sacramento. There he won the support of four storekeepers, Leland Stanford, Collis P. Huntington, Mark Hopkins, and Charles Crocker. Unimpressed— surely those rustics were incapable of completing so monumental a task —the San Franciscans ordered their own construction crews to begin the more realistic job (as they saw it) of pushing the Sacramento, Placer & Nevada extension from Folsom on toward the expectant town of Auburn.

Ill luck soon deluged them. In January, 1862, floods tore out great chunks of their track, and work on the extension halted six miles short of Auburn. The city of Sacramento, which had always resented control of the railroad by San Francisco, added to the burden. It increased transfer taxes on goods moving from the river docks to the railroad and laid down arduous rules about repairing street crossings and maintaining the right-of-way. When Congress awarded generous loans to the Central Pacific as builders of the western half of the transcontinental, the whole city paraded in delight. The election of Leland Stanford, president of the Central Pacific, as governor of California added still more power to the arsenal of this sudden rival. As a final blow, the directors of the CP

Leland Stanford,
first president of
the Central Pacific,
later became governor
of California.

snatched from under their noses the franchise for building the north-side wagon road from Dutch Flat to Virginia City.

Stunned by the heaped misfortunes, the directors and stockholders of the Sacramento Valley Railroad decided to offer the property to the Central Pacific. Stanford rejected them out of hand. Several reasons were given, one being that the Central Pacific could draw government loans for building a new line but not for buying an old one.[8] Beneath that argument, however, lay deeper jealousies: the Central Pacific was to be a Sacramento railroad, not a mere adjunct to San Francisco's overweening ambitions.

The rejection left the Sacramento Valley people with little choice but to fight. Their first move was to pull their railroad out of the unfriendly city of Sacramento and create, four miles downstream, the new town of Freeport, which they hoped would intercept the boats of the California Steam Navigation Company. For carrying the traffic thus intercepted, they built a new line from Freeport to Folsom. Because the CP controlled the Dutch Flat roadway on the north side of Lake Tahoe, they abandoned the still incomplete Sacramento, Placer & Nevada and concentrated their energies on the south-side extension to Placerville.[9] Ralston, of course, participated in all these belligerent decisions.

They were not without strength. Several firms that would be hurt if Sacramento city became the chief distributing center of traffic arriving by train from the East rallied to the firm's support—the Pacific Mail

Collis Huntington raised enough money to keep the CP moving when Ralston's friends were predicting failure.

Steamship Company, the California Steam Navigation Company, and the Pioneer Stage Company, which operated from Folsom through Placerville to Virginia City. Prodded by Louis McLane, a friend of Ralston's and an incorporator of The Bank of California, the Pioneer Stage Company and its powerful ally, Wells, Fargo & Company, even offered to underwrite some of the costs of construction. Because the Central Pacific planned to build a telegraph line in conjunction with the railroad, the California Telegraph Company, of which Ralston was a director, added its urgings. By no means least, the residents of El Dorado County, of which Placerville was the county seat, voted a subsidy of $300,000 to speed the work of laying track in the precipitous foothills.[10]

This was a formidable array, and at first the Sacramento Valley Railroad seemed on the point of triumph. Investors in San Francisco refused to buy even token amounts of stock in the Sacramento-based Central Pacific. A vigorous sales campaign by brokers in the employ of the CP resulted in the sale of only fourteen shares. Charles Crocker went in person to Virginia City, where San Francisco influence was strong, and managed to dispose of only one share! By contrast, 230 residents of Sacramento subscribed to CP stock with a face value of nearly a million dollars.[11] Unfortunately for the Central Pacific, however, most of those sales were in the form of pledges. Only 10 percent of the total price had to be paid at the time of the agreement, and so the transactions produced only a fraction of what the railroad needed in addition

191

*During the final days
of construction
Mark Hopkins, as
treasurer, drew heavily
on Ralston for funds.*

to its government loans—loans it could not draw until it had completed a designated amount of track.

Failure might have come to the Central Pacific then, except for the ordinary citizens of California. Swayed by personal considerations rather than by the economic rivalries underlying the struggle, they wanted direct rail connections with the East. They believed that through trains would reduce living costs, that mail and newspapers would reach them in days instead of weeks, that friends and family would no longer seem so remote. True, they did not have money for buying stock. But they did have votes. In spite of energetic opposition during the election campaigns, they authorized the city of Sacramento, the city and county of San Francisco, Placer County, and the state of California to issue bonds that were to be used for the purchase of Central Pacific stock.

The friends of the Sacramento Valley Railroad promptly challenged the constitutionality of the bond issues in the courts. Their attacks delayed the payment of the subsidies to the Central Pacific and thus delayed the progress of construction. In the end, however, the courts decided every case in favor of the CP.

Other triumphs followed quickly. In mid-June, 1864, while Ralston was completing in secret the organization of The Bank of California, the Central Pacific opened its subsidiary Dutch Flat wagon road. Curious teamsters turned that way, liked what they found, and drew large volumes of traffic away from the south-side road. Meanwhile the CP had

*Charles Crocker's driving
energy in the field pushed
the western half of
the transcontinental to
completion in May, 1869.*

pushed its railhead far enough so that it could begin drawing government loans. On top of that, the Union Pacific and the Central Pacific,
working together, obtained from Congress on July 2, 1864 (three days
before The Bank of California opened its doors), legislation allowing
them to issue first mortgage bonds of their own—$1.25 million worth
initially in the case of the CP.[12] The business of handling those bonds
went not to The Bank of California but, pointedly, to Ralston's estranged
former partners, Joseph Donohoe and Eugene Kelly.[13]

At this point, D. O. Mills, the president of The Bank of California,
stepped in as peacemaker. Because he was still a resident of Sacramento
and an acquaintance of the principal owners of the Central Pacific, he
was able to take a wider view of the situation than were the embattled
San Franciscans. From his vantage point he could see only disaster
ahead for the Sacramento Valley Railroad if the rivalry continued.

He did not want Ralston involved in a collapse of that sort at a time
when the new bank and its high-riding cashier were being carefully
watched by many doubters. So he urged Ralston to help him persuade
the directors of the Sacramento Valley Railroad to end the fight.

In Mills's opinion—and he had good pipelines to the Central Pacific
—that road would be willing now, as it had not been before, to buy the
Sacramento Valley line if the terms were reasonable. The CP, too,
needed peace. The San Franciscans' opposition had seriously delayed
its work program and was threatening to choke off all possibility of aid

Crocker speaks while Stanford poses with a shovel in this imaginative painting of the CP's ground-breaking at Sacramento.

The Central Pacific prepared the way for its steam cars with the widely advertised and profitable Dutch Flat Wagon Road.

from the Nevada legislature. Of equal concern, the CP could also increase its current revenues by purchasing its rival, for then it could divert still more traffic over its own slowly advancing tracks and through the tollgates of its Dutch Flat wagon road—matters well worth considering.

The arguments swayed Ralston. In many ways the fight was a negative one, devoted more to hurting a rival city than to building up San Francisco. Mills was right; Billy's energies were needed on more constructive projects.

The first overt indication of his new cast of thinking was his departure from the Valley line's board of directors. He did not lose his voice for peace, however, for he was replaced in March, 1865, by Ralph Fretz.[14] Another strong ally on the new board was Jonathan Hunt, who owed his position as president of the Pacific Insurance Company largely to Ralston's influence. Working diligently, they swung the railroad's president, George Bragg, to their way of reasoning. That clinched matters. After a long series of conferences between Bragg and Stanford, the Central Pacific agreed to buy the Sacramento Valley Railroad's assets for $800,000.[15]

So that reef, too, was cleared and channels were open now for the bank's officers to try to woo the Central Pacific's potentially profitable business away from Donohoe and Kelly. Victory from a lost battle, bullion still flowing across the mountains from the Comstock—by the time The Bank of California was a year old several questions about its viability had evaporated.

CHAPTER 14

In Full Command

The personal satisfaction that Ralston derived from the sale of the Sacramento Valley Railroad was climaxed by an opportunity to show off his city to influential easterners. During the Civil War most news from the West had been overshadowed in the nation's papers by dispatches from the battlefield. Now that peace had come, war-weary investors and potential tourists were eager to adjust the balance. Sensing this, a group of potent opinion makers traveled during the summer of 1865 toward the Pacific to discover any developments in the West that might be worth writing about.

The make-up of the investigating party guaranteed an enormous audience of readers. At the head of the group was amiable Schuyler (often called Smiler) Colfax, a six-term congressman from Indiana and Speaker of the House of Representatives. Accompanying him were William Bross, lieutenant governor of Illinois and publisher of the Chicago *Tribune;* Albert Richardson, top correspondent of Horace Greeley's famed New York *Tribune;* and Samuel Bowles of the influential Springfield, Massachusetts, *Republican.*

Whatever dispatches those journalists telegraphed to their papers would later be expanded into speeches and books distributed throughout the United States and western Europe.[1] Accordingly it behooved San Francisco and all other cities along the party's route to make ready.

From Ralston's standpoint as a banker engaged in assembling funds for investment, the timing of the visit was marvelously opportune. The brief faltering brought to the economy by the collapse of Comstock stocks had ended. All around the bay, business was humming again. He could claim some credit, both as an individual and as the chief executive of The Bank of California, and he wanted the results of the work known.

The year before, 1864, he had rescued the foundering San Francisco & Pacific Sugar Refinery from bankruptcy and had made possible its reorganization under the capable presidency of George Gordon, creator of the residential district of South Park. He had helped finance the expansion of iron foundries and the completion of the long-delayed railroad between San Francisco and San Jose at the southern tip of the bay. Thanks in part to the bank's liberalized policy of lending money to Comstock mines and mills, gold and silver bullion was still crossing the mountains in undiminished quantities. (The total value for 1865, like that for 1864, would be $16 million.) To find additional outlets for that silver he had arranged through The Oriental Bank of London to ship several consignments directly to China and India.[2] Soon $7 million worth of silver bars were moving across the Pacific each year, most of them handled by The Bank of California. So much precious metal demanded scrupulous care in its treatment. To render this essential service, The Bank of California had joined several other financial houses (including Donohoe, Kelly & Co!) in forming the San Francisco Assaying and Refining Works, managed by Ralston's good friend, Louis A. Garnett, In time most of California's bullion would be purified and tested by that one concern.

Another enterprise of which Billy was proud was the Mission Woolen Mills. Founded in 1859 by a Scot named Donald McLennan, the Mission company had boomed during the war by making cloth for army uniforms. The approach of peace brought a sharp break in the company's stock. Fortified with money from The Bank of California, Ralston swept up control. Retaining McLennan as president of the company, he set about converting the mills to peacetime products— red flannel shirts for miners, and blankets for the Indian Department, army installations on the West Coast, and domestic use generally.* His goal was the production each year of half a million yards of flannel and 32,000 pairs of blankets, at which point the company would be grossing more than $1 million annually. At the same time he insisted on quality with remarkable results. In 1867, two years after his acquisition of the company, Mission blankets, as they were known throughout the West, won first prize in their category at an international exhibition in Paris.[3]

At the bank, business was so brisk that the cramped quarters at Washington and Battery streets no longer sufficed. Ralston, always an exuberant builder, wanted a new structure magnificent enough to epitomize the opportunities he felt lay ahead, yet for some time he hesitated over a location. Should he stay in the same neighborhood, as

---

*Somewhat earlier Ralston had also gained control of the rival Pacific Woolen Mills and installed his wife's foster father, John D. Fry, as president. Although the Pacific and Mission mills occupied adjoining factories, they did not combine operations until 1875.

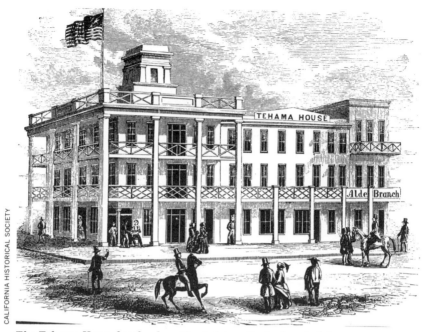

CALIFORNIA HISTORICAL SOCIETY

The Tehama House hotel, where the Ralstons lived after their honeymoon, was moved to make room for The Bank of California.

Donohoe and Kelly had done when setting up their competitive organization? Or should he follow the handful of savings banks, real estate brokers, and the new London & San Francisco Bank, managed locally by Milton Latham, southward toward Market Street?

In the end he chose the latter course, selecting as a site the northwest corner of California and Sansome streets. The ground was already occupied by the old Tehama House hotel, in which Lizzie and he had spent the first post-honeymoon days of their marriage. He bought it for $67,500, had it jacked up on rollers and moved eight blocks north to a deteriorating neighborhood on Broadway near Kearny.[4] He then hired architects and was discussing plans for the new bank building when he learned of the approach of the eastern journalists.

Predictably he responded with enthusiasm to a request that he help entertain and instruct the visitors. The prospect appealed to his ebullient spirits and love of display. But there was more. He shared in full the conviction of most nineteenth-century westerners that they were creating a new, potentially ideal civilization in what recently had been an untamed wilderness. In such a setting boosterism became a virtue. A man fulfilled himself and justified his work by extolling his city and his state. Many of Ralston's friends later recalled that characteristic in him above all others. His brother Andrew Jackson quoted him as saying once, "Anything that is calculated to promote the interests of this coast is the thing that I am working for, and I will use all the powers at my command to accomplish this." True prosperity, moreover, needed the broadest of bases. In a letter to Milton Latham, Ralston declared vehemently, "We hold that what is for the good of the *masses* will in the *end* be of *equal* benefit to the Bankers."[5]

For the sake of all California then, he and his fellow committeemen racked their imaginations for ways to impress their distinguished visitors. What could they do that other aspiring cities along the route— Denver, Salt Lake City, Portland—could not do?

One stunt that evolved was a welcoming banquet presented on Thursday evening, August 17, 1865, at the Hang Hoong restaurant on Clay Street by the presidents of the Six Companies, tightly-knit fraternal organizations controlled by San Francisco's principal Chinese merchants. Attending the festivities with the visitors were such distinguished local leaders as William Ralston and Joseph Donohoe.

The restaurant's chairs and serving tables were draped with gold-embroidered scarlet cloth. The dining tables were fragrant with fresh flowers. There were three sittings, each replete with exotic fare. After each sitting, the guests went into the anterooms to enjoy Chinese-made cigars while the tables were cleared for another flood of dishes. All told, according to a reporter from the daily *Alta California,* a diner could have chosen, if his taste buds and capacity allowed, from 336 different dishes. Meantime Chinese singers and a Chinese band supplied entertainment. There were numerous speeches, made still more interminable by being interpreted for everyone's sake. At midnight the party finally ended. Afterwards, said Bowles, "a leading banker" (Ralston, perhaps? Or Joe Donohoe?) took the suffering editors across the street to an American restaurant for "a good square meal."[6]

The next day the party set out, under careful guidance, to survey what Bowles later spelled, to the shuddering dismay of Bay Area readers, as "Friscoe." He was not wholly smitten. "The town sprawls roughly over the coarse sand-hills that the Ocean has rolled and blown up, and is still rolling and blowing up." He disliked (as did Liz Ralston) the perpetual wind with its burden of dust. The same wind that flipped up the ladies' hoopskirts, Mark Twain grumbled, also filled the would-be spectator's eyes with sand, a matter Bowles did not mention. But Bowles did have much to say about what he considered the unattractive gridiron pattern of the streets. The residents, he thought, should have let nature determine the contours of the boulevards. Instead the city clung stubbornly to its rectangles, mercilessly attacking the hills in order to reduce thoroughfares "to a grade that man and horse can ascend and descend without double collar and breeching help."[7]

It was a raw town, in Bowles' estimation. The citizens had not yet had time to "tame down." Society was rough and materialistic, characterized by "fastness and loudness" and by "a sort of gambling, speculating, horse-jockeying morality." The women were given to scandalous gossip and garish dress: "rich, full colors [and] the startling effect that the Paris demi-monde seeks." Intense feminine rivalry led to expensive, daring ball and opera gowns. "Their point lace is deeper, their moire antique stiffer, their skirts a trifle longer, their corsages an inch lower, their diamonds more brilliant—and more of them—than the cosmopolite is likely to find elsewhere."[8]

He was surprised at the amount of alcohol consumed. A drink of whiskey in an ordinary saloon cost ten cents (the smallest coin in circulation was a dime) and twenty-five cents in one of the more aristocratic hotels. "Champagne is mother's milk indeed to all these people"—imported French champagne rather than the harsher product of the Buena Vista Vinicultural Society that Ralston backed. At Sam Brannan's resort hotel at Calistoga in the Napa Valley, the editor was astounded to see a handsome, well-dressed young woman from San

CALIFORNIA HISTORICAL SOCIETY

Montgomery Street, 1865. Despite its energy San Francisco was, in the opinion of eastern visitors, still raw and untamed.

*A sight tourists wanted to see—and Ralston was always glad to show—
was the Cliff House, poised at the far edge of the continent.*

Francisco march to the bar and "down a nightcap with some of the
first gentlemen of California."[9]

The coin had its other side, however. Although the wind might be
troublesome, its rising swept the skies clear of mist, turned the views
sparkling, and alerted the senses. He found the hotels as good as any in
the East and the restaurants better. The food markets were filled with
luscious fruits, crisp vegetables, fish and game birds and animals of
many kinds. Churches flourished, and as a part of their civic pride the
citizens lavished money on school buildings and hospitals. The visitors
particularly enjoyed a brisk buggy ride across the tip of the peninsula to
see the seals that swarmed over the wave-swept rocks beyond the Cliff
House. The United States Mint also intrigued the party. "It was
decidedly refreshing," William Bross later told the New York Chamber
of Commerce, "to see a mass of gold worth $75,000 melted in a
single retort."

Most of all Bowles was struck by the businessmen with whom he
talked. They were marked, he wrote, by "a wide, practical reach, a
boldness, sagacity, a vim that can hardly be matched anywhere in the
world"—a sweeping declaration that specifically included the men who
guided the destinies of The Bank of California, "the financial king of
the Pacific States."[10]

The businessmen responded by hurrying the visitors through the
docks, the switching yards of the newly completed San Francisco &
San Jose Railroad, and the principal commercial houses and manufacturing plants of the city, including the Mission Woolen Mills. There

Ralston showed his own sagacity by presenting each of the guests with a brand-new suit of clothes.

The guests wore their new raiment to the elaborate farewell parties given for them on September 1. Ralston was host at the first event, a banquet held in a private dining room in the new Occidental Hotel. The ceremony was praised at the time as the most splendid entertainment ever presented in the city. A score of prominent San Franciscans listened with warm pleasure to Smiler Colfax's sonorous approval of the city's enterprises. Said the speaker, "I am prouder of the suit in which I am clothed tonight, of California cloth, from wool on the back of California sheep, woven by the Mission Woolen Mills, and made here, than of the finest suit of French broadcloth I ever owned." He went on to urge his listeners to do what they had already started—to foster local manufacturing. Delighted with his nod of recognition, the audience applauded lustily.[11]

After the dinner the group adjourned to the grand ballroom for a dance open to anyone who paid $25 gold for a ticket. Ralston was head of the committee of reception. With Lizzie beside him he stood at the entrance to a transfigured chamber banked with flowers, evergreen boughs, flags, caged canaries, goldfish in lighted bowls, and hung with paintings of the California scenes that the tourists had enjoyed most— Yo Semite, as the name was spelled then, the geysers of Sonoma Valley, the Big Trees of Calaveras County. Some three hundred merry-makers participated, refreshing themselves now and then with "hot-beef tea with just a smack of claret in it." At midnight they all sat down to yet another banquet.[12]

Well content with the California part of their excursion, the party moved on to Portland. Even after they had gone, they continued to be fed rosy-hued data. Of particular import in Ralston's mind were two separately prepared scientific reports about the Comstock Lode issued in the fall of 1865. William Ashburner of the California Geological Survey was the author of one; Baron Ferdinand von Richthofen of Germany penned the other.

Both men confirmed in technical language what common miners on the lode had been telling each other for many months: spots of barren ground were characteristic of silver deposits. But the scientists were more precise than the folklorists. They named specific mines in Mexico, Peru, Germany, and Hungary that over the centuries had kept striking new bodies of ore as their shafts pierced greater depths. Why should not the mines of the Comstock produce similar results, once management had solved the technical problems of draining impeding water from their lower workings?

Ralston rushed a copy of Ashburner's report east to the journalists. Bowles published it in his new book *Across the Continent*—he identified Ashburner as "the confidential mining engineer of the leading bankers of San Francisco"[13]—and William Bross drew heavily on it when addressing the New York State Chamber of Commerce, January 25, 1866, on "The Resources of the Far West."

Nothing, Bross implied in his grandiloquent talk, was impossible out yonder toward the sunset. He described the Central Pacific Railroad struggling upward through the Sierra Nevada. He extolled the proposed opening of steamship service to the Orient. Soon "the Queen of England and the Empress of France will order their teas and their silks by the American line." But what really fired him to eloquence were the mines. "In all the countries where silver mines are worked they have never been exhausted." That being so, there were obviously no limits to the future. Within fifteen years, he predicted on the basis of no evidence whatsoever, the West's output of gold and silver would reach half a billion dollars per year. "The production of so vast an amount of the precious metals will give to this nation a power to control the commerce and civilization of the world far beyond all that the wildest imagination ever dared to picture."[14]

How much of this bombast Bross's New York listeners swallowed —the eastern representatives of The Bank of California were in the audience—is impossible to say. But when copies of the speech reached California, heads nodded in agreement. Certainly the time for expansion had come.

For Ralston this meant, first of all, pushing ahead with the new bank building at the northwest corner of California and Sansome streets. On that recently cleared ground workers began sinking 300 pilings as support for what Ralston intended to be the most opulent edifice in the West. Almost simultaneously in May, 1866, the bank's board of directors announced that on July 1, at the close of the firm's second fiscal year, the paid-in capital would be increased to $5 million in gold. It was also revealed that during the preceding twenty-two months the bank had earned a net profit of $1.2 million, of which $1 million was paid to the shareholders in the form of a 50 percent stock dividend. This was no inconsiderable sweetener since regular dividends amounted to 1 percent a month. The balance of the profits, which reached $300,000 by July 1, was retained as surplus.

Ralston's decision about the location of the new bank building confirmed the southward drift of San Francisco's financial district. "It was with pride," banker Zoeth Eldredge later wrote, "that men spoke of their connection with The Bank of California." Stockbrokers, who were particularly dependent on the bank's credit, the stock exchange, and several related enterprises immediately began erecting quarters for themselves in the vicinity. By the end of 1866 California Street was known throughout the Pacific states as the Wall Street of the West.[15]

Ralston wanted the classic lines of the new Bank of California to reflect the institution's strength and stability.

The construction was part of a feverish building boom that swept across the city in 1866 and 1867. Capital, much of it from the Comstock, had been accumulating rapidly. Part was lavished on a thousand new public and commercial buildings, including three large hotels, eight theaters, and forty-six churches. None, however, came close to matching the elegance of the two-story bank building. Solid, Roman-style stone columns flanked the arched entry and the rows of tall, arched windows. The exterior was faced with a bluish stone quarried on Angel Island in the bay. A stone balustrade crowned with ornamental vases circled the roof.

The ceilings of the main room were nineteen feet high and painted in what was called "Italian style." A large counter, its corner curved rather than square, fenced off most of the main chamber. No grills existed. Near each teller's elbow were stacks of gold and silver coins that could be scooped up with little trowels as needed. At the rear of the work area were four massive vaults of chilled iron. Tables were of mahogany; chairs were upholstered with green morocco leather. Upstairs in the directors' room hung huge paintings of Yosemite Valley.

The course of construction was punctuated for Ralston by personal sorrow. His brother James died in Virginia City on August 25, 1866, and

CALIFORNIA HISTORICAL SOCIETY

Open counters and a sense of opulence marked the bank's interior.
(Ralston stands just to the right of the teller's sign.)

was brought to San Francisco for burial in the Lone Tree cemetery beside the baby Edna Louisa. Then, in June 1867, three weeks before the scheduled opening of the new building, Ralph Fretz also died. Since Panama days he had been Ralston's most steadfast friend. Other partners—Garrison, Morgan, Donohoe, Kelly—had split away for various reasons, but those two had remained together.

At the time of his death, Fretz was 58 years old. (Ralston was then 41.) He had never married. Quiet and unobtrusive, he had not attracted the attention of the city's newspapers. But his cool judgment and restraining hand had been good for Billy Ralson—better by far **than** Cornelius Garrison's flamboyant plunging and corner cutting. The two had prospered together. The papers estimated the value of Fretz's estate at more than half a million dollars. Judge O. C. Platt, D. O. Mills, and William Ralston were named in his will as executors. Most of

Fretz's holdings were bequeathed to relatives in Pennsylvania. But he did leave $20,000 to the United States in compensation, he wrote, for his inability during the war to help defend with arms "the best Government man ever had."[16]

Several nights after the funeral the bank staff piled ledgers, files, and heaps of gold coin into satchels, wheelbarrows, and wagons and hurried them from the old quarters to the new. When the doors swung open the following morning, even staid Stephen Franklin, the bank's secretary, felt that a new era was beginning. As William Bross and Samuel Bowles had said, opportunities were boundless.

Ralston's spectacular progress kindled envy as well as awe. Banker John Parrott, one of the wealthiest men in California, declared in a letter to Joseph Donohoe, who had never forgiven Billy for the fragmentation of their partnership: "Ralston is a man of wonderful resources, people look upon him as on a King. He has a ring formed of very strong people. . . . Such as the Barrons, Bell, Butterworth, Hayward, Sunderland, Tevis, and their stripe, who are going in for a New Gas company or depress the Stock of the old one until they buy upon their own terms and get the control. . . . They stop at nothing these days."[17]

Yet, as Parrott well knew, kings can be challenged. In shipping, mining, real estate developments, and in banking itself fierce struggles for dominance would arise. Rules would be few, for this was the dawn of the Grant era, the jungle days of America's notorious laissez-faire economic competition. No single individual or institution could expect to win all the battles. Just winning enough to survive would be a noteworthy accomplishment, dependent on skill and boldness, on the effect of worldwide political and economic developments, and, above all, on luck. But at least Billy Ralston had this assurance as he faced the future: few men entered those rough-and-tumble arenas any better equipped than he was.

CHAPTER 15

To the Seas Again

One March day in 1861 a tall, rawboned wagon freighter named Ben Holladay strode into the office of what was then Fretz & Ralston and asked for a loan he could use in putting together a steamship company.

Ralston's fancy was caught. Holladay, aged forty-two that year, wore black broadcloth adorned with diamonds, as many San Franciscans did, but the trappings did not hide the fact that he was essentially a frontiersman from the alkali plains bordering the continental divide. He was sandy-haired, weather-marked, and calloused. The incisiveness of his mouth was partially hidden by a moustache and a thick spade beard. Like other sanguine promoters who from time to time fired Ralston's enthusiasm, Holladay was also devious. Billy did not always notice such characteristics, however. What swayed him were a man's potentials for accomplishment.

Holladay's past suggested a spectacular future.[1] Kentucky born, unschooled, and lacking in social graces, he had made his first money during the war with Mexico by hauling supplies for the army during its invasion of the Southwest. He had trailed beef cattle across Nevada to gold-rush Sacramento, and shortly thereafter had made still greater profits as a contractor furnishing draft animals, wagons, grain, flour, and related items to Russell, Majors, and Waddell, a freighting monopoly whose wagon trains served every army installation between El Paso, Texas, and Fort Hall, Idaho.[2] He also furnished the firm with carefully-chosen saddle horses and some money when it launched the famed Pony Express in a vain hope of winning government mail subsidies.

Now, in 1861, Holladay's imagination was captured by still another transportation challenge—supplying southern Arizona, which in those days was one of the most isolated sections of the United States. The normal method was to send goods by steamer or even sailing vessel from San Francisco around the tip of Baja California to the port of Guaymas, Mexico, from which point wagon roads led north to Tubac and Tucson. Another approach from the Gulf, though a difficult one, was to transfer supplies to shallow-draft steamers and push up the Colorado River as far as Fort Yuma.

The drawback to the Gulf service was the hit-or-miss scheduling of the tramp ships that provided it. Holladay wanted to reduce this element of risk and systematize the commerce.

An essential ingredient of the plan was a clutch of obsolescent ships that had just come onto the market at bargain prices. After competing fiercely throughout 1859, the Pacific Mail Steamship Company and Cornelius Vanderbilt had decided to amalgamate rather than continue fighting. The peace left the new combination oversupplied with vessels. Among those approaching the end of their days were the pioneer steamers of the gold rush, the *California, Oregon,* and *Panama,* and three others that must have brought nostalgic memories to Billy Ralston, the *Cortes, Orizaba,* and *Sierra Nevada.* Those six ships, which had a value of $561,512 on the company books, were offered to Holladay for $250,000.[3]

Would Fretz and Ralston provide him and a partner, Edward R. Flint, with some of the financial help they needed to complete the purchases and organize what they planned to call the Mexican Coast Steamship Company? As collateral for the loan, Ben offered 120 shares of stock in the Ophir Silver Mining Company.[4] According to legend he had won the certificates in a poker game.

Billy agreed. It was the beginning of a long and often stormy relationship. Holladay expanded marvelously. (His partner, Flint, died during the burning of the Pacific Mail steamer *Golden Gate* off Manzanillo, Mexico, in 1862; Ben was luckier and survived, one of fifty out of 242 passengers to do so.) From Mexico he reached north into British Columbia, reorganizing his line as the California, Oregon, and Mexico Steamship Company. On land he took over the once-powerful freighting firm of Russell, Majors, and Waddell. Throughout this period Ralston handled most of Holladay's financial affairs, first as a partner of Donohoe, Ralston & Company and later through The Bank of California.

Awkward dilemmas for the profitable association arose with the discovery of rich goldfields in Idaho and western Montana—goldfields that during the last half of the 1860s produced more than 50 percent of the precious mineral found during that period in the United States. Which transportation companies, those based in Oregon or those based in California, would dominate the carrying of supplies to the lucrative new markets?

*Flamboyant, hard-driving Ben Holladay involved Ralston deeply
in shipping on the Pacific and railroad building in Oregon.*

At first the advantage seemed to lie with the Oregon Steam Navigation Company. Supported in large part by Ralston and The Bank of California, John Ainsworth and his partners in Portland had grown vigorously, building extensive warehouse facilities in several riverside communities and enlarging their fleet to 29 steamers, 13 schooners, and 4 barges.[5] When the rush to the new goldfields began, OSN stern-wheelers were ready on a moment's notice to thrust hundreds upon hundreds of tons of merchandise through the Cascade mountains to various unloading docks beside the upper Columbia and lower Snake rivers. There the material was turned over to packtrains and wagon freighters for the rest of the journey to the interior.

As the mountains of freight grew, the California Steam Navigation Company, of which Ralston was a director, determined to compete for them. The CSN pattern went like this. Its ships carried cargo across San Francisco Bay to boat landings on the upper Sacramento River. There freighters loaded it aboard wagons for transport to southern Idaho and southwestern Montana.[6]

As if this weren't problem enough for the Oregonians, the Central Pacific Railroad also entered the fray. Hoping to divert traffic to its slowly climbing rails in the Sierra, it entered into price agreements with the California Steam Navigation Company.[7] Preferential rail rates were given to freight from San Francisco that the CSN deposited at the depot in Sacramento. The railroad carried the merchandise on to the end of its line in the mountains, then transferred it to wagons for the trip over the CP's new Donner Pass road and on through central Nevada to the goldfields.

Thus the war was on: the California Steam Navigation Company and the struggling Central Pacific against the Oregon Steam Navigation Company. Costs were roughly the same by any of the routes. The key to success was service, and that was where Ralston's main dilemma lay. The situation on the ocean was such that he was bound to offend one good friend or another.

Most of the manufactured items that were distributed by Portland merchants to storekeepers in the goldfields originated in San Francisco. This freight was carried from the Bay to the Columbia by two potential rivals. One was Ben Holladay's California, Oregon, and Mexico Steamship Company. The other was the California Steam Navigation Company, a late entrant into ocean shipping. Competition between the two firms should have been keen, but wasn't.

Although the point can't be documented, one suspects Ralston's influence. He was banker for both companies and a director of one. In Panama and Nicaragua he had learned how harmful unrestrained warfare between ship owners could be. In his opinion a struggle on the northwest coast was certain to injure both his clients. Would not a mutually beneficial understanding be more healthful for the two firms if not for their customers? Anyway, that was apparently what happened; the companies entered into an agreement about rates and schedules and then settled down to peaceful coexistence.

Because no real competition existed, service was wretched. The coastal ships were old and overcrowded; delays were frequent. The chief sufferers were Portland middlemen handling merchandise ordered by the impatient miners of Idaho and Montana. When complaints about the abominable service brought no improvement, the Oregonians developed dark suspicions. The two noncompetitive coastal lines, they concluded, were deliberately trying to discourage the movement of traffic by way of the Columbia River in order to divert it to the new, expensive facilities of the California Steam Navigation Company. Holladay did not object because his stagecoaches benefited from increased passenger and express traffic fed them by the California concern. Neither did Ralston, who in spite of his many ties with Oregon was essentially a Californian and a director of the rival shipping company.

Confirmation of the Oregonians' doubts came (in their minds at least) during the summer of 1865. On July 30 of that year, the California Steam Navigation Company's sidewheeler *Brother Jonathan* struck a submerged rock off the coast of northern California and sank so rapidly that of the 200 persons aboard only 19 reached land. As a replacement for the vessel the CSN purchased from Ben Holladay the obsolescent *Orizaba*. Traffic to Portland via the coast declined still more.

Dissension split the board of directors of the Oregon Steam Navigation Company. The bolder members argued that the only way to break

A recurring motif in Ralston's seafaring enterprises was the steamer
Orizaba, *painted in 1876 by artist Joseph Lee.*

the impasse was to enter the coastal trade themselves, even at the cost of building a big, new oceangoing vessel. To the more timorous members the proposal seemed wildly reckless. Suppose that Holladay, Ralston, and the California Steam Navigation Company reacted by invading the Columbia? That would be disastrous. "You know the stuff the Cal Co is made of," one wrote in agitation, "and if they start in it will be no boys play."[8]

The aggressive ones carried the day and sent representatives east to contract for a luxury liner to be called the *Oregonian*. (Its costs eventually reached $403,000, an awesome sum for the times.) They also sought to hide their intentions by having their agents register the ship in their own names. The hope was that Holladay, Ralston, and the California Steam Navigation Company would suppose that the *Oregonian* was a private venture and not a corporate challenge from the OSN. Lulled thus, the Californians would refrain from entering the Columbia in retaliation.

Surmising at once what was afoot, Ralston wrote a vigorous protest to his friend Ainsworth. First he waved a club. The California Steam Navigation Company was determined to maintain its hold on the coastal trade by whatever means were necessary. In other words, beware of an invasion of the Columbia. That point made, he held out a carrot. No one wanted to endure the costs of unbridled competition. Therefore he was prepared to discuss any reasonable accommodation that Ainsworth proposed. "I say this not only on my own account, but am authorized to say it for the [CSN] Comp'y."[9]

Ainsworth replied that the large property owners of Portland felt that improvement of the San Francisco run was essential to their interests. Since the promises of the California Steam Navigation Company had proved unreliable in the past, those property holders had at last been forced to contract for a suitable ship of their own. He did not believe that the OSN was in any position to persuade the owners of the new ship to call off the competition, much as he deplored it.

Ralston was not fooled. Ainsworth knew it and, in writing to an associate, predicted trouble. Nevertheless the OSN would not yield. "We are busying ourselves with preparations to resist a siege, and flatter ourselves that our works are strong and guns reliable."[10]

A nose-to-nose confrontation—and yet at the same time that the challenges were being hurled Ralston was helping Ainsworth on another front. The president of the Oregon company and his three closest associates, W. S. Ladd, Simeon G. Reed, and R. R. Thompson, had grown weary of the constant carping of the firm's cautious shareholders. Now they made plans to get rid of them.

Times were ripe. To the consternation of all concerned, the growing volume of freight along the West Coast had lured in new competition

Ralston's lifelong friend John Ainsworth (center), S. G. Reed (left),
and R. R. Thompson dominated Columbia River navigation.

from the outside—the Anchor Line, a Maine corporation controlled by
shipbuilding brothers, G. Y. and J. Patton. The Pattons' inspiration
was clear from the names they gave their vessels—the *Montana,* which
they sent around the Horn early in 1866, and the *Idaho,* which was
still on the ways in the East.

The immediate result was a price-cutting battle almost as ferocious
as those once waged between the Panama lines in the 1850s. Freight
rates from San Francisco to Portland were cut in half to $3.00 a ton;
passenger tickets dropped even more.

In addition to cutting rates, the California Steam Navigation Com-

213

pany and Holladay tried to smother the new opponent with sheer volume. During the year the CSN added two secondhand ships to its Oregon-Washington-British Columbia run. Holladay, as usual, was more flamboyant. He had just received, late in 1865, the *Del Norte,* the first oceangoing steamship ever built entirely in San Francisco's shipyards. (Liz and Billy Ralston were aboard when the *Del Norte* took a gala trial run through the bay, which suggests that The Bank of California probably had something to do with financing the construction.) Ben also brought over from China the sumptuous *Oriflamme.* In Washington, D.C., he picked up the *Continental,* a troopship which Asa Mercer planned to use for carrying unwed maidens—the famed Mercer girls of northwest history—around the Horn to bachelors eagerly waiting in Seattle.

All told, the CSN and Holladay's ships made forty round trips between San Francisco and the Northwest during 1866, as compared to the *Montana*'s eighteen.[11] But when the *Idaho* arrived the numbers would become more nearly equal. Pointing out that there simply was not enough freight to support so many ships, the dissidents within the OSN argued that they should sell the *Oregonian* for whatever they could get.

Ainsworth, Ladd, Reed, and Thompson reacted by setting out to buy control of the company. To disguise their intent and thus keep stock prices down, they proposed to act through Alvinza Hayward. Hayward, who was a part owner of the fabulous Old Eureka Mine in the Sierra foothills and a director of and major stockholder in The Bank of California, was to pretend that he was representing a group of California investors in search of a bargain.

Events continued to aid the plot. The new *Oregonian* arrived in San Francisco Bay on December 2, 1866. Almost simultaneously the Pattons announced that in February their newly-built *Idaho* would join the *Montana* on the San Francisco—Portland run. The California Steam Navigation Company then declared publicly that it would defy all comers with a new ship of its own, the *Ajax.*

On top of those developments came disquieting news that an eastern shipowner named William H. Webb had decided to reestablish the old Nicaragua route between the Atlantic and the Pacific. Needing help on the West Coast end of the run, Webb sought out a veteran of the old days in Nicaragua, Billy Ralston. His selling point: success in Nicaragua would force Pacific Mail to reduce its monopolistic rates across Panama. Because that in turn would stimulate travel between San Francisco and the East, Ralston jumped at the idea.

Details concerning the new crossing had not been completed when 1867 opened, but speculation was rife. Webb's two Pacific steamers, the *Moses Taylor* and the *America,* so the stories ran, would not terminate their Nicaragua runs at San Francisco but would continue north as far as British Columbia. Such a development would, of course, mean still more competition for the Portlander's *Oregonian*.

The threats brought Ainsworth's scheme to fruition. Blocks of OSN stock began appearing on the market at discounts of 10 percent to 25 percent below par. Hayward swept them up. His expenditures amounted to somewhere between $887,000 and $1.5 million, according to the reminiscences one chooses to believe. Whatever the sum, Ralston —that is to say, The Bank of California—provided much of it, or so Ainsworth wrote many years later.[12] To the schemers in the OSN it was all very worthwhile. To celebrate their control of the company, they declared a dividend of 36.84 percent on the stock they owned and had purchased, and increased the capitalization of their company from $2 million to $5 million.[13]

Ainsworth does not speculate in his memoirs as to why Ralston, who had been fighting him through the California Steam Navigation Company, had suddenly decided to support him. The following guess is not unreasonable, however. Billy wanted to create a climate of cooperation among the shippers of the northwest coast. As the one man who had direct ties to three of the contending groups—only the Pattons' Anchor Line lay outside his immediate sphere of influence—he saw no gain in a furious quadrangular fight. His friend William Norris, who had just resigned as secretary of the California Steam Navigation Company in order to become agent of Holladay's shipping interests, agreed, and together they set about trying to bring peace.[14]

Ben Holladay was the key figure. He had just sold (November, 1866) his stage operations to Wells, Fargo & Company for $1.5 million cash plus $300,000 worth of Wells, Fargo stock. Now he wanted to devote his energies and his fortune to creating a shipping monopoly as all-embracing as his stage company had been. What evolved, with Ralston's help, was this. For an undisclosed sum Holladay bought all of the California Steam Navigation Company's "outside" ships.[15] He purchased the Pattons' two steamers. Largely at Ralston's behest, one suspects, he paid the Oregon Steam Navigation Company $50,000 for its promise not to use either the *Oregonian* or any other of its ships against him in the Pacific. He then bundled all his steamers—there were sixteen or seventeen now—into a new company, the North Pacific Transportation Company, incorporated for carrying on business from San Francisco to Alaska. Ralston's services in bringing about the amalgamation were recognized by his being given a seat on the new company's board of directors.

There still remained the matter of William Webb's North American Transportation Company. There Ralston ran into obdurate resistance from his associates in both New York and San Francisco. The Pacific

Mail Steamship Company, which he proposed to challenge south of San Francisco, was entrenched on both coasts. Webb, an upstart, lacked adequate backing in the East for attacking such a Goliath. The prospect of Ralston's using Bank of California money for making up the deficiency brought agitated telegrams from Lees and Waller in New York: *Don't do it!*[16] Mills and Louis McLane, whose brother Allan McLane was president of Pacific Mail, added more persuasion. In the end Ralston dropped the proposal, feeling, so reported banker John Parrott, more than "a little mean about it."[17]

Billy wasn't quite through with Webb, however. He negotiated the sale to him of the OSN's now very white elephant, the *Oregonian,* for $312,000, and the ship was kept busy running first to the west coast of Nicaragua and then, when that route failed to attract profitable trade, to Panama. Finally, in November, 1868, the would-be David gave up and left the New York–California battlefield entirely, probably in exchange for a small subsidy from Pacific Mail.[18]

Also, Webb had developed other strings for his bow. In 1867, Holladay's lobbyists in Washington had won from the government contracts for carrying mail from Portland and San Francisco to Honolulu. Webb joined Holladay in providing the service. Later, with help from The Bank of California, the two men expanded the service to Australia and New Zealand. Results were mediocre, largely because

SOCIETY OF CALIFORNIA PIONEERS

West Coast grain king Isaac Friedlander depended on Bank of California money to keep his complex shipping operations afloat.

"Harvest Time" by William Hahn idealizes the hard work of threshing the wheat that was so important to California's economy.

they could not compete successfully with English fleets heavily subsidized by the British government. Lees and Waller, in short, had been right in advising Ralston to be wary of Webb's bottomless pit.

But if the shipping ventures with Webb did not quite jell, an even bolder one with the grain king of California, Isaac Friedlander, did, and spectacularly so. Friedlander was one of the remarkable men of early California. Raised in South Carolina by German-Jewish parents, he had been swept to the West Coast by the gold rush. Though scrupulously honest, he was a ruthless battler for each penny and soon became wealthy through shrewd speculations in flour and grain. He was equally imposing physically. He stood six feet seven inches tall and weighed three hundred pounds. His handsome wife, also from South Carolina, was a notable hostess. Her banquets at their South Park mansion, which held guests to damask-covered, silver-laden tables for hours, were the talk of San Francisco society. Billy and Liz Ralston were fixtures at most of those affairs.

More clearly than other Californians, Friedlander grasped the opportunities inherent in the unique nature of California wheat. The West Coast climate produced a flinty, durable grain capable of surviving long journeys around Cape Horn in slow, cheap sailing vessels. Since Liverpool was not much farther away by that route than New York, where competition with midwestern wheat was keen, Friedlander decided to seek markets, as a broker, in England. Two things were requisite: ample shipping and hundreds of thousands of burlap sacks imported each spring for holding the grain.

Chartering ships was risky. If Friedlander brought in too many, he would lose his shirt. If he failed to produce enough, other brokers would rush to fill the vacuum and his would-be dominance of the trade would collapse. So he needed to anticipate the quantity of each year's harvest well in advance, and also outguess the market: would farmers hold back in the spring in the hope of better prices, or would they hurry their output to the docks to take advantage of a rise in prices? The same considerations also governed the number of sacks he bought.

It was a fluid operation demanding large sums of readily available capital. Ralston, who had full confidence in Friedlander's widespread sources of information and in the conclusions that the broker drew from the data, supplied the money through The Bank of California and, in London, through The Oriental Bank. Success was phenomenal. In 1868, two years after the operation began, 192 sailing vessels left San Francisco Bay with $8.5 million worth of wheat.[19] Well over half of the grain was bound for Liverpool in ships chartered by Isaac Friedlander with the bank's support.

All in all, it was a very satisfactory substitute for the Webb operations, and indicative of the way in which Ralston's concepts were expanding during those years of mounting optimism. Everywhere that Billy looked, on the high seas, in the West's valleys and mountains, in the cities and on the rivers, he saw still more alluring promises that in his zest he thought he could easily embrace and direct for the benefit of the bank, himself, and—what was the same thing in his thinking—the state of California.

CHAPTER 16

Rainbows Everywhere

A wry appraisal of Ralston's exuberance during this period of bursting optimism came from George Gordon, president of the San Francisco & Pacific Sugar Refinery. The company's affairs had not prospered as well after the reorganization of 1864 as some of the stockholders wished, and in 1866 Ralston offered suggestions for further change. Afterwards Gordon wrote a friend as follows (the misspellings are Gordon's):

"His [Ralston's] fertility of invention . . . is enormous . . . but it will probably be disasterous for any of our people to take charge of his ideas and bring them forth. It would be like a mascular giant impregnating a female dwarf—the germ might be perfect in itself, but the mother would burst as it grew in her keeping."[1]

The characterization was apt, not only for Ralston but for many of San Francisco's chance-taking entrepreneurs. The times favored them. Wealth was accumulating rapidly; immigration was quickening. Expanded steamship lines and railroads either under construction or projected promised to extend the city's reach from Central America to Alaska, from the Orient to the Rocky Mountains. When Gen. Edward McCook was appointed territorial governor of Colorado in the spring of 1869, he wrote Ralston that his main purpose in going to the mountain area was "to *annex* it to the Pacific Coast."[2]

Geographic scope was only part of the exhilaration. The West Coast was either receiving from the East or was developing at home awesome new technological devices for exploiting natural resources. Concurrently California's more aggressive developers were acquiring a political sophistication that enabled them to lay hands on those resources in ways best suited to their own purposes—and to the

Hydraulic mining was another of the awesomely expensive enterprises that commanded Ralston's attention during the 1870s.

discomfiture of their rivals. Although failures were frequent, loss seldom served as a restraint because one great success could compensate for many stumblings.

A good example of what could be wrought with advanced technology was the North Bloomfield Gravel Mining Company, of which Ralston was part owner. Situated on a timbered ridge between two deeply canyoned forks of the Yuba River, North Bloomfield was a hydraulic operation. Powerful jets of water were used to tear up gravel hillsides and wash the sludge into sluice boxes where the minute amounts of gold in the earth could be recovered by standard methods. The key to profits was volume.

Before the Civil War hydraulic mining had been limited by two factors. One was the inability of hoses and nozzles to withstand the pressures brought on them. The other was the difficulty of disposing of the mountains of debris created by the process.

The first problem was solved by the invention of flexible iron pipe attached to awesome nozzles that looked and acted like pieces of field artillery. Called variously Monitors and Little Giants, these cast-iron spouts, each manned by a single slicker-clad worker, could hurl a jet of water across four hundred feet of space. When a blast hit a gravel bank, a corona of mud, sand, and stones flared like a soiled sunburst. Undercut banks hundreds of feet high collapsed with a din that overwhelmed even the thunder of the water hurtling through the nozzles. Sluice boxes for handling the muck grew from the modest troughs of the early days to massive conduits five or six feet wide, three feet deep, and thousands of feet long. The waste was disposed of by dropping it into tunnels that carried it underneath the mountains to some canyon big enough to hold the syrupy piles. What the reckless disposal process did to the land farther downstream was a matter that seldom troubled the reveries of the operators.

In 1866 three of the men who had been active in the old Sacramento Valley Railroad—Ralston, L. L. Robinson, and F. L. A. Pioche—joined Samel Butterworth, Thomas Bell, and two or three other San Franciscans in acquiring several hundred acres of gravel hillside near the town of North Bloomfield. To obtain as much water as they needed for operations on an unprecedented scale, they spent $350,000 buying water rights and easements for their canals. During 1868 and 1869 they employed 1,100 workers and spent $750,000 digging forty-seven miles of ditch to a reservoir constructed deep in the Sierra. The tunnel for disposing of waste was 8,000 feet long and cost another half million dollars.[3]

Operations were dramatic. One of the pits gouged out by the water, the huge Malakoff, was so weirdly eroded that it has since been apotheosized as a state historical monument. Costs were high, however. During Ralston's lifetime he did not receive a penny in dividends from an investment of well over $250,000.[4] Those of his associates who lived longer were luckier.

AN ENTERPRISE THAT BEGAN MORE PROFITABLY, and one that required political manipulation rather than technological muscle for success, was the Pacific Insurance Company, which specialized in fire and marine insurance. Ralston and Jonathan Hunt had founded the firm in 1863, after the legislature at Sacramento had obligingly passed a law placing severe handicaps on out-of-state companies. From California they pushed its operations into Oregon and then Nevada. Its progress in the latter state was quickened by a typical Hunt deal. He promised that if certain laws the company disliked were repealed by the legislature, Pacific would buy, at par, $100,000 in Nevada state bonds. The legislators responded with alacrity. Their treasury was bare, and unless the state's first issue of bonds sold quickly they would receive no pay.[5]

Farther east the going was harder. Companies resentful of California's discriminatory laws against outsiders had prevailed on their legislatures to pass retaliatory measures against California firms seeking to do business in their states. By this time Pacific had grown so magically that Hunt and Ralston decided they could risk competition at home for the sake of new markets in the Midwest and along the Atlantic seaboard. More deals resulted: Pacific would persuade the California legislature to repeal the very laws it had passed at their request if the eastern states would respond in kind.

The result was chaos. As agents of outside companies swarmed back across the state borders, new wildcat companies sprang up at home. Alarmed by the price wars that resulted, Ralston sat down with the heads of California's leading insurance companies and worked out a state regulatory code. But when they presented these proposals to the legislature they found they had to deal with a monster of their own making. California's unruly solons had received payoffs for passing and repealing earlier laws dealing with insurance. Why not for this code, too, even though everyone admitted its merits? Ralston had to spend somewhere between $80,000 and $100,000 to put the new regulations into effect.[6] But at least he got what he was after. Freed of the jungle warfare at home, Pacific and several other California insurance companies resumed their aggressive and profitable drives into the Midwest.

Another chimera that fascinated Ralston during those exuberant yars was the fur trade of Russian Alaska. His first associate there was a mysterious San Franciscan named Louis Goldstone. Goldstone's past is murky. Apparently he obtained most of his pelts from petty traders who filled small ships with contraband liquor and guns, and ghosted north with them to trade with the Indians. This was an illicit activity, forbidden by both the Russian government and by the Hudson's Bay Company of England, which leased the Panhandle from the czar's quasi-official representative at Sitka, the Russian American Company. Because it was illegal, it was also risky. Goldstone wanted to remove the clouds by buying all Alaska for himself and his friends. He could then make his own laws.

In 1859 he and a San Francisco concern known as the American-Russian Company offered Russia, through the offices of Senator William Gwin of California, $5 million for the huge territory. Nothing came of the proposal, but in 1865 Goldstone was ready to try again on a more modest scale. According to stories he told later, the idea occurred to him when he was in Victoria buying pelts and heard that the Hudson's Bay Company's lease would not be renewed when it expired later in the year.

Excited, he sent two ships north to survey possibilities. Without awaiting results—time was of the essence—he hurried back to San Francisco to form a company strong enough to step into the shoes of the English firm. By early June he had brought into being the California

Russian Fur Company. In addition to himself the incorporators included William Ralston, D. O. Mills, Sam Brannan, General John F. Miller, the Collector of the Port of San Francisco, a capitalist named Louis Sloss, a contractor named George Nagle, and, not by coincidence, a Judge E. Burke, whose brother-in-law, Cornelius Cole, was one of California's congressmen.[7]

At that point they were battered by contradictory developments. First the Hudson's Bay Company discouraged them by unexpectedly renewing its lease to the Panhandle for another year and entering into talks with the Russians about continuing the rental into the future.[8] Almost simultaneously Goldstone's survey ships returned triumphantly to California with encouraging bundles of maps, data on good trading centers, and, presumably, valuable pelts gathered to show how profitable the trade could be.

After anxious discussions Ralston and his associates decided to undercut the English by offering the Russians a better price for a long-term lease than their rivals were likely to offer. Early in 1866, Congressman Cole carried their proposal to Baron de Stoeckl, the Russian minister in Washington. Stoeckl's American counterpart in St. Petersburg, Cassius Clay, lent his support, and of course the American secretary of state, William Seward, was kept informed.

Alas for hope. A bigger deal, the sale of Alaska to the United States, was also under consideration at the same time. The secret bargain was concluded during the closing days of March, 1867, and on May 30 was presented to the Senate for ratification. That of course ended any possibility of leasing the Panhandle from the Russians, and the California Russian Fur Company expired.

It was an expensive loss. Goldstone sued the United States for $183,700, claiming that he had spent that much compiling information which Seward later used in convincing his government to purchase the territory—a contention backed in part by Cornelius Cole, who of course was desirous of consoling his influential constituents. Presumably Ralston and others of the California Russian Company had provided Goldstone with part of that $183,700 and would have shared in the settlement if the suit had succeeded. It did not. Goldstone had not been as all-persuasive as he thought. Several other sources of information and several motives, including military considerations, had led to the acquisition.[9]

In spite of the defeat, Ralston was not yet through with Alaska. On June 5, 1867, less than a week after the Senate's ratification of the treaty of purchase, he incorporated a new firm, the North Pacific Fur Company. His intent, at first, was a simple elaboration of the lease approach. Although the company could not rent what was now public territory, it could buy the widespread installations of the Russian

American Fur Company. Using those installations as bases, its ships would then hunt the coastal waters of Alaska as originally planned.

For reasons that have not survived, the members of the expired California Russian Company were not willing to go along with the new campaign. Instead Ralston chose as his associates in the adventure men with whom he was more accustomed to work—William Barron, Lloyd Tevis, Ben Holladay, L. L. Robinson, and J. Mora Moss. Moss, like Robinson, was a member of the old Sacramento Valley Railroad–Pioche, Bayerque ring. He was also the inaugurator, in 1852, of an enterprise that cut ice from glaciers near Sitka and shipped it south to San Francisco bars, restaurants, and food wholesalers. Because he knew the Russians he was elected president of the fur company.

Straightaway he hurried to Sitka to treat with Prince Maksoutoff, head of the Russian American Company and, as such, the former governor of Alaska. A brief talk convinced Moss that Maksoutoff would sell the North Pacific Fur Company its warehouses, shops, and furs, but one foggy morning a little later on he learned that he had been overbid by two other Alaska familiars, Hayward Hutchinson and William Kohl, plus Louis Sloss of the old California Russian Company. They had offered the prince $350,000 for the property and he had closed the deal without giving Moss a chance to enter a counter bid.[10]

The losers adapted as best they could. From a now unknown base they sent one ship, perhaps more, in and out of the craggy fiords of the Panhandle, dickering with the Indians for the land furs coming along aboriginal trade routes out of the interior of British Columbia. They had company at times—a government steamer, the *Saginaw,* which was taking soundings in some of the channels.

The commander of the *Saginaw* was Richard W. Meade, Jr., who had become friendly with Ralston in San Francisco. Meade disliked his Alaskan assignment and hoped that Ralston could prevail on the admiral in charge of the Department of the Pacific to relieve him. As a bit of flattery in aid of his cause he gave the name Ralston to a mile-long island in the Lynn Canal 27 miles northwest of present Juneau.[11] The name still clings, though whether or not the gesture helped Meade win his transfer does not appear.*

A more popular region for exploitation than the Panhandle was the

---

*More would-be flattery: on September 15, 1869, the territorial governor of Colorado, Edward McCook, wrote Ralston that he had named a creek near Denver for him so that Ralston would live forever on the maps of Colorado.[12] This was arrant nonsense, as McCook must have known. The creek, already firmly inscribed on Colorado maps, had been named in 1850 for a mixed blood Cherokee Indian, Lewis Ralston. What the two incidents do indicate is that varied people in widely scattered places felt that Ralston's goodwill was worth cultivating.

Pribilof Island group north of the Aleutian chain. Until the purchase, the fur seal fisheries there had been closed to outsiders. Now a rush began. The first small ship to arrive, early in 1868, was one that had been outfitted in San Francisco by R. H. Waterman and banker John Parrott. Parrott's share of the pelts, gleaned in a few months by dousing the Indians with liquor, sold for $60,000. Such a bonanza naturally invited competition.

Ralston's entry in the Pribilof race (or perhaps the entry of the North Pacific Fur Company) was the ship *Lewis Perry,* captained by one of the bank's leading employees, Edney S. Tibbey. Tibbey left San Francisco in March, 1868, and returned in February, 1870.[13] How well he fared is unknown. He must have picked up something, for the total harvest of Alaskan seals in 1868 alone has been estimated at more than 200,000 animals.

The slaughter was so dreadful, indeed, and the rivalry so ferocious that Congress began considering bills designed to bring order to the trade. Several of the bloodied competitors thereupon decided to form an organization that would promote monopolistic hunting under the supervision of the government. This organization, the Alaska Commercial Company, naturally hoped to be the monopoly to whom the rights would be granted. Among its incorporators were John Parrott and two members of the expired California Russian Company, John F. Miller and Louis Sloss. Neither Ralston nor any other founder of the North Pacific Fur Company was included. They intended to apply for the franchise on behalf of North Pacific.

Miller was elected president of Alaska Commercial and sent to Washington to lobby for the necessary bill. Since Ralston had a stake in seeing the act passed, Miller reported the course of events to him and solicited Ralston's help in urging the San Francisco Chamber of Commerce to lend its weight. Unctuously he appealed to Ralston's affection for the city. Miller's whole intent in backing the legislation, he said, was the good that would come to all San Francisco if the city emerged as the leading fur mart of North America.[14]

The bill passed. Under its terms an exclusive privilege to harvest 100,000 seals a year would be awarded to whatever company submitted the highest bid to the secretary of the treasury. Thirteen firms, the North Pacific Fur Company among them, made offerings. The low bidder turned out to be Alaska Commercial Company. But then one of those mysterious changes that occurred so often during the Grant administration took place. Alaska Commercial was allowed to revise its bid and, lo, it emerged as the winner.[15] At that the North Pacific Fur Company passed out of existence as quietly as had the trailblazing California Russian organization. For Ralston and his unlucky associates there was to be no pot of gold on those fog-bound shores.

ANOTHER QUEST—perhaps running dogfight is a better metaphor—
was for a monopoly in quicksilver, an essential ingredient in recovering
free gold and silver from placer sand or crushed ore by amalgamation.
The story begins in the mountains fifteen miles southeast of San Jose.
There in 1845 a Mexican cavalry officer, Andrés Castillero, stumbled
onto a deposit of cinnabar. He promptly applied to the governor of
Mexican California for a mining grant covering the mineralized area
and named the place New Almaden, after the fabulously rich Almadén
quicksilver mine of Spain.

New Almaden soon fell into the hands of a group of English traders
then living in Mexico. Among them were three men destined to become
incorporators of The Bank of California, the brothers William and
Joseph Barron and one of their clerks, Thomas Frederick Bell. The
mine began production in 1850, a great boon to California gold seekers
who had been paying $100 a flask for imported mercury. It was a boon,
too, for Barron & Company, which became the chief distributing agency
of mercury in all North America.[16]

Any valuable property whose title was based on a Mexican grant was
bound to draw attacks in California during the 1850s and 1860s. In the
case of New Almaden the plot grew complex. Through chicanery two
different American companies acquired title to separate Mexican land
grants in the vicinity of the mine. Each hoped to have the title to the
mine declared invalid. That done, it would try to have the bounds of its

*The dedication of the Enriquita Quicksilver Mine, part of the New Almaden
complex, attracted this festive crowd in 1859.*

own grant extended so as to embrace the coveted quicksilver claim.

The controversies grew so fierce that in November, 1858, the attorney general of the United States intervened and ordered mining to cease until determination of title could be reached. The intricate maneuvers that followed are irrelevant here, except for the ending.[17] In 1864 the New Almaden company agreed for a consideration of $1.7 million to amalgamate with its leading contender, the New York Quicksilver Mining Company, headed by Samuel Butterworth. The company that resulted kept the name New Almaden. Although the Barrons retained a substantial interest in the property, Butterworth became the president. Nominal capital was set at $10 million. Ralston handled the financial arrangements through The Bank of California. Because of that involvement, Ralston also figured largely in the mine's subsequent attempts to control quicksilver production throughout California.

At this point it becomes necessary to backtrack to another group of cinnabar deposits located high in rough, parched, lonesome mountains some ninety miles southeast of New Almaden. Those claims had been discovered in 1851 by three Mexican cowboys roaming a particularly inhospitable part of the area known as Panoche Grande.

An opportunist named Vincente Gomez sought to grab the deposits by swearing, probably falsely, that in 1844 he had been issued a grant to the area by Manuel Micheltorena, then governor of Mexican California. On December 23, 1857, Gomez sold his Panoche Grande claim, as he called it, to William McGarrahan, a San Francisco grocer, for $1,000. At the time of making the purchase McGarrahan was well aware that the title was subject to question.

On January 28, 1858, five weeks after the McGarrahan purchase, the Barrons formed what they called the New Idria Mining Company, after the famed Idria quicksilver mine in what was, in Ralston's time, the Austrian province of Carniola, now Yugoslavia.* With much more capital at their command than McGarrahan had, they were able to buy the "rights" of several squatters who were working in the Panoche Grande district and begin operating on a large scale.[18] Their timing was fortunate, for when the attorney general closed New Almaden later in the year, they were able to step up production at New Idria enough so that their distribution agency, Barron & Co., did not suffer unduly.

In 1861, McGarrahan formed the Panoche Grande Quicksilver Mining Company, issued several million dollars' worth of stock, and scattered handfuls of the certificates among senators, congressmen, and influential bureaucrats in the General Land Office, a branch of the

---

*At the time of his death Ralston owned 69 shares of New Idria stock, valued at $1,200 a share. The date on which he acquired the shares is unknown.

Department of the Interior. This stock would have value only if McGarrahan's Mexican-derived title to the land was confirmed by the Commission on Private Land Claims. It was confirmed. According to testimony offered years later by Congressman (later General) Daniel Sickles of New York, President Lincoln himself thereupon ordered that a United States patent to the land be issued to the applicant.[19]

The officials of New Idria were equal to the occasion. By bribery—so it was charged later on the floor of Congress—they persuaded clerks in the land office to filch the voluminous records of the case from the files and then to mutilate the patent itself by obliterating the signatures and writing across the face of the document, "Suspended, March 1863."[20] This crude hanky-panky turned out to be needless, however, for New Idria also appealed the ruling of the land commissioner to the Supreme Court. The justices decided that Gomez' title, and hence McGarrahan's, was invalid. New Idria's occupancy of the land was thus confirmed.

Throughout these years western miners held the mineral rights to the ground they worked only by the sufferance of the federal government. Since no method existed whereby they could obtain full title, tens of thousands of them were, in effect, ordinary trespassers on the public domain. This absurdity was rectified in 1866 by a law that allowed, among other things, miners to buy from the government, at $5.00 an acre, the claims they were working. Hoping to perfect its title, the New Idria company promptly sent $2,400 to the U.S. land commissioner to pay for the 480 acres it had been holding since 1858. McGarrahan, making much of the patent Lincoln had authorized, countered by asking Congress to pass a bill for his relief (had he not been grievously wronged?) that would allow him to purchase, for $1.25 an acre, the 17,000 acres covered by his outlawed grant. All this placed the government in a dilemma, for obviously both patents could not be allowed.

For Butterworth, the Barrons, and Billy Ralston the timing of the conflict was inopportune. Production of quicksilver had increased to the point that prices were on the verge of a drastic decline. Hoping to forestall the collapse, the managers of New Almaden, New Idria, Barron & Co., and the Redington mine north of San Francisco Bay, plus a few smaller operators, were drawing up an agreement to limit output.[21] The Bank of California, which had helped bring the operators together—it handled financial matters for most of them—watched over the proceedings like an anxious midwife.

If Congress heeded McGarrahan's appeal, both New Idria and the pricing agreement would collapse. Consequently Ralston also watched McGarrahan with anxiety. He asked for and received regular Washington reports from one of California's congressmen, Samuel Axtell, and from Senator Eugene Casserly. Two lobbyists, Christopher J. Hutchinson and Francis A. Smith, added their accounts.[22]

Strangest of all was a man named Warrick Martin. Martin appeared out of nowhere on August 10, 1869, stating by letter that he had befriended Ralston in Louisiana when Billy had been a steamboat clerk and adding that he could help him again in the McGarrahan affair. For, said Martin, he was investigating graft cases for the government on a contingency basis. He was to receive half of whatever the government collected from culprits he exposed. He had $500 million worth of fraud cases ready for the courts and should realize at least $50 million from them. If Ralston wished, he would add the McGarrahan fraud to his list. Meanwhile, continued Martin, he needed a small loan so that he could continue his work—say $10,000.

Billy complied. He authorized Martin to draw on him for $10,000 and within less than a year added $2,000 more. Martin produced nothing (his graft cases all collapsed), but he kept wheedling until 1874, when Ralston finally exploded and cut him off.[23]

By using stock in Panoche Grande as a bribe, McGarrahan several times pushed a bill for his relief through the House, only to have it stalled in one or another of the Senate committees to which it was referred. Bribery by New Idria was used in setting up those blockades.

The matter became a national scandal in 1870. One of McGarrahan's opponents was Secretary of the Interior Jacob Cox, one of the few honest men in the Grant administration. When Grant expressed himself strongly in favor of McGarrahan, Cox, who was already at odds with the president over other matters, resigned in outrage. Newspapers hostile to the administration made capital of the tempest. The New York *World* accused Grant of driving away a good man in order to abet a fraud. The *Nation* declared that the president was forever soiled: "The wreck of his fame is a national misfortune."

The bank, too, suffered stain, for McGarrahan's supporters (whether bribed or not) made much of his being a lone but dauntless individual battling for his rights against soulless corporations. "The New Idria Company," roared Representative J. B. Beck of Kentucky in February, 1871, "is in fact The Bank of California, with its millions of capital, a corporation which runs the state of Nevada, controls the press and opinions of the Pacific Slope, which, if successful in this case, holds an absolute monopoly of the quicksilver mines of the continent."[24]

Following the lead of such congressmen, the muckraking New York *Sun* printed scurrilous attacks on the bank, not all of them restricted to the mercury affair. The New York *Evening Post* added other uncomplimentary tales. Each morning during the 1869 debates someone placed marked copies of the Washington *Chronicle,* which supported McGarrahan, on the desks of every senator and congressman in the capitol building.[25]

Although Ralston's associates were deeply concerned about the effect of the attacks on him, he weathered the storm.[26] The uproar, he wrote one acquaintance, was motivated by small-minded people— plural, not just McGarrahan—who had personal grudges to gratify.[27] Yet neither he nor the bank nor the New Idria company could have taken much pride in the victory they won. Though New Idria's title was indeed superior to McGarrahan's, the company had not depended on rightness to carry its case. Government being what it was, perhaps the mine owners had to resort to devious tactics to save their property— just as Ralston had been forced to stoop in Sacramento in order to obtain good insurance laws for the benefit of the Pacific Insurance Company. Even so, as historian Claude Bowers suggested when commenting on the McGarrahan case in his study of the Grant administration, *The Tragic Era,* corruption is indeed rife when evil can be fought only with evil.[28]

THROUGHOUT THESE YEARS Comstock silver engrossed Ralston's attention even more than did New Idria's mercury. The great lode tantalized with promises. Although most of the ore in the district grew leaner after 1863, there was always one mine that kept renewing hope for all. First it was the Yellow Jacket, which Sharon had managed to absorb for The Bank of California late in 1864. Then, as the Yellow Jacket's profits began to slip, the Hale & Norcross and its neighbor to the north, the Savage, boomed into prominence. From 1866 into 1868 the pair paid out $4.1 million in dividends while producing stacks of gold and silver bars worth $10.2 million.

Such figures seemed to bear out the predictions made by William Ashburner and Baron von Richthofen that as the Comstock's shafts probed deeper, additional bonanzas would be revealed. Formidable blockades stood in the way, however—stifling heat, poor ventilation, and repeated gushes of water. Unless those obstacles could be overcome, the future would not be as limitless as stockbrokers kept saying when urging shares on their clients.

In the opinion of Adolph Sutro, a man as persistent in his own way as William McGarrahan, the intertwined problems could be unknotted with a single massive drainage tunnel. He possessed few scientific qualifications for making such an assertion. Tall, swarthy, and muscular, he had arrived in San Francisco from his native Aachen, Germany, when he was twenty-one.[29] After selling cigars and tobacco with moderate success for half a dozen years, he had joined the gold rush to the Fraser River in British Columbia. Though his venture was not profitable, it put the fever of stampeding into his blood, and he tried again in Nevada. There, on the banks of the Carson River at the mouth of Six-

Adolph Sutro fought long and stubbornly to break what he considered to be The Bank of California's Comstock monopoly.

Mile Canyon, he built a small stamp mill, one of many in the area.

From riding up and down Six-Mile to sell his services to the mine owners, Sutro learned of their problems with water and ventilation. He noted the topography of the steeply rising land and watched early efforts to punch inadequate drainage tunnels into the workings from the side hills. Like a handful of other visionaries, he concluded that the problem could be solved only by a huge tunnel that would run from the floor of Carson Valley 3.9 miles into the mountains and intersect the lode at a depth of approximately 1,700 feet.

Unlike the other dreamers, Sutro acted. He persuaded the state of Nevada to grant him the necessary franchises, and then went to Ralston for advice about corporate organization and finance. Ralston helped him with his prospectus and then persuaded such influential men as Senator William M. Stewart of Nevada and geologist Louis Janin, Jr., to act as directors of the tunnel company that Sutro incorporated in July, 1865.[30] Billy was not ready, however, to back the scheme with Bank of California money. What he hoped was that Sutro could raise the necessary funds in the East and in Europe. That is to say, he wanted the tunnel to succeed for the sake of the Comstock and ultimately of San Francisco, but he was not convinced enough of its feasibility to risk his depositors' money on it.

The bank's moral support was enough, nevertheless, to stimulate Sutro's energies. After a year of effort he persuaded twenty-three of the leading mines of the Comstock to sign contracts agreeing to pay him, in the event that he drained their workings, $2.00 a ton for all the ore they mined. To that fee they promised to add smaller sums for using the bore to transport men, ore, timber, and waste rock between the sites of their work and the outside. On his part Sutro guaranteed to raise $3 million by April, 1867, and to begin work promptly thereafter.

Armed with letters of recommendation—Ralston gave him one to The Oriental Bank of London[31]—Sutro traveled to Washington by way of Panama. Aided by Stewart he prevailed on Congress to grant his tunnel company a right-of-way through the public domain. That technicality completed, he moved on to New York, meanwhile sending reports about his progress to Ralston.[32]

In New York he was set back hard. The financiers to whom he applied for help pointed out the damaging fact that no westerners were supporting the plan with cash. To remedy the defect Sutro hurried back to Nevada. There he talked the legislature into giving the project its stamp of approval in the form of a memorial to Congress asking for federal support. He also prevailed on the directors of eleven mines to pledge $600,000 of the $3 million he needed and to extend by one year his deadline for raising the balance.

So far, so good. But suddenly, on June 7, 1867, the stockholders of the Crown Point mine, most of them closely associated with The Bank of California, refused at their annual meeting to ratify their directors' pledge of $75,000 to the tunnel company.[33] At about that same time Senator Stewart resigned from the tunnel company's board of directors.

Completely astounded, Sutro looked for an explanation. He thought he found it in the formation, also in June, 1867, of the Union Milling and Mining Company. Its directors, too, were closely associated with The Bank of California.

What had happened was this. There were more custom mills in the vicinity of the Comstock than there was profitable ore to support them. In May, 1866, the little Swansea, unable to repay money loaned it by William Sharon of The Bank of California, submitted to foreclosure. Others followed suit. By May, 1867, the bank owned seven or eight small properties that it did not wish to operate and that no one was willing to take off its hands.

Seeking a solution, D. O. Mills and Billy Ralston crossed the Sierra to consult with their Virginia City representative. Of necessity, since his generosity with loans had created the problem, Sharon had a plan ready for them. Would it not be well, he suggested, for a group of wealthy San Franciscans to put together a company capable of absorbing the properties? The new owners would move as much of the machinery as was practicable down to the Carson River, where water could be used for motive power. Hauling ore down the hill to the relocated mills would undoubtedly be cheaper than lifting cordwood up the mountain by ox power for creating steam.

If the new company also purchased the two mines the bank controlled, the Yellow Jacket and the Crown Point, it could benefit from its own economies by grinding their ore. If those mines did not produce enough ore to keep the mills working at capacity, the company could acquire additional ones. Sharon already had his eye on the several likely prospects, the Chollar-Potosi, the Bullion, the Kentuck, and the Hale & Norcross. The first two could probably be obtained quite cheaply by purchasing stock that had been forfeited through the original owners' refusal to pay assessments. Since the last-named was in bonanza, it would cost more.

All this added up to considerable risk. Before taking the jump, Sharon's listeners wanted reasonable assurance that the mines they acquired could continue operating. What about floods in the lower workings, for instance?

Except on the northern reaches of the lode, where the soggy Ophir was located, the problem of water, Sharon said, was no longer so acute. The mines he had named lay farther south. Their deepening shafts seemed to be entering drier ground, and, besides, powerful new pumps capable of handling unprecedented flows of water were being developed in San Francisco.[34]

If that proved so, then obviously there was no need to burden the mines with pledges and contracts with Adolph Sutro for a tunnel that might take years to reach the workings. The Crown Point made the reasoning overt, to Sutro at least, by canceling its agreement with the tunnel company. Senator Stewart clinched the point by resigning from the company's board of directors. Almost simultaneously the Union Mill and Mining Company took legal shape. Its chief stockholders were Sharon, Mills, and Ralston. Among the company's other five directors, three—W. E. Barron, Thomas Bell, and Alvinza Hayward —were principal stockholders in The Bank of California.

Sutro steadfastly refused to believe that changed conditions on the lode had anything to do with the bank's breach of faith. He was convinced that Ralston and the others were deliberately stealing his thunder. In a bombastic pamphlet published in September, 1866, the promoter had predicted that his tunnel would make Virginia City and Gold Hill obsolete, for he would establish in their stead a new milling complex and town beside the Carson River, near the portal to his great bore. What need then for towns high on the windswept mountainside? Virginia City and Gold Hill were, according to him, as good as dead.

Naturally, Sutro's argument continued, neither the business houses up on the hill nor the bank that battened on them liked the prospect. Accordingly they had attacked him. Their strategy was to ape his economic foresight by building new mills in the Carson Valley but at the same time to keep the archaic towns on Mount Davidson flourishing for their own selfish purposes. To that duplex end they had fomented among merchants, mine owners, and financiers a diabolical plot to deprive him of support.

Although Sutro poured out these convictions in pamphlet after pamphlet, he never proved that a formal conspiracy existed.[35] Probably none did. Visions of monopoly, however, did dance through the imaginations of Ralston and his associates. One boost to their speculative spirits came from a slight upturn in the Comstock's mineral production—from $12 million in 1866 to $14 million in 1867. Hoping that the figures signaled an end to the slow decline of the past years, investors grew suddenly frenzied. Stock prices soared; the number of sales made by stockbrokers in 1867 doubled those of 1866. Sharon gave another fillip to the furor by coaxing a special session of the Nevada legislature to enact new tax laws favorable to the Comstock mines.[36]

Amidst this rising fever the Union Mill and Mining Company set about consolidating its position. First it reduced, both through foreclosure and purchase, the excessive number of the Comstock's highly competitive mills. By 1869 it had acquired seventeen. Some it closed. Others it adapted to serve as auxiliaries to its riverside operations.

In order to find ore enough for filling the voracious maws, the company (or men connected with the company) acquired the mines Sharon had recommended. As matters developed, his record as a seer was well short of perfect. Although the Kentuck produced well, the Bullion did not. Even worse was the Hale & Norcross. The battle to gain control there shot stock prices as high, in March 1868, as $2,900 a share. In spite of that Sharon finally won command, installed a handpicked board of directors—and then learned that bonanza had given way to borasca. Within six months stock values had tumbled to $41.50 a share.[37]

234

Although the new owners of the Hale & Norcross took only 16,500 tons of low-grade ore from the property during the balance of 1868, the situation in general was favorable to the Union Milling and Mining Company. Its operators were able to make highly favorable contracts with themselves as owners of mines whose ore needed treatment. No concerned outsider existed to demand a close check on the amount of bullion that the mills sent back to the mines after reduction. No impartial auditor examined the cost sheets that formed the basis of the milling company's charges. Thus Sharon, as manager of Union Mill and Mining, was able to pay himself and his associates good dividends from the beginning.

The arrangement naturally suggested the desirability of acquiring more mines and more mills. This the company did. On gaining control of a mine, it placed complaisant men on the board of directors. (John D. Fry, Sharon's close friend and Ralston's father-in-law, made a fortune while serving as a director of more than a dozen Comstock mines.) When a mill that the Union company wanted proved resistant, the Sharon-manipulated mines starved it into submission by refusing to send ore to it.[38] The Bank of California added to the pressures by the way it placed its loans.

Within the ever-expanding arch of this rainbow, Sutro's projected tunnel cast a very distant shadow, one that would become dangerous only if the promoter found large sums of money. Aware by now that private sources of money were not likely to heed him, Sutro shifted his appeal to the federal government and asked Congress for the sort of subsidy then being awarded to ambitious railroads throughout the West. The directors of the major Comstock mines checked him by sending telegrams to Washington stating that the tunnel was unnecessary and unwanted. To Sutro this opposition was proof of a conspiracy and he denounced it far and wide as such. To the ring whose center was the Union Mill and Mining Company, it was one more small incident on their march toward mastery of the entire Comstock.

For Ralston the dazzling vision necessitated piling heavy financial commitments on top of his wide array of other expensive dreams. Still unconsidered is the boldest of these—a project for controlling, for his and the bank's benefit, the new growth patterns of San Francisco, even at the cost of uprooting his own home atop Rincon Hill.

CHAPTER 17

The City Shapers

From his hilltop home at 324 Fremont Street, Billy Ralston could see very clearly the dilemma that faced his dynamic city. Each section—residential, commercial, industrial—had become so overcrowded that it had to find new space somewhere. The men who proved able to control the expansion—and Ralston was determined to be among them—would not only benefit financially but would also leave behind a refashioned city as their legacy.

One of the most unstable areas lay to the northwest of his home, between the base of Rincon Hill and the broad diagonal of Market Street, a section that the pioneers of '49 had misnamed Happy Valley. After the shanty dwellers there had moved out, industry had moved in, reclaiming the tidal swamps near the bay front so as to be near the new docks and warehouses south of Market Street. One feature of the new order was a gas plant (in which Ralston was a major stockholder) that manufactured illuminating gas from coal and then dumped its tarry residue into the bay. Adjoining the gas plant on its inland side was the tallest man-made structure in San Francisco, a shot tower 200 feet high built in 1864 by Thomas Selby, a fabricator of lead and the father-in-law of Andrew Jackson Ralston. Since Rincon Hill was only 100 feet high, the top of the tower interfered with Ralston's view when he looked across Market Street toward the ornate new building occupied by The Bank of California.[1]

Still farther inland, pinched between Market Street and Rincon Hill, was a clutter of small foundries, livery stables, sailors' boardinghouses, lumberyards, workers' homes, and the small shops that met the district's needs. This sprawl extended for several long blocks to the vicinity of the abandoned Spanish mission of San Francisco de Asís, generally called Dolores. There another cluster of factories, Ralston's woolen mills

236

The shanties of Happy Valley (foreground, looking north from Rincon Hill) were soon replaced by early industrial plants.

among them, was grouped around the marshaling yards of the San Francisco & San Jose Railroad. The cluttered section between the shot tower and the rail yards was expendable and was being eyed hungrily by businessmen in the congested urban core north of Market Street. Why not hop across Market Street, in spite of its unusual width, and build new banks, brokerage houses, hotels, and fashionable shops in what had once been called Happy Valley?

If that happened, then the builders of new factories would have to search elsewhere for room. To Ralston it seemed evident that the best place to look was the Potrero Nuevo district on the opposite, or southern, side of Rincon Hill.

Potrero Nuevo had many allures. There was room for docks along the bay shore, and though the land looked unattractive—some was swampy and some was warted with sand hills—all could be leveled and filled, a speculator's dream. Railroads were another possibility. Because the San Francisco & San Jose Railroad entered the city by an inland route over the San Bruno hills, there was room for more tracks near the bay shore. Two such lines were already taking shape on paper. One, the Western Pacific (which had no connection with today's road of the same name), was designed to connect San Francisco with Sacramento by circling the southern arm of the bay. The other, the Southern Pacific, had been incorporated in 1865 to thrust south to San Diego and then veer east to a connection with a recently chartered transcontinental, the Atlantic and Pacific. If either the Western or Southern Pacific—or both—became a reality, its managers could surely be persuaded to build their depots, yards, and machine shops in Potrero Nuevo just south of Rincon Hill.

A gas plant, shot tower, and new commercial buildings north of the hill, rail yards and factories south of it—to anyone visualizing the scene from Fremont Street, Rincon Hill must have seemed like an anachronism, an irrelevant island of gentility amidst a rising sea of industrialism. Besides, Ralston had a new enthusiasm. He had bought country acreage twenty-two miles south of the city at a place he called Belmont. There he could indulge his passions for raising fine horses and building yet another dream house. So in spite of Lizzie's dismay (of which more in the next chapter), he decided to sell the Fremont Street house, which was only five years old, and rent temporary quarters in the city until the country mansion was finished.

He easily found a buyer, Asbury Harpending, who after the transaition soon turned into a kind of private demon, leading Ralston on from one wild speculation to another. Harpending, the reader will recall, was the Confederate sympathizer who had been imprisoned briefly during the Civil War for his harebrained scheme to seize California gold bound for New York. After his release, Asbury had prospered as a mine developer in Kern County. In 1866 he returned to the city and married, aged 27. Able now to afford a plush home, he snapped up Ralston's Fremont Street offering. Billy then turned to reshaping the city as he had envisioned it from the hilltop.

He had already made a start. The year before, in 1865, he had put together a syndicate to buy what was known as the de Haro land claim. The intent of the purchasers was to have the claim recognized by the federal government and then manipulate its boundaries in such a way that it would embrace the parts of Potrero Nuevo that they desired. They would then order all squatters out of the area, subdivide it, and sell the lots to the new industrialists.

The hitch in the scheme was the dubious legality of the de Haro tract. Many of the purported Spanish and Mexican land grants that pretended to embrace various sections of San Francisco were fraudulent, and all had been challenged in front of the U.S. Board of Land Commissioners. Even before Ralston became interested in the de Haro grant, the commissioners had ruled that its title was clouded. The purchasers knew, accordingly, that they may have purchased nothing more than shadows. To strengthen their chances, so it was charged later, Ralston worked assiduously to put a complaisant friend, Charles Felton, into the United States Senate, where a special bill (like the one sought by William McGarrahan to confirm his title to the New Idria quicksilver mines) might be passed in favor of the buyers. The effort failed. Nothing remained then but to appeal to the Supreme Court of the United States.[2]

While the case was making its slow way upward through the legal thickets, Ralston produced, like a huge rabbit from a hat, another attraction for industries contemplating a move to the south. This was the Hunter's Point Dry Dock.

Hunter's Point was the bay end of a gentle ridge that formed the southern boundary of Potrero Nuevo some four miles south of Rincon Hill. The area was unique for that section of the bay in that the water was deep enough for ships to lie to almost beside the shore. The backbone of the ridge, moreover, was composed not of sand, like so many of the peninsula's hills, but of solid rock. In 1864 an engineer named Alexander Von Schmidt suggested carving an artificial basin out of the easily approached snout of the ridge and using the resultant bowl as a dry dock for repairing large vessels—a facility San Francisco lacked.

Ralston responded with enthusiasm. He bought the necessary land, prevailed on the directors of The Bank of California to finance a con-

Ralston's huge dry dock at Hunter's Point, completed in 1868, filled a major need long felt by maritime San Francisco.

struction company dominated by himself, and in September, 1866, at about the time he sold his home to Harpending, he set his men to gouging out a hollow 421 feet long, 120 feet wide, and 22 feet deep, space enough to hold all but one or two of the largest vessels then afloat.[3]

Though costs were projected at $1.2 million, the sum did not seem excessive. Ralston's close connection with the California Steam Navigation Company and with Ben Holladay's proliferating shipping interests assured him of their business. He probably could count on the Pacific Mail Steamship Company as well, even though he had been

Rincon Hill (left foreground) and the Market Street diagonal show clearly in this 1868 bird's-eye view of the city.

intermittently battling that potent concern ever since his days in Panama. As he knew, the company was seeking a mail subsidy from the United States government so that it could expand its scheduled services as far as China, and there was no place other than Hunter's Point on either side of the Pacific where its fleet would be able to find adequate services.

The debris blasted from the excavation was used as fill to supply foundations for the small community of workers that would be attached to the dry dock. At the time the spot was isolated enough to look like a separate village. Ralston never conceived of it as such, however.

In his mind the long stretch between Hunter's Point and the city would soon be filled with an orderly array of planned businesses. The backbone of the expansion, as Ralston envisioned it, would be a wide boulevard running from the financial center of the city southward through the Potrero to the vicinity of Hunter's Point.

There would be difficulties. The main one resulted from the radical shift in the city's layout that had been created years before by the wide diagonal of Market Street. North of Market, the streets ran due north and south, or east and west. On the south side of Market they slanted so as to run parallel to Market's course. The blocks just south of Market were not only askew in respect to those in the north but were also much larger and broken here and there by erratic subsidiary streets.

Ralston wanted his grand connecting boulevard to begin at the lower end of Montgomery Street and strike due south past the inland (western) tip of Rincon Hill. Such a route would avoid the construction difficulties that would otherwise be occasioned by the hill. But in order to drive due south, the new boulevard—he called it Montgomery South—would have to smash through the slanting blocks beyond Market Street without regard for patterns already established there.

The gain, as he saw it, would outweigh the disadvantages. The congestion of the city's urban core would be relieved as financial houses, fine hotels, and elegant shops crossed Market to new locations beside Montgomery South. Then, as the traveler continued south, parallel to the bay shore, the scene would shift from merchandising to industry— factories, rail yards, and the shipbuilding works Ralston believed would spring up around Hunter's Point. No other city in the world, he declared, would have a boulevard equal to Montgomery South. Meantime he would find a material reward for his vision in the sale of strategic lots he acquired alongside the grand new street.

Clearing a way for Montgomery South would entail condemning great deal of property, and of course only the government could do that. Ralston accordingly had the necessary legislation prepared and submitted to the Board of Supervisors of the City and County of San Francisco on October 29, 1866.[4] The board reacted by appointing a five-man committee of its own members to study the proposal and make a report.

A series of hearings at the city hall during March and April, 1867, drew forth such vehement protest from citizens whose property stood in the way of the juggernaut that the committee delayed its report until September 23, 1867. On that day it presented a lukewarm 3–2 recommendation in favor of the extension. The full Board of Supervisors accepted the findings by an equally narrow margin, 7–5. Not so Mayor Coon. On October 14 he vetoed the bill, pointing out that the proposed street would chop the blocks it crossed into unmanageable gores. If other extensions followed, unjustified confusion would result.

*This official 1851 map (the dark line marks the original shore) shows
the break in street patterns that hampered city planning.*

When the bill went back to the board, a mysterious change of mind
took place. The mayor's veto was quickly overridden by the necessary
two-thirds majority, a vote of 9–3 as compared to the earlier tally of
7–5. Montgomery South now seemed to be a viable entity.[5]

Early in 1868 surveyors and assessors moved into the area to determine the exact route of the street and the amounts that should be paid
for the condemned property. It was slow, complex work. Every foot of
the way was contested by leagues of property owners whose lawyers

stormed through the courts hoping to produce a blizzard of injunctions that would halt the extension.[6] The Catholic Church, which owned a key building in the section, became a particularly obstreperous opponent. Then, to top the difficulties, the state supreme court rejected the de Haro claim. At that point Montgomery South seemed very much in danger of dying.

As Ralston contemplated the wreckage, wondering how to salvage part of the dream, he remembered hearing that Asbury Harpending was also busily purchasing property along the south side of Market Street but a little farther east than were the lots Ralston wanted. Curious about Harpending's intentions, he asked the young man to meet him at the bank one summer morning in 1868. Even Harpending, whose tales of his financial prowess never suffered from understatement, admitted to being awed.

Ralston thoroughly charmed him. In his memoirs, written more than forty years after the event, Harpending left this picture of the banker as he remembered him from that meeting.

"He wanted to see his state and city great, prosperous, progressive, conspicuous throughout the world for enterprise and big things. I think it was this imagination, this ambition that kept hurrying him into one big undertaking after another, many of which were way ahead of their time. . . . Nothing seemed to disturb his imperturbably good humor. He was at once the best winner or loser in the world—could pick up or drop a million with equal gaiety and nonchalance. He always smiled in conversation, but in moments of repose his features settled into an expression that was half-thoughtful, half-sad. . . . He had wonderful manners, frank, cordial, magnetic, and handed out the same quality to everyone alike. He avoided, either by design or inclination, all the pomposity and circumstance of greatness."[7]

During their conversation it developed that Harpending, too, envisioned a new financial and shopping section south of Market, and a new boulevard that would thrust from there on to the bay. Unlike Ralston's street, however, Harpending's proposed avenue which he called New Montgomery Street, would not cut across established patterns but would veer southeast so as to run parallel to thoroughfares already in existence. After crossing Rincon Hill—Asbury said he had a plan for that, too—New Montgomery Street would continue directly to the bay, reaching the shore well north of Hunter's Point and within easy range of waterfront developments already under way.

Harpending says that he thought all this up by himself. More probably he was improving on the designs of a certain John Middleton, who owned bay shore land near the corner of First and Townsend streets, just south of Rincon Hill, where the Pacific Mail Steamship Company was building new wharves. The drawback to the site was the difficulty of moving goods and passengers back and forth to the center of the city. Teamsters either had to struggle over Rincon Hill's steep flanks or circle them. If a level, direct route could be provided, the value of dockside property, Middleton's included, would soar.

An ingenious schemer, Middleton had himself elected to the state legislature in the fall of 1867. There, by scandalous means, he prevailed on his fellow lawmakers to pass a bill authorizing the "modification" of the Second Street grade across Rincon Hill. Modification as interpreted by Middleton meant gouging a 75-foot canyon through the heart of a hill only 100 feet high. Although a few men like Thomas Selby, owner of the shot tower, protested the desecration, most of the hilltop residents accepted the cut as one of the inevitabilities of progress.[8]

One way through Rincon Hill was the unsightly Second Street cut. Ralston would have preferred leveling the entire barrier.

SOCIETY OF CALIFORNIA PIONEERS

What Harpending wanted to do was outdazzle Middleton, whose project he decried as "a sordid bit of real-estate roguery, carried through without a moment's thought of other people's rights." Because of the threatened cut, many of the monied people of the hill were scattering to other sections of the city, and real estate values were falling. Therefore, since the hill was neither useful any longer nor prohibitively expensive, why not remove it entirely, sacrificing his own newly purchased home along with the rest?

Exhilarated by the boldness of the idea, Ralston offered to become a partner in the project by purchasing a quarter interest in Harpending's real estate holdings south of Market Street. Or so Harpending recalled the division of interests forty years later.[9] Inasmuch as Ralston and his associates had also accumulated considerable property in which Harpending now became a sharer, and in view of the heavy expenditures looming ahead, the division may have been more evenly weighted. In any event, the two men began assiduously taking up options on the additional land they wanted.

Even nature helped them. At 8:00 A.M. on October 21, 1868, an earthquake shook the peninsula. Five persons were killed in San Francisco by falling bricks. Buildings on "made" (reclaimed) land suffered considerable damage.[10] The Bank of California lost the ornamental stone balustrade that enclosed its roof. Ralston calmed the terrified clerks and then ordered the balustrade replaced by one made of painted wood. False fronts of any sort were distasteful to him, but in this case he preferred pretense to maimings in the event of another tremor.

Several aftershocks followed. Afraid to go home, hundreds of terrified people camped for several days in the city's public squares. Whistling in the dark, a veteran real estate dealer, Charles Carter, declared that the effect on property values was negligible. Harpending tells matters differently in his memoirs. He says that Selim Woodworth, owner of a lot that Ralston and he particularly wanted, was so alarmed by the quake that he fled from the city. Just before leaving, Woodworth sold for $150,000 the land that a few days earlier he had been holding for half a million.[11]

Neither nature nor friendship could overcome sentiment, however. Banker Milton Latham, recently widowed, refused to leave the family home. To turn aside the importunities of his old friend, Billy Ralston, he asked a price that left the new partners "aghast," to use Harpending's word. Another banker, John Parrott (his bank would soon be absorbed by Latham's) was plain stubborn. He and others like him had believed, when building their homes on the hill or in the vicinity of South Park, that they were re-creating cherished forms of civilized living amidst the crudities of the new West. To Parrott the leveling of a long-established residential hill merely to gain easy access to a new industrial area was

The sharp earthquake of October 21, 1868, shook real estate values as well as buildings.

one of the insensitivities of those reckless times that should not be tolerated. Accordingly he refused even to meet the would-be purchasers.[12]

As a final resort the frustrated partners appealed to civic ambition. Let San Francisco issue $12 million in municipal bonds. Five million of the sum would be spent buying the hill—the Parrott and Latham properties could be condemned if the men stayed recalcitrant—and the remaining $7 million would be used for leveling the hump. The excavated material would be carted to the bay shore for reclaiming 200 blocks of swamp and tidelands southward from the new docks of the Pacific Mail Steamship Company. Everyone would benefit. The city could sell the "made" land along the bay shore for enough to redeem the bonds. Thereafter taxes on the lots would keep the municipal tills filled to overflowing. Middleton's Second Street cut, an abominable eyesore, would be swallowed by the leveling; business would have room in which to expand; and the men who had proposed the plan would profit from their vision by obtaining, before prices skyrocketed, choice lots on either side of the eventual line of New Montgomery Street.

To Ralston's surprise, the newspapers almost unanimously damned the plan. When bills authorizing the measure were presented to the state legislature—that many bonds could not be issued or that much land reclaimed without state permission—a great hue and cry arose about selfish interests and corruption. There was some cause. Forty years later Harpending admitted in his reminiscences that he had spent $35,000 to form what he called "treaties of alliance" with key members of the assembly. Ralston, he added, spent a great deal of time entertaining and charming state senators. Wasted money. Governor Henry Haight, brother of Lizzie Ralston's bridesmaid Sarah Haight, vetoed the measure, and that scheme, too, was dead.[13]

A healthy heir remained, however. During the slow progress of the legislation the two men spent $853,720 acquiring, through purchase and long-term leases, a choice rectangle that reached from Market Street southeast for 1,100 feet between Second and Third to Howard Street at the foot of Rincon Hill.[14] Though the hill had escaped them, they could at least develop that fine block according to their lights. Their idea was to raze all structures in the area and then run New Montgomery Street through the middle of the square as the axis for a carefully planned urban construction program.

They promised to surface the new avenue with the finest quality Stow wooden paving blocks, build drains and sewers, and maintain all this at their own expense for ten years. They also promised to build, at a cost of between $400,000 and $500,000 a fine hotel, to be named the Grand, on the south side of Market between Second and New Montgomery. On the ground floor of the Grand Hotel, they said, would be quarters for the finest shops in San Francisco. The rest of the land in the area would then be offered for sale at auction. Purchasers would have to agree that any buildings erected in the area would conform to the same exacting standards of architectural design that would govern the appearance of the hotel.

The entity created for handling the program was the New Montgomery Street Real Estate Company, formally incorporated on December 24, 1868. Its nominal capital was $7.5 million. Ralston was president, L. L. Treadwell was vice-president, Harpending was actuary. Among the directors was a man whom Ralston had made almost ubiquitous, his wife's foster father, J. D. Fry.

Unfortunately for themselves, they developed their plans just as San Francisco's postwar economic boom underwent a sudden cooling. Reaction to excess was one cause of the downswing. Another was the failure of a railroad scheme as grandiose as the Ralston-Harpending plan to level Rincon Hill.

The Central Pacific, it will be recalled, was a Sacramento corporation. Ever since it had demonstrated its vigor by breaching the Sierra, a fear had existed that it might not extend its facilities to San Francisco but instead would build its western terminus on the inland side of the bay. By 1868 the Southern Pacific was also showing signs of life. Suppose it, too, decided to locate its terminus at, say, Oakland. A harbor could be dredged out there or at nearby Goat (Yerba Buena) Island, and ocean liners would then go directly to those docks with only a passing whistle for San Francisco. Isolated at the tip of the western peninsula and deprived of both rail and sea commerce, the once proud city would dwindle into an anachronism.

No one in San Francisco was prepared to accept such a fate, of course. As noted earlier, the Western Pacific Railroad had been designed to capture transcontinental traffic by running its tracks from Sacramento south through Stockton to San Jose and then north beside the bay to San Francisco. By June, 1867, the partially built line was in the hands of the Central Pacific. Hoping to make sure that the Central Pacific used those tracks to the city's advantage, several prominent San Franciscans, Ralston among them, suggested that the state make available to it—and, more importantly, to the Southern Pacific—ample land south of Rincon Hill for docks, shops, yards, and depots.

The idea was sound, but its execution was hoggish. The bill that was presented to the legislature would have allowed the two railroads to buy for a mere $100 an acre a strip of tidelands eight miles long and up to a mile and a half wide—6,620 acres altogether. Since the railroads would need only a fraction of that amount for their own purposes, it seemed evident that they hoped to use the balance for speculation.

Alienate priceless waterfront to enrich a handful of connivers! San Francisco roared protest. Taken aback by the vehemence of the opposition, the legislators retreated into niggardliness. On March 30, 1868, they donated thirty acres to the Western Pacific and another thirty to the Southern Pacific, with the provision that each company spend $100,000 improving its swampy gift. The grant also imposed onerous restrictions on the railroads' access to the actual waterfront.[15]

The ordinary voters of San Francisco thought they had won a great victory. Not so investors in real estate. Their courage, already shaken by the earthquake, sank still lower. If the directors of the railroads were really considering placing their main facility on the inland side of the bay, the condition-hedged promise of thirty acres to each line was not likely to change their minds.

By May 6, 1869, when the New Montgomery Street Real Estate Company offered its first lots at auction, confidence in the future had collapsed. Bids were so low that auctioneer Maurice Dore, following Ralston's orders, withdrew the land from sale. But the pause, Billy insisted, would last a short time only. Harpending agreed. San Francisco was still the queen city of the West. To prove their faith they vowed to go ahead with digging sewers, paving New Montgomery Street, and building the Grand Hotel as if no hitch had occurred in their plans.[16]

Even men who knew Ralston well were dismayed. The poor showing at the auction was not the result of temporary whims. A new depression was creeping across the coastal states. After a brief upswing, the output of Comstock ore was dropping radically again. Moreover, many of Billy's other adventures—the North Bloomfield hydraulic mines, the Alaskan seal fisheries, the New Idria quicksilver company—were either bogged down in expensive development work or were under attack from the outside. Even romance was conspiring against him. The daughter of George Gordon, manager of the Ralston-controlled San Francisco and Pacific Sugar Refinery had eloped, and Gordon was so despondent that he was letting the business go to pieces.[17]

In spite of these discouragements, however, Ralston had launched two other extravaganzas—the building in the city of the most lavish theater west of the Mississippi and the creation at Belmont of a home that he was determined to make one of the showplaces of the world. To persist with New Montgomery Street, including the building of a half million dollar hotel, seemed, under the circumstances, like the wildest kind of recklessness—a recklessness that some acquaintances blamed on Harpending.

More probably the stimulation was mutual. For when had Ralston, even acting on his own, ever been cautious?

CHAPTER 18

Extravagances

In order to keep abreast of his maze of interests, Ralston drove himself relentlessly. According to one of his friends, A. A. Cohen, he arose at six o'clock every morning to study reports preparatory to inspecting one of the companies in which he held an interest or which had applied for a loan from the bank. During his examinations he visited not just the managers' offices but the workshops as well. If the factories belonged to one of his own companies he was able to call most of the laborers by their first names. Asbury Harpending put it thus: "As to the industrial classes, they simply worshipped Ralston. He was their constant provider, philosopher, and friend."[1]

He tried to finish the morning inspections in time to be at the bank by nine. From then until four or five in the afternoon he entertained a stream of business visitors. Afterwards he made appointments relative to his own affairs, until finally he had to rush off to a dinner that very often was a civic or philanthropic function rather than a relaxing meal. Frequently he had more appointments afterwards, so that by the time he sank into bed he had put in a sixteen-hour day.

He took good care of himself. Whenever he could, he swam in the cold waters of the bay. He grew fairly stout as the years advanced, though less so than many of the hearty feeders of the time. He drank sparingly. His nerves stayed sound; his capacity to concentrate showed n diminishing.

Needing occasional escape from his pressures, he found it in the related fascinations of raising fine horses and in erecting an opulent mansion at Belmont, twenty-two miles south of San Francisco. Originally the Belmont site had belonged to an Italian count named Leonetto Cipriani. Because the building trades in gold-rush California had been

*"Belmont," painted by George Albert Frost, shows Ralston's
country estate as it appeared in 1874.*

crude at best, Cipriani had fabricated a house in Italy in 1852 and had
shipped all 120 tons of it in carefully marked packages to San Francisco.
He hauled the pieces down the peninsula in wagons to a glen where
Diablo Canyon broke out of the oak-clad hills of the Coast Range.
There, on rising ground that commanded a spectacular view of the
southern arm of the bay, he reassembled the far-traveled domicile.[2]

In 1864 he offered land and house for sale. Ralston snapped them up
and christened the place Belmont. For awhile Cipriani's prefabricated
building grew like Topsy—additional rooms first, then wings, then
upper stories. Each increment suggested another. Finally, at about the
time that Billy's Montgomery South plans were crystallizing, he began
visualizing Belmont as one of the superlative mansions of the state.

Lizzie did not share his enthusiasm. Although she had never really liked San Francisco's brisk climate and raucous energies, she dreaded the isolation of Belmont even more. Besides, an iciness was congealing between Billy and her. His work absorbed him. She rarely saw him by day, and at night when he returned to the house they were renting on Leavenworth Street while Belmont was under construction, he was abstract and tired. Except for the children, to whom he was overly indulgent, he had little to share with his wife. Under the circumstances, their onerous social obligations were a relief, for the parties gave them something to do while they were together.

After an unknown number of flare-ups, interspersed with periods of chill, they decided it would be wise if they spent several months apart while reassessing their marriage. Excuses for the neighbors were readily manufactured. Ralston was a member of a commission charged with selecting California products—his Mission blankets among them—to be sent to the Paris international exhibition of 1867. Lizzie could be a sort of quasi-official shepherdess for the goods. And while she was in Paris, she told her acquaintances brightly, she would find a French tutor for the children. On March 30, 1867, they sailed on the ship *Golden Age*—Lizzie, Sam, William Jr., and little Emelita, not yet two. Two maids went with them.[3]

Architects had been summoned meanwhile to impose some sort of pattern on the sprawl at Belmont. What emerged after considerable reshaping was a mansion classified as Italian Renaissance, adapted to the Victorian tastes of the time—a style, in the words of one architectural historian, that accurately reflected "the heavy meals, strong drink, elaborate clothes, ornate furniture, flamboyant art, melodramatic plays, loud music, flowery speeches, and thundering sermons of mid-nineteenth-century America."[4] Belmont did not go the full route, however. Possibly because Ralston had an instinctive dislike of frills, the building escaped much of the overblown gingerbread that was popular throughout the country during the same period.

The extensions were constructed of redwood cut on the peninsula. Windows were numerous and large, many of them bays. The center section rose four stories high and was topped by a rectangular tower. Guests could draw up to the massive main doorway under an arched porte cochere. Out front were paths lined with rose bushes. Broad stone stairways dropped to descending levels of terraces where flowers bloomed in season, shrubbery hung heavy, and fountains sparkled amidst a mélange of huge Chinese vases and classical urns. Curved stone benches invited wanderers to pause for a view of the bay. Uncomfortable breezes were shut away in time by long lines of pines and cedars.

To the east of the house were a bowling alley and a tile-roofed Turkish bath. The stables were to the west. On the hillside in the back were greenhouses and a massive brick building where gas was generated from coal for illuminating hundreds of chandeliers. Eventually some of the gas was piped as far away as the hamlet of Belmont, a station on the San Francisco and San Jose Railroad. The servants lived in Little Belmont, a fifty-room dwelling located half a mile from the main house. Projected for the future was a private telegraph line (telephones had not yet been invented) to Ralston's office in The Bank of California.

Water was a problem. Ralston had to drill several wells more than 500 feet deep before he developed a modest supply. Eventually he built a reservoir in Diablo Canyon and hooked its stored waters to an elaborate system of fire plugs and sprinkler heads. In spite of the protection, the wooden stables burned in 1874 and had to be replaced with brick.

Belmont's mirrored ballroom, ornate chandeliers agleam with gas jets,
was the scene of San Francisco's most gala parties.

The verandah that embraced most of the house was modeled after
the promenade deck of a Mississippi River steamboat. Unlike those
windswept decks, however, the verandah at Belmont was enclosed with
glass and filled with greenery, wicker furniture brought directly from
China, and much bric-a-brac. Wide doors opened from it into an airy
drawing room; a library walled with leatherbound books chosen for
their looks rather than their content; a music room that contained a
grand piano handmade of Hawaiian koa wood by a master builder in
San Francisco; a huge pale-green ballroom with a high arched ceiling
and skylight; and a dining room capable of seating, at a pinch, 110

guests. An ingenious system of overhead ventilation kept fresh air moving through disguised louvers into each main room, a conditioning system far in advance of the times.[5]

In many ways the interior of the house echoed the prevailing tastes of post-Civil War America. Draperies were heavy and carpets thick. The window seats in the bays were covered with bright upholstery. Scattered about in convenient niches were classical-style busts on pedestals of Carrara marble. Paintings were large and framed in gilt. There were ostentatious displays of bronze objets d'art (both Oriental and European), of silver candelabra, silver tea services, silver goblets, and silver and cut-glass vases filled with flowers.

The house shimmered with mirrors. In the ballroom they rose from within inches of the floor almost to the curved ceiling, so that women could see their dancing feet. They were set at angles in the corners. Those on the opposite walls were not placed in a direct line with each other but were offset slightly so that the room took on an extraordinary sense of depth, with radiant suggestions of multiple joy and Cinderella-like unreality. The dining room, too, had its enormous mirror. Cunningly placed in its center was a clock that consisted, so far as the viewer could tell, of only golden hands and golden numerals. The smaller rooms had mirrors above their fireplaces. Reflections everywhere: were they an unconscious expression of vanity, or part of Ralston's never-outgrown effort to bedazzle and amuse?

He placed equally loving care on the woodwork, a trait that would emerge again in the hotels he built. The floors at Belmont, even some of those destined for carpets, were intricately inlaid and highly polished. The mantels above the fireplaces were carefully chosen for texture and grain, as were the commodes, bookcases, chairs, tables, and the cabinets in which china and silver were displayed. He demanded high quality even in wood soon to be covered by enamel—the legs of the window seats, the bannister of the staircase that mounted grandly to the second floor.

Lizzie and the children returned to this breathtaking new abode after ten months in Europe, landing in San Francisco on February 2, 1868. Presumably they went straight to Belmont. The house was not finished— Billy projected space enough for at least a hundred overnight guests —but thirty rooms were ready for occupancy, and after their long separation he was eager for her to see what he had wrought.

Their first notable party took place less than two months later. Representative of many gatherings that would follow, it was a sort of state welcome to distinguished visitors, and was designed to impress them with what had been accomplished in California during the past few years and what could still be done by men willing to bet their investment dollars on the West's future.

*Diplomat Anson Burlingame
was so intrigued by Belmont
that he bought land nearby,
thus giving his name
to a modern suburb.*

The principal guest on this initial occasion was Anson Burlingame. A noted orator and one-time congressman from Massachusetts, Burlingame had been appointed United States minister to China in 1861. Ralston had met him on his trips to and from his post. In 1866 he had whisked the traveler down the peninsula to see Belmont and the rolling lands surrounding the embryo mansion. Charmed, Burlingame had bought 1,000 acres adjoining Ralston's property. His intent, which speculator Ralston applauded, was to subdivide the land into sites for country estates.[6]

In November, 1867, Burlingame lost his job as minister. The Chinese, who liked him, promptly made him their own Envoy Extraordinary and Minister Plenipotentiary to the United States and the nations of Europe. Accompanied by several Oriental nobles, he crossed the Pacific to win diplomatic recognition for China and suitable civil rights for Chinese citizens living abroad. He also hoped to persuade the United States government to reduce the restrictions imposed on Chinese immigration. American labor opposed any lowering of those barriers, but Ralston, like most West Coast employers, favored a more liberal policy as a means of holding wages to what they considered a reasonable level.

The Burlingame mission reached San Francisco on its way to Washington on March 24, 1868. Ralston called on his old friend at once and invited the entourage to dine with him and several San Francisco notables at Belmont on Saturday evening, March 28. Though Billy normally worked on Saturdays, he probably went out ahead this day to oversee arrangements. Legend says that he liked to race the train from San Francisco to Belmont depot. This may have been one of the occasions, particularly if one of the guests went with him.

We know the kind of horses he drove—high-blooded animals between five and nine years old, preferably black, that were capable of trotting for sustained periods of time at a rate of 12.9 to 16 miles per hour while pulling a light carriage holding two people. He had several such horses among the forty or so housed at the Belmont stables. As soon as one passed the optimum age, it was replaced.[7] Ralston himself handled as much of the training as his schedule allowed.

Even animals like his could not trot all the way from California Street to Belmont. Whenever Billy decided to challenge the train, he had to arrange for relays along the way, with attendants specially alerted to make lightning switches. In those days no California locomotive traveled very fast. Furthermore the San Francisco–San Jose train made frequent stops. So, by averaging fifteen miles an hour behind his high-stepping

One of Billy Ralston's favorite relaxations was driving a carriage pulled by high-stepping, blooded horses.

blacks, Billy probably could have made better time across the twenty-two mile course than the steam cars did. It was the sort of stunt that would appeal to him, and no doubt he tried it once he had learned the train's schedule, but it seems unlikely that the "race" (the train wasn't racing) occurred as regularly as legend says.

In any event, he probably went off ahead of this particular group. They followed by the evening train. Ralston and several other drivers met them at the depot with a convoy of char-a-bancs, long, open-sided coaches capable of carrying at least eight passengers each. As the cavalcade wound up the hill, the early spring darkness closed down. The mansion, its hundreds of gas jets aflame for the occasion, blazed gorgeously against the black wall of the mountains.

Awed, the group dismounted and eddied self-consciously through the reception room and the central court into the library. Lizzie met them looking very bored, Gertrude Atherton says.[8] How many other women graced the occasion does not appear. There was a long pause while the new acquaintances exchanged pleasantries. Then Ralston gave a signal. An entire wall slid softly upward, revealing a banquet hall luxurious with damask, silver, choice porcelain, and flowers grown in the greenhouses out back. Behind each chair stood a Chinese waiter in a white uniform. What the two groups of Orientals thought as they faced each other is not a matter of record.

If routine patterns held sway the next day, Ralston loaded his char-a-bancs with as many of his visitors as felt like an outing and took them for a drive through the surrounding countryside, lush green with the rains of spring. Burlingame looked contentedly at his land and pictured a future he was not destined to see. Later, in Washington, England, Denmark, Sweden, Holland, and Prussia, he concluded the treaties that were the purpose of his mission. But in Russia, in February, 1869, he died suddenly. His proposed subdivision faltered in the hands of his heirs. The sums they asked for land were too high, and, Gertrude Atherton says, the elite who might have been his customers were too riven by jealousies to settle in a homogeneous colony. The name stuck, however, and today the suburb of Burlingame stands on part of the site that the ambassador had bought at Billy Ralston's urging.

Shortly after the mission had gone its way, Billy began adding another guest wing to the mansion. So far the place had been totally his, and at times Lizzie felt like a stranger in it. But one day when she knew her husband would be gone for an extended period to Virginia City, she asserted herself. She called in carpenters, tore down the walls at the head of the main staircase, and circled the ballroom with a spacious balcony divided into protruding bows like the facades of box stalls in an opera house. On his return Billy was delighted.[9] "Bully!"—his invariable exclamation of approval. An unenthusiastic dancer himself, he ever afterward enjoyed sitting in one of the bows with friends to watch the merrymakers below swirl through the glade of mirrors.

Concurrently with the new wing he launched another extravaganza in the city—the California Theater. San Francisco, irresistible magnet for miners, seafarers, and ranchers with money to spend, had always been a good theater town, even though the strain of reaching the West Coast discouraged many of the distinguished stars the audience would have liked to see. The 1860's equivalent of burlesque flourished, of course, but so did theaters offering such fare as Shakespeare, "The Count of Monte Cristo," "Mazeppa," and light opera.

For nearly two decades the autocrat of the San Francisco stage had

The balcony at Belmont, designed by Lizzie Ralston, allowed guests to sit and watch the dancers swirling below.

been Thomas Maguire. No one had successfully challenged his monopoly for years. But as soon as the railroad was completed—so Billy reasoned—noted stars would be less reluctant to journey west, especially if they were promised one of the world's outstanding theaters in which to perform. To his sanguine boosterism the thought was electrifying. He would erect such a theater, spread San Francisco's fame as a cultural center far and wide, and in the process topple Tom Maguire.

In hindsight it seems strange that he did not place his rococo temple near the New Montgomery Street holdings he was trying to boom. He owned ample land there (which, to be sure, Harpending and he hoped to sell); he was projecting a plush hotel for the area; and the best of the city's existing hostelries were just steps away on the north side of Market. But perhaps he thought that Kearny Street, recently widened and filling with fashionable shops, would draw better crowds. In any event, he leased a block of land on Bush Street between Kearny and Dupont (now Grant Avenue) for $1,000 a month and went to work.

By opening his pocketbook wide, he hired away from Maguire two popular actors, Laurence Barrett and John McCullough, whom Maguire had imported to serve as the nucleus of a first-class stock company. The two were to perform the same function for Ralston's California Theater. In addition McCullough was to manage the business side of the enterprise. As a final fillip Billy offered a $1,000 commission to a rising young author named Bret Harte to write a new play as the theater's initial offering to the city.

The massive building with its Corinthian facade turned out to be as elegant as even Billy Ralston could have wished. The stage was vast, the scene-changing mechanisms ingenious and complete. Footlights consisted of 81 Argand burners with glass chimneys—white, green, and red—arranged in three rows of 27 each. Overhead were more burners fitted with large parabolic reflectors. A local artist of repute, G. J. Denny, filled the paneling between boxes and the fronts of the curving balconies with colorful paintings. Denny also covered the drop curtain of the stage with a monumental painting of the bay as seen from an imaginary balcony overlooking the Golden Gate. The first three rows of the dress circle pampered the occupants with what amounted to high-backed rocking chairs. Altogether the auditorium could seat 2,479 people.[10]

There was one disappointment. Although Bret Harte extracted another $1,000 from Ralston, he failed to produce a play. He did hand over a dedicatory poem that was read on the opening night by Laurence Barrett, a small, large-headed man with an extraordinarily resonant voice. The opening play, however, chosen at the last minute because the actors knew it, was Bulwer-Lytton's comedy *Money,* a perennial San Francisco favorite.

Bret Harte failed Ralston by producing a poem instead of the play he had promised for the opening of the California Theater.

BANCROFT LIBRARY, UNIVERSITY OF CALIFORNIA, BERKELEY

The audience did not mind the staleness. Opening night, January 18, 1869, was the social event of the decade. All the elite were there with Lizzie and Billy Ralston. The grand stairway that swept up from the foyer was banked with white camellias. The chandeliers glittered. Most of the people were in costume, for the stage performance was to be followed by a masked ball. Ralston led the way as the Doge of Venice.

The California Theater played to packed houses for the next 300 nights, a record run for the time. The high point was a six-week stand by tiny Lotta Crabtree, a product of the mining camps and the darling of the West Coast. Her *Little Nell and the Marchioness,* through which she romped, sniffed one critic, "with a reckless abandon of the laws of taste," jammed every niche of the house. Almost as sensational was the *Firefly* which filled the stage with marching troops and the roar of cannon. Lotta's earnings were such that she invested $7,000 buying a lot 50 by 137 feet on Turk Street at a time when most San Franciscans were shying away from real estate as if from a plague.[11]

Lizzie did not see *Little Nell.* Not long after the opening night she abruptly bundled up the children and with her maids left again for Europe.[12] The story this time was that she was going to buy furniture for Belmont, which indeed she did. More probably, however, she had discovered what was such common talk in San Francisco that even Ambrose Bierce had alluded to it in one of his newspaper columns. During Lizzie's first absence in Europe, Ralston had taken a mistress, whom he continued to see for at least a time after Lizzie's return.[13]

Apparently Lizzie's swift and icy departure shook Ralston. At least

Despite the photographer's careful posing, Elizabeth Ralston,
mistress of Belmont, shows the impact of the sorrows in her life.

there is in existence a letter from a friend, T. Scott Stewart, a United States consul in Japan, in which Stewart stated that he was glad that Billy had "not gone back to the other." That letter was followed by another wherein Stewart stated he had heard that Ralston had "settled down and changed wonderfully. What means all this?" Was Billy "tired of the gayeties and frivolities of life?"[14]

When word of the reformation reached Lizzie in Paris, it shook her in her turn. She had been consoling herself there, again according to gossip, with a handsome artist.[15] Now she dropped him (if he existed), made arrangements for shipping home the $25,000 worth of furnishings she had purchased, and on August 12 caught a liner to New York. There she did a remarkable thing. She took the children to visit the Thornes, parents of Ralston's first sweetheart, Louisa.[16] After all, Emelita was the namesake of Louisa's mother, Emma Thorne.

That obligation completed, she boarded a Pullman palace car leased for her use by her husband. Accompanied by an uncle, Gen. James B. Fry, and sped along by special dispensations, she set out for the West Coast—and, quite unconsciously, for an American travel record.

When San Francisco passengers on the transcontinental reached Sacramento, home base of the Central Pacific, they faced a number of alternatives. They could catch a river boat for the rest of their journey. They could change to the cars of the California Pacific, cross the river, and slant southward to Vallejo before boarding a ferry that would carry them to their destination. Or, beginning in mid-September, 1869, they could stay in their seats and ride over the newly completed tracks of the Western Pacific south through Stockton and on to Oakland, where ferries waited to whisk them directly west across the bay to San Francisco.

Lizzie chose a fourth way, one that few others wanted to waste time on. Staying in their luxurious Pullman car, her party continued along the Western Pacific tracks to San Jose, near the southern tip of the long bay. At San Jose the train was shunted onto the northbound rails of the San Francisco & San Jose road. Although there is no corroboration for this point, it seems highly probable that if Lizzie and the children had continued to San Francisco, they would have been the first persons of their sex and age to travel from the leading metropolis of the East to that of the West without once changing cars.

Records were not on Lizzie's mind, however. On September 20, 1869, she got off the train at Belmont, 22 miles short of the bay city.[17] Billy was there. Once the couple were alone, their repentful reunion must have been emotional and satisfying. It came, too, at a time when Ralston badly needed a wife's sustaining hand. California's sharp recession of 1869 was pinching hard on his far-flung enterprises. His extravagances had caught up with him, and he would have to exercise all the ingenuity he possessed if he were to save the bank and himself from ruin.

CHAPTER 19

The Railroad Morass

The railroad that carried Lizzie Ralston home was in large measure responsible for the troubles that afflicted her husband. Anticipating that the spanning of the continent would bring a rush of prosperity to the state, San Franciscans had overbuilt recklessly. Then, as we have seen, second thoughts came. Some were ushered in rudely by the earthquake of September, 1868, and some by the fear that a rival city on the inland side of the bay would steal San Francisco's thunder by becoming the western terminus of the transcontinental.

Equally shocking was the arrival, in the spring of 1869, of a mass of traveling salesmen from the East. Smiling and eager, they flooded through retail outlets once dominated by the city's wholesalers. The prices they quoted for hats, shoes, blankets, shovels, furniture, and dozens of other commodities rang like the clang of doom. For years the high cost of transportation had protected San Francisco's budding industries, but the golden spike that linked the rails at Promontory, Utah, ended the security, and local business cringed under the impact of a competition it had never known before.

An unbroken flow of bad news from the Comstock intensified the gloom. First was a disastrous fire in the Yellow Jacket Mine, owned by the Union Mill and Mining Company, which in turn was controlled by Ralston, Sharon, and D. O. Mills. The cause of the fire, as nearly as could be determined, was a candle that some careless miner had left burning near a pile of timbers. The flames must have smoldered for some time, because a long span of wooden sets in a tunnel 800 feet below the level of the surface were eaten through. As the day shift dropped down the shaft on the morning of April 7, 1869, a massive cave-in occurred. Billows of smoke and poisonous gas surged throughout the

BANCROFT LIBRARY, UNIVERSITY OF CALIFORNIA, BERKELEY

Ralston's investment plans for the Comstock were upset in 1869
by a disastrous fire in the Yellow Jacket Mine.

lower levels of the Yellow Jacket and on into two adjacent mines also controlled by Union Mill and Mining, the Kentuck and the Crown Point.

A few men clambered to safety, but a quick check of rosters showed that some three dozen still remained underground. Firemen and miners led by John P. Jones, superintendent of the Crown Point, made repeated efforts to reach the trapped men but were driven back each time by heat and smoke. At noon on August 9, all hope of saving lives being gone, Jones sought to quell the flames by ordering the shafts of the mines closed while boilers on the surface pumped the caverns full of steam. On the 12th the Yellow Jacket was reopened. Three bodies were recovered. Then drafts caused by the opening of the shafts fanned the fire alive again and forced another closure. This one lasted for several weeks. No more bodies were recovered. It is not certain how many there were. The number of deaths given in various accounts ranges from 34 to 45.[1]

Ralston was stunned, first by the scope of the tragedy and then, as the magnitude of the destruction became known, by the blow to his own prospects. He had held great hopes for the Yellow Jacket, erratic though its record had been. In 1867 it had produced ore worth $2.7 million. In 1868 the figure had dropped to $628,000, but in November miners had uncovered leads that looked promising. Development work had been proceeding at full speed when the fire closed the mine. It stayed closed for much of the rest of the year. Its neighbors also suffered. The Crown Point, which had been paying small dividends until the disaster, was so crippled that its workers produced only 5,680 tons of ore throughout 1869, much of it taken out during the three months preceding the fire.[2]

Worse, the holocaust was not an exception amidst general prosperity. Sound mines were also running out of ore. By the end of 1869, the lode's annual output had dropped from a heartening $14 million in 1867 to less than $7 million.[3] The pangs were not alleviated when the miners refused to countenance a cut in the $4.00-a-day wage they had won (up from $3.50) during the optimistic days of 1867. Indeed, the fire had made their tempers so explosive that Sharon and Ralston decided against pressing the issue, costly though the high pay scale was to them.

Meanwhile cracks were appearing in the monopolistic edifice, the Union Mill and Mining Company, that Sharon was trying to erect. As noted earlier, he had spent hundreds of thousands of dollars winning control of the Hale & Norcross, only to run out of pay ore almost immediately thereafter. Stock prices skidded. While he was engrossed in other problems, four Irishmen, John W. Mackay, James G. Fair, James C. Flood, and William S. O'Brien, swept up enough shares to elect their own board of directors at the company's annual meeting of stockholders in March, 1869. Simultaneously, they bought two small mills, overhauled and enlarged them, and prepared to treat their own ore in defiance of Union Mill and Mining. Still more distressing, from Sharon's point of view, was the fact that they quickly found good ore in the Hale & Norcross. During the next two years they paid themselves nearly a quarter of a million dollars in dividends and used part of the profits to wrench control of the Virginia City water company from Sharon's grasp.[4]

During this period Adolph Sutro set about making capital out of the Yellow Jacket disaster. In August he harangued a mass meeting of miners about the wickedness of The Bank of California ring that so carelessly held their lives in its greedy palms. They opposed his tunnel, he said, for the sake of their profits, little caring that a well ventilated tunnel would provide their workers with an escape hatch in the event of another major fire. He illustrated his points with grisly cartoons, and after he had lifted his audience to roars of anger, he urged it to subscribe funds to the tunnel project both as individuals and through their unions. To Ralston's incredulity, they pledged $50,000.

In October Sutro held a triumphant ground-breaking ceremony and then hurried to Washington to ask Congress to subsidize the rest of the work. Ralston didn't think he would succeed—the West Coast's senators and congressmen ought to be able to checkmate the plea—but he might prove troublesome if he took to spreading ugly tales about the bank among New York's financial community.

Comstock miners, hoping Sutro's Tunnel would provide an escape route from future blazes, bought $50,000 worth of his stock.

Sutro's persistence and the raid of the four Irishmen on the supposedly fading Hale & Norcross illustrated a curious attitude: no matter what happened, men's faith in the Comstock would not die. Mine and mill owners kept right on sinking money into their properties, and not always for the sake of rigging the stock market. Some of the funds needed for the development work were loaned by the bank. More came from assessments levied on stockholders. The last device was particularly painful to investors less affluent than the members of the bank ring. There is, for instance, in the archives of The Bank of California, this frantic, unsigned note addressed to William "Sharron."[5]

"Your time and mine is short. I have hoped that the assessment would be rescinded and save me from ruin. To come to poverty and misery, NO, NO, I will die first, you force me to it. The assessment is unnecessary—you and your party are now trying to freeze out the weak ones for 18 months I have held on but now alas the worst is upon me & the Day of Grace is a short one and you shall have it. *So help me God.*

"PS You will not Believe this till you see the muzzle of my Revolver and then it will be too late."

REOPENING THE INJURED MINES while faced with decreasing revenues would have been onerous enough for Ralston and his associates. In addition they also had to push ahead with the railroad that Sharon had been promoting since the middle of 1867 as an essential step in reducing freight cost for the milling and mining company.

His first step had been a masterly bluff. He had leaked word that he planned to send tracks north over the mountains to the Truckee River, where they would connect with the Central Pacific. North! True, that was the shortest way to a San Francisco connection. On the other hand, Nevada's two most populous counties lay south of the lode. Eager to be served by a railroad and afraid that Sharon really meant what he said in spite of the mills he was building in Carson Valley, the voters promised

The town of Sutro, the main tunnel, and the branch tunnels that
Adolph Sutro promoted so diligently show in this 1866 map.

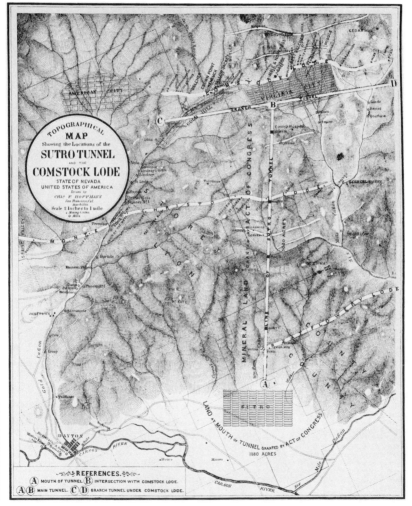

to put up the sum of $500,000 if he would take a more roundabout route —down the south side of the mountain to Carson City and then back north through the Washoe Valley.[6]

This guarantee safely in hand, Sharon called a meeting for February 26, 1868, at The Bank of California office in Virginia City of all persons interested in subscribing to the proposed railroad, the Virginia & Truckee. Ten persons showed up, among them Ralston and John D. Fry. They'd had a hard trip across the mountains. Snow was halting the Central Pacific locomotives as far down the eastern side of the Sierra as Cisco, and they crossed the summit in sleighs, wrapped in buffalo robes. The town they came to, pitched steeply on a barren mountainside, was wind-swept, grimy with the soot from many tall factory chimneys, and proud of its gambling dens and extensive red light district. A railroad, built in times of depression, would make it even grimier—and even prouder.

During the next few days, the men concerned with the railroad incorporated their company, elected officers, and formulated plans for borrowing additional construction money from the mines, to be paid back in the form of reduced freight charges once the road was operating. Ralston subscribed to 3,500 of the 30,000 shares of $100 par value stock authorized by the articles of incorporation.[7] He probably paid for it in instalments, and the price per share most likely was quite a bit below the $100 appearing on the face of the certificates. Even so, the investment was a burden for him at that particular time—as it was for Sharon and Mills, who subscribed to comparable amounts. The remainder of the stock was divided among eighteen other shareholders.

They ordered rail from England in January, 1869, and a month later broke ground at Gold Hill. By the time of the Yellow Jacket fire, 750 men were at work, mostly Chinese supervised by white bosses. Fearful that the low-paid Orientals would be moved into the mines next, several hundred hardrock stiffs marched behind a brass band to the nearest camp, intending to frighten the Chinese into flight. Sharon met them with a placatory speech—no, of course the Asiatics would not compete with whites underground—and jollied the would-be attackers into dispersing. Within another month 38 camps were strung down the mountainside and along the Carson Valley, housing roughly 1,200 Chinese.

They faced a demanding job. The tracks had to climb 1,575 feet within little more than 13 miles. To attain a practicable grade, the workers had to blast out six tunnels aggregating 2,400 feet in length. The number of degrees through which the spiraling tracks swung equalled those in 17 full circles. A wisecracking journalist from Reno wrote that the company would save half its engine power by having a locomotive push at the back end of the train while pulling at the front, an idea devised by Sharon from "his long connection with rings in the mining, milling, and stockjobbing—alias banking—businesses."[8]

By October the company was out of money. Its grant of $500,000 in county bonds, sold at a 25 percent discount, had netted only $375,000, and assessments on the stockholders failed to keep pace with costs, which were running upwards of $50,000 a mile. To make up the difference, the directors of the Virginia & Truckee borrowed heavily from The Bank of California. But the bank was in trouble, too. To ease the situation the railroad directors voted, on November 24, 1869, to issue a million dollars' worth of 7 percent bonds.[9] Thus invigorated, the V & T paid off most of its debt at the bank and crept on toward Virginia City, arriving there on January 29, 1870. The railroad also imported by wagon (as yet it had no outside rail connections) enough freight and passenger cars and locomotives to inaugurate service between Virginia City, the mills in the valley, and the state capital, Carson City, 21 miles away. But it was not able as yet to bend back north toward Reno.

The effect of those 21 miles of track was dramatic. The cost of hauling wood uphill to the mine boilers fell from $15 to $11.50 a cord; of transporting ore downhill to the mills from $3.50 to $2.00 a ton. These were significant gains, not just for the Union Mill and Mining Company, but for every business on the mountainside. Without that boost at a time of deep depression, many a firm would have gone under.

A Virginia & Truckee ore train, 1874. Though expensive to build, the line was one of the best investments made by Ralston, Mills, and Sharon.

To Ralston, however, savings were not enough. He needed immediate income, and the debt-burdened V & T was not likely to produce any for years.* He must have reflected wryly that of the many quicksands threatening him during 1869, railroads were the most treacherous.

He had become entangled in several lines. The first in point of time was the California & Oregon, brainchild of an energetic surveyor and rascally promoter named Simon G. Elliott. Elliott's plan was to build from a junction with the Central Pacific near Sacramento northward to Portland. Although he went through the motions of consulting several Oregonians about the project, they were suspicious of him. He had overloaded the California & Oregon's board of directors with residents of San Francisco —Ralston was one—and the northerners feared that the trade of southern Oregon, which they wanted, would be pulled into the bay city's ever-expanding orbit. Accordingly they incorporated a defensive company, eventually known as the Oregon Central, designed to run southward to the California border.[11]

The promoters of the line then wrecked their own strategy by announcing that they would lay their track along the west side of Oregon's Willamette Valley. This aroused property owners on the east side of the valley, who promptly incorporated a rival railroad to run through *their* hamlets and past *their* farms on its way to California. Simultaneously both companies sought land grants from Congress to aid in the construction of their competitive lines.

Congress dodged the issue by saying that the land, some 3.8 million acres, would go (after specified amounts of track had been laid) to whichever of the companies was chosen by the Oregon legislature. Intrigue grew wild then, with Simon Elliott in the middle of it. Representing himself as the agent of Albert J. Cook & Co., railroad contractors, he persuaded the east side Oregon Central that the best way to woo the legislature was to let Cook & Co. push ahead with track building before their rivals could start. Without even bothering to check on Albert J. Cook & Co., the bemused East Siders gave Elliott a contract and then issued several million dollars' worth of stocks and bonds to pay for the initial stretch of railroad.

There was no Albert J. Cook & Co. Elliott assigned the contract and bonds to himself and went to San Francisco to raise cash by selling the paper at a discount. Inasmuch as The Bank of California had once offered to help Elliott if he formed a "sound" company in Oregon, the promoter presumably offered some of the bonds to Ralston.[12] Though Billy wasn't always wary, he backed off this time. Not so his good friend Ben Holladay. Ben acquired a satchel full of the worthless paper and then sailed to Portland to see what he had bought.

---

*As matters turned out, the V & T paid its first dividend on August 1, 1874.[10]

The prospects excited him—3.8 million acres, if he could gain control of the company and build the line. The first part was easy. The stock was cheap—there was nothing behind it but hope—and he quickly obtained as much as he needed. He also bought, with lavish entertainment and other expressions of good will, the favor of the legislature, which designated his east side Oregon Central as the proper recipient of Congress's land grant. For a time he kept Elliott on his payroll as chief engineer, but then found an excuse for firing him.

What Ben could not do was extend by any appreciable amount the time that Congress had allowed for laying the first twenty miles of track. Before he had finished his conniving, the deadline was only eighteen months away, and he had almost no equipment on hand with which to begin work.

One major consideration was rail. Shipping what he needed around Cape Horn would create insuperable delays. Off he rushed to California to see Ralston. Could Billy, who had many railroad connections, help him find enough iron in California for launching the job? In addition could The Bank of California help him with a loan of, say, a quarter of a million dollars?

The timing of the requests was bad. San Francisco's business recession was sinking toward its nadir. Money was tight, and locking up capital far from home could have unfortunate repercussions. On the other hand, Ralston liked Holladay. He admired the way in which Ben had put together his stagecoach lines and, afterwards, his steamship empire, culminating in the North Pacific Transportation Company, of which Billy was a director. Whether or not he was aware of the shady means Holladay had employed in winning the Oregon legislature to his side cannot be said. In any event, he did know that Ben had been tapped as the potential recipient of 3.8 million desirable Oregon acres. If a boost at the beginning of the adventure would put the prize in Holladay's grasp, Ralston was willing to take the chance.

He located and financed the purchase of 2,000 tons of iron from A. A. Cohen, who controlled two shortlines on the east side of the bay. He then authorized additional loans, so that by the fall of 1869, Holladay's railroad account with The Bank of California stood at $280,000.[13] Considering the other morasses surrounding Ralston at the time, it was a risky step indeed. Characteristically, however, Billy made his decision on what he considered to be the railroad's potentials, not on its dangers.

The ultimate success of the road would depend in large measure on making connections with a line leading through northern California to Sacramento and San Francisco. Fully aware of this, Holladay changed the name of his company from the Oregon Central to the Oregon and California. The reason was clear. He wanted to echo the name of

Elliott's original creation, the California & Oregon, which Congress had already designated as the recipient of federal land grants between Sacramento and the Oregon border. The similarity in company names, Holladay reasoned, would suggest that a treaty of alliance existed between the two lines. This assumption would, in turn, enhance the attractiveness of the bonds he was on the point of issuing in order to raise money for construction purposes.

Circumstances thrust Ralston into the midst of the program. Elliott had proved incapable of breathing life into the California & Oregon, and his fellow directors had long since ejected him. Then they found they could not finance the railroad either. Losing their courage, they turned to Ralston. Could he help them dispose of the line and its potential land grant to the most logical prospect in the West, the Central Pacific?

Billy agreed to try. The sale, if consummated, would lend an attractive shine to Holladay's coming bond issue. More importantly, as far as Ralston was concerned, the negotiations would provide him with a new approach to the increasingly powerful owners of the Central Pacific—Leland Stanford, Collis P. Huntington, Charles Crocker, and Mark Hopkins.

Billy had been trying to woo the quartet away from the banking firm of Donohoe and Kelly ever since the collapse of the old Sacramento Valley line. Along with other San Francisco financiers he had provided Stanford and Huntington with letters of recommendation designed to help them sell their securities in New York and Europe. In October, 1867, he had instructed Lees and Waller to treat Huntington, the road's financial and purchasing agent in New York, as the bank's most favored customer. By endorsing Stanford's personal note, he had persuaded the Pacific Insurance Company to lend the railroad president $100,000 for use on the project.[14]

Equally important, both Ralston and Mills understood the desire of the CP's owners to defend future stock prices by keeping competitive railroads away from the rich markets of central California. Several potential rivals, recently chartered by Congress to span the continent north and south of the central route, already had their eyes on the traffic originating in the bay area. The best way to tap it would be to join forces with one or another of the little short lines radiating north and south through central California. Some of those lines were in process of construction, others were mere paper corporations whose value lay chiefly in the charters they possessed. All were potential threats to the Central Pacific. By becoming salesman first for the California & Oregon and then for every other short line in northern California, Ralston assured himself of a hearing in the offices of the worried organizers of the first transcontinental.

He worked adroitly, serving his clients well while at the same time winning the esteem of the Central Pacific's president, Leland Stanford, and its treasurer, Mark Hopkins. The transcontinental took over everything he offered them, including the California & Oregon, and Holladay's proposed bond issue looked, from Holladay's standpoint, better than ever.[15]

The success contained its perils, nevertheless. The directors of the Central Pacific were going to be annoyed when Holladay offered Oregon and California bonds in Germany at the same time that the CP was trying to sell California & Oregon bonds in the same market. Sensing this, Ralston made no effort to handle Holladay's paper but let the marketing fall into the hands of Milton Latham's New York and San Francisco bank, working in conjunction with the Seligmans of New York. Sure enough, Huntington was outraged, but not at Ralston. Billy stayed friendly with everyone—perhaps even too friendly with the Central Pacific, as will shortly appear.[16]

One reason for the continuing friendliness was Ralston's and Mills's help during the railroad's relentless drives to dominate southern as well as northern California. As noted earlier, the CP first acquired the Western Pacific's tracks from Sacramento to San Jose. Simultaneously they bought from A. A. Cohen, with Ralston serving as intermediary, a pair of vital shortlines that gave the Western Pacific access to the twin towns of Oakland and Alameda on the eastern shore of San Francisco Bay. More significantly, the would-be monopolists also gobbled up the Southern Pacific, a paper corporation whose strength lay in the fact that Congress had designated it as the potential recipient of enormous grants of land in southern California.

With Ralston's help the Western Pacific and Southern Pacific (that is to say, the Central Pacific as parent company of both lines) applied for the right to purchase more than 6,600 acres of waterfront land in the Potrero Nuevo district south of Rincon Hill. The proposal, it will be recalled, was turned down. In partial compensation for the loss, Ralston and A. A. Cohen thereupon purchased for the railroad a $200,000 block of property on the bay front southeast of Rincon Hill, beside the new docks of the Pacific Mail Steamship Company.[17]

To complete its encirclement of the southern part of the bay, the CP again utilized Ralston's services as a broker in winning an option to buy the San Francisco & San Jose Railroad for $3.25 million in gold. And finally the directors of the Central Pacific chartered a new line of their own, the San Joaquin Railroad, to build south along the eastern side of the San Joaquin River. Its purpose was to head off any intruder that might try to avoid the Southern Pacific by striking north along the valley. As a gesture of their appreciation for Billy's services during all this wheeling and dealing, the Big Four of the Central Pacific proposed to give the name Ralston to one of the first towns that took shape along the new San Joaquin line. He declined the honor at a public meeting attended by the local citizenry, whereupon, so California folklore insists, the town was called Modesto in recognition of his great modesty.[18]

So far Ralston's participation in the railroad's drive to monopolize transportation in California had been limited to his services as a broker. In 1868, however, he became financially committed, joining with a group of friends to form the construction company, the Santa Clara and Pajaro Valley Railroad, that built the first stretch of the Southern Pacific's line, a thirty-mile hop from San Jose to Gilroy.[19] As soon as the tracks reached the latter town he fell under the spell of still a new excitement, tobacco raising. Experimental fields were just then being planted around Gilroy, and he immediately joined the activity, both as a lender of money through The Bank of California and as a purchaser of tobacco fields in his own name. The day would come when that enthusiasm, too, would backfire. At the time, however, he saw it only as one more resource to be developed for the good of the state—and, as a corollary, for the bank and Billy Ralston.

Still another ill-judged enthusiasm that sprang from his railroad associations was the Kimball Car Manufacturing Company. The plant had been founded originally to build light carriages and buggies, but when Ralston acquired control, he introduced broader goals—railroad cars. In 1868 he built a new factory in San Francisco two acres in size and three stories tall. There he turned out a few cars for the San Francisco & San Jose and for the Virginia & Truckee railroads. His dream, however, was the building of better sleeping cars for the Central

The Kimball Manufacturing Company, which Ralston converted from making wagons to railroad cars, never met his expectations.

Pacific than even George Pullman could produce. He created a luxurious model, resplendent with the fine woods he loved, but he was never able to land an order.[20] The Central Pacific could obtain cheaper cars in the East, where Pullman and Huntington worked hand in glove, and against that lure craftsmanship was not enough. Inexorably the Kimball Company sank deeper and deeper into debt.

These many intertwinings placed heavy strains on both the bank and on Ralston's personal fortunes at a time when he was already over-burdened with projects—the North Bloomfield hydraulic mines, the

Though dressed resplendently for one of Belmont's famed masquerade balls, Ralston seems here to be weighed down by his many problems.

Alaska seal fisheries, the New Montgomery Real Estate Company, the fire-gutted Yellow Jacket Mine and the Virginia & Truckee Railroad, his palatial home at Belmont, his theater, the sugar refineries, woolen mills, and so on. It opened the bank to insatiable calls for money as the Central Pacific quickened its race with the Union Pacific. At times the CP's fluctuating account at the bank topped $1 million, while the personal accounts of Stanford and Mark Hopkins stood above $100,000 each.[21]

As San Francisco's feverish optimism turned to gloom late in 1868, Ralston tried to rein in his rampaging client. Predictably the restraints annoyed Huntington. In a series of angry letters to Mark Hopkins, he criticized both the policy and the capabilities of the man who made the policy. The Bank of California, he growled, was showing insufficient concern for its best account. Ralston, Mills and the rest needed a lesson. "We should do business with three or four banks in San Francisco and build competition and let them know we expect them to carry us through tight money markets." He said that unfavorable rumors were abroad in New York about the bank's officers speculating too freely in unsound ventures, notably mining. Then, his impatience mounting, he snorted, "I think time will show that Ralston has got a larger institution than he is able to run."[22]

When Hopkins conveyed a watered down version of the remarks to Ralston, Billy replied crisply that he could not run the bank for the benefit of a single customer. Others were calling for money, too, with the result that in May, 1869 (the month when the first land offerings of New Montgomery Street Real Estate Company failed to sell), The Bank of California had $11 million out on loan. Instead of expecting favoritism, the Central Pacific should relax its demands. After all, he told Hopkins, "'tis the business of the bank to do all that is possible for our legitimate commercial trade and important social interests of various kinds. . . . In fact, we do not see where they can go or what they could do if we do not help them. Therefore we must on behalf of all these things ask you people not to lean on us for awhile."[23]

Not to lean on us: what that meant among other things was go easy with its requests for gold coin with which to pay bills and wages. Because of a strange conjunction of events, California, the nation's primary supplier of gold, had become so depleted of coin that on many mornings Ralston was not sure the bank had cash enough in its tills to finish out the day's business. If this physical shortage became widely apparent, it might well be as a sign of the bank's instability. Then, if a run developed. . . . There were sleepless nights for Billy Ralston that summer. He had never faced a crisis quite like this before, and he knew that the boldest sort of improvisation would be necessary to solve it.

CHAPTER 20

Not Enough Gold

Throughout the trying summer of 1869, the beleaguered officials of The Bank of California worked hard at presenting to the public an air of easy confidence. Though the bank was then losing money, the monthly dividend of 1 percent on each share of capital stock was paid regularly. Influential visitors from outside the state were entertained lavishly in the hope that they would return home impressed by the energy and prosperity not only of the West's best known financial institution but of all California.

This glad-handing became the special province of Billy Ralston. To help him meet the financial demands involved, the bank allotted him, according to Leland Stanford, an expense account of $20,000 a year.[1]

The visitations with which he had to cope reached flood proportions following the completion of the transcontinental railroad in May, 1869. Of necessity Ralston devised mass-production patterns for handling the different groups.

Congressional committees and delegates from the boards of trade or chambers of commerce of major cities were first shown the sights of San Francisco. Then at eight o'clock on some specified morning the visitors currently in hand were put aboard the train for a run to San Jose. After a sumptuous breakfast in the leading hotel there, the visitors climbed into waiting carriages for a drive northward along the stately Alameda to Santa Clara and thence past orchards and elegant country estates to Belmont and another heavy repast. The tour ended with an evening train ride back to San Francisco. California wine was served throughout the day to whoever wished it. Sometimes consumption slipped out of hand. "Well," clucked Lizzie's uncle, Gen. James B. Fry, to Ralston on one occasion, "you *did* put the delegations through!

Some fair drinkers sh . . . a pity to pour that fine wine into some of those ratholes." But, reported Ezra Clark Carr, who was present on one of the junkets, Ralston himself, though lively, was abstemious—"one of the noblest and most generous of men."[2]

Individual travelers also clamored for attention—governors, statesmen, English military officers bound to and from the Orient, artists, writers, businessmen, each with a letter of introduction that he expected to be an open sesame. If a visitor merited special attention, Billy drove him (or her, as in the case of writer Grace Greenwood) out to watch the sea lions where the Pacific crashed against the palisades below the Cliff House. More energetic sightseers were escorted by the bank's secretary, Stephen Franklin, to the geysers in Sonoma County or even as far as Yosemite. When former Secretary of State William H. Seward and his entourage passed through San Francisco on their way around the world Ralston entertained them as a matter of course at Belmont and then provided them with special deck chairs to use on the steamer that took them to the Orient.[3]

To James Lees in New York he confessed that at times the activity palled. Lees sympathized: "When you already have enough, and indeed far too much to look after and care for, I am amazed that you can stand it." Then he explained why the assault was likely to continue. "Everybody talks about you, your princely hospitality, and large scale of expenditures. . . . All who go to California want to see you and want letters of introduction," which Lees and Waller found difficult to refuse. Rather than impose on Ralston, he finished, the bank should establish a visitors' bureau to help with the entertaining.[4]

Not every visitor was a nuisance, however. One who appeared at an opportune time during the late summer of 1869 and helped extricate Ralston from the financial morass into which he was sinking was Dr. Henry R. Linderman, the leading expert on money matters in the United States.

Linderman was one of the ablest men of his times. Though he had studied to be a surgeon, he had become fascinated with the problems and theories of coinage. He grew so learned in the field that although he was a lifelong Democrat, Andrew Johnson appointed him director of the mint at Philadelphia. When Grant took office, Linderman was ousted to make room for a party stalwart. Unwilling to lose so good a man, George Boutwell, Grant's secretary of the treasury, made Linderman his special deputy with multiple assignments. He was to examine all the mints in the United States, pump leading bankers for their ideas concerning monetary reform, and then join the deputy comptroller of the currency in preparing a sweeping new coinage bill for presentation to Congress.

Immediately after reaching San Francisco in August, 1869, Linder-

CALIFORNIA HISTORICAL SOCIETY

H. R. Linderman, ambitious director of the Philadelphia Mint,
became Ralston's close personal and business friend.

man sought out Ralston. The two men liked each other at once. Linderman was tall and athletic. His lean face sported the kind of imperial beard that European royalty would popularize years later. He was a good politician, an affable companion, and something of a bon vivant. Underneath his geniality was an incisive yet flexible mind. He knew how to listen, and Ralston had much to tell him about money reform, as did Billy's principal adviser on the subject, Louis Garnett of the San Francisco Assaying and Refining Company—but more of that in a later chapter. At the moment, Ralston's chief worry was the government's insane policy, as he considered it, concerning its supplies of gold.

THE BANK OF CALIFORNIA

Only two of these negotiable gold ingots from the Comstock Lode still exist—this one in The Bank of California's money museum.

The situation, as he explained it to Linderman, was not only complex of itself but was rendered even more difficult by local jealousies and local politics. Its roots went back to the Civil War, when California had refused to accept paper money—greenbacks—as a circulating medium. Thus specie was required for nearly every West Coast transaction from buying groceries to disbursing wages.

The banks of San Francisco acted as intermediaries in providing this gold coin. They collected much of what they supplied in the form of deposits and then redistributed it to their customers during the day's work. They also gathered unrefined bullion from the mines and from gold purchasers operating in the Sierra foothills. They took this dust, or bars as the case might be, to the mint to be refined. Afterwards they stored some of the refined metal in their vaults, where it functioned as a liquid asset. The rest they had struck into new gold coins to meet the needs of their growing city and state.

Because The Bank of California handled more gold bullion and more gold coin than any other institution in the West, Ralston had cultivated friendly relations with the officials of the United States Sub-Treasury and Mint in San Francisco. His competitors felt that he used these associations to their disadvantage. Their charges of wrongdoing brought a congressional committee to San Francisco in November,

Some of Ralston's enemies thought that his ties with the San Francisco branch mint were altogether too close.

1868, to investigate. Ralston and the officials of the mint were exonerated—both Secretary of the Treasury George Boutwell and Congressman A. A. Sargent of California issued public statements to that effect—but the backbiting was by no means quieted.[5]

One continuing source of contention was the San Francisco Assaying and Refining Company, founded in 1866 by a consortium of West Coast bankers that included both Donohoe, Kelly & Company and The Bank of California. The two firms were not compatible bedfellows and Donohoe, Kelly & Company soon withdrew from the refinery. At about the same time, Ralston and the manager of the assay plant, Louis A. Garnett, asked the government to grant it an exclusive contract for refining all bullion handled by the San Francisco Mint. To speed the passage of the necessary legislation, they sent a special representative, John

Hewston, the company's chemist, to Washington to act as lobbyist.

If the law passed, the refinery at the mint would be closed and every ounce of western bullion destined for coinage would have to pass through the hand of Ralston's company. A howl of protest went up, led by Joseph Donohoe in San Francisco and Eugene Kelly in New York. Ralston, they charged, was proposing an intolerable monopoly, for by controlling the treatment of bullion the assay company—in other words The Bank of California—would also be able to control the mint.[6]

While this controversy was at full heat, another quarrel was precipitated by President Grant. After his inauguration in March, 1869, the president began putting his own followers into positions formerly held by appointees of Andrew Johnson. Among the departments slated for a shake-up were the Treasury and the Mint.

The prospect of the turnover touched off a fierce internecine struggle in California. To whom would the new civil servants in the San Francisco Sub-Treasury and Mint owe their allegiance? What effect might this have on clipping the wings of The Bank of California?

For Ralston there were short-term considerations as well. In common with bankers throughout the nation, he was experiencing difficulty in obtaining enough coin for the conduct of the bank's daily business. Shortages of specie had always been chronic in America because of the country's rapid expansion. The fevered postwar boom in the East intensified the problem. Imports were leaping. Greenbacks could not be used in making purchases abroad or in paying duties at the country's customhouses, and so gold was drained from circulation for those purposes. The government, too, needed gold for paying interest on the swollen national debt.

The result of these demands on a limited supply was a rapid increase in the price of gold and a consequent acceleration in its flow eastward from California. The state's annual output, which during the latter part of the 1860s stabilized at roughly $18 million, did not compensate for the drain.[7] Because California still refused to accept greenbacks as legal tender, the state's businessmen needed more gold for daily use than did those in the rest of the nation. Hence the pinch of the money shortage was particularly severe on the West Coast, and Ralston, as director of the area's largest bank, inevitably bore the worst of it.

By April, 1869, his scramble for coin was so obvious that rumormongers predicted that The Bank of California was on the point of calling in half its outstanding loans.[8] Ralston vigorously denied the tales, yet he knew that there was this stark shadow of truth in it: if he lost his one dependable, if shrunken, supply of coin—the vaults of the United States Mint on Sacramento Street—he would be in serious trouble.

That was exactly what loomed because of President Grant's reshuffling of personnel. If Ralston's friends were turned out of the San Francisco Mint, the doors would probably be closed while auditors checked accounts for the new officials. In agitation over the prospect Billy wired California's delegation in Congress to object to the new appointments and thus forestall the closure. He also wired his New York correspondents, Lees and Waller, to use their influence to the same end.[9]

The effort failed. The new appointments were announced, and the mint was closed. While the auditors went slowly about their business, the supply of coin at The Bank of California dwindled away until, one evening in July, not enough remained on hand to meet the next day's needs.[10] If customers were refused specie on request, a disastrous run on the bank might develop. Meanwhile more than two tons of raw gold were locked in the bank's vaults, as useless there as so much sawdust.

Ralston went about meeting this newest crisis with characteristic recklessness. He summoned two men to meet him at the bank shortly after midnight. One was Asbury Harpending. The other was Maurice Dore, the auctioneer who was helping Ralston and Harpending handle the disappointing land sales connected with the New Montgomery Street Real Estate Company. The trio spent the next several hours of darkness furtively lugging bars of gold to the mint, trading them for sacks of double eagles, and carrying the sacks back to the bank. The two doorways were only 400 steps apart, but the sustained, nerve-racking effort was as exhausting as a prospecting trip in the Sierra. According to Harpending, they handled close to five tons of metal that night. The value of the coins which they obtained in exchange for the bullion came to nearly $1 million.[11] The records at the mint were presumably doctored by Ralston's friends there in such a way as to make the trade appear legal, and inasmuch as no values were tampered with during the exchange, the sleight of hand went undetected by Ralston's enemies.

Harpending always believed that their pre-dawn activities saved The Bank of California from closure and the entire West Coast from a financial panic. Like many of his estimates, this one was overblown. Perhaps a run and its attendant troubles were averted, but no long-range problems were solved. The million dollars soon disappeared in the course of daily transactions. In the meantime fresh supplies of coin became harder than ever to obtain because of the machinations of Jay Gould and Jim Fisk of New York.

The two money sharks had concocted a breathless plan. They would corner the nation's supply of gold, drive prices to unprecedented heights, sell at the top of the market, and make a killing for themselves. The plan would not work, however, unless they could keep the government from releasing its supplies from the various mints around the

*Jay Gould's attempt
to corner America's
gold supply caused
acute financial crises
in San Francisco.*

BOTH PAGES: CULVER PICTURES

country. This Gould did by persuading President Grant and key officials of his administration that if gold were kept locked in the government's vaults, its price would rise. This escalation, the schemer argued, would deflect enough newly harvested American grain to market in England to benefit this country's balance of payments.

Through Lees and Waller, the bank's agents in New York, Ralston knew that something drastic was afoot, but what it was he hardly cared right then. His need, and the need of all California bankers, was to get enough gold coin out of the mint in San Francisco to keep their city from being strangled economically. "Alas," he wired Lees and Waller in New York, "millions locked up in subtreasury here," most of it obtained through duties paid at the customhouse.[12] But none of it could be used—just currency, and San Francisco would not accept that.

A midnight transfer like the one he had engineered with Harpending and Dore a month earlier would not work again, and even if it did it would not help the other bankers in the state. This time the breach had to be legal and open to all.

That was where Linderman came in. At once grasping the nature of the emergency from Ralston's explanations, he urged George Boutwell, secretary of the treasury, to authorize transfers of gold from the East Coast to the West by telegraph. The first step was for a businessman in the East who owed money (or would loan money) in California to deposit gold coin at one of the subtreasuries near his place of business. The official who received the gold would wire a statement of

Gould's fellow conspirator in the gold scheme was Jim Fisk. Tight money everywhere almost ruined Ralston's New York agents.

the amount to the head of the mint in San Francisco. The western official would then allow the designated recipient to draw from the mint the amount of gold specified in the telegram, less a service charge of three-quarters of one percent.

The plan did not put any more gold into circulation but simply shifted its locus. Accordingly Boutwell accepted the idea, although he was nervous about his officials letting loose large sums of money on the receipt of a mere telegraphic order, even one in cypher.[13] Enormously relieved, Ralston put pressure on the bank's largest debtor, the Central Pacific Railroad, to start depositing gold in the East, even though the specie cost Collis Huntington heavily in terms of greenbacks. Within a few days the railroad's financial manager had deposited $700,000, meanwhile grumbling sourly to Leland Stanford, "I think if The Bank of California was not in quite so many things as they are, they could do their friends more good than it is in their power to do as they now conduct their business."[14] Ralston had revenge of sorts for that remark. In the coded telegrams he exchanged with Lees and Waller he used the word "Hungry" for Huntington.*

---

*Thinking up code names for people amused Ralston. Lees and Waller, who were very nervous during this period, were called "Palsy," until they objected and became "Lexicon." Mills was "Monarch." The Bank of California was, appropriately, "Bullion"; The Oriental Bank of London, "Opulent." Harking back, evidently, to his Mississippi days, Ralston called himself "Eddy."

Other San Francisco banks obtained coin through similar processes, and the city's economy quickened again. For Ralston, there was a backlash. During the crisis he drew heavily on Lees and Waller—so heavily that he left those loyal friends stripped of their gold reserves just as the Gould-Fisk conspiracy was accelerating during September. They wired frantically for him to send back some of the gold he had drawn. "We are absolutely out of money," went a typical message. "Some depositors want their balances. Send us transfers today at any cost to extent of $500,000." Now it was Ralston's turn to scramble in a desperate effort to save the men who had saved him. The two concerns barely stayed afloat until Black Friday, when Gould's attempted conspiracy failed, the treasury opened its doors, gold prices plummeted back to normal, and the nation's economic transactions returned to their accustomed channels. As James Lees said to Ralston and Mills, it had been a terrible squeeze "and such an one I hope neither you nor I will ever be in again."[15]

Severe as the gold problem was, it was only one jaw of the vice in which Ralston was gripped. The other was The Bank of California's indebtedness to The Oriental Bank of London.

When The Oriental Bank had agreed to act as the London agent for The Bank of California, its officers had said that the Americans could draw on it to a limit of £250,000 sterling—approximately $1.25 million. During the spring of 1869, just as the gold shortage in California was growing acute, Ralston exceeded that amount by a full 100 percent. His excuse: the record grain harvest that the state produced that year.

The latter part of the decade had been marked by higher than average rainfall. The deluges lured farmers into purchasing half a million acres of new farmland in the San Joaquin Valley during the short space of two years. They were rewarded with bounteous harvests of wheat.[16] The climax came in 1869. Urgent calls flooded into San Francisco for record amounts of money to move the grain to the bay and load it aboard ships chartered in the main by Isaac Friedlander, who also depended on The Bank of California to finance his operations.

In an effort to meet the requests Ralston stretched the bank's credit with Lees and Waller until his obligations there reached $1 million and James Lees began objecting strenuously. Simultaneously Ralston was drawing on The Oriental Bank until his credit there had reached its stated limits. Needing still more money, he asked James Lees to help him persuade the English financiers to open their purses even wider.

Lees refused.[17] Money was tight everywhere, he said; the times called for contraction, not expansion. Thus rebuffed, Ralston determined to go ahead on his own. He would not—could not—be a party to leaving grain standing in the fields and businesses stagnating in the cities. Well aware of the repercussions that would follow, he began deliberately overdrawing The Bank of California's account with The Oriental Bank.

On July 6, 1869, Charles F. J. Stuart, the head of the London corporation, reacted with sharp letters of reprimand, directed not to Ralston, but to the bank's president, D. O. Mills, and to James Lees. For the safety of their own organization, Stuart said, he and his directors were forced to demand that The Bank of California reduce its indebtedness to the £250,000 limit by November 30, 1869.[18]

This gave Ralston less than five months in which to produce $1.25 million from a bank currently operating in the red! Mills and Lees both wrote Stuart soothing answers and then forwarded his ultimatum to Ralston. What now?

It was a miserable question. So far as Ralston could foresee, there was no possibility of the bank's raising the necessary money within the time allowed.

At that point another opportune visitor appeared in San Francisco. He was William W. Cargill, The Oriental Bank's head officer for eastern Asia, and he was on his way from Yokohama to London for consultations. As had been the case with Linderman, Ralston entertained him at Belmont and thereafter got on famously with him. There was even talk for a time of Cargill's accepting a high position in The Bank of California.[19]

Because of this mutual trust, it was easy for Ralston to be candid with his visitor. He admitted that the fevered postwar boom had led The Bank of California to be overly liberal with its loans. As a result it had been placed in a difficult position by the sudden recession of 1869. On top of that the unexpected gold stringencies, coinciding with the bountiful harvest, had created artificial hazards that made affairs look worse than they were. He went over all the bank's liabilities and assets with Cargill and in the end convinced the Englishman that long-range prospects demanded more consideration than Stuart had shown.

Together they worked out a plan for Cargill to submit to his bank on arriving in London. First Ralston promised to make an all-out effort to cut the indebtedness immediately from £500,000 to £400,000. In return the Oriental people would grant The Bank of California an additional three months—that is, until February 28, 1870—for whittling the sum down to the prescribed £250,000. The difference between that figure and the £400,000 that was Ralston's first target would be covered by a loan of £150,000 from The Oriental Bank to The Bank of California. Interest was to be 1 percent more than the prime rate being charged during the period by The Bank of England.

Then came the sticker. Since Ralston alone was being blamed for placing The Bank of California in jeopardy, he was going to be held responsible for its rehabilitation. For the protection of The Oriental

Bank, he was to place in the hands of two trustees, Darius O. Mills and Thomas Bell, enough of his own securities to cover the £150,000 loan.* If The Bank of California failed to repay the amount, then those securities, valued at some $750,000, would be surrendered to The Oriental Bank. Finally, Ralston agreed to the appointment of an executive committee from The Bank of California's board of directors that henceforth would review every loan he made.[20]

Because Cargill had come from his talks with Ralston with complete faith in the Californian, The Oriental Bank accepted the proposal. Ralston thereupon began the urgent, tedious process of squeezing the water out of the bank's accounts and calling in enough loans to meet the various deadlines. He did this in the face of widespread rumors in eastern financial circles that there was no hope for The Bank of California. Even James Lees was so shaken by the pessimistic talk and by the effect that it was having on Wall Street that he almost lost confidence in Billy, too.

The event that precipitated Lees' doubts was this. Ralston was accustomed to endorsing commercial paper in California and then sending it to Lees and Waller in New York for sale. During September, 1869, this paper became almost impossible to place. Lees could not understand why until a "spy" named George Bradbury appeared from the potent financial house of Brown Brothers, normally a heavy purchaser of Bank of California paper, and began asking questions about Ralston. From Billy's standpoint, no better an investigator could have been dispatched. Bradbury, at one time the president of the Pacific Mail Steamship Company, was a friend of Ralston's and a stockholder in the Ralston-created Hunter's Point Dry Dock Company. As a result he told Lees as much as he learned. Rumormongers, he said, were filling Wall Street with predictions that The Bank of California was more deeply involved in speculative adventures, especially mining, than it should be. Its officers, meaning Ralston, were reputedly lax in their personal lives; often they did not appear at the bank until afternoon and sometimes not at all. Until such tales were squelched, Brown Brothers would be reluctant to deal in the bank's paper.

Lees denied the charges and Bradbury, drawing on his own knowledge of Ralston, returned to Brown Brothers with a favorable report. Lees, however, remained disturbed by the episode. To think that

---

*Thomas Bell, the second of the trustees, was a Scot who as a young man in the 1840s had joined a trading firm in Mexico that also employed William and Joseph Barron. He and the Barrons acquired an interest in the New Almaden quicksilver mines before the American conquest of California. From there he branched into many fields—like the Barrons, he was an incorporator of The Bank of California—and became wealthy. A bachelor, he consorted with Mammy Pleasants, the handsome, financially shrewd, part-black owner of San Francisco's most elegant bordellos.

*Wealthy Thomas Bell,
an incorporator of the bank,
helped rein Ralston in
when he grew too sanguine.*

Brown Brothers would do such a thing! Was there cause? In agitation he wrote a joint letter to Mills and Ralston. "For months and months your balance with us was from $500,000 to $800,000 and sometimes a million, and with the Oriental it has hardly been less than $2,000,000 and sometimes 2½ millions—when I asked myself what has the bank done with all their capital and surplus, I was entirely at a loss what to think."[21]

At that point William Cargill came to the rescue again. He stopped in New York before sailing to London, called on Lees and Waller, and gave them the reassurances they craved. Lees made sure the good word reached other bankers. This was followed a month later by news that The Oriental Bank had extended Ralston's deadline for reducing his debts. Suspicion in Wall Street eased off, and for the first time in months Ralston's gala entertainments and the bank's bland air of well-being had more behind them than Billy's optimism about his ability to handle the threats confronting him.

The swing came just in time to fend off determined attacks by his enemies. Several were converging on the East that fall. Sutro was there, lambasting The Bank of California to anyone who would listen as a "fortified monopoly" sucking out the lifeblood of the Comstock. William McGarrahan poured forth vitriol concerning the New Idria quicksilver mines. More was added by men eager to remove Ralston's friends from the San Francisco Mint and at the same time block any government legislation that might grant to the San Francisco Assaying and Refining Works preferential contracts for treating the tens of millions of dollars' worth of bullion handled each year by the West Coast mint.[22]

If the attacks had come during the low ebb of Billy's fortunes in August, they might well have damaged him severely. At the year's end it was too late. Sutro raised no capital that winter to add to the $50,000 pledged him by the miners of Virginia City. McGarrahan, as we have seen, did not gain control of New Idria. Ralston's good friend, Charles Felton, stayed on as subtreasurer in San Francisco (but some minor officials in the mint were removed), and the San Francisco Assaying and Refining Works won its contract. Meanwhile Ralston was succeeding in his reformation of the bank. Outstanding accounts were reduced (Holladay, for one instance, pared his loan from $280,000 to $40,000), doubtful assets were winnowed out, and by December, 1869, the bank was again showing a profit.[23]

At that point another unexpected hurdle arose. Darius Mills shook Ralston badly by selling 1,500 of his 2,000 shares of bank stock and asking that he be relieved as president. James Lees, his confidence in Ralston fully restored, urged Billy to accept the decision and move into Mills's place as president.[24] Ralston refused. Affairs were indeed improving, but not so much that the bank could afford a new spate of rumors occasioned by the withdrawal of its internationally known president. Talking earnestly, he persuaded Mills to stay on—no onerous request, since Ralston had always done most of the bank work anyway.

By February, 1870, Ralston had shown enough progress that The Oriental Bank raised no fuss about letting him have another four months in which to complete his work. By summer the job was done and the trustees turned back to him the personal securities they had been holding. It had been a notable performance, and both Lees and Stuart wrote him fulsome letters saying so.[25] Billy, however, was not satisfied. He was no longer drowning, true, but neither was he swimming ahead, and for a man of his sanguine temperament a cautious treading of water was not enough.

He was particularly restive concerning his personal affairs. The New Montgomery Street Real Estate Company still languished. The extension of the Virginia & Truckee Railroad from Carson City to Reno had been indefinitely postponed. Even the discovery in the Comstock's Chollar-Potosi Mine of a small but very rich ore body (it paid, during the next two years, nearly $2 million in dividends) was not truly heartening, for the mineral lay in a neglected section of the upper workings. Thus the strike gave neither Ralston nor anyone else encouragement about the lower levels of the great lode.

Miners still kept whistling in the dark, nevertheless. Another eminent geologist, Raymond W. Rossiter, predicted that big blocks of profitable mineral still awaited discovery in those hot and odorous depths. Believing Rossiter because such belief was a psychological necessity at the time, Billy urged Sharon to keep looking. They had to have another bonanza, he said.[26] He wanted it for a lifting of everyone's spirits as well as for money, and he approved of Sharon's levying of $240,000 in assessments on the stock of different mines they controlled so that the search could be pressed.

While Sharon delved deeper into the Comstock, Ralston began looking further afield. It says much about him—and about men's attitudes toward the American West of his era—that he never for a moment doubted that he could somehow tap, somewhere in that vastness, whatever fortune he needed. There is even a kind of airy disdain for his past experiences in his optimism. He knew perfectly well, from remarks that he'd been hearing from conservative eastern bankers, that mine speculation was a demerit in their eyes. But those men had not experienced with their own senses what Sierra gold and Comstock silver had done for California. He had, and he felt that such results merited risk. And so, strangely unscathed by his close brush with disaster, he prepared to plunge in again.

CHAPTER 21

Why Not Diamonds ?

Three names keep bobbing up in the tale of Ralston's search for quick new wealth. One we have encountered before, Asbury Harpending. The others are Philip Arnold and George D. Roberts.

Like Harpending, Philip Arnold was a native of Kentucky. Ten years older than Asbury, he had joined the army in August, 1847, had served in Mexico for a year, and then had gone to the Pacific Coast. The two men first encountered each other after Harpending, still in his teens, had started hydraulic mining in Yuba County in 1857. Arnold, then twenty-eight, was one of his employees.

The Civil War separated them, but they were together again in 1867 at another mine, owned jointly by Harpending and George D. Roberts. Located near the hamlet of Lincoln in Placer County, the diggings were known variously as the Gold Quarry Mine, the Banker Mine, the Harpending Mine, and the Lincoln Mine.[1] Again Harpending was the boss, Arnold the employee. He was a very good employee: tough, self-reliant, and knowledgeable about the practical aspects of his rugged work. Probably he was in charge of operations at the mine, while Harpending advised him from his San Francisco office.

Harpending's fellow proprietor in the Lincoln Mine, George D. Roberts, had often been at the edge of fortune but had never achieved it. As a poor prospector fresh from the East, he had discovered, in October, 1850, a quartz mine in Grass Valley, California. Unable to raise money for developing it, he sold the property two years later for a pittance. Named the Empire by its purchasers, it operated continuously for more than a century and produced $70 million.

Hunting wistfully for a similar strike, Roberts joined the rush to the Comstock in 1859. He failed, but did find a niche for himself as a mine

*Asbury Harpending was
Ralston's ingenious friend
and, some thought,
his evil genius as well.*

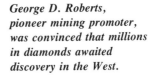

*George D. Roberts,
pioneer mining promoter,
was convinced that millions
in diamonds awaited
discovery in the West.*

broker—bringing poor mine owners and eager investors together in ways that at times were beneficial to all concerned. Some of his earnings he used for purchasing islands in the Sacramento Delta, where the rivers of the Central Valley mingle before pouring into San Francisco Bay. His hope was to drain the marshes, build levees to keep out floods, and thus turn the rich peat soil into an agricultural bonanza. First, though, he had to have money, and because of that perpetual need he was ripe for plucking.

He was as eager to please as a spaniel. He had gentle, wide-set eyes in a broad face. He wore his thin hair cut short and combed flat to his head. He had a gray moustache and a thin gray beard cropped off just below the bottom of his chin. Ralston enjoyed his talk, and occasionally lunched with him in order to tap Roberts' encyclopedic fund of information and rumor about mining developments throughout the West. Billy also took an interest in some of the delta land that Roberts owned, but because of his own financial straits could not help reclaim it.

The Lincoln Mine, in which George sank more money than he could afford, proved to be another disappointment. Hoping to unload it at a profit, Harpending and he offered it for sale in England for $250,000. Their agent there handled the matter badly, extolling the property beyond reason in the promotional literature he issued. The London *Times* sneered at the offering as a swindle, and the two owners withdrew it from the market. They did not escape unscathed. A man named I. L. Pechy, who had invested $10,000 in the mine, sued them for fraud, implying that Harpending, Roberts, and of necessity their foreman Philip Arnold had salted the ore in order to make it appear more valuable than it was.[2]

Inasmuch as Pechy did not collect, it may be that no deliberate dishonesty was involved. Certainly the episode did not diminish Ralston's esteem for the two men. It was after the London fiasco that he became associated with Harpending in the New Montgomery Street Real Estate Company. He also continued to lunch intermittently with Roberts.

As the decade of the '60s drew to a close they found much to discuss. For the past few years prospectors had been fanning eastward across Nevada, opening new mining districts of undetermined richness and extent. Ralston followed developments eagerly. When the White Pine district flashed into prominence near the Utah line late in 1868 (in three months frenzied Californians incorporated 170 White Pine mining companies with a paper value of $250 million[3]) he opened two bank agencies in the area, only to close them sheepishly when the excitement burned out eighteen months afterwards. A little later, to James Lees' sharp annoyance, he sank $370,000 of the bank's money into financing a smelter and other installations at Eureka Consolidated, a lead-silver mine in the central part of the state.[4]

A property in which Ralston became personally involved, along with Roberts, was Mineral Hill, 45 miles north of Eureka. The prospect had recently fallen into the hands of William Lent, another name that figured importantly in subsequent events. One of the original incorporators (along with Ralston) of the Comstock's first bonanza mine, the Ophir, Lent went by the nickname of Uncle Billy. It was too homey for him. He was majestically formal. He wore snowy-white shirts, a white bow tie, and suits of expensive black broadcloth, their wide lapels faced with satin. He was chunky and sallow, his stolid face adorned with a trim white Prussian moustache and a small goatee. His single concern in life, some people thought, was Uncle Billy.

So that he would not have to assume the entire risk of developing Mineral Hill himself, Lent sold 12,000 shares of stock in the company to Ralston and another 8,000 shares, held jointly, to Roberts and Harpending.[5] As the shaft deepened during 1870, the underground promises shone brighter and brighter. All four owners grew very hopeful for the future, none more so than George Roberts.

Another alluring mine in which most of the same men became involved bobbed up at about the same time in the extreme southwestern part of New Mexico, two or three miles south of present Lordsburg, in barren hills that government surveyors named the Pyramid Range but that local people called the Burro Mountains. Late in 1869 silver had been discovered there by a man named W. D. Brown, who came to San Francisco to seek financing. The upshot was Harpending & Company, formed to exploit Brown's claims. The principal owners of Harpending & Company were Brown, Harpending, Roberts, and Philip Arnold.[6] Ralston's financial interest at first was minor, yet from that casual beginning would spring his involvement in one of the most bizarre episodes ever to occur in the freewheeling West, the so-called great diamond hoax.

An expedition led by Brown and captained by Arnold reached the Burro Mines in March, 1870. There the men laid out what they called (echoes of the Comstock!) the Virginia Mining District and platted a town site with the obvious intent of selling lots to an influx of stampeders. That job done, Arnold returned to San Francisco with thirty-two samples of ore for assaying. Roberts grew so ecstatic over results that he somehow raised $25,000 and bought Arnold's share of the property. It was a transaction they would all look back on with mortification some months later.[7]

Having given up his financial interest in the mine, Arnold also lost his job as superintendent and was replaced by Brown.[8] The new manager pushed development work hard. Among other things he ordered from San Francisco a diamond drill, a machine used for boring deep holes in connection with underground exploratory work. That drill, too, would cause wry reflections later on.

By August, Brown had thirty men at work under the broiling sun. He was also beginning to encounter threats from disgruntled outsiders, who insisted loudly that the original Arnold-Brown discovery expedition had not followed territorial law when entering its claim and that therefore the ground, including the town site, was open to jumping. At that point Harpending & Company began talking of hiring professional gunmen to defend its property, a step it took a few months later.[9] It is another point to be remembered.

The company directors also decided to shore up the status of the town site by formally incorporating it so that normal municipal functions, including police service, could be installed. In order to take that step they had to have a name for the place—one that could be submitted to the Post Office along with an application for mail service. The designation they chose was Ralston. On December 8, 1870, after several weeks had been spent ironing out the preliminaries, Ralston, New Mexico, became a legal entity.[10] All this suggests that Billy's monetary interest in the company, and particularly in the town site, had increased materially since the formation of the firm.

After the name had been chosen but before it was affixed to the tumultuous town, the San Francisco owners of the mine decided that one of them should have a look at the place—and at the work of the partner they scarcely knew, W. D. Brown. Asbury Harpending, the youngest of the group (thirty-one in the fall of 1870 as compared to Ralston's forty-four), was chosen for the mission.

He took with him two persons destined to bring radical alterations during the next two years to his own affairs and to those of his associates. One was James B. Cooper, an employee of the company that manufactured the diamond drill that Brown had ordered. Presumably Cooper was going to the Burro Mines to check on the machine's operations. The other wayfarer was Henry Morgan, an amiable Englishman six feet six inches tall who professed to be a mining engineer on vacation, touring the American West to see the sights. Harpending undertook to show him a few.

When the travelers reached the town of Ralston, Harpending found that Phil Arnold had returned there. With Arnold was his cousin, John Burchem Slack. Slack, too, had worked for a time at Harpending's hydraulic mine in Yuba County, California. During the Civil War, Slack had drifted east into Arizona and had been in the territory ever since. For a time he had been in charge of a mine near Prescott, and he had sat for a term in the Arizona legislature—which is to say he was more than a common prospector.[11] Inevitably James Cooper, the diamond-drill expert, met both cousins.

During the following week, Henry Morgan, the English engineer, grew wildly excited about the Burro Mines. He vowed that he could sell the property in England for $3 million. Harpending was dubious— or so he wrote in his memoirs—but agreed that the proposal was worth submitting to his partners in San Francisco.[12]

When they reached the city early in November, they found Billy Ralston the talk of the town for having engineered a triumph that typifies the speculative fevers of the times. The Mercantile Library, with which he was philanthropically involved, had needed $500,000 for paying off a mortgage on its new building and for providing an endowment for the future. Aware that no such sum could be raised through standard appeals to a handful of wealthy men, Ralston had proposed selling tickets to a million-dollar lottery. Under his plan half the proceeds would be distributed as prizes and half would be retained by the library. He helped prevail on the legislature to pass the necessary bill, and organized a campaign that quickly disposed of 200,000 tickets at $5.00 each. On the day of the drawing, November 1, 1870, business stopped throughout the city and an enormous concourse of people gathered to watch a blind boy draw the ticket stub designating the winner of the first prize of $100,000, a blind girl draw the second of $50,000, and so on.[13]

The luck of the draw. Perhaps the Burro (or Pyramid) mines were the partners' winning number in their mining lottery. They authorized Morgan to hurry to London and set up the necessary sales organization. Harpending would follow to answer technical questions about the mine.

Harpending then suggested that while he was abroad, he should try selling some mines himself. Being a very plausible young man, he managed to collect in a few days quite a portfolio of offerings.[14] The only one that concerns us here is Mineral Hill, owned jointly, it will be recalled, by Uncle Billy Lent, William Ralston, George D. Roberts, and Asbury Harpending himself. Then, during the latter part of November, off he went to London, dreams of fat commissions whirling in his head.

Far stranger dreams were meanwhile shaping up in New Mexico. About ten days after Harpending and Morgan had left the Burro Mines, their ex-foreman, Philip Arnold, and the diamond-drill expert, James B. Cooper, also started for San Francisco. Apparently John Slack was not with them; at least his name does not appear in the skimpy records that survive.

In Tucson the two travelers showed to a newspaper reporter from the *Weekly Arizonan* some crystals that they said were diamonds.[15] Cooper added that rubies and other precious stones abounded in the area from which the crystals came. He did not say where this area was.

The *Arizonan* printed the item on November 19, 1870, with what amounted to a shrug. Semiprecious stones—garnets, quartz crystals, topaz, turquoise, even occasional rubies—occurred throughout Arizona Territory. Greenhorns were always thinking they had found fabulous jewels.[16] Quite probably Arnold and Cooper were, at that point, no different from the others.

Just what was the source of those crystals? Arnold could have picked them up in the Burro Mountains. A more likely point of origin, however, is John Slack, who had been in Arizona for the past ten years. As a miner Slack would have been attracted by unusual specimens either on the ground or in jewelry made by Indians. During the course of the decade he could have put together a handsome collection. He might well have shown that collection to Arnold and Cooper while they were at the mines, and the sight might have set their imaginations afire.

Cooper worked with diamond drills. Low-grade diamonds were attached to the bits of such drills to enhance their cutting power. Thus Cooper should have known what rough diamonds looked like. Perhaps —we are in the realm of pure speculation—perhaps that very fact fooled him. He may have supposed that the crystals really were diamonds.

There is another point. Cooper surely knew, as perhaps Arnold and Slack also did, that the first discovery of a diamond in South Africa had occurred only three years before, in 1867. (Before then the bulk of the world's supply had come from Brazil.) By 1870 a full-scale rush to the African diamond fields was under way, and American newspapers carried frequent stories about the excitement.

Why shouldn't comparable fields exist in the American West? It had already produced several breathtaking bonanzas—the California placers, the Comstock Lode, the diggings of Idaho, Montana, and Colorado, and, for timber cutters, the unbelievable redwoods. So why not diamonds, emeralds, rubies, sapphires? The very tone behind that rhetorical question is essential to understanding the diamond hoax. If Arnold, Slack, and Cooper could ask themselves "Why not?" when turning the crystals in their hands, then they would assume that others would respond in the same way. In other words, a predisposition toward belief was already in existence in the sanguine atmosphere of the boom-time West.

Enthralled by that belief—this is still speculation—Arnold and Cooper persuaded Slack to let them take some of the choicest crystal to San Francisco for testing. The results were negative. Fooled! . . . and then this thought: if two men as knowledgeable as themselves had been taken in so easily by the crystals, then others could be, too.

They set the stage swiftly. It was a simple matter to either buy or steal a few rough, uncut diamonds from the stock at the drill company where Cooper worked. They mixed these stones with the original crystals, and then—we are leaving speculation now for recorded fact—they went in search of Harpending.[17]

Presumably the novice swindlers chose Harpending because through him they would be able to approach really big money, namely William Ralston and The Bank of California crowd. A crucial question is this. Did they intend to make Harpending their dupe? Or did they have reason to suppose that he would be willing to participate in the swindle?

Arguments can be produced to support either contention. Harpending had suddenly become a supersalesman of mines, abrim with a promoter's zeal. While in that exuberant frame of mind, he might not question too closely the authenticity of a diamond discovery presented to him by a long-time friend and valued employee.

On the other hand, Harpending had shown, in such instances as the Lincoln Mine promotion, a disposition to shave the edges of the truth, as Arnold knew. Phil may have reasoned, accordingly, that Harpending could be prevailed upon to join a diamond fraud if it looked profitable.

Whatever the truth, Arnold and Cooper learned that for the time being Harpending was out of reach. So they used George Roberts instead. They let him take their small stock of crystals to a local jeweler, who of course noted the genuine diamonds that had been planted among them. At Robert's behest the schemers then sent two or three of those real, raw diamonds to lapidaries in Boston for cutting and appraisal.[18] But whenever they were asked about the site of the mines, they "shut themselves up like a jackknife," to borrow a phrase that Ralston used in a letter some months later.[19]

They were afraid, they said, that if they even hinted at the location, the news would leak and catapult a horde of prospectors into the area. Look at what was happening at Ralston town, where the company was hiring gunmen to defend its claims. Until they knew a better way to protect their discovery, they would reveal nothing about the site. In fact, they said, the whole problem of protection was one of the things they wanted to talk over with Harpending.[20]

Meanwhile the only word that came from Harpending was a request for $10,000 to be used for starting what he called the *London Stock Exchange Review*, wherein speculative offerings from the United States —notably Harpending's own—would be analyzed for the benefit of English investors. Reluctantly Asbury's backers sent the money, although Roberts had to borrow from Ralston in order to raise his share.[21]

When the crystals that had been sent to Boston came back sparkling like icy fire, accompanied by unassailable word that the largest among them was worth $3,000, George became feverish.* He poured out letters to Harpending. Why hang around London, where he seemed to be accomplishing nothing? Come home! "Your presence here," he wailed in writing, "will insure our chances in the diamond discovery, which I consider to be worth millions."[22]

Unable to stand the suspense, he violated his promises of secrecy to Arnold and Cooper and showed the cut stones to Lent and Ralston. Arnold may have been counting on this all long. In any event he learned what he wanted to know about the reactions of monied people. Lent was mildly interested. Ralston, as his correspondence shows, was not.[23]

It is easy to guess why. Billy was used to thinking in terms of steamship lines, railroads, and Comstock mines whose shafts dropped more than a thousand feet into a wider vein than men had ever seen before. A few sparklers from what was probably shallow gravel in the remote Southwest did not challenge him.

---

*An industrial diamond probably could not have been cut into a gem worth $3,000. The true source of that stone is thus another of the frustrating mysteries of the strange hoax.

It is a measure of Arnold that he grasped the problem immediately. You do not hunt elephants with popguns. If he hoped to command Ralston's attention he would have to overwhelm him with diamonds.

The awareness lifted him completely out of Cooper's sphere. Overwhelm? The drill expert backed off. They could not draw on his company's limited stock for that many diamonds, and he had no money for going somewhere else to buy more. Besides, the long delays had given him time to grow nervous about the whole business.

At that, Arnold, who still had most of the $25,000 he had received for his share of the Burro Mines, prepared to drop Cooper. He told Roberts that the fellow didn't count. Phil's cousin, John Slack, was the one who had made the discovery—and was the only one who knew its exact location, some three hundred miles north of the newly christened town of Ralston. Arnold then sent for Slack—at least his name now bobs up for the first time in Roberts' correspondence—and early in March they departed, ostensibly for the Southwest to do some more prospecting.[24]

Their real destination was probably London. As they either knew themselves or had learned from Cooper, the city was one of the world's principal marketplaces for cheap industrial gems. In addition there is this piece of flimsy evidence. In August, 1872, when the London *Times* was raising questions about the American diamond strikes, an English correspondent wrote Samuel Barlow, a New York lawyer who had become involved in the affair, a curious letter. In the spring of 1871— the correspondent recalled March as the month—an American had been buying diamonds in London without indicating what the gems were for.[25] Jewelers liked to have that information because it helped them serve their clients. Silence on the subject was odd—and remembered. But of course that trifle is not enough to identify Arnold or Slack as the purchaser, even though they did return to San Francisco late in May with a sackful of rough gems to show to their intended victims.[26]

Meanwhile Asbury Harpending had launched his *London Stock Exchange Review*. Shortly thereafter, on January 22, 1871, Henry Morgan issued a prospectus that purported to describe the newly discovered Pyramid Range Silver Mountain Company Mines of New Mexico— nothing so prosaic as Burro Mines for Morgan. The mountains in the vicinity of the mines, his brochure said, were composed almost entirely of silver ore that assayed more than $4,000 a ton. The outcroppings were not buried deep in the earth. "The miner," the prospectus declared, "has but to select the most desired locality for his blast, and then quarry out the ore-bearing rock without timber or windlass in the broad light of day." In other words neither shafts nor tunnels would reduce profits.[27]

Later Harpending claimed that he had nothing to do with those sweeping claims. His own *Exchange* belies him. In its columns he commented on Morgan's offering as follows: "One pauses for want of breath in the contemplation [of the mine], and we will merely add that the enterprise is introduced under such thoroughly respectable auspices that there can be no shadow of suspicion of intentional exaggeration."[28]

Marmaduke Sampson, the financial editor of the London *Times*, disagreed. On January 28 and again on January 30, he attacked the offering ruthlessly. He compared the overblown prospectus with the one that had been issued on behalf of the Lincoln Mine of Placer County, California, in 1867. He pointed out that George Roberts and Asbury Harpending were on the board of directors of both the Lincoln and Pyramid mines. Sarcastically he asked what had become of the gaudy ore that the Lincoln Company had promised to investors. Would the same sorry fate befall the people who bought Pyramid stock? By the time he was through, Pyramid was dead.

Billy learned the news from clippings sent to him by William Cargill of The Oriental Bank.[29] Since Ralston's name did not appear in the *Times'* stories, no veiled reprimand was intended. Cargill had simply

This diamond (enlarged in photo) may be one of those used in the hoax; it is now owned by the California Division of Mines and Geology.

thought that Ralston would be interested, as indeed he was. Possibly he even squirmed a little when he read the clippings and recalled his promises to the Oriental people that he would be more careful about mine speculations.

He was also angry. Roberts and he both wrote sharp letters to Harpending asking for details. When Asbury did not answer, Ralston wired The Oriental Bank, requesting them to locate the fellow and tell him to get in touch with San Francisco.[30]

None of this perturbed Harpending. Through contacts unnecessary to describe here he had gained the ear of the most notorious English promoter of the nineteenth century. Born Albert Gottheimer, the fellow had purchased an Italian barony and went by the name of Baron Albert Grant. He sympathized with Harpending over Sampson's slaying of Pyramid and said that *he* could handle the editor in case Harpending had another mine to offer. At that Harpending brought up Mineral Hill. Grant was immediately interested. By April, affairs had progressed far enough that Asbury and a representative of Grant's company decided to journey to San Francisco and wind up the details with the principals there. The sale, if it went through, would amount to more than a million dollars.

Because he was the bearer now of good tidings, Harpending did not worry about the Pyramid fiasco, but airily shifted the blame onto Morgan. And then there were the diamonds. Had he seen Arnold and Slack in London, either as their dupe or as a willing participant in their proposed swindle? Or was he simply responding at last to Roberts' feverish letters? None of the questions can be answered with assurance. In any event, by spring he was excited. To Alfred Rubery, the young Englishman who had shared his privateering misadventures during the Civil War, he said he had wind of a discovery that would astonish the world.[31]

With such thoughts to buoy him he sailed for America. He was in San Francisco when Slack and Arnold returned from their prospecting trip laden with enough diamonds, they hoped, to seduce Ralston, with or without Harpending's help, and thus bring life to their scheme.

CHAPTER 22

Bedazzled

One of the stones that Arnold and Slack brought to San Francisco was an irregularly shaped, dull-looking pebble that weighed 108 carats. They showed this gem to Roberts and Harpending and then let one or the other of them submit it to Shreve & Company, respected San Francisco jewelers, for appraisal.

They were taking a calculated risk. Wherever that rough diamond had come from, it had cost Arnold and Slack no more than a few thousand dollars. But would the experts at Shreve & Company recognize its poor quality? San Francisco jewelers seldom handled raw stones, but bought their stock already cut from wholesalers in the East. Their tendency, as Cooper probably had told Arnold, was to overvalue rough gems.

In spite of their hopes the conspirators must have been astounded by the appraisal rendered—$96,000, a sum roughly comparable to $1 million in terms of today's inflated prices.[1]

How does one explain so extraordinary a miscalculation? Possibly the appraiser was bribed. Possibly the appraisal papers were forged, although later investigations turned up no evidence of that kind of hanky-panky. More probably the bluff worked because, as has already been indicated, the milieu was right. Nothing was impossible in the West of Billy Ralston's time. Given that atmosphere, a man radiating confidence might well march into a jewelry store, say firmly, "I think I found a good diamond back on the mesas; what do you think?" and receive an affirmative answer from an appraiser who recognized the stone as a diamond but had no satisfactory way of testing its worth.

In any event, $96,000 was what the appraiser said. At that Roberts, Harpending, Slack, and Arnold promptly came to terms. Each man was to own a quarter interest in the mine, Slack and Arnold on the strength

William Lent, leading California and Nevada mining figure, was completely taken in by Arnold's and Slack's "discovery."

of their discovery, and Roberts and Harpending in return for producing investors willing to pay enough for a part interest in the property to make the activities of all of them worthwhile.

The first candidates for the sales pitch were Uncle Billy Lent and a friend of Lent's, Gen. George S. Dodge. One evening in early June, Lent and Dodge met with Roberts and Harpending at the latter's Fremont Street home—Ralston's former dwelling. Arnold and Slack were not present, probably because they didn't wish to appear too eager to sell so grand a property.

The drama was carefully prepared. Harpending upended a bag of gems onto his billiard table. The slithering pile, he said, consisted of 80,000 carats of rubies (most of the "rubies" were probably garnets) and several diamonds, some of which were certainly white topaz and quartz. Roberts held up the stone that Shreve & Company had valued at $96,000 and then estimated that the value of the whole collection was somewhere in the neighborhood of $600,000. In other words, the promoters were wisely not pretending that the average stone was as valuable per carat weight as that one spectacular.

Roberts—poor gullible George had really been taken in—then applied the clincher. He said, and probably believed, that Slack wanted to sell out quick for $100,000. The prospector was old and worn by his rugged life. Moreover a spiritualist had warned him that he would not live long if he made many trips to the mine.

Lent asked, cannily enough, why the promoters didn't sell the gems on the table and divide the proceeds. If the jewels were worth $600,000, Slack's share would bring him more than he was asking for his quarter interest in the whole discovery.

The promoters were offended. Slack wouldn't do that to his friends. Dumping so many jewels on the market at once would attract attention. They'd be followed wherever they went. They wouldn't be able to visit their own mine without revealing the secret of what might be the most extraordinary find in the United States.

Lent and Dodge still hesitated. Could they examine the mine?

Again the promoters recoiled. Arnold and Slack, they said, had been turned intensely suspicious by their experiences with the claim jumpers at Ralston town. They did not want a similar experience at the diamond mines. For one thing, the field was too large for two mineral claims to cover it. Hence they refused to reveal the site to anyone until they could protect all of it.

The argument did not budge Lent or Dodge. They insisted on seeing the gems in the ground with their own eyes.

Word of their intransigence was carried to Arnold and Slack, who grew indignant. Was their honor being questioned? Give them three months, they said hotly, and they would go to the mines, dig up $2 million worth of stones, and bring them back to show the doubting Thomases. But first they wanted evidence of good faith on the part of Lent and Dodge—namely $100,000.

Two million dollars worth of diamonds! At that point the victims caved in. Before clucking over the ease of their seduction, however, we should remember that they were not dealing directly with two hardcase miners. They were working through intermediaries, Roberts and Harpending, whom they trusted and with whom they had had business associations over many years. Harpending was on the point of selling for more than a million dollars the Mineral Hill mine in which Lent held the major interest. Naturally Uncle Bill was disposed to listen to him. Finally, as security against the pair's absconding, there was that $96,000 stone, plus the rest of the jewels in the sack.

Dodge drew on The Bank of California for $50,000 and handed the draft to Slack for one-half of his interest in the discovery. Lent promised to pay another $50,000 as soon as Dodge and he saw the stones the two men brought back.

Once again Slack and Arnold disappeared, this time with $50,000 to invest. Again they traveled to England. In July, according to later revelations, a man who had "all the appearances of a hardworking digger" and who said he was a railroad contractor bought with cash several thousand dollars' worth of rough diamonds from the London jewelry firm of Pittar, Levinson & Company. At approximately the same time the firm of Leopold Keller & Company sold to two rough-looking individuals about $15,000 worth of inferior diamonds. One of the pair gave his name as "Arundle," which is vaguely like Arnold. The other said his name was Burchem. Burchem, probably not by coincidence, was John Slack's middle name.[2]

In August the pair returned to San Francisco. Notified by telegram of their approach, Harpending met their train in Lathrop, a station sixty miles or so east of Oakland. He found them travel-stained and weary. They had dug up $2 million worth of stones, as promised, but, they admitted, they had lost half the treasure when the homemade raft on which they were crossing a flooded stream flipped end over end. They hoped, however, that what was left would be enough to convince the doubters.

Convince them it did—a cascading million dollars in jewels! On Lent's behalf (Uncle Billy was out of town) Dodge paid Slack the promised $50,000 for his remaining one-eighth interest in the discovery. They then besought Ralston to join them in setting up a company to handle the property. For the prestige of his name they were willing to give him a one-sixth interest. They proposed to break down the shares of the others as follows. Arnold would hold a quarter interest as discoverer. Harpending and Roberts would each receive, like Ralston, a sixth. Lent and Dodge, the only ones who had yet paid actual cash for their shares, would continue to hold what they had bought from Slack— a one-eighth interest each—all of which says something about the wages of promotion.[3]

Ralston agreed. He did not even ask to have the mine examined.[4] His reasons were much like those that had swayed Lent and Dodge. He had seen the earth-stained gems with his own eyes, and he assumed almost automatically, that so many precious stones—one valued at $96,000— could have come from no other place than the earth of his beloved West. In order to exploit the gems he was joining experienced mining men whom he had known for a long time and in whom he had confidence.

Did not Harpending's sale of Mineral Hill justify that confidence?

Beyond that was the imponderable but very potent element of Ralston's faith in himself. He believed in the intuitive urgings that other men call their lucky stars. His star was rising again. The sale of Mineral Hill was one indication. Spectacular developments on the Comstock, of which we will hear more in the next chapter, were another. As fresh stacks of money flowed steadily into the bank, he soon became his old irrepressible self, eager for new adventures in what was still a largely undeveloped land.

The pattern that the group proposed to follow was standard for mine promotions of the time. They had already taken the first step when they had organized an informal company to own the discovery. The next move was to form an exploitation company that would obtain capital for its operations by persuading wealthy investors to buy its stock. The exploitation company would use part of this new capital for buying the interests of the discovery group. The six owners of the discovery company—Arnold, Harpending, Roberts, Lent, Dodge, and Ralston, with Slack now eliminated—would also be given stock in the exploitation company. Thus they would be paid not only for their efforts but would also share in whatever profits the new company developed.

They proposed to incorporate the new company for what was then a breathtaking sum—$10 million, represented by 100,000 shares of $100 par value stock. True, the stock would not cost the initial purchasers its full face value. Even so, the totals involved were so high that Ralston did not believe the money could be easily raised in San Francisco, where the effects of the business downswing of 1869–70 still lingered. On his recommendation, therefore, they decided to incorporate in New York.

The lawyer Ralston chose for handling the critical details of organization was one of the era's most colorful and famous attorneys, Samuel L. M. Barlow. Barlow was wealthy, debonair, and fat, his bushy sideburns framing a double chin and handlebar moustaches. His specialty was corporate organization and finance. When he needed favors from Congress, he generally worked through Representative Benjamin Butler of Massachusetts, a corrupt politician but a brilliant lawyer with an unrivaled knowledge of behind-the-scenes Washington. An ardent Democrat, Barlow was also an intimate of Gen. George B. McClellan and had worked assiduously to have McClellan elected president over Lincoln in 1864. He was also adept at finding lucrative, nonmilitary jobs for the general.[5] Ralston had known Barlow ever since his days as a Vanderbilt steamship agent, and so it was natural to seek Barlow's assistance in establishing the diamond company as a New York corporation.

Oddly, Ralston did not go east. Neither did Roberts. Both gave their powers of attorney to Harpending, who joined Lent and Dodge in New York for the discussions with Barlow. Philip Arnold also journeyed to

New York, but, as had been true in San Francisco, he let Harpending do his talking for him. As visual evidence that they were not completely mad, the westerners took with them the bag of gems that Arnold and Slack had produced in August after their purported misadventure with the upset raft. The other bag, the one containing the $96,000 diamond, remained behind in The Bank of California.

The sight of the gems and the eloquence of the visitors failed to convince Barlow, and he wired Ralston for additional details.

Ralston replied on October 16, 1871, with a telegram that Barlow found incomprehensible, probably because Billy used circumlocutions rather than mention diamonds in a public telegram. Barlow again wrote, urgently this time.[6] Ralston replied on October 24 with another telegram and a letter. Only a flimsy letterpress copy of the letter survives. Parts are illegible, much is incoherent, all is agitated. In none of its five pages did Billy mention the stones in the bank. He admitted very candidly that there was an "*utter want* of anything like business information for your guidance." He pointed out the fact that Harpending was the key to the affair, since he was the only effective contact between the purchasers and the discoverers. But said Ralston, he had faith in Harpending and was willing to follow the lead of Lent and Dodge in putting money into what he considered "a *legitimate mining* investment." He finished by saying, "This letter *must be* kept as confidential . . . as I don't want to be counted as crazy."[7]

Today the letter hardly seems persuasive, but it suited Barlow, partly because of what had happened just before its arrival. After receiving Ralston's telegram of October 24, which must have been reassuring, he had summoned a distinguished group of New Yorkers to meet with the San Franciscans at his palatial home at 1 Madison Avenue. Present were Gen. George McClellan, Congressman Benjamin Butler, a Mr. Duncan, partner in the banking firm of Duncan, Sherman & Company, Horace Greeley, editor of the New York *Tribune* (who must have been sworn to secrecy), and Charles Tiffany of the famed jewelry house of Tiffany & Company—plus, of course, Harpending, Lent, and Dodge, but not Arnold.

The easterners listened to what was now a well-worn tale and then watched Charles Tiffany paw through the stones. The samples looked good, he said, but he would not commit himself on values without consulting his lapidaries. Could he take about a tenth of the pile for testing?

Two days later he was back with a report that is the most incredible part of the whole tale. His gemologists were evidently as ignorant of rough stones from South Africa (none had reached America as yet) as were the jewelers of San Francisco—and as susceptible to suggestion about the marvels of the West. They valued the collection at $150,000. Tiffany himself concurred.[8]

If the sample Tiffany had checked was worth $150,000, then the whole sackful of gems, which had been deposited for safekeeping in Duncan, Sherman & Company's vaults, should be worth $1.5 million. In California there was another sackful. Included in it was a stone appraised by the reputable firm of Shreve & Company as worth $96,000. The implications disarmed the victims completely. Such figures were clearly out of the range of common bunco artists. Against that background, Ralston's confidence in the "legitimate mining venture" seemed sound, and Barlow straightaway began organizing what the participants named the Golconda Mining Company.

The six owners of the discovery site—Arnold, Dodge, Lent, Harpending, Roberts, and Ralston—transferred to Golconda every interest they possessed, except the $96,000 stone in San Francisco. This was to be sold and the proceeds distributed: one-third to Arnold, one-third to Slack, and one-third in roughly equal portions to Lent, Dodge, Harpending, Roberts, and Ralston. The special treatment of the big stone, along with its tacit admission that Slack had sold out too cheaply, was clever psychology on someone's part, for it strengthened the aura of authenticity surrounding the whole affair.[9]

Barlow was to be paid $250,000 in Golconda Company stock for his services. He received another $100,000, also in stock, to be used in wheedling from Congress whatever legislation was necessary for obtaining full title to an extensive tract of ground surrounding the discovery site.

The next step was to learn where the fields were. This faced Arnold with a real problem. He had been spending his time, money, and ingenuity in producing gems enough to hook his victims, and in all probability had not yet decided where to locate the reputed treasure house. To cover his quandary he grew stubborn. He was vulnerable, he said. How could he be sure that these powerful men would not cheat him out of his discovery once they knew where it was? He would not reveal the location unless given $250,000 in cash—$100,000 down and the balance after he had guided a geologist of the company's own choosing to the secret field. Because of snow, he said, the trip could not take place until April. (The April date suggests that he was still thinking in terms of the Southwest.) If he failed to appear in April, the company could reimburse itself from the bags of stones in San Francisco and New York. Meanwhile he was going back to Kansas to relax from the rigors of the past year by hunting buffalo.

Who was to provide the initial $100,000 down payment? Lent said he would put up half if Ralston would match the sum. Contacted by telegraph, Ralston agreed. Early in November, Barlow handed the prospector $100,000 in greenbacks. Arnold distributed the bundles about his person under his shirt and walked calmly out of the door.[10]

One has to admire the man's aplomb. He could have disappeared then, well paid for his troubles. Instead he decided to buy more jewels in London, salt some convenient field, face down an investigation by whatever eminent geologist the company chose to send with him, and collect another $150,000.

By December, as later investigations would show, he was in both Paris and London, buying at least $8,500 worth of inferior gems. In December, Asbury Harpending also went to London, this time with his wife, to revive his *Stock Exchange Review* and resume selling mines. A witness testifying during a later lawsuit swore to seeing Arnold and Harpending together on the streets during that time.[11]

Of itself the meeting does not mean that Harpending knew why Arnold was in the city. What is troublesome (if the meeting indeed occurred) is Harpending's silence about it in view of the crisis which Arnold's disappearance was creating for the new Golconda Company.

One of the reasons that Arnold had given for not revealing the location of the diamond fields was their size. They extended, he said, across 3,000 acres, far too much to be covered by the small claims authorized by the mining laws of the United States. There was even some doubt that those laws, which dealt with ground containing valuable metals, would be elastic enough to embrace precious stones. Until those loopholes were plugged, Arnold insisted, he would not reveal the discovery.

Barlow's first task following the organization of the Golconda Mining Company was the closing of those gaps. He used part of his expense money to support amendments liberalizing the claim laws.[12] This was a contingency measure, however. What the company really wanted to do, if possible, was engross the entire area for itself.

The best method for doing this, Barlow decided, was to obtain from Congress the right to run a railroad through the region, together with the supplementary right of purchasing 3,000 acres scattered along the route. The company's purpose, it was given out by Congressman Benjamin Butler, was the acquisition of coal.[13] All seemed so well, indeed, that several potent investors—notably bankers August Belmont and Henry Seligman of New York and certain wealthy friends of Barlow's in England—made down payments on Golconda stock. Imagine being able to control the only considerable diamond fields in North America!

Unfortunately for the company, the request for railroad legislation had to be accompanied by a map showing the line's approximate route. But where were the fields? A frantic search began for Arnold, the only person able to provide the information. Since he was assumed to be hunting buffalo in Kansas, Barlow hired a Kansas City detective agency to run him down. Naturally they came up empty-handed.[14] Why no one informed Harpending of the search—he knew Arnold better than did anyone else in the company—or why nothing resulted if he was informed, those questions constitute just one more enigma surrounding Asbury's true role in the conspiracy.

The lapse was costly. Congress shelved the railroad bill; Belmont and Seligman grew restless. Barlow took alarm, for if those two declined to support the company, others would also shy away. Desperately he urged patience: Arnold was a strange sort, but he would reappear in April as he had promised. An expedition would then go with him to the diamond fields and stake sound claims, for at least Congress had passed, in March, 1872, the amendments to the mining laws that the company desired. Later, if the step seemed wise, the railroad legislation could be revived.

Alas for that hope, too. Arnold showed up in San Francisco in March —where he rejoined Slack—but he flatly refused to start for the diamond fields until the end of May. Too much snow, he said. Meanwhile he had better things to do, mainly moving his wife and children, who were living in San Francisco, back to their old home at Elizabethtown, Kentucky.

Unable to budge him, Ralston, Roberts, and Barlow all cabled Harpending to hurry home and talk sense to the recalcitrant fool.[15] Wondering what on earth was up, Harpending sailed for the United States on April 17, taking with him his English friend, Alfred Rubery, who had just caught his wife in his own bed with a seventeen-year-old boy and who felt in need of distraction.

It was too late. Arnold had disappeared again, this time with his family.[16] Belmont, Seligman, and several others thereupon withdrew from the Golconda Mining Company.[17] Furiously Ralston wired Harpending in New York, "A[rnold] pledged his honor as a man to carry out faithfully programme as agreed. We did not then nor do we now believe he intended doing so . . . [and] consider ourselves swindled out of the fifty we paid."[18]

The message is revealing. Ralston was not questioning the existence of the diamonds, which by then he fiercely wanted to be real. Rather, he feared that Arnold, for scoundrelly purposes of his own, was not going to reveal their source in spite of the money he had collected. The brainwashing, in short, was complete, and does much to explain the persistence of the victims.

Arnold's shifting of dates from April until May probably means that he had given up the Southwest as a site for his presumed discovery. As yet no railroad entered either New Mexico or Arizona, and accordingly Slack's and his movements would lack anonymity, especially since both were relatively well known in the area. What they needed for their salting was a sizable region that they could approach quickly without attracting attention, and yet one that was isolated enough so that chance wanderers were not likely to stumble across traces of their activities.

One good place that Arnold had noticed during his travels back and forth across the continent was the section south of the Union Pacific's line through southwestern Wyoming. As far as he could learn, the area was scarcely known. Slack and he could step off the train a few score miles east or west of where they wanted to go, rent horses, mix up their tracks, and then vanish into the wilds, traveling far enough to be sure of leaving the area of the Union Pacific's land grants. Unhappily, the region was also 7,000 feet above sea level and would be heaped with snow for weeks to come. Until he was sure he could prepare his ground for inspection, he was not going to say anything about its location.

The company officials for their part were growing increasingly anxious to hurry him into the field with a geologist so that they could produce a report that would lure the lost investors back into the fold. Stung by Ralston's anger, Harpending somehow got in touch with Slack, who was then in St. Louis. Through him he made arrangements for Arnold to meet an investigating party in that city in mid-May, two weeks earlier than Arnold's date, and lead it to the diamond fields.

Now for a geologist. By great good luck Asbury met in a New York hotel one of the country's best earth scientists, Henry Janin, who had already done a good deal of consulting work for Ralston.[19] If a man of Janin's stature reported favorably on the discovery, Golconda would soar again.

Janin agreed to examine the fields for a fee of $2,500 and an option to buy 1,000 shares of Golconda stock at $10 a share.[20] In company with Dodge, Harpending, and Rubery, he then headed for St. Louis to meet Arnold and Slack. The pair did not appear for two weeks. Almost certainly they had been using the time to salt their hurriedly chosen ground. How they calmed the impatient group in St. Louis does not appear, but about June 1 the investigating party, now consisting of six men—Janin, Harpending, Rubery, Dodge, Arnold, and Slack—boarded a Union Pacific train for Rawlins, Wyoming. This must have surprised those who were still thinking in terms of the Southwest.

At Rawlins they rented horses and camp equipment and zigzagged southwestward for four days, until they reached the sagebrush and piñon mesas that border the northern arm of what is now Dinosaur National Monument, Colorado. (It would have been possible to get there in one day from the railroad, but Arnold did not want the trip to appear too easy.) Finally they camped and the prospectors put them to digging. All told they produced in two days of frenzied activity about four pounds of rubies and 1,628 carats of diamonds, many of poor quality. They then stopped digging in order to stake out the maximum number of homestead, mineral, and water claims that the law allowed each man. The total fell far short of covering the whole field, but the railroad legislation having failed it was the best they could do.

As soon as the staking was finished, Harpending announced that they were running short of supplies and should leave. Besides, his wife, who had returned from England with him and was visiting in Tarryton, New York, had not been feeling well and, he said, he was worried about her health.[21]

Janin was dumbfounded. Although the digging had been good, it had been confined to a narrow section and he wanted to test the full area over which their claims extended. The others, their hands blistered and their backs aching, overruled him, and back they went.

In presenting his report to Barlow, Ralston, and the others, Janin said cautiously that it was preliminary and confidential. "I desire," he wrote, "to particularly impress on the mind of any potential purchaser that I am not in a position to say, owing to the limited time allowed me for prospecting the ground, how extensive the area of rich gravel is." But then his excitement took over and he concluded, "I consider this a wonderfully rich discovery. . . . Any investment at $40 per share [is] a safe and attractive one."

How could he possibly have thought so? Well, for one thing, he did not know diamonds. For another, he could not believe that men like Barlow and Ralston would be mixed up in such a venture without sound reason. Like the others, he believed that anything was possible in the wide open West. Seeing is believing. He had hefted the gems in New York. When he later picked salted diamonds out of a Colorado anthill with his own fingers, his duping was complete.

Arnold demanded and received from the owners of the discovery site the $150,000 due him for guiding the party to the field. He then sold through Harpending, acting as agent for unspecified parties, 15,000 of his 18,750 shares in the Golconda Company. He received $300,000. Part of these substantial sums—$450,000 altogether—was met by Lent, who drew on Ralston for $75,000, and by George Roberts, who gave Arnold a note for $150,000 payable thirty days from July 17, 1872. Roberts covered the note when it fell due by borrowing from Ralston.[22] The source of the remaining $225,000 is uncertain, but it is reasonable to assume that Ralston provided much of it.

All told Arnold had plucked $550,000 from his prey—say $5 million in terms of today's currency. Slack had picked up another $100,000. How it was divided between them we do not know, but it should have been enough to suit even Arnold. Incredibly, however, money had ceased to be the main allure. Unlike Slack, who fled Kentucky, Phil had become fascinated by the forces he had set in motion, and he wanted to see what happened next.[23]

For a time it seemed that nothing would transpire. Chilled by the reservations in Janin's report, bankers Duncan, Seligman, and Belmont refused to join the company. That news would soon filter along Wall

Street and frighten off other investors. Golconda lay dying on the threshold of success. To Phil Arnold, the creator of the hoax, so dull an anticlimax was intolerable. He relished the excitement of the affair and was eager to set things rolling again. At least how else can one explain his hanging around New York, repeatedly offering his services to the disappointed promoters?

At that point Ralston stepped in. Let Golconda die. He would organize and finance another company in San Francisco—one that would need Arnold's help.

Billy's motives were complex. He believed in the diamonds and in Janin, and he was not a man to give up easily. He wanted to show that his beloved San Francisco, rapidly recovering its energies under fresh transfusions of Comstock silver, was capable of doing what New York would not do. Pervading all this was his insistent trust in his own luck.

Working swiftly, he had the new company incorporated under the laws of California on August 1, 1872. Its nominal capital, like that of the deceased Golconda Company, was $10 million, represented by 100,000 shares of $100 stock. Because Barlow, General McClellan, and Charles Tiffany wished to maintain their connections with the discovery, they were appointed the company's New York agents, and, as a concession to them, the firm was named the San Francisco and New York Diamond Company—San Francisco first, at Billy's insistence. The House of Rothschild was named the firm's London agency. Rothschild's San Francisco representative, Alfred Gansl, became one of the mining company's directors, along with such Ralston familiars as Maurice Dore, Louis Sloss of the Alaska Commercial Company, Milton Latham, and Thomas Selby, Andrew Jackson Ralston's father-in-law. Lent was elected president, Ralston treasurer.

An elaborate scheme of exploitation was worked out. First, twenty-five wealthy men were solicited to invest $80,000 each. They responded swiftly. Subscriptions were then closed (except for Barlow, who continued selling some stock in New York and England) and the money was placed in escrow in The Bank of California.[24]

The company officials still clung to the notion that the fields extended across 3,000 acres—the amount of land that Barlow had hoped to acquire by incorporating a railroad. The firm decided that instead of trying to work the entire area on its own, it would divide the land into nineteen 160-acre tracts, develop one of those tracts itself, and lease the other eighteen units to subsidiary companies for $1 million cash each, plus royalties on the precious stones extracted.[25] The 160-acre figure was chosen because it was a basic unit in the government's disposition of the public domain to purchasers and homesteaders.

It was the company's intent to use government land scrip for obtaining title to that part of the field not covered by the claims staked earlier by the Janin group. Land scrip consisted of certificates which the government issued to war veterans and others as bonuses. The certificates enabled them to obtain acreage in the public domain. Since thousands of recipients did not wish to use the scrip themselves, they offered it for sale through brokers. Ralston, Isaac Friedlander, W. S. Chapman, and others were currently buying up enough to acquire huge agricultural tracts in California's San Joaquin Valley. Why not divert some to the acquisition of diamond land in Wyoming? First, however, the acreage the company wanted would have to be surveyed, a step the original Golconda group had hoped to avoid because of the conspicuousness of the surveyors. The responsibility for this assignment was given to George Roberts.

Another necessity was the compiling of detailed information for the use of the subsidiary companies to whom the ground was to be leased. Janin was hired to return to the fields and complete a thorough examination. His guide—Philip Arnold! Arnold, moreover, was to hire twenty-five blacks to serve as roustabouts and bodyguards against the Ute Indians of Colorado, who were then very restive because of an incursion of miners into their reservation south of the diamond fields.[26]

So far, so good. From then on, however, everything was cross-purposes and confusion. With fanfare the company announced the discovery, published Janin's preliminary, confidential report, opened plush offices, and placed piles of precious stones (presumably from the sack in The Bank of California) on display in its own offices and at the bank. Intense excitement filled the West.[27] When the company refused to reveal the location of the fields, dozens of pretenders sprang up, saying that they had the information, and solicited subscriptions to their companies.

So many spies dogged Janin's and Arnold's every move that they never went to the fields at all. Irritated by the publication of his preliminary report, Janin threatened to resign—he sold his 1,000 shares of stock at a profit of $30,000—but was placated and promised to take the trip with thirty-five men the following spring, after things had quieted down.[28]

Trying to rectify its mistakes, the company sent a diversionary party into the Southwest. Screened thus, Roberts' big, awkward group of surveyors left San Francisco secretly and in sections late in August. They had scarcely disappeared, with the Englishman Rubery as guide, when shocking news arrived from London. On August 27, 1872, the *Times* of that city commented adversely on the diamond company, which it linked to Harpending and Roberts of the earlier, notorious Lincoln and Pyramid mine fiascos. The story brought a rush of mail to the newspaper from jewelers who had sold raw diamonds to rough-looking Americans during the very periods when Arnold had been out of sight.[29] The *Times* printed these letters, and Rothschild cabled Barlow and Ralston for data. Was this the fraud it seemed to be?

Ralston cabled back firm assurances. He believed Janin. Barlow tried to keep faith, but was so shaken that he wrote Billy four letters on August 30 alone. He was doing his best to keep the people to whom he had sold stock happy, he said, but he wanted the last $100,000 he had sent Ralston returned immediately.[30]

The return of the Roberts party from the fields early in October seemed to justify Ralston's faith. Although the men had spent most of their time surveying and laying out a town site called Brilliant City, they had prospected on the side and had unearthed nearly 400 small gems, as they took the crystals to be.[31] Ralston wired Barlow, who

U.S. GEOLOGICAL SURVEY

Prior surveying along the 40th parallel gave Clarence King (right) the background he needed for exposing the hoax.

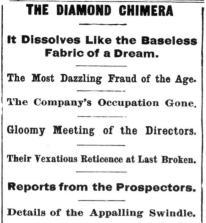

THE DIAMOND CHIMERA

It Dissolves Like the Baseless Fabric of a Dream.

The Most Dazzling Fraud of the Age.

The Company's Occupation Gone.

Gloomy Meeting of the Directors.

Their Vexatious Reticence at Last Broken.

Reports from the Prospectors.

Details of the Appalling Swindle.

The Evening Bulletin *of November 26, 1872, told San Franciscans of the collapse of the swindle.*

triumphantly wrote to one of his own correspondents that there was nothing more to fear. On the strength of that joyous word he even sold some more stock.[32]

The end was near, however. Unknown to anyone in the company, and certainly to Arnold, a government surveying party under Clarence King was examining the natural resources along the line of the transcontinental railroad. Rumors that Roberts and Janin had found diamonds in the area trickled to them from roustabouts along the line and worried them. If they missed so startling a find—and they had seen no evidence of precious stones—it would cast discredit on all their work.

By chance two of King's party boarded the same train on which the Roberts group was returning to San Francisco. By indulging the prospectors in casual talk, the federal men unearthed several revealing hints about the location of the supposed fields. They also gleaned more bits of data from Janin when he came out from San Francisco to meet Roberts. After they had arrived in the city, they compared notes with King, who had also developed suspicions. The upshot was that King returned to Wyoming with some of his men. They followed Roberts' tracks to "Brilliant City" and after working three days in bitter cold convinced themselves that the whole affair was a monstrous fraud.[33]

Back in San Francisco, King stayed up all night with Janin, persuading him that he had been victimized. Red-eyed and trembling, Janin the next morning, November 11, 1872, summoned Ralston and the other directors of the San Francisco and New York Mining Company to an emergency meeting. Stunned at what they heard yet still unbelieving, the directors prevailed on King to return to the desolate area with Janin and three of their own men: surveyor John Bost, David Colton, the company's new general manager, and Edward M. Fry, Lizzie

Ralston's cousin—or possibly her brother (his identity is uncertain).

The report of this special party completed the debacle. The company returned to its stockholders the money it had been holding in escrow. Arnold fled to Kentucky, where he felt safe from extradition—and where he vociferously denied any wrongdoing. Lent pursued him there and finally wrung $125,000 from him for himself and Ralston. Barlow thought he should have shared in that money, but little was left after meeting legal fees and the expenses of uncovering the fraud, and he received nothing. He was also outraged over the bag of stones at The Bank of California. Surely it was worth something. But although he railed about it several times, the San Franciscans never responded to his satisfaction.[34] Indeed, the ultimate fate of the $35,000 or so worth of stones used in the salting is still a mystery.

Barlow always thought that Harpending was as guilty as anyone in the affair.[35] Ralston stoutly defended his friend. When the grand jury met to consider indictments, he used his influence with the prosecuting attorney to keep both Harpending and Roberts in the clear legally. Even so, the atmosphere in San Francisco became so intolerable to Asbury that he decided to leave, whereupon Ralston and Sharon bought from him his share of the New Montgomery Street Real Estate Company at what Harpending said was a painfully low price.[36]

Roberts fared even more poorly. In one of a series of unhappy letters to Harpending, he moaned, "I owe Lent—Latham—Fry—and Ralston in the aggregate near $200,000." (This after receiving his share of the Mineral Hill sale.) But, he admitted, Lent and Ralston acted liberally. First they gave him time to try to raise funds. When that failed, Ralston and Maurice Dore furnished him with still more money for reclaiming 32,000 acres of Sacramento delta land he owed. Their hope was that the work would raise the value of the land enough so that its sale would cover, in Roberts' words, "a large part of their losses in the cursed diamond matter." It was a hope that by the time of Ralston's death had not been realized.[37]

In hindsight that cursed matter appears almost symbolic. In a sense Ralston, who personally had lost something like a quarter of a million dollars, and his associates had seduced themselves. Swindlers think of their hoaxes because the basic premises on which the schemes are founded are already part of their milieu. Victims succumb for the same reason: they are preconditioned by their times. For the entire West, and particularly for California, the decades since 1849 had been gaudy, greedy, improbable, naive, and wonderfully exuberant. Why be careful when nothing seemed impossible? But the days of reckless expansion were ending—just as the dream of diamonds had ended—in chill disillusionment, and it would be marvelous indeed if Billy Ralston, with his plunge-ahead spirit, managed to escape unscathed.

CHAPTER 23

Coin of Two Realms

Although Ralston and his associates found no diamonds in Colorado, those among them who were connected with the Comstock Lode did stumble, at unprecedented depths, onto new bonanzas of silver ore. The outpouring of wealth that resulted helped restore Ralston's faith in himself as one of fortune's favorites and produced a true Greek hubris leading toward disaster. He rushed with reckless confidence into schemes for new railroads, a cigar factory, and a massive system of canals designed to change the face of the San Joaquin Valley. He clung with renewed stubbornness to his floundering real estate plans, to his hardluck carriage manufacturing company, to his increasingly disorganized woolen mills and the overly ambitious California Theater.

Strangely, or so it seems in hindsight, he missed the irony inherent in his enthusiasms. As a financier and statesman, he realized that too much silver flooding out of the mines of the West could be harmful both to the United States and to The Bank of California. With special agent Henry R. Linderman of the U.S. Treasury Department and John Jay Knox, deputy comptroller of currency, he worked hard and astutely to avert the danger threatening the country's monetary system. Yet he did not sense that the sirens of almost unlimited silver were simultaneously tempting him into riskier personal investments than he had ever embraced before.

The story of the Comstock's resurgence begins with an act of faithlessness. During the fall of 1870, John P. Jones, the burly, black-haired superintendent of the Crown Point Mine (and the hero of the Yellow Jacket fire of April, 1869), discovered at the 1,100-foot level of the workings he supervised tantalizing indications of rich ore. Inasmuch as the Crown Point was controlled by Ralston's, Sharon's, and Mills's monopolistic Union Mill and Mining Company, Jones should have reported the discovery to one of them or to their representatives. Instead he singled out Alvinza Hayward.

Although Hayward was a friend of Ralston's and a stockholder in The Bank of California, Jones and he decided to keep the information to themselves. Quietly they began buying Crown Point stock, which at that time (November, 1870) was selling at $2 a share. Under the impact of their purchases, the price rose to $180, at which point they owned, by the thinnest of margins, enough stock to control the mine.

Sharon, who had been caught napping, decided against trying to regain mastery. The effort would be expensive, and he wasn't sure it would succeed. Moreover, he had somehow learned—he had spies in every mine on the lode—that the ore body lay in such a way that it probably extended into the Belcher Mine which adjoined the Crown Point on the south. Accordingly he went to Hayward and offered to sell him 4,100 shares of Crown Point stock for $1.4 million (roughly $341 a share) if Hayward in return would sell him, at an unrecorded but smaller figure, Hayward's stock in the Belcher.[1] Seeing fat dividends ahead for Crown Point shares, Hayward agreed.

The bargain, which was struck in May, 1871, drove a second wedge into the monopoly that Union Mill and Mining was trying to maintain on the Comstock. (The first had been the acquisition of the Hale & Norcross by Mackay, O'Brien, Flood, and Fair.) The cracks in the monolith were worries for the future, however. At the moment the transaction brought Ralston and his Comstock partners a considerable sum of money when they badly needed it. Beyond that was the far more stimulating gain in hope. Ore at depth! That lure had led Union Mill and Mining and The Bank of California to sustain Virginia City—in effect, all Nevada—for more than two years. Now they could reap the rewards of their faith.

Promptly they undertook to have the Belcher cleared of water and its shafts deepened. By August, 1871, they knew, in spite of Jones' and Hayward's efforts at secrecy, that the Crown Point was on the verge of opening what might be the greatest ore body yet found in the giant vein. Moreover, every indication suggested that a considerable part of the bonanza—perhaps even a major part—extended into the Belcher. It was at that point that Ralston, agog over the potentials he glimpsed in the Nevada earth, agreed to join Harpending, Roberts, Lent, Dodge, and Arnold in their proposed diamond mining company.

Fortune's favorite: when disaster threatened in other fields, he wriggled out of it. On October 8, 1871, a wind-driven fire destroyed $200 million worth of property in Chicago. One of the major underwriters of insurance in the stricken city was the Pacific Insurance Company of San Francisco, in which both Billy and Andrew Jackson Ralston were deeply involved. As claims poured in from Illinois—eventually they totalled $3.2 million—it became evident that Pacific's assets could not cover more than half of its liabilities.

Under California law an owner of shares in a corporation was personally liable for the debts of the company in proportion to his stockholdings. If the claimants in Illinois enforced that provision, the blow to the Ralston brothers would be shattering. It was safe to assume, however, that few policyholders outside of California were aware of their advantage. Hastily Ralston called for help on H. D. Bacon, a St. Louis banker who had recently moved to San Francisco. Because Bacon knew Chicago well, Ralston offered him $30,000 if he could persuade claimants to settle for what Pacific was able to pay, fifty cents on the dollar.

Bacon succeeded marvelously. Although Pacific, in the words of a contemporary, "went out like a candle" after meeting the claims, the stockholders escaped with whole hides.[2] Jack Ralston, secretary of the defunct firm, found new employment in Virginia City as assistant to William Sharon. Again irony was involved, for while Billy Ralston was evading responsibility on the one hand he was simultaneously heading a San Francisco relief committee that raised $25,000 in voluntary contributions to send to sufferers of the conflagration.

During those successful maneuverings, the weather turned benign. After two dry years, so Billy wrote R. G. Dun of what became Dun and Bradstreet, "Rain puts laughing faces on *every* body. You can add from *25* to *40%* during the next twelve months to the entire natural increase of wealth of this coast . . . from 6 to 7 hundred thousand tons of *Wheat additional alone*." Gold mines that for two years had stopped operations for want of water were humming again. "We feel happy!"[3] The euphoria was such that it reached to The Oriental Bank of London, which increased the credit it allowed The Bank of California from £250,000 to £300,000.[4]

At home, affairs were just as joyous. Nearly seven years after the birth of her last baby, Lizzie, aged 34, was pregnant again. The child, another girl whom the parents would name Bertha, was due, as events turned out, on March 28, 1872.

Against this background of fair weather at home and outside, Ralston achieved an international coup that set all San Francisco abuzz. Early in January, a delegation of 105 Japanese diplomats, financiers, and scholars arrived in San Francisco from Tokyo, accompanied by Charles DeLong, the American minister to Japan, and by an American adviser named George B. Williams. The travelers represented Japan's new Meiji ("Enlightened Rule") government, which had come into power in 1868 and was in the throes of remaking the nation after western models. This particular group, whose studies would take it as far as Europe, was burdened with many duties. In addition to studying western in-

COLLECTION OF DOROTHY PAGE BUCKINGHAM

*Bertha, the youngest
of the Ralstons' children,
was born only
three and a half years
before her father's death.*

dustry, art, education, public works, and tariffs, its members were also charged with gathering information about currency reform and, if possible, with floating a loan of between $15 million and $20 million. On the strength of recommendations from agents of The Oriental Bank in Yokohama and from Minister Charles DeLong, a one-time California miner who knew Billy, they turned first to Ralston.

As usual Ralston mingled entertainment with business. First he and Mills talked at length at the bank with the ambassador, Tomomi Iwakara; the minister of public works, Hirobumi Ito (later Premier of Japan); the minister of finance, Toshimichi Okubo; and his vice-minister, Yoshida Kiyonari. Then, in a formal printed invitation Ralston stated that he would "be happy to receive His Excellency [Iwakara] and such members of his Embassy as His Excellency may be pleased to designate at his residence at Belmont on Sunday Morning next, the 21st inst., under the escort of Mr. Mills."[5]

Iwakara selected about 25 of his fellows to participate. Originally Ralston hoped to follow the routines he had established when entertaining official members of boards of trade from eastern cities. First there would be a train trip to San Jose. After a reception there, provided by that town's suitably awed dignitaries, Ralston and his drivers would transport the visitors in a fleet of carriages to Belmont for the most lavish banquet yet held in the mansion.

To his angry dismay San Jose's business leaders declined to participate. Bitterly he wrote one of them that the city "evidently required a Normal School in her midst to teach them the Common Civilities due to their Elder Brothers." The town replied with a newspaper editorial. Their citizens, the writer said, had suffered long enough "stuffing the skins of visiting businessmen with tipple and victual." The time had come to end "the same old selfish welcoming, the same calculating hospitality. . . . They [the Japanese] will trade with us if they find it to their advantage, but this lionizing will not make them perceive the advantage."[6]

Behind the disdain was the prejudice that California's small towns and country folk had long felt toward Asiatics. Ralston shared none of it. Belmont was filled with Oriental furniture and art sent to him by business friends in Asia. Through those same friends he had been able to develop a lively trade with China. A substantial part of that nation's tea harvest for 1872 would shortly be landing at the San Francisco docks, and, as usual, The Bank of California would handle the lion's share of the financial arrangements.[7] Appreciable quantities of Comstock silver moved to China and India each year. When J. Ross Browne, the minister to China from 1868–70, had proposed that geologist Ferdinand von Richthofen of Germany lead a prospecting expedition into the interior of China, Billy helped finance it—without results.[8] During the previous fall he had endeavored to place orders in Japan for streetcars and railway cars manufactured by his Kimball Carriage Company.[9] So far he had had no luck. But the Meiji government's new interest in all things western promised to broaden opportunities in every field, and he was determined not to let the churlishness of one small town imperil the flowering.

He postponed the date of the festivities to January 25 and filled part of the intervening time personally escorting Ambassador Iwakara and the vice-minister of finance, Yoshida Kiyonari, around San Francisco to see the sights, including the mint and the plant of the San Francisco Assaying and Refining Works, in which Billy held a dominant interest. He ordered the staff at Belmont to outdo themselves in preparing for the banquet. Because of the interest the Japanese had in railroads, he invited Mark Hopkins of the Central Pacific to be one of the guests of honor. He prevailed on the mayor of San Francisco, William Alvord, who was also a director of The Bank of California, to make the welcoming address, an assignment that Alvord handled with grace. The whole affair passed off beautifully. When the magnificence of Belmont burst upon the visitors, Iwakara murmured, so the story goes, "It seems like a dream."[10]

Possibly the calculated hospitality helped more than the resistant businessmen of San Jose thought it would. One of the problems that concerned the delegation was finding ways and means to modernize Japan's system of coinage. By coincidence, the United States was also considering at that same time significant changes in its monetary system. As will be noted shortly in more detail, Ralston and Louis Anicharsis Garnett of the San Francisco Assaying and Refining Works had helped agents of the Treasury Department draw up for presentation to Congress the bill that was necessary for effecting the changes. That bill had recently passed the United States Senate, and the delegation's coinage expert, Hirobumi Ito, was anxious to study it.[11] Ralston went over the legislation with Ito in detail.

Even the physical problems presented by the changeover were formidable to the Japanese. The basic unit of the country's archaic coinage system was the niboo, whose subsidiary coins were based on a quaternary system. Ito believed—and his talks with Ralston reinforced the belief—that the new system should be metric (that is, a decimal system) based on a round gold coin to be called the yen.

How could those yen be best produced? In 1870 the Meiji government had erected a mint at Osaka and had hired a group of Englishmen to operate it. The English proposed to obtain a major part of the metal needed for the new coins by melting down and refining the old niboos still in circulation—some $20 million worth, it was estimated. As matters developed, however, refining procedures in Japan could not achieve the standards of purity desired. Could that essential work be done in California?

Indeed it could. The Bank of California would be glad to handle the program through the San Francisco Assaying and Refining Works. As

A Ralston company refined several million dollars' worth of niboos like these during Japan's drive to modernize her coinage.

THE BANK OF CALIFORNIA

part of its pay it agreed to accept the silver it recovered from the niboos during the process of refining. It would then dispose of this silver, currently worth $1.32 an ounce, as it did bullion from the Comstock, either to industrialists in the United States, by direct shipment to India, or through the complex system of exchanges handled by The Oriental Bank of London.

Eager to start minting their new yen, the Japanese asked The Bank of California to ship to Osaka at once $500,000 worth of pure gold. They would pay interest on this until gold refined out of the first consignment of niboos began coming back from San Francisco. Thus Ralston was, in effect, loaning half a million dollars to Japan and at the same time could look forward to a year or more of profitable work from the refining operations. The contract covering the arrangements was signed on January 30, 1872—the first agreement ever entered into between an American business organization and the government of Japan.[12]

A far better piece of business would have been handling the $15–$20 million loan that the Meiji government wanted to float. As Ralston himself admitted, however, there was no possibility of his finding that much surplus capital right then on the West Coast.[13] California enterprises, not all of them wise, were clamoring for every dollar he would let them have. He had no choice, accordingly, but to recommend that his visitors go elsewhere in their search for money.

Where? Billy had to tread carefully in giving his answer. The logical place was The Oriental Bank of London. In 1870 that corporation had arranged the first foreign loan to Japan, a modest £913,000 that was being used for building a railroad between Tokyo and Yokohama.[14] Why not float a second loan through the same company—especially since Oriental would recognize Ralston's assistance in the matter by asking The Bank of California to handle many of the details involved?

Unhappily for that idea, the Japanese were suspicious of the English. They had seen what had happened in China, where English money was followed by economic dominance and threats of military intervention. If they must deal with outsiders, they preferred to do it with Americans.[15]

Americans, who knew little about Japan and who on the basis of that skimpy information doubted the country's stability, did not reciprocate. Aware of the feeling—and also of his obligations to The Oriental Bank —Ralston with consummate tact persuaded his visitors to give up their hopes of floating a loan in the United States and to turn to London instead.

Having accomplished what he considered a noteworthy feat, he was astounded to discover that the English scorned it. John Robertson, an official in The Oriental Bank's Yokohama office, said publicly that Billy had been outwitted by the Japanese. They had used the niboo contract —Robertson doubted that Japan had $20 million worth of niboos available—merely to impress America with their empire's wealth. Actually, the country was not wealthy. Anyone recommending a loan on the strength of those reputed $20 million in niboos was displaying, Robertson said, a large measure of ignorance. Furthermore, the terms of the refining contract were ridiculous; no one else would have been so generous with the wily Asiatics.

Enraged by what he considered the insults in Robertson's remarks, Billy fired off protests to both Yokohama and London. The top officials of The Oriental Bank, Charles Stuart and William Anderson, replied with soothing letters and cablegrams. Yes, Robertson had spoken out of turn. But though they deplored the man's methods, it was quite clear that they agreed with his basic conclusions: the loan was not advisable, and the refining contract, with its provision for part payment in silver, gave undue advantages to the Japanese.[16]

Piqued by this challenge to his judgment, Ralston switched stands and made a desperate, last-minute effort to have the loan floated in the United States. Early in May he sent urgent letters to financier Jay Cooke in New York and to Hamilton Fish, President Grant's secretary of state. In these communications he pointed out as strongly as he could the advantages that would accrue to this country, and particularly to the West Coast, if America took the initiative in developing friendly relations with Japan. He entreated James Lees to spread the same message among leading New York financiers in addition to Cooke. "You observe," he finished his agitated letter to Lees, "we are desperately in earnest on this business."[17]

Earnestness was not enough. The government and the financiers rejected the proposal, and the disconsolate delegation, which had halted in the East awaiting developments, sailed on to England to try to change Stuart's mind. Bitterly disappointed, Ralston put the affair aside for the time being.

THERE WAS PLENTY TO OCCUPY HIM. By the spring of 1872 both the Crown Point and Belcher mines had done enough development work to realize that they had penetrated an ore body rich enough to have supplied the funds the Japanese wanted. There was no possibility of any such cooperative action, however. An intense rivalry had developed between the owners of the two mines. Alvinza Hayward of the Crown Point withdrew from The Bank of California and used part of his new wealth to beef up San Francisco's newly founded Merchants' Exchange Bank. In the same way, on the Comstock he and Jones challenged the Union Mill and Mining Company by creating what they called the Nevada Milling and Mining Company.

In order to obtain more ore for the Nevada Milling Company, the new bonanza kings wrested control of the Savage Mine from Sharon, Mills, and Ralston. Soon whispers sped through Virginia City and on over the Sierra to San Francisco that the Savage, too, had struck rich ore.

The stock market went wild. Between mid-January, 1872, and the end of April, the price of Savage stock soared from $62 a share to $725, almost a twelve-fold increase. During the same period Crown Point rose from approximately $800 to $1,825; Belcher from $300 to $1,525.[18]

This dizzy acceleration led Jones and Sharon to carry their rivalry into the field of politics. In the spring each announced that he would campaign for legislators committed to electing him as the next senator from Nevada. (In those days state legislatures chose U.S. Senators.)

Politics was not a new interest for either man. As early as 1869 Sharon, whom columnist Ambrose Bierce characterized as a "nuzzler of hot paps by instinct," had discussed with Ralston the advisability of his trying for a senatorship.[19] Jones's ambitions were even older. He had run frequently for office in California—as sheriff of Trinity County and as a member of the California state senate. Dejection over his failure to be elected lieutenant governor in 1864 had prompted him to go to Nevada in the hope that he could build up a new following there. The fame he earned by his courage during the Yellow Jacket fire and then his sudden wealth had made him feel that the moment had come. And so he challenged Sharon.

Jones was popular in Nevada. Sharon was not. Hoping to overcome that handicap with sensationalism, Sharon found a miner who said—or was bribed to say—that Jones was no hero and, indeed, had deliberately started the Yellow Jacket fire, in which 35 or more men had died, for the sake of influencing stock market prices to his advantage.

The charge, aired first by the San Francisco *Chronicle* on May 8, 1872, stunned the West Coast. Reporters swarmed around the principals, including Ralston. Excited curbside gossip declared that Jones confronted Sharon inside the offices of The Bank of California and would have gunned down his traducer except for Mills's intervention. A Nevada grand jury began an investigation of the charges, and Mills and Ralston announced through the *Chronicle* that unless Sharon could prove that he was not guilty of malicious libel, either he or they would leave The Bank of California.[20]

While reverberations from the episode were shaking the city, news arrived from the Comstock that the Savage did not contain good ore. Jones and Hayward had been bulling the market for their own ends. Prices cracked. Shares in the Savage dropped almost overnight from $725 to $175. Comstock values as a whole shrank from an overinflated $81 million to about $20 million. In anguish James Lees, who had never been happy about Ralston's mining activities, wired to know how seriously the bank had been hurt.

Ralston reassured him. Both the Crown Point and the Belcher, he said, were weathering the storm. Although stock prices in the first had dropped from $1,825 to $833, they had soon climbed back to $1,125. The Belcher's pattern was comparable; its shares dropped from $1,525 to $750 and then swung back to $1,080. To give his assurances a final gloss, he added that his brother, Andrew Jackson Ralston, erstwhile secretary of the defunct Pacific Insurance Company, had recently moved to Virginia City and would keep a close eye on affairs there while Sharon went about his politicking.[21]

By that time the grand jury in Nevada had cleared Jones of Sharon's charges of arson. When Ralston and Mills declined to disown their Virginia City partner in spite of their promise to the *Chronicle,* Jones shifted to the attack. Hayward and he, he vowed publicly, would build a new railroad to compete with the Virginia & Truckee, of which Sharon was president. To show he meant business, Jones sent surveyors into the field, then threatened to stir the Nevada legislature into investigating the Virginia & Truckee's rate structures.

Possibly he was bluffing, but Ralston did not want to risk calling him. The directors of the V & T had just borrowed enough money to extend the line from Carson City to a junction with the Central Pacific at Reno, and the last thing they wanted was harassment from the legislature. For weeks Billy and Andrew Jackson Ralston (who at Billy's behest had been named vice-president of V & T) tried to persuade Sharon to give up his headstrong ambition. On August 16 they finally succeeded. Profoundly relieved, Ralston sent the following memo to Mills, who was in New York.

> Sharon withdrew [from the senatorial race] without any entanglements whatever with anyone & has nothing to say or do with political fights. Both Jones & Hayward pledged themselves in writing to me to do all in their power to aid us in the maintaining of our Rl Rd fares, freights, and in the extension of the road, and in every way to help us in *all* our interests with the legislature, pledging good faith, etc., etc., but this of course must be confidential, *sacred, no one* outside of Sharon, Jones, Hayward, myself know of this. . . . All of us felt great relief at the consumm—[sic] of Sharon's withdrawal as did you of course.[22]

Unharried by the legislature, the bank ring finished building the railroad to Reno during the late summer months of 1872. No traffic could move into or out of Virginia City except on their terms. By the time of the senatorial election in January, 1873—Jones won easily, after spending between $500,000 and $800,000 putting the legislators he wanted into the state house—the V & T was running thirty or more trains each day between Virginia City and the mills in Carson Valley. It was the richest railroad per mile in the United States. On July 20, 1874, Ralston received his first dividend check of almost $300,000. Thereafter he received each month another $1,800 from that source alone.[23] Sharon and the other stockholders—there were only a score all told—of course reaped equally well.

Ralston meanwhile was involved in politicking of his own, albeit less odorously. The occasion was another visit from his friend, Henry R. Linderman, special agent for the United States Treasury Department. Ostensibly Linderman had come to San Francisco to supervise the installation of new equipment in the mint. Actually, he was more interested in discussing with San Francisco businessmen changes that they wanted in a coinage reform bill that had recently passed the Senate—a bill Ralston had discussed earlier with his Japanese visitors—and which was still under consideration by the House of Representatives.

The bill, an important one for the nation, had had a checkered past. The initial motive prompting it had been a desire evinced by many Americans to get rid of the inconvertible, legal-tender greenbacks that had been introduced during the Civil War, and to stabilize the country's currency by resuming specie payments—that is, to make metallic money the only legal money in the nation. The dollar would still be the basic unit, but what kind of dollar, of silver or of gold—or both?

That fundamental question had led to a maze of other considerations about monetary policy. Finally, late in 1869, George Boutwell, secretary of the treasury, had instructed Linderman and John Jay Knox, deputy comptroller of the currency, to draw up a bill that would overhaul the entire body of laws dealing with American coinage.

The two men hammered out a preliminary draft and then sent copies of it for study to about 30 "gentlemen [who] are known to be intelligent upon metallurgical and numismatical subjects." As stated earlier, William Ralston and Louis A. Garnett, head of the San Francisco Assaying and Refining Works, were among those consulted.

Of the two, Garnett was the better theoretician. He was excruciatingly shy, however, a strange little man whose thin face was framed by enormous sideburns and a tiny goatee. He might never have been heard at all if Ralston had not undertaken to urge Garnett's ideas on visitors to San Francisco—Knox and Linderman among them—and to distribute to influential statesmen and financiers copies of the pamphlets Garnett wrote to expound his ideas.[24]

Theoretically the United States was still on a bimetallic standard, with silver's value pegged to that of gold at a ratio of 16 to 1. Actually, the California and Australian gold discoveries had so reduced the value of gold that, on a 16 to 1 ratio, the silver in a silver dollar was worth $1.03. Inevitably silver dollars, being more valuable as metal than as coin, disappeared from circulation. Even the miners in Virginia City, the most famous silver camp in the world, seldom saw a silver dollar.

Farsighted economists—among them Linderman, Knox, Ralston, and Garnett—wished to make gold the only legal standard when the government resumed specie payments. Their reasons varied. In California, gold was symbolic of a sound economy; the state, it will be recalled, had refused to join the rest of the nation in accepting greenbacks as legal tender during the war. Only the stability of gold, Californians were convinced, would maintain the price of domestic bonds, real estate, and foreign exchange.

Linderman had additional reasons for preferring gold. Like many other conservative economists, he was sure that the price of silver was going to drop. Before the discovery of the Comstock Lode, the United States had never produced more than $51,000 worth of silver in any one year. By 1864 the output had soared to $11.4 million, with Colorado and Utah contributing largely to the flow. In 1870, government geologist Raymond Rossiter had predicted that although the Comstock was then in the doldrums, its great years still lay ahead—a prediction given sharp reality by the opening of the Crown Point and Belcher bonanzas.

If this outpouring reduced the price of silver while bimetallism was still legal, the owners of gold coin would melt their holdings into bullion and trade it at the mint for cheap silver dollars. They would use those silver dollars for paying debts. Price structures would collapse, trade with Europe (which had to be conducted in gold) would suffer, and the Treasury would soon be emptied of its stores of yellow metal.

To prevent this, the Linderman-Knox-Garnett school of economists decided that the new mint bill they were preparing should drop the silver dollar from the list of coins that the government would mint. Ralston and Garnett also sought other privileges that would benefit the West and themselves. They asked first that the government aid California's faltering gold mining industry by dropping all minting charges for coining gold pieces. (The Bank of California, it is worth remembering, handled more gold bullion than did any other private institution in the country.) Next they sought to provide a market for Comstock silver by urging the government to strike off, under the seal of the United States, "commercial" or "trade" dollars for use in the Orient. Although the trade dollars would not be legal tender in this country, they could perhaps be substituted in Asiatic transactions for Mexican pesos, at that time the preferred coin in the Orient.*

After intermittent, apathetic debate, the bill passed the Senate in

---

*American merchants trading in China had to import Mexican pesos at a premium of 7 1/2 percent. This placed a heavy burden on Asiatic commerce, and the San Francisco mercantile community was eager to find some other medium, preferably an American coin.

January, 1871. It was complicated, dull, and long—it contained more than 70 clauses—and the House seemed inclined to let it die of inertia. Agitated by the slowness, Ralston hired lobbyists to work on its behalf, put pressure on West Coast congressmen, and even paid Linderman $5,000—at Linderman's request—to stir up activity. Inasmuch as Linderman already had a vested interest in the bill (he was a government employee, he had helped write the bill, and he would become director of mints if it passed), his pumping of Ralston for more benefits raises questions about his standards.[25] Ralston, however, never complained. It was, in Mark Twain's phrase, a gilded age.

As Congress dawdled, the German government announced its intention of going onto the gold standard in 1873. This meant that the German treasury would melt down some $350 million worth of silver coin and dump the bullion onto the open market. The flood would so shake the price of the white metal that other countries in Europe decided to follow Germany's lead. Meanwhile the West's production of silver was mounting steadily. By the end of 1871 its annual value had soared from 1864's $11.4 million to $35.87 million—and the Crown Point and Belcher were not yet in full production.

Apprised by Linderman in May, 1872, of these developments, Ralston decided that perhaps the recently departed Japanese delegation had indeed taken advantage of the San Francisco Assaying and Refining Company in offering to pay in silver part of the cost of refining the niboos. Promptly he wrote the delegation's American advisor, George B. Williams, urging that the contract be modified to meet the new conditions. What resulted does not appear in the records.[26] Simultaneously he redoubled his efforts to achieve action on the coinage laws.

When the bill at last reached the House of Representatives, he—and the rest of the West—found that it did not meet their desires. For one thing, the proposed law would retain the old coinage charge of 0.5 percent of the bullion's value for striking off gold pieces. For another, the silver trade dollar which it authorized weighed only 384 grains as against the Mexican trade peso of 419.25 grains. Obviously a dollar of so light a weight would stand little chance of acceptance by tradition-minded Orientals, particularly the Chinese, and hence would be of no benefit either to San Francisco merchants or to the Comstock mining industry.

When Linderman appeared in San Francisco in the fall of 1872 on mint business, Ralston and his financial allies fell on him. Look here, Henry —and off they took him to the Comstock.

By that time the rivalry between the Crown Point and Belcher had extended to output. Geologist Rossiter in his annual report criticized both companies for their wasteful methods and "pell-mell digging." But the Comstock's mood had never been conservative. Why be cautious when, in the grandiose words of John P. Jones, it seemed certain that "the vein will penetrate the earth . . . to an indefinite depth?" Ride high—but in the meantime that silver somehow had to find additional markets. In Ralston's opinion, only a trade dollar of 420 grains—just enough heavier than the Mexican peso to be alluring—would provide adequate relief. As for the bill's arbitrary coinage charge, it amounted to a tax on the honest miner's labor and should be eliminated.

Linderman carried the message back to Washington. When the bill at last passed Congress and was signed by President Grant in March, 1873, it came very close to being what the West wanted. Coinage charges were cut to 0.2 percent of the value of the bullion handled—enough, Linderman calculated, to save California miners $90,000 a year. The San Francisco Assaying and Refining Works retained its privileged position as refiner for the San Francisco Mint. The silver dollar was dropped from the list of American coins (the so-called Crime of 1873, though at the time no one protested), and as a substitute of sorts a trade dollar of 420 grains of silver for use in the Orient was authorized.

Three people, Linderman declared exultantly, were primarily responsible for these many gains—himself (he was rewarded by being named director of all the country's mints), Louis Garnett and William Ralston. With mock ingenuousness he added that having finished his work, having "fought the good fight," he would let Ralston decide whether "to do much, little, or nothing at *all*" in the matter of additional compensation.[27] Ralston's answer has not survived, but, his nature considered, he probably paid generously for what Linderman should have done without pay.

The trade dollar would be of no benefit unless the Chinese accepted it. As rapidly as the mints of Carson City and San Francisco turned out the new silver coins, Billy rushed shipments of them to the agents of The Oriental Bank in China. He urged American diplomats to use all their

Ralston worked diligently to have American trade dollars of silver introduced into the Orient.

THE BANK OF CALIFORNIA

Family legend avers that the Emperor of Japan sent Ralston this Meiji cabinet in gratitude for Billy's financial advice and aid.

resources—even "tipping" if necessary—to persuade local mandarins to declare the new coins legal tender within their areas of influence. His energy was so relentless that some of his correspondents in China took to referring to the heavy silver discs as "Ralston dollars." Soberly they warned him not to make America's new Oriental money appear to be the exclusive concern of The Bank of California.[28]

Although the trade dollars did not spread inland, they did take root in China's great harbor cities, particularly Shanghai and Hong Kong. The times helped account for the acceptance. American commercial contacts with the Orient were spreading vigorously. Silver had not yet started its precipitous decline, and the trade dollar filled a needed place. In 1874 American mints turned out $3.6 million worth of silver trade dollars. In 1875 they added another $5.7 million. The bulk of the coins went to the Orient through The Bank of California, and for that consider-

335

able triumph Billy Ralston could claim the major part of the credit.

One other triumph occurred at the same time. In January, 1873, the month the House passed the coinage bill and sent it to a joint committee for a resolution of its differences with the Senate version, the Japanese delegation won a $12 million loan from The Oriental Bank of London. So Billy had been right after all. The new government of the island empire did merit the help of the Occident.

He had stayed in touch with both the delegation and The Oriental Bank of London throughout the negotiations. The appreciation that the Japanese felt for his services was given concrete expression by its adviser, George B. Williams, who sent to him for addition to the Oriental treasures at Belmont two large, black lacquered pedestals and two large Japanese bronze vases to put upon them. (Ralston had previously sent Williams a carriage and harness; in fact, Ralston supplied, free of charge, buggies and fine horses to many of his contacts in Asia, particularly those connected with The Oriental Bank.) Family legend says that he also received from the Emperor of Japan, presumably in connection with the same services, a handsome Meiji cabinet of lacquer and gold.[29]

It was pleasant to contemplate the lovely objects and remember the victories they represented, especially since the hill ahead sloped down and there were not going to be many more spectacular triumphs to savor.

CHAPTER 24

Soft Spots

Gifted with hindsight, we can detect more cracks in California's economy during the mid-1870s than were visible to William Ralston and his associates. They were blinded by their own desires. Convinced that San Francisco was on its way to becoming one of the great metropolises of the world, they heeded only those statistics that reinforced their beliefs.

The figures were imposing. The city's population was climbing rapidly —from 149,473 according to the U.S. census of 1870 to 191,716 in 1875. In 1873 more people arrived in California than had come during any other year since the great gold-rush influx of 1852—and still more would arrive in both 1874 and 1875.

Builders grew frenzied again, piling the sidewalks with bricks and lumber as they replaced the old iron-shuttered business structures of the 1850s with modern edifices ornate with gimcracks. Vendors crowded the streets, dodging among carriages to shout out their offers to grind razors, carry luggage, or sell Los Angeles oranges. In 1873 eight omnibus companies transported customers in horse-drawn cars over more than eighty miles of track. That same year Andrew Hallidie put into operation the first of the city's cable cars, designed to conquer the peninsula's windswept hills. Throughout the state, business failures declined from 80 in 1872 to 68 in 1874. Though drought had impoverished thousands of farmers during the winter of 1870–71, "normal" rainfall soon returned and for the next two years wheat harvests were bountiful.[1]

The arts flourished. The San Francisco Art Union, which Ralston had helped found in 1865, was absorbed in 1871 by the more sophisticated San Francisco Art Association, which by 1874 had 700 members, 100 of them holding life certificates that cost $100 each. The group held four glittering receptions each year, two of them exhibitions at which the crowds were so dense that the pictures could scarcely be seen. In March, 1872, a group of newspapermen and writers inaugurated the city's still prestigious Bohemian Club. Laymen clamored to join and were gradually admitted; Billy Ralston became a member on February 3, 1874. After all, he could claim to be a patron of sorts of pen-wielders. Hadn't he, Collis Huntington, and Ben Holladay together subsidized travel writer Charles Nordhoff in turning out a popular book called *Northern California, Oregon, and the Sandwich Islands?*[2]

The theater, always intensely competitive in San Francisco, continued to draw sterling entertainment. Because Ralston's pocketbook and pride were deeper than Tom Maguire's, his California Theater generally outdrew the latter's Grand Opera House. Lotta Crabtree returned repeatedly to ecstatic plaudits. Judge Matthew Deady of Oregon, who spent a weekend at Belmont with Ralston, boasted of going on two successive evenings to see a then-famous Shakespearean actor named Fletcher play a stirring Hamlet.[3] When Billy's fancy was touched, he was insatiable. In March, 1874, he sat through twenty straight nights of Adelaide Nielsen's attendance-shattering stand at the California, then invited her and her husband to Belmont for a week. There he presented her, out of pure admiration, a $10,000 diamond necklace. He also held in her honor a banquet so lavish that it aroused one San Francisco newspaper to satire:[4]

> The center [of the main dish] was a humming-bird filled with baked almonds, surrounded by a Spring linnet, which in turn was enveloped by an English snipe . . . covering which were two canvas-backed ducks raised in a celery garden, the whole placed within the bosom of a Chicago goose. Soaked in raisin wine for six days, then larded, and smoked three weeks over burning sandalwood, it was at last placed on the spit and roasted with pig-pork drippings. The sauce was of truffles stewed in *Private cavé;* the garnish was moss-rose buds.

Although the spoof was not meant to be taken seriously, some somber souls did believe it and were angry. Their feelings reflected the discontent that was coming to a head throughout California. In large measure the restlessness was the product of disappointment. Most of the new immigrants who streamed westward during the early 1870s were men and women left unemployed by the gathering depression in the East. They had heard that a new subsidiary of the Central Pacific, the San Joaquin Railroad, was opening huge tracts of rich agricultural land in the southern reaches of the Central Valley, and they believed that good farms were readily available there. They believed, too, that

CALIFORNIA HISTORICAL SOCIETY

One expensive element in Ralston's dream of beautifying San Francisco was the California Theater (background) on Bush Street.

placer mining still offered opportunities to a poor prospector. Some sanguine migrants even expected to share in the silver magic of the Comstock Lode's newest bonanza.

In California they found that the land on which they hoped to settle was controlled either by the railroads, by such Ralston familiars as William Chapman and Isaac Friedlander, or by cattle barons like Henry Miller and Charles Lux, and was not to be had at prices they could afford. They learned, through the speeches and writings of ardent reformers, that 122 men, most living in mansions in San Francisco, owned farms of between 70,000 and 1 million acres each.[5] Great chunks of those ranches were held in idleness as a speculation, awaiting the coming of a railroad or the development of irrigation water, at which time they would be subdivided and sold at high prices. Other chunks were plowed and harvested not by owner-occupants but by contractors

*Lotta Crabtree, one of
the California Theater's
greatest attractions, grew
up in the mining camps.*

SOCIETY OF CALIFORNIA PIONEERS

who hired labor as needed from the drifting itinerants who called at their desolate camps. Still other plots were rented to sharecroppers who, hoping for quick returns, bled the life from the soil with over-plantings of wheat, the state's great money crop.

The workers, many of them newly arrived immigrants, were the victims. In 1871, in a scathing book called *Our Land and Land Policy,* journalist Henry George, who later would become a fellow-member of Ralston's in the Bohemian Club, described their plight thus: "Over our ill-kept, shadeless, dusty roads . . . plod the tramps, with blankets on backs—the laborer of the California farmer—looking for work in its season, or toiling back to the city when the plowing is ended and the wheat crop is gathered."

Having reached the city, the men endured the winter largely on charity, of which Ralston dispensed his share. As they shivered around their tiny fires, they grew convinced that the state's industrialists were deliberately inducing labor to come to California so that the resultant competition for jobs would reduce wages. In particular they resented the Chinese, whose numbers had been rising swiftly ever since Ralston's friend Anson Burlingame had persuaded the government of the United States to remove its restriction on immigration from China. By 1875, there were more than 60,000 Chinese in the state. Half of them were grubbing out a living on mining claims already exploited by the whites—claims the newcomers from the East had supposed, quite unreasonably, might be their own salvation. The other half of the Orientals held low-paying jobs that hungry immigrants thought they could have had at higher wages if the Chinese hadn't snatched the work from under their noses.

Too many people, too few opportunities for livelihood—no, immigration was not a sign of prosperity. That recognition came later, however. When Ralston and his associates saw the rising population figures, they extrapolated them as proof of the state's essential soundness and were encouraged to press ahead even more vigorously with their majestic schemes.

Some of those schemes brought forth unexpected opposition. One involved the expanded activities of the North Bloomfield Gravel Mining Company, a hydraulic operation that had not paid a dividend since its incorporation in 1866, and one in which Ralston was a major stockholder. Tantalized by each month's cleanup of the massive sluice boxes—the yield was *almost* enough to meet expenses—the managers kept groping for higher returns through greater volume. They linked efforts with adjoining companies faced with the same problem, enlarged their reservoirs, canals, and debris tunnels. All told they spent $3.5 million dollars chasing the yellow rainbow.[6] Tomorrow . . .

Meanwhile incalculable tons of sterile waste were being spewed into the canyons, not just by North Bloomfield but by dozens of other hydraulic mines—North Bloomfield was simply the largest of them.* Spring floods each year rolled the syrup farther into the lowlands. Fields and orchards were smothered; salmon disappeared; roads were obliterated; once navigable streams could no longer be negotiated. In the early 1870s, farm groups began protesting. They sought court injunctions and appealed to the legislature for help in checking the headlong exploitation. Mining interests were still dominant in California, however, and during Ralston's lifetime the farmers achieved nothing. Relief did not come until the late 1880s. Meanwhile the rising antagonisms drew new class lines across the state's social and economic structure and added one more element to the uneasiness that was corroding California's economic fabric.[8]

---

*Ralston was interested in at least two other hydraulic companies, the El Dorado Water and Deep Gravel Mining Company (2,500 shares of stock) and the La Grange Ditch and Hydraulic Mining Company (5,000 shares of stock).[7] None paid him very well, though after his death North Bloomfield became enormously profitable.

Isaac Friedlander, California's grain king, was another target. Financed with hundreds of thousands of dollars loaned him each year by The Bank of California, Friedlander imported the millions of sacks the farmers used and chartered the scores of ships that carried their wheat to overseas markets. Convinced that he was holding up prices through his monopoly on sacks and that he juggled his charter rates so as to absorb the profits that good prices in England would otherwise have brought them, the farmers girded for battle. Their weapon was the Grange, which by 1873 boasted 104 chapters in California. Its managers set up cooperatives for buying sacks and other supplies, and employed agents to charter ships. The Grange even founded its own bank in the hope of freeing itself from what it considered San Francisco's monolithic financial establishment. These were not pursuits the grangers understood, however, and their efforts failed.[9] Enthusiasm turned to sullenness, and that too acted as a drag on the state's prosperity.

Greatest villain of all, in the minds of many Californians, was The Bank of California's best account, the Central Pacific Railroad. By 1872 that line and its subsidiaries (the Southern Pacific, the San Joaquin, and the California & Oregon) were clearly intending to monopolize rail transportation throughout the state. As a monopoly it indulged in practices that stirred the ire of a large part of the state's population. It published its rates as the law demanded, but then gave secret kickbacks to large shippers. It influenced legislators by handing out passes to them and their families. It won low tax charges by easing obliging assessors into county offices. Its long-haul system was a scandal. It carried

The transcontinental railroad brought California excitement and economic stimulation, as suggested in William Hahn's "Sacramento Railroad Station."

merchandise from the East to San Francisco at a lower cost than from the East to Reno. As a result Reno distributors had to ship what they wanted from San Francisco back across the Sierra. This helped keep Central Pacific freight cars full as far as the bay city, but it also ended the protection that isolation had once afforded San Francisco manufacturers and forced many of them out of business. To a firm that had failed from that cause and to its former workers, who now had to compete for jobs with the rising influx of immigrants, California hardly seemed as prosperous as the Chamber of Commerce boasted.

Gradually the heterogeneous antagonisms found a unified voice in a new political group called the People's Independent party, or Dolly Vardens, after a character in Dickens's *Barnaby Rudge* who favored costumes of mixed bright colors. Principal target of the Dolly Vardens was the old-line Republican establishment that with minor exceptions had dominated California politics since the Civil War. Inevitably Ralston was caught up in the turmoil, not only through his business connections with railroads, irrigation projects, hydraulic mines, and wheat shipping but also through his supposedly nonpolitical work as one of the first regents of the University of California.

The university had sprung from seed planted by Congress's Morrill Act of July 2, 1862, which granted to each state public land that could be sold for the support of higher education. California's share of the largesse was 150,000 acres—once the legislature had ended its squabbling and had accepted the grant on March 31, 1864. The troubles that followed were manifold, largely because free land did not prove to be a magic fund raiser. Much of California was already claimed by the successors of old Mexican grants, by the railroads, and by speculators who were snapping up huge areas by means of land scrip. Eastern colleges were entitled to locate Morrill Act land in western states, and their scouts too were invading California. Finally there were the homesteaders. The nascent university had to find land in competition with all those searchers.

While the hunt was going on, the university acquired its organizational shape. By law ultimate power rested in the hands of twenty-two regents. Six of the regents held office by virtue of their governmental positions—the governor of the state, the superintendent of public instruction, and so on. Eight more were appointed by the governor. These fourteen then chose eight additional members. William Ralston was one of the eight elected in the spring of 1868. His term was to run for fourteen years. On taking his seat he was named treasurer of the university.

There was little to be treasurer of. Although the state's land locaters had at last found good tracts, sales at a reasonable price moved slowly. Before enough money was on hand to launch a building program, the

Voucher No. 1 of the University of California was signed along the left side by W. C. Ralston, university treasurer.

deadline specified by the Morrill Act loomed ahead. Unable to erect a new college in the time that remained, the regents decided to take over one already built.

Their choice fell on a debt-ridden private institution in Oakland called the College of California. (In 1868 there were no publicly supported colleges in the state. The few private ones that existed were sectarian, given to curricula weighted toward the classics, relatively expensive for the students, and strictly segregated according to sex.) The Oakland college was no great shakes physically, but it did own 160 acres of beautifully located land where Strawberry Creek sparkles out of the Coastal Mountains on its way to the bay—a section soon to be called Berkeley. The dream of the college was to build a new plant on the site, but it could not raise the money and so it reluctantly sold its Oakland campus and Berkeley land to the new state university.

Forty-two students opened their books in the decrepit Oakland buildings in September, 1869. Meanwhile the regents began struggling with the problems of building a university and setting its directions. Unable to find a president, they appointed from among their own members in January, 1869, a three-man executive committee to take charge of affairs. The temporary rulers were Horatio Stebbens, a San Francisco minister; Samuel Butterworth, the ruthless head of the New Almaden quicksilver mines; and William Ralston.

The trio worked rapidly—perhaps too rapidly. Headlong speed was a characteristic of the times. "When we [Californians] have wanted a thing," said Andrew Hallidie, one of Ralston's fellow regents, "we have wanted it badly and we scarcely had time to breathe until we got it."[10] In that mood of precipitance, the executive committee sent an agent to Europe with $15,000 to assemble books for a library. It announced an architectural contest, first prize $1,000, for plans for the first building in Berkeley, the College of Agriculture, and then fell into an acidulous quarrel with the winner when it sought to apply his prize money to his fee. Changing architects, the trio let contracts for the building, only to run out of money when nothing more than the basement had been completed. Covering the excavation against the weather, they besought Congress to remove certain restrictions from land sales, in the hope that this would speed the disposal of their federal holdings, an objective that was eventually achieved.

Concurrently they tackled the thorny problem of the curriculum. After deciding that the university proper should emphasize liberal arts, they fulfilled the demands of the Morrill Act for practical education by sending out the head of the College of Agriculture to lecture on a regular schedule to farm groups throughout the state, and by opening highly popular night classes in the mechanical arts in San Francisco. Discovering that applicants for admission to the university proper were lacking in academic qualifications, the group established preparatory "fifth classes" (freshmen were the fourth class) whose tutoring sessions were held at five branches scattered throughout the state.

After a year and a half of this arduous work—jobs piled on top of their personal affairs—the committee members had had enough. They appointed an interim president, 68-year-old Henry Durant, a man long associated with education in California, and in November, 1870, disbanded—but then kept on looking over Durant's shoulder as he assumed his duties.

In terms of percentages, the university's growth was rapid. The third scholastic year opened in September, 1871, with a student body of 147. Of these, 26 were—and it was a radical step for the times—females. Even the majority of the male students were loath to mingle with what they called "stiff-necked and misguided young women." In spite of covert harassment, however, 21 of the coeds stuck out the year.[11] Women's lib, with Ralston voting in its favor, was on its way in California.

As money became somewhat more plentiful in 1871–72, the regents appointed a new building committee headed by Samuel Merritt of Oakland. Two projects were now on the boards: finishing the College of Agriculture and erecting a building to house the College of Letters. Although Merritt went through the motions of calling for bids, the successful contractors turned out to be friends of his who obligingly bought the brick and lumber they needed from his supply firm.

Cost overruns became severe. Funds tightened, and the specifications for the College of Letters were changed from brick to wood. Students were employed whenever possible. When money for their wages was not available on payday, Ralston personally advanced them cash against the certificates of indebtedness the university issued them.[12]

Wasteful pressures attended the program, for the regents had promised the university's new president, Daniel Coit Gilman, former head of the Sheffield Scientific School at Yale, that the buildings would be ready by the opening of the academic year in September, 1873. Gilman had first come to California to look over the naked campus late in the summer of 1872. He spent time at Belmont and on leaving thanked Ralston effusively for the kindness, courtesy, and inspiration given him.[13] Yes, he would take the job as soon as he could wind up his affairs in New Haven.

Early in November he was back. On the sixth he attended a reception at Ralston and Harpending's Grand Hotel and then was escorted to Oakland by Billy and several other regents. There he was met by fire engines, brass bands, President pro tem Henry Durant, the faculty, and the entire student body. In his speech to the gathering he promised that the new university would rise above California's many diversities in race and religion and would be the servant of all the people of the state.[14]

The Dolly Vardens snorted their doubts. They saw little to be proud of in the two new buildings, prominently ugly on a badly scarred hilltop. The campus was dust in dry weather, mud in wet. The town of Berkeley consisted of one small restaurant and a ramshackle hotel. There were no sidewalks, no newspaper, no doctor, and, at the university, no living quarters. Students and faculty had to travel back and forth between Oakland and Berkeley in horse-drawn omnibuses until dormitories and residences could be built. Worst of all, the Dolly Vardens charged, was the exorbitant cost that had been involved in achieving so little. Talk of corruption filled the State House at Sacramento. Backed by the Grange, the People's Independent party demanded and won a legislative investigation.

The grilling of the regents began in San Francisco early in January, 1874. A leading witness for the Dolly Vardens was sociologist Henry George, later author of *Progress and Poverty,* who was then editor of the San Francisco *Evening Post.* He accused Merritt of manifold misdeeds and then created a modern-sounding controversy by refusing to reveal the sources of his damning statements. His bitterest vitriol swirled around philosophies. He scorned Gilman's theory of education as being courses that enabled students "to distinguish the useless, the false, and the fragile from the good, the true, the lasting." The university's duty, he insisted, was to present the youth of the state with a practical education as specified by the Morrill Act. Instead the institution had been captured by San Francisco's power establishment and put in the charge of a genteel aristocrat from Yale who did not understand the needs of the West. It was a school for rich men's sons who, George implied, were being trained to perpetuate California's inequitable social and economic systems.

Gilman retorted with a messianic speech defending what the regents had accomplished. The faculty split down the middle. Most of San Francisco's newspapers supported George. The sole major exception was the *Bulletin,* a surprise because that paper, as we shall note, generally found delight in excoriating everything with which William Ralston was connected.

The debates closed with a legislative resolution absolving the regents from wrongdoing and praising them as "men of integrity of character and honest of purpose, and who have at heart not only the interests of the University, but the educational interests of the whole State."[15] So much for those obstreperous Dolly Vardens and for Henry George—or so it seemed to California businessmen who still refused to see the depths of discontent which this attack on the state's first public university represented.

One reason for the blindness was the speculative mania released by the Crown Point and Belcher discoveries on the Comstock Lode, and by new silver and copper finds in eastern Nevada. The stock exchange, which long since had replaced the faro tables of the forty-niners as an outlet for San Francisco's penchant for gambling, was again thronged with the purchasers of hope. Millionaires dealt in $1,000 shares; parlormaids and bootblacks scrambled to buy penny stocks. Blind chance rewarded many, and that clouded the fact that far more were ruined. For a sizable portion of the population thrift ceased to be a virtue. Much worse was the siphoning away of time, energy, and money from more constructive enterprises. And yet—such were the paradoxes of the Comstock mania—this was the period when San Francisco consolidated her position as the queen city of the West.

So frantic a situation could not last. As the inequalities between classes grew more pronounced and the hope of lucky riches proved less soothing, there would be race riots, new vigilante activity, and a swelling demand for a revised state constitution that would end corporate dominance of the political as well as the economic systems. Ralston would not live to see those developments, but the forces that brought them into being were an integral part of the background against which he launched his last flamboyant and mostly futile enterprises.

CHAPTER 25

Paths to Disaster

For nearly two years promoter Alfred A. Cohen tried diligently to put together a syndicate of San Francisco capitalists capable of buying the Central Pacific Railroad and its subsidiaries. Among the men he sought to involve were Ralston, Sharon, D. O. Mills, Lloyd Tevis, and Michael Reese.[1] All were tempted. If the $27 million purchase went through, it would be by far the biggest financial event in the lives of any of them. For Ralston it would also involve a notable act of self-levitation, for by the beginning of 1872, when interest in the deal was soaring, he lacked enough capital to participate. His sole hope of becoming a railroad magnate, a prospect that had always intrigued him, was somehow to manufacture the necessary funds out of thin air.

Opportunity came from what he described to Mills as a gigantic "muddle."[2] The vital question of where the Central Pacific would locate its western terminus had not yet been resolved. San Francisco's donation of a small piece of land south of Rincon Hill for depots and marshalling yards had not been enough to compensate for the difficulties inherent in swinging from Sacramento all the way around the southern tip of the bay. Accordingly the owners of the Central Pacific still favored ending their line on the inland side of the bay. By 1870 they had even succeeded in selecting the exact spot—a small island in the bay west of Oakland.

Its name in Spanish was Yerba Buena; in English, Goat Island. The water surrounding it was deep on the side facing the ocean, shallow on the side facing land. Thus it would be easy to run a causeway for rails from Oakland out to navigable water on the far side of the island, where berths for the biggest ocean liners could be constructed with a minimum of dredging. San Francisco would then be isolated, and Oakland would become the principal distribution center of the West Coast—if the CP could persuade the federal government to part with the property.

In spite of testimony from the navy that Goat Island was an essential part of the bay's defense system and should not be alienated and in spite of evidence presented by the Coast and Geodetic Survey that a causeway would seriously affect tidal patterns, the railroad's political juggernaut rolled toward victory in Washington. In April, 1872, by a vote of 101 to 86, the House of Representatives agreed to let the Central Pacific have the land it wanted. If the Senate concurred, the job was done.

San Francisco opponents of the railroad immediately formed a Committee of One Hundred prominent citizens to find some means of staving off disaster. Three alternatives presented themselves. One was to put such pressure on the Senate that it would cancel the House's generosity. Another was to bribe the railroad into forgetting the island. This involved persuading the voters of the city to approve a subsidy of $2.5 million in municipal bonds for building an access bridge across the southern arm of the bay near a point called Ravenswood.

The third alternative centered on speeding the approach of a rival transcontinental, the Atlantic & Pacific. The A & P had been chartered by Congress in 1866 to build from Missouri through northern New Mexico into California at or near the town of Needles. Until the 1870s nothing had happened, even though the road's 35th parallel route was relatively free of snow—a constant plague to the Central Pacific in winter—and it had received from Congress a promise of generous land grants once it started laying track. Recently, however, the company had reorganized, and its new officials were guaranteeing action at last.[3]

Some of the Committee of One Hundred proposed to stimulate that action by offering the A & P $10 million in municipal bonds for building the western end of the track between Needles and San Francisco. The bay would not interfere, for the line would approach the city by way of the southern peninsula. Oakland would be bypassed and, of equal importance in the eyes of the monopoly-hating Dolly Vardens, the presence of a competing transcontinental would force the CP to behave in a more socially responsible manner.

The relationship of the leading supporters of the A & P subsidy plan to Ralston is of some interest. They were all opponents of his. One was R. G. Sneath, head of a rival bank; another was Caspar T. Hopkins, the insurance executive who had recently opposed Ralston vigorously in that field. A third was Alvinza Hayward, who with John P. Jones had wrested control of the Crown Point Mine away from the Union Mill and Mining Company.

Hayward had worked himself into such a lather of excitement over the railroad that Ralston grew concerned about him. "This will in my opinion kill Hayward," he wrote Mills, who was in New York City.

"His friends have done all in their power to get him out but all of no use, he seems determined—and his financial affairs are by no means in a satisfactory shape."[4] They were so unsatisfactory, indeed (Crown Point dividends had not yet begun rolling in), that Hayward even appealed to Ralston for help. Swallowing his resentments about the mine, Billy generously gave it to him, helping him raise almost overnight half a million dollars.[5] The day was not far distant when Ralston himself would need comparable aid—but would not get it. At the moment, however, this is a digression.

Abrim with excitement, Sneath and a subcommittee of the Committee of One Hundred hurried east to check on the soundness of the A & P. Officials of the A & P traveled west to check on the Committee of One Hundred.[6] (Ironically, both groups traveled over the Central Pacific.) Banquets, mass meetings, and long orations about the values of unimpeded intercourse between East and West kept that part of San Francisco that was interested in such things—and it was a large part— in a tizzy of suspense.

The Central Pacific of course did not want free and easy exchanges between East and West. It had acquired the Southern Pacific and its potential land grant from the road's original incorporators just so that it could build south to the Colorado River and block the A & P or any other eastern railroad that sought to approach the Bay Area from that direction.

As originally conceived, the Southern Pacific was to have paralleled the coast to Los Angeles before swinging east to the river. A land grant in the coastal area was of little worth, however, because most of the acreage was already in private hands and hence unattainable. Accordingly the new owners of the line sought and received permission from the secretary of the interior to reroute the tracks from Gilroy southeastward into the San Joaquin Valley.[7]

The shift of the Southern Pacific's route gave Ralston and some of his ring an idea. Why not incorporate a new line, the San Francisco and Colorado River Railroad, whose announced purpose would be the filling of the gap along the coast? After running as far south as San Diego, the tracks would veer east to the Colorado River. There they would meet whichever transcontinental arrived first, either the A & P or its equally slow-starting rival, the Texas Pacific. Because Congress was no longer doling out land grants, the San Francisco and Colorado would ask the voters of San Francisco to help it with $10 million in municipal bonds on the grounds that it was a home corporation, which the A & P was not, and hence offered a better answer to the CP's Goat Island threat than did the easterners.

The birth of the hopeful new line was announced in the spring of 1872. Incorporation was for $50 million. Of that sum, the line's officers said, $3.9 million was already subscribed. Although Ralston's name appears only as one of the directors of the company, his subsequent activities indicate that his voice was the real force in the new scheme.

This is not to imply that he was surrounded by nonentities. Quite the contrary. Among the other incorporators were Michael Reese, reputedly the richest man in California and a notable skinflint (he later died in Europe of a heart attack suffered when he tried to scale a cemetery wall to avoid a small admission charge); wholesale merchant William T. Coleman, leader of the vigilantes of 1851 and 1856; J. Mora Moss of the Sacramento Valley Railroad and the banking firm of Pioche, Bayerque & Company; J. O. Earl, incorporator with Ralston of the first two Comstock bonanza mines, the Ophir and the Gould and Curry; Peter Donahue of the San Francisco & San Jose Railroad, recently absorbed by the Southern Pacific; and Henry D. Bacon, who was currently helping Ralston escape from the catastrophe brought on the Pacific Insurance Company by the Chicago fire. Less easily accounted for in this group was banker John Parrott, who had helped undercut Ralston's hopes of gaining commercial concessions in Alaska and of extending New Montgomery Street past Rincon Hill.[8]

The sudden appearance of this new company among the opponents of the Central Pacific's Goat Island grab created a sensation. Exactly what was afoot?

Caspar Hopkins, one of the Committee of One Hundred who favored the A & P, and Hubert H. Bancroft, who would soon set about compiling a 39-volume history of the West from Alaska to Central America, jumped to the conclusion that Ralston was really trying to help the Central Pacific, not combat it. Inasmuch as the CP then owed The Bank of California $1.1 million, there was some logic to the supposition. Ralston naturally wanted to protect his client, and one way to do it was to defeat any issue of municipal bonds to the rival transcontinental.[9]

The reasoning was incomplete. Ralston was willing to help the Central Pacific, but he also wanted to fulfill his long-standing desire to own a large part of a major railroad. He could not afford to join Cohen's syndicate for purchasing the entire Central Pacific. (As matters developed, the syndicate never materialized.) The next best thing was to buy what promised to be the CP's most lucrative subsidiary, the Southern Pacific. He could do it if the city's voters authorized $10 million in bonds for aiding the new corporation.

His idea was to use the bonds not for building a new line, but for making a down payment on the Southern Pacific. In return for that and for a mortgage whose amount was to be determined by negotiations, he and his associates would receive the SP's charter, its land-grant rights, its share in the Mission Bay land donation south of Rincon Hill, the property of the San Francisco & San Jose Railroad, which the SP had recently acquired, rolling stock, depots, and the track that had been laid to Gilroy and beyond. The purchasers would also assume the SP's debt, most of it in the form of corporate bonds and notes of indebtedness to the San Francisco & San Jose.

Even Collis Huntington, the vice-president and extraordinarily able financial magician of the Central Pacific, was caught by surprise. He adjusted quickly, however, a process stimulated by the Senate's refusal to join the House in donating Goat Island to private profiteering. He agreed to part with the Southern Pacific for $15 million, to be raised by the San Francisco bonds and a first mortgage on the railroad property, *if* the CP received as consolation for the lost island $2.5 million for building the Ravenswood bridge and if the new owners promised to honor the bonds that the SP had already issued. At least $1 million in commissions would be involved, part of which would go to Ralston and The Bank of California.[10]

At that point word of the proposal leaked to the *Bulletin,* a main supporter of the A & P. The paper, in Ralston's words, "pitched into me personally at a fearful rate."[11] The attack was gleefully extended throughout the nation by James W. Simonton, an implacable enemy of Huntington's and part owner of the *Bulletin,* of Western Union, and of the Associated Press. What kind of outrageous conniving was this? If Huntington could not get his hands into the federal treasury through the Senate, then he would milk the city through the conniving of toadies like Ralston. And so on.

The vituperation served mainly to confuse the voters. Fearful that the end result would be a rejection of all subsidies at the polls, the visiting officials of the Atlantic & Pacific went into a huddle with their supposed rivals, Ralston's group. Their reasoning was pragmatic enough. They wanted to be on friendly terms with whatever California corporation built to the Colorado River, and this might well turn out to be the Southern Pacific, controlled by Ralston's ring if its powerful members won the city's $10 million gift. But no one would benefit if the *Bulletin*, in its frenzy of righteousness, continued muddying the waters. Could Ralston somehow calm down the editors, men named Fitch and Pickering?

Billy agreed to try. "At the behest of both sides & many of our friends," he wrote Mills, "I went to see the Bulletin people had two long sessions with them all pleasant, as I was determined *not* to get excited. I felt well satisfied with myself afterwards."[12]

The overtures came too late. Excitable San Franciscans had always diverted themselves by attending mass meetings, where they were harangued on current issues by spellbinding orators. Small-fry politicians, eager to take advantage of the current uproar, gathered audiences on street corners and in public halls, and stirred them with wild denunciations of all railroads. Chanting mobs marched against the city hall, where the supervisors were discussing which of the subsidy measures, if any, should be placed on the ballots—and where the marchers were turned back by a cordon of police supported with artillery.

No weapon existed for overcoming antagonism at the polls, however. All three subsidies—to the CP for the access bridge, to the A & P and the San Francisco & Colorado for construction work—all were defeated.[13] Ralston's dream of a railroad was gone.

Equally frustrating was the gigantic San Joaquin and Kings River Canal Company, in its way a bolder concept even than the plan to seize the Southern Pacific with municipal money. The idea was to draw water out of the Kings River and Tulare Lake in the southern part of the San Joaquin Valley, add more from the San Joaquin River where it made its big bend northward after pouring out of the Sierra Nevada, and carry the fluid as far as tidewater at Antioch, beside the Sacramento delta. The distance, counting windings, was roughly 200 miles. Water flowing northward along that hot, almost flat expanse would irrigate hundreds of thousands of acres, mostly planted to wheat. When the growing season was over, the huge ditch—it would be at least six feet deep and twenty-eight or more feet wide at its bottom—could be used to float bargeloads of grain to ocean schooners waiting at Antioch and to bring back lumber for building fences, houses, and barns in the treeless valley.

The scheme had been in the air for some time. In 1866 the state had surveyed the Sacramento Valley with the idea of fostering a combined irrigation-transportation canal in the northern part of the Central Valley. Inevitably the proposal stirred talk of a similar project southward in the San Joaquin. No one acted in either section, however, until a husky six-footer named John Bensley took hold and posted a notice at a key point on the San Joaquin River, declaring his intention of diverting part of its water into a canal.

Ralston knew Bensley well. A native of New York, he had gone to Mexico in 1839 as a trader. During the war between that country and the United States he had profited handsomely by buying supplies and mules from Mexican ranchers he knew and reselling the acquisitions to the American army. He was one of the first to hurry north from Mexico on learning of the gold discoveries in California. He flourished as a merchant in Sacramento and then moved to San Francisco, where he helped develop the city's first water system. He was one of the incorporators of the California Steam Navigation Company, and it was through that mutual interest that Ralston met him.[14] When Bensley conceived of his huge canal, he turned naturally to Billy for aid in setting up a company capable of building it.

The stockholders whose support Ralston enlisted included, in addition to himself, two directors of The Bank of California, Nicholas

*John Bensley initiated
an irrigating canal
in the San Joaquin Valley
that drew more energy
and money from Ralston
than he could afford.*

BANCROFT LIBRARY, UNIVERSITY OF CALIFORNIA, BERKELEY

Luning and lumberman A. J. Pope, and such business familiars as J. Mora Moss, Isaac Friedlander, and Lloyd Tevis. Also included, for the sake of obtaining a right-of-way through their land, were cattle barons Henry Miller and Charles Lux, whose livestock grazed across more than a million California acres.

The ditch company hired, at $1,000 a month, an English civil engineer, R. M. Brereton, to supervise the work. Brereton began modestly with a 38-mile stretch of construction leading from Fresno Slough north to Los Banos. Hundreds of men employed at $30 a month and board ($50 a month for those that furnished work horses) settled in grim camps on what was then a sun-smitten, wind-whipped desert. Supplies and tools came by boat when the San Joaquin River was high with Sierra snow melt and during the rest of the year in long strings of wagons toiling from the railroad at Gilroy through Pacheco Pass to Los Banos.

Those were years of drought. The winter of 1871–72 was particularly bad. By the end of February, 1872, the grain was only six inches high and turning sere. Farmers desperately cut unauthorized subsidiary ditches into the new canal and saved the crops on about 20,000 acres. It was not enough to rescue Friedlander, however. He went bankrupt —and then, with Ralston's help and in the face of attacks from the Grange, whose members wanted to break his monopoly in sacks and ships, began the arduous task of recovery.[15]

Leaders of the People's Independent party, the Dolly Vardens, joined the Grange in denouncing the irrigation company as the tool of unconscionable land speculators. (The approach of the ditch did boost the price of farmland from $2.50 an acre to $25.00–$30.00.) Discouraged by the hostility, the bad weather, and Friedlander's collapse, Ralston prevailed on the company directors to send engineer Brereton overseas to sell the canal to English investors. The effort failed. Charles Stuart, head of The Oriental Bank of London, wrote Ralston a six-page letter explaining why. English capitalists suspected western enterprise of being shoddily run for the sake of quick profits from stock speculations. They preferred slower, surer returns from conservative operations. Moreover, Brereton's timing was bad. He had arrived in London, said Stuart with a cutting reference to Harpending's recent Burro Mine promotion, just "when John Bull was suffering from a credulous belief in Pyramids of Silver." Another fancy promotion like that—or like the empire-sized San Joaquin and King's River Canal Company—simply would not be swallowed right then.[16]

The exposure of the diamond hoax shortly thereafter completed British disenchantment. Brereton returned to the United States. Aided by California's congressional delegation, who in turn had been primed by letters from Ralston, he made an appointment to appear before the Committee of Public Lands as a first step in a drive to obtain a federal subsidy for the canal. On March 3, 1873, a five-man commission was appointed to investigate the proposal, but that was as far as the matter went.[17]

The scrambles to raise money for the railroad and canal schemes came at a time when all of Ralston's affairs were once again in perilous shape. The first rumbles of warning came from James Lees of Lees & Waller in New York as early as April, 1872. Ralston had asked the New Yorkers and The Oriental Bank of London to increase the amount of capital available to him. Lees snapped back a refusal. As far as he could see, he said, the request was unwarranted. What was going on out there on the Coast?

History's unhappy repetitions: just as he had done three years before, Ralston began overdrawing the accounts without authorization. By fall The Bank of California was $3.5 million in debt to The Oriental Bank—an amount "grossly out of line," scolded Oriental's president, Charles Stuart. Lees meanwhile was protesting sharply and continually about the "extreme pressures" that Ralston's demands were placing on the New York house. Both men demanded that he shape up immediately.[18]

Ralston responded with what he hoped were soothing words. The burning of a tunnel on the Virginia & Truckee Railroad had delayed ore shipments from the Comstock, but the problem was about solved and he would soon be able to send enough silver bullion to London to clear up his cash accounts there. As soon as Californians quit hoarding money to meet tax bills due at the end of the year and as soon as ships could be found to move grain still standing in the warehouses, his capital would become fluid again and he would not need so much credit. Please be patient. All would be well. As a partial step toward making it well, he demanded that his own principal debtor, the Central Pacific, take steps to reduce its account, which stood at more than $1 million.[19]

His creditors were not placated. The Bank of California, Lees railed, "appears always to be hard run and absolutely lies down and asks its creditors to have patience in the face of loud calls for remittance. To me this is galling and humiliating in the extreme." To Mills he wrote crossly that it simply was not possible for the San Francisco bank to carry all California financially, as Billy seemed to be trying to do. He ended by demanding that Mills, Ralston, and Thomas Bell execute a bond that would guarantee Lees and Waller "against loss by reason of any personal liability incurred in handling the accounts of The Bank of California"—a request with which the chastened trio complied on December 6, 1872.[20]

At that juncture Ralston fell critically ill. What the affliction was and how much of it was brought on by overwork and nervous tension does not appear in the records. Whatever the trouble, it was alarming enough that newspapers carried word of it as far as Italy, where California's senator-designate, Judge John S. Hagar, was spending his honeymoon, and to Yokohama, where Charles DeLong was about to be replaced as American minister to Japan.[21]

While Ralston was laid up, the worried directors of the bank did what they should have done earlier; they checked its books. As soon as Billy returned to work, they gathered angrily in his office—it was February 19, 1873—and faced him with the shocking discoveries. He had loaned to three businesses which he controlled a total of $3,518,176—$578,580 to the Kimball Manufacturing Company, $967,900 to the Pacific Woolen Mills, and $1,971,696 to the New Montgomery Street Real Estate Company. All three firms had defaulted on their interest payments, and the loans looked shaky indeed. Although the Central Pacific was meeting its obligations, the income wasn't enough. The Bank of California was close to collapse. What did Ralston, the principal debtor of the very institution he managed, propose to do?

He was rescued by his wife's foster father, John D. Fry. Fry had grown wealthy through Comstock connections that Billy had made for him. He was president of the Belcher Mine and was a director of twelve other mines controlled by the Union Mill and Mining Company. Drawing on these resources, he agreed to pay the bank $3.4 million. In return he was given the notes that the bank held against the three debtor firms—Kimball, Pacific Woolen, and New Montgomery—and

John D. Fry,
Lizzie's foster father,
whom Ralston made wealthy,
tried to rescue Billy financially
at a time of great need.

the collateral that had been offered as security.[22] Ralston, in other words, now became indebted to his father-in-law for nearly three and a half million dollars.

Fry took the step with full knowledge of the extraordinary bonanza that was being opened in the Belcher. During 1873 the mine would pay $6.7 million in dividends on ore that grossed $10.5 million. (The Crown Point, where the strike had first been made did not do quite as well: $5.3 million in dividends on ore valued at $7.3 million. At times the thought must have crossed Ralston's, Mills's, Sharon's, and Fry's minds that it would have been most pleasant if they had managed to hang onto both mines.) And of course mine dividends were not the whole story. The milling company and the railroad flourished. It has been estimated that by 1875 those enterprises had paid Sharon and Ralston $4 million each and Mills $2 million in addition to what the partners drew from the Belcher.[23]

The effect was marvelous. The Bank of California, which even in its darkest moments had not once skipped its dividend of 1 percent a month, recovered smartly. The bond that Ralston, Mills, and Bell had executed on behalf of Lees & Waller was cancelled on March 26, 1873, and the letters that came from London were again filled with compliments. Presumably Ralston reduced his obligations to his father-in-law with equal dispatch.

Officers and staff of The Bank of California, 1874, in the directors' room. Ralston is seated in the center under a portrait of Darius Mills.

Yet shadows lingered. Dissatisfied with the roller-coaster career of the bank and eager to devote more time to his personal affairs, Darius Mills determined to sell his last 500 shares of stock and resign as president. This time Ralston could not change his mind and the separation came in July.

Ralston became president of the bank in his stead. He bought Mills's stock, but did not note the transfer on the bank records. Because the stock still stood in Mills's name, it was possible to elect him, without his knowledge, to the board of directors. The reason for the deceit probably went as follows. Mills had an international reputation. If he

were to leave the bank so soon after its time of trouble, harmful rumors would spread. If, however, he appeared to have faith in the institution, not only California businessmen but also Lees & Waller and The Oriental Bank would be reassured.[24] The fact that the other directors stayed silent about the matter suggests that Ralston either held them in the cup of his hand or that they were again content to leave the entire running of the bank to him. In view of his recent troubles, either explanation is next to incomprehensible except on the grounds of Billy's dazzling powers of persuasion.

Late in September, 1873, less than three months after Mills's departure, James Lees died. Of the two losses, his was the more serious. Like the other directors of The Bank of California, Mills had never paid much attention to daily operations, but had given Ralston full latitude. By contrast, James Lees as senior partner of the house that acted as New York agent for both The Bank of California and The Oriental Bank of London knew much of what was going on in the West. He spoke out when he thought he should, with the kind of wisdom that made Ralston stop and listen. Now, just as enough money to excite a far duller imagination than Billy's was flowing across the Sierra, the last restraint was gone.

Under the stimulus of that excitement, Ralston might not have heeded even Lees. Once again he became his old sanguine self, convinced in the rightness of whatever appealed to him. Plans for the city and state—and for himself—tumbled out in dizzying sequence. Fear? Of what? The West was boundless.

Even the canal no longer seemed like a drag. True, he wrote a friend, it did take continual supervision and endless money. But its design was so tremendous that the struggle, whose reward would be "positive and perpetual prosperity for our coast," was well worthwhile. Nor was the gain something for the distant future. "Five years time will see much of it in actual and practical operation."[25]

He agreed instantly with Sharon's proposal that the bank group spend part of its Belcher profits in an attempt to control the insatiable Comstock lumber market. Through a corporation called the Carson & Tahoe Lumber and Fluming Company, they acquired 50,000 acres of timber near the southern and western sides of Lake Tahoe, built trains for hauling the logs they felled to the water's edge, and towed the logs behind steam tugs to three sawmills the company erected at Glenbrook, Nevada, on the eastern shore. A narrow-gauge railroad lifted the wood to Spooner Summit. There it was shifted to a twelve-mile-long flume filled with water and swished down the mountainside to a spur track of the Virginia & Truckee for the final stage of its journey to the mines.[26] The expense of the system was staggering, but once again Ralston saw only prosperity at the end.

Once more his penchant for building swept him up. Tired of living in an apartment when he had to stay in San Francisco overnight, as often happened, he decided to build a town house at the corner of Pine and Leavenworth streets. It began modestly but under the radiance of the Belcher sun expanded until its four stories contained thirty rooms warmed by steam heat (a rarity in those days) and serviced by an elevator. Gossips estimated that costs exceeded $200,000. It was finished in time for Lizzie and him to entertain King Kalakaua of Hawaii twice in 1874 as the island monarch passed through San Francisco on his way to and from Washington on a state visit.[27]

Of Billy's many plans during those years the one that most stirred the imagination of his fellow San Franciscans was his well-publicized determination to build for his city what would be, literally, the largest and most sumptuous hotel in the world, to be called the Palace. Though boosterism and personal vanity were mingled in the decision, his main purpose was practical. He wanted to save the foundering New Montgomery Street Real Estate Company.

The exposure of the diamond fraud, it will be recalled, had resulted in Sharon's and Ralston's purchase of Asbury Harpending's share of the real estate project. Hoping to entice clients into the area, the new partners had offered to erect a stock exchange building and rent space at low rates if the city's brokers would shift their activities south of Market Street.[28] The lure failed, and so Ralston turned back to the idea of using a hotel as a magnet.

Inasmuch as Harpending and he had already tried that approach by building the Grand Hotel, the idea seems uninspired for Ralston. But the notion's lack of originality was compensated for by magnificence. Neither New York nor London would be able to boast of so opulent a hostelry. He would connect the Palace to the Grand by means of a covered passageway above New Montgomery Street. Together the two hotels would offer well-heeled visitors more than a thousand rooms. He would fill their ground floors with the most elegant shops in the country and in that way start a drift of retailers toward the languishing mass of real estate.

Sharon agreed to go along, although costs would run into the millions. Prospects, moreover, were not encouraging. San Francisco was overbuilt with hotels. Besides that, whispers of trouble were beginning to come from Virginia City. Miners probing the ore body in the Belcher had reached what appeared to be its outer limits. Behind them were reserves enough to keep the mine operating for two more years. After that—who could say?

By nature Sharon was chill and calculating. He must have seen some of the pitfalls surrounding the Palace project. On the other hand, the New Montgomery Street company was $2 million in debt, and something had to be done to save it. The Palace might be the magic wand.

Finally, despite his reserve, William Sharon was as susceptible as anyone else to Ralston's magnetism. Worry? Ridiculous! Notice how San Francisco was growing. As for the Belcher, ore bodies were always exhausted in time. But a new one would surely turn up somewhere else. One always had, hadn't it?

CHAPTER 26

Collapse

San Franciscans watched the growth of the Palace Hotel with fascination. In the cavernous excavation for the basements and then in the rising red brick walls they saw proof that their city, population 191,000, was ready to take its rightful place among the sophisticated urban centers of the world. The edifice also gave reassurance about Ralston and The Bank of California, nerve centers of the financial West. Limitless funds were surely necessary for so imposing a work.

Nearly every day journalists found new statistics over which to marvel. The building was going to be impervious to fire and earthquake. The hotel's own artesian wells would fill a 630,000-gallon reservoir in the sub-basement. Tanks capable of holding another 130,000 gallons were to be placed on the roof and attached to a circulating system that led to 350 outlets equipped with 20,000 feet of fire hose. All walls, exterior and interior, were to be thicker than the average. Their bricks were to be glued together with mortar of special strength and then reinforced with parallel bands hammered out of 3,000 tons of strap iron.[1]

The eight hundred rooms in the seven-story building would be airy with ceilings fifteen feet high. Most would boast individual fireplaces and toilets equipped with "an arrangement by which the water is carried off without producing the horrid noise one usually hears." Because San Francisco was a city of bay windows, designed to catch every fleeting ray of sunshine that pierced the mists, Ralston decreed that each of the Palace's exterior rooms was to have its own glassed-in bay. The result was an amazing look of shiny corrugations across the facade.

There were to be three interior courts. The central one, surrounded by seven floors of balustrades and covered by a soaring roof of opaque glass, opened off New Montgomery Street. Its marble floor was shaped

Ralston's last monumental project for San Francisco was the Palace Hotel, touted as one of the world's most lavish hostelries.

like a keyhole. Carriages could drive in through the broad entrance and deposit their passengers amidst a forest of potted plants. Once inside the visitors glided upward in one of five elevators elegant with padded benches for comfort and with mirrors—a Ralston hallmark—for last-minute examinations of coiffures and neckties.

Every brickyard in the Bay Area was drawn on for the 300,000 bricks laid each day. Fifteen firms furnished marble. Suites and the big public rooms—the main dining room was 155 feet long—were covered with carpets woven in France. C.F. Haviland, also of France, contracted to furnish 30,000 dishes of various kinds. Nine thousand cuspidors were on order. Ralston created one special company, the Adams Lock Company, to manufacture the building's door and cabinet fittings, and another, the West Coast Furniture Company, to turn out tables, chairs, bedsteads, chiffoniers, and washstands. Silk hangings and upholstery came from his own silk company in San Jose, blankets from his woolen mills in San Francisco.

By mail he asked the agents of The Oriental Bank in Shanghai and Yokohama to search out suitable wood for paneling. He sent to Manila for teak and mahogany. Hearing of a foothills ranch covered with stately oaks, he bought it, only to discover that the gnarled trees that grew there did not produce wood suitable for flooring. For the furniture he

*Arriving guests were brought by carriage into the Palace's soaring
interior court, roofed seven stories up by opaque glass.*

finally chose light, strong, yellow primavera imported from Mexico.[2]

Rather than run the establishment themselves, Sharon and he leased
it to one of the best hotelmen in the country, Warren Leland. Recruiting
one hundred skilled laborers in Chicago, he sent them west to put the
last touches on the interior. He also decided to staff the Palace with
trained blacks, an innovation for San Francisco, whose hotels employed
either Chinese or what one newspaper termed "impudent" whites.[3]

Then, as the huge walls climbed higher, so did doubts. The hotel's
own grandeur was likely to be its undoing. In the opinion of the *San
Francisco Real Estate Circular* for November, 1874, it was likely to
block civic expansion southward, not invite it. "It stands," declared
the writer, "like a dark menace to Montgomery Street, as though it said,

'Thus far shalt thou go and no further.' " Worse, it was ugly, "with as little architectural embellishment to adorn and soften its flaming red brick face as any building we have ever seen"—a criticism that may have led the builders to paint the walls white. To no avail. Retailers examined the 18 unfinished shops on the ground floor, found them inconveniently small, and declined to pay the rent that was asked.[4]

Sharon complained of the costs, which were mounting toward $5 million. But there was no way to back out. Moreover, Ralston remained stubbornly sure that the carpers were wrong. The average passerby was proud of the Palace. Where else in the land could such a monument be found? Of course it would succeed.

He needed success. Everything he touched was failing. The factories he created to produce goods for the Palace could not meet the standards he decreed at a price the hotel could afford, nor could they expand their markets in the face of cheap imports from the depression-battered East. Outside competition killed the Cornell Watch Company, which he had located first in San Francisco and which later had to move to Oakland because the windy air of San Francisco was filled with dust. Gradually the San Joaquin and King's River Canal Company slipped away from Friedlander, Bensley, and him to become, in the main, an appendage of the enormous ranching operations of Henry Miller and Charles Lux. Though the California Theater continued to put on sterling programs, its manager, actor John McCullough, spent excessive sums to attract famous names, muddled his accounts, and each month sank deeper into debt.

Grimmest note in the tale was the Consolidated Tobacco Company. A rank-tasting tobacco flourished near the town of Gilroy. Billy first encountered it during his involvement with the construction company that extended the tracks of the Southern Pacific into the area. When a man named J. D. Culp claimed to have discovered a curing method that would overcome the plant's disagreeable qualities, Ralston grew excited. Another home product to boom! Promptly he formed the Consolidated Tobacco Company, set out 1,000 acres of Gilroy tobacco, bought Culp's patents, built curing sheds, warehouses, and a cigar factory.

Boasting that he would drive Cuban tobacco and Havana cigars not only out of California, but out of the United States, Billy flooded acqaintances in the East with cigars during the winter of 1873–1874. They answered politely but sales languished. The Culp process was full of bugs, and the Coast's Chinese cigar makers, using southern tobacco, proved impossible to undercut. Consolidated closed after losing, with dismaying speed, a million dollars.[5]

Even the Comstock Lode was no longer dependable. The attack this time came from the four Irishmen, John W. Mackay, James G. Fair, James C. Flood, and William S. O'Brien, who had caught Sharon napping

365

in 1869 and had wrenched control of the Hale & Norcross Mine from Union Mill and Mining. After netting close to $1 million from their acquisition, the quartet began searching for new properties. While attention was fixed on the Crown Point and Belcher mines at the south end of the lode, they went to its northern end and spent somewhere between $50,000 and $100,000 acquiring an ill-regarded group of small claims called the Consolidated Virginia.[6]

Inspired by the Crown Point and Belcher bonanzas, they dropped deep underground and in the face of suffocating heat began slow, methodical, thorough explorations. By the end of 1873 they knew that a block of ore that might prove to be one of the great bonanzas of all time lay at their fingertips. Hoping to extend their mastery to its farthest limits, they quietly bought up a controlling interest in four adjoining claims to the north. These they incorporated as the California Mine. Much of the ground embraced by the California, like the Ophir Mine just to the north, had once belonged to Union Mill and Mining. Discouraged by lean ore and a constant struggle with flooded shafts, Sharon had let the properties, the Ophir included, go to speculators who in their turn sold to the Irish quartet.

In May, 1874, Consolidated Virginia declared its first dividend of $3 a share on 108,000 shares. The payment was repeated each subsequent month until March, 1875, when it went up to $10 a share each month. (At that point the California was still in development stages.) To handle the ore of the two mines, the four silver kings, as they came to be called, incorporated the mills that they already owned or were building into the Pacific Mill and Mining Company. Everyone assumed, quite rightly, that they intended to compete with the bank ring's Union company for control of the lode.

Throughout the summer of 1874 the prices of Con Virginia and California stock climbed steadily, dragging quotations on the rest of the mines with them. In August Sharon decided to regain the Ophir, whose stock was then selling at about $20 a share. Presumably he acted because he thought that the Consolidated Virginia's big bonanza spread northward through the California into the Ophir.

Presumably. Some of his contemporaries believed, however, that his interest in ore was secondary and that he planned an unprecedented manipulation of the stock market.[7]

Although Sharon had lived in San Francisco for the past two years, he still wanted to be elected to the United States Senate from Nevada. Opportunity came when one of the two incumbents, William M. Stewart, decided not to run for reelection. Immediately Sharon laid the groundwork for his own campaign. He purchased the Virginia City *Enterprise,* which had vigorously opposed his candidacy during his contest with John P. Jones in 1872. Charges that have never been substantiated state that he paid Nevada's favorite son, Charles DeLong, recently retired as U.S. minister to Japan, a large sum to stay out of the race.[8] He then sent agents throughout Nevada to learn how much it would cost to send to the state senate at Carson City enough legislators to give him the national seat he craved.

Because of Adolph Sutro the price was high. One way or another the persistent German had scraped together enough money, mostly in Europe, to keep driving his would-be drainage tunnel toward the 1,650-foot level of the Comstock. Although Congress regularly considered helping him with federal funds, the necessary bill never carried. The reason, Sutro remained convinced, was the opposition of The Bank of California and of its subsidiary, Union Mill and Mining. He certainly did not want a key member of that group sitting in Congress when he next appealed for aid. So he sought to block Sharon by running for the same seat as a candidate of the People's Independent party, the Dolly Vardens.

The third party was strong that year (Democrats were never much of a threat in post–Civil War Nevada) and Sutro was popular with miners. The campaign promised to be, and was, vicious and bruising.

All this took money, possibly as much as $800,000.[9] Though Sharon was wealthy, millions of his capital were tied up in such currently non-liquid enterprises as the Carson and Tahoe Lumber and Fluming Company, the New Montgomery Street Real Estate Company, and the Palace Hotel. The quickest way to raise funds, if one had sufficient credit to begin with, was to shake the stock market.

The first step was to push up the price of Ophir shares. He began buying heavily. His friends, Ralston included, followed eagerly. Hadn't Sharon been right in predicting that the Crown Point bonanza would extend into the Belcher? By November their purchases had lifted the price of Ophir stock from $20 to $133. At that point Sharon and Ralston gained control of the Ophir by paying Elias Jackson Baldwin, ever afterwards known as Lucky Baldwin, $2.64 million for 20,000 shares.[10] During that same wild period, Ralston, Sharon, and their associates spent another $1.7 million to acquire Alvinza Hayward's share of the Crown Point, only to discover that its bonanza was even nearer exhaustion than the Belcher's.[11]

On the face of things the purchases looked good. The Con Virginia was staggering men's imaginations. Engineer Philip Deidesheimer, inventor of the timbering system used in all Comstock mines, declared that the Consolidated Virginia, the California, and the Ophir together would produce during the next few years at least $1.5 billion. Journalists who visited the Con Virginia returned to the surface filled with extravaganzas. San Francisco speculators—and that included a large part of the population—went into a frenzy.

On January 7, 1874, Consolidated Virginia stock, which the silver kings had begun buying at $1 a share hit $710. Stock in the California, which could have been picked up in September, 1873, for $37 reached $780. Ophir touched $315. All told, the stock value of the Comstock's 31 leading mines reached, that delirious day, $253 million. Of that sum the Con Virginia, the California, and the Ophir accounted for $194 million—$4 million more than the assessed valuation of all the real estate in San Francisco![12]

Such prices, which far exceeded the amount of West Coast capital available for investment, were totally unrealistic. On January 8 the market broke. By the end of the month California was down to $240. Consolidated Virginia, which was still paying $300,000 a month in dividends, sagged to $497. Ophir dropped to $116.

There was nothing new about such violent seesaws on the Comstock. The unanswerable question raised by this one is whether or not Sharon timed the collapse to suit his own purposes, in complete disregard of what might happen to his friends.

The preceding November Nevada's voters had elected a legislature committed to sending Sharon to Washington. Now he was faced with paying off his commitments. While still recommending that his friends buy Ophir stock, he began secretly selling his holdings short at prices ranging from $200 to $250, delivery to be made in 90 days. As the time neared, so later accusers said, he had his rumormongers leak word that there was no bonanza in the Ophir. (There wasn't, but it seems unlikely that Sharon could have discovered this fact in the time available.) Down went the overinflated market. Sharon delivered on schedule, reaped a handsome profit, and then bought back the shares at low prices from those who had been ruined by the decline. "If this be true," Charles DeLong wrote his wife about the episode, "the man is a demon and deserves destruction."[13]

It was Ralston, however, who was destroyed. He evidently knew nothing of what Sharon was doing—if, indeed, Sharon was doing anything more than following a reasonable hunch that the overheated market was due to cool soon and suddenly. Less perspicacious and desperate for cash, Ralston held his rising stock too long, was caught, and lost what one newspaper guessed to be $8 million.[14] The figure was probably excessive, but Billy was so deeply in debt that the point is academic.

He faced the debacle with no other family at home than his youngest daughter, Bertha, not yet three. The boys, Sam, 15, and Willie, Jr., 12, had for the past two years been attending a private school in Newton, Massachusetts.[15] Instead of bringing them home for the Christmas holidays of 1874, Lizzie decided to join them in the East. Leaving Bertha in charge of a nursemaid, she bundled up nine-year-old Emelita and about December 10 boarded a train for Boston. Billy's brother, Andrew Jackson Ralston, traveling on business, went part way with her. Along

Dapper, shifty, politically ambitious William Sharon, the bank's agent in Virginia City, was Ralston's partner in many ventures.

the way they encountered, somewhat to his surprise since he had recently been entertained at Belmont without hearing of the trip, the new Japanese ambassador to the United States, Kyonari Yoshida. After gathering in the boys, Lizzie spent the holidays with her uncle, Gen. James B. Fry, then commander of the Military Division of the Atlantic, with headquarters in New York City. The general considered the lads hellions. "Your decision of character," he wrote Ralston, "does not show as much in educating your boys, as it does in other things."[16]

The episode suggests that Lizzie and her husband were still having difficulties and that she still punished him, as she had during the days of his mistresses, by walking out with the children when her patience reached an end. Be that as it may, he was alone.

He was alone, too, when he received a strange charitable request. A group of fifty Scandinavian women had decided to buy for $7,000 a house on Clay Street that they could turn into a haven for destitute natives of their own countries. The spokeswoman of the group asked Billy by mail to launch the campaign with a contribution of $1,000.

Across the bottom of the appeal Ralston wrote with sweeping strokes, "I have plenty and can do it *all*."[17] He sent the full $7,000 and the astonished Scandinavians rejoiced. Ralston, the magnificent, as a newspaper once called him. But he did not have plenty. Just determination and one last bright hope, the Spring Valley Water Company.

By buying out its competitors, including a pioneering delivery system created by John Bensley, the Spring Valley Company had become San Francisco's sole dispenser of water. Its principal source of supply was a series of reservoirs in the rugged peninsular mountains south of the city. It was a profitable firm. In 1870, it collected $816,859 from its patrons and distributed $479,967 in dividends to its stockholders, a 59 percent return. By 1875 the figure had risen to $1,032,890 collected and $640,000 dispersed, for a 61 percent return.[18]

Naturally the company wished to retain its franchises. It was running into trouble with the city, however. One squabble was over an old promise to supply free water for public purposes. Successive dry years and the extensive development of Golden Gate Park made this agreement seem archaic to the company, and in 1869 it said it would no longer abide by the franchise terms. The city retorted that in view of the company's earnings it had no cause to complain.

The dispute was underscored by everyone's awareness that the company's limited supplies would not meet the needs of the growing city much longer. New sources would have to be developed somewhere outside the peninsula. Instead of letting Spring Valley do the work, presumably at exorbitant profit to itself, San Francisco's Board of Supervisors decided to buy the company, turn it into a public service, and undertake the expansion program under municipal auspices.

In 1874 an eastern engineer named T. R. Snowden was hired to seek out the best new source. After spending eight months studying various sites, Snowden recommended purchasing the Calaveras watershed on the northeastern slope of Mount Hamilton, near San Jose. Despite its name, the watershed had nothing to do with either Calaveras County or the Calaveras big trees, where Ralston had spent part of his honeymoon. It lay a short distance east of the southern extremity of San Francisco Bay, mostly in Santa Clara County. One of its prime values, aside from the area's heavy rainfall, was a splendid reservoir site from which water could easily be piped 28 miles to the existing Spring Valley system on the peninsula.

Before the city was ready to move, William Ralston and a friend named Charles N. Felton stepped in and bought the entire 2,250 acres of the Calaveras watershed from its owners for approximately $100,000. Simultaneously they set out to gain control of the Spring Valley Company. Since they had no cash available (this was just after the Ophir disaster), they resorted to an ingenious device. They offered more than the market price for stock and paid for it with certificates bearing 9 per cent interest. Until the certificates were paid for, the stock was held in escrow in The Bank of California in the name of the buyers. When an occasional seller sought to cash his certificate—not many did, since the certificates were ostensibly worth more than the stock—Ralston met the demand by borrowing from one of the city's savings banks.

In this way Ralston and Felton swept up 49,000 of Spring Valley's 80,000 shares. In May, 1875, they sold the Calaveras land they had recently purchased to the company they now dominated for $1,012,000, a profit of $900,000. This acquisition, valued at what the company paid, lifted the physical worth of the Spring Valley Company to roughly $10 million. Ralston and Felton offered these assets to the city for $15 million. At that price they could pay off the certificates of indebtedness and still have a profit of $2.5 million or so each to show for their troubles. Fortified by the quick windfall, Ralston could, he believed, fight his way back into the clear financially.

The city's newspapers, most particularly the *Call* and the *Bulletin* raised a howl: taxes and water rates would rise fearfully just to enrich speculators who were already wealthy enough. San Francisco did need more water, but there were better and cheaper ways of getting it. Swayed by the uproar, the supervisors rejected the offer.

Ralston was not unduly shaken. A new city administration, including a new Board of Supervisors, was to be chosen at the September elections, and it should not be difficult to fill the seats with men favorable to the sale, which various engineers declared was not exorbitant. His candidate for mayor was ex-Congressman Charles Clayton. The Dolly Vardens responded by nominating Andrew Hallidie, inventor of the cable car and a regent, with Ralston, of the University of California. The *Bulletin* and the *Call* supported Hallidie mostly by attacking Ralston and his alleged corruption of the electoral processes. Billy had already drawn barbs from the two papers during the debate over a municipal subsidy to the San Francisco and Colorado River Railroad Company, but this new assault surpassed anything in his experience. Not the least of his dismay was for Lizzie and the children, who were home again.

During this period, the financial depression that had begun in the East during the fall of 1873 reached California in full force. Ralston's problems became compounded. The gold that California businessmen demanded for their transactions once again became hard to produce in needed quantities. Premium prices in the East drained $30 million in gold and coin from the state, twice the amount that had been exported the year before. Another $4 million was absorbed by farmers and shippers preparing to move their wheat to market.[19]

Even more insidious was a creeping lack of confidence in the future, in The Bank of California, and in the man on whom San Franciscans had once looked, in the envious words of banker John Parrott, "as on a king." The price of silver, on which so much of San Francisco's well-being depended, was beginning its long decline. Alarming competition for Ralston's so-called ring was gathering strength. Not satisfied with challenging the Union Mill and Mining Company with their own reduction works, the silver kings had formed a lumber company with which to fight Ralston's and Sharon's Carson & Tahoe Company. Worse, they were preparing to open in the fall the Nevada Bank of San Francisco, with a paid-in capital of $5 million. Providing that capital drew still more gold from circulation. Buffeted by the adverse factors and by the *Bulletin's* unremitting attacks—the newspaper by now was questioning the bank's solvency—the institution's stock, which for years had stood as firm as the Sierra at $150 a share, slid downward for the first time, touching $119 in July.[20]

Groping for cash with which to stay the widespread deterioration, Billy resorted to illegal expedients. To overcome a shortage of gold pieces, he ordered all the bullion in the San Francisco Assaying and Refining Company, some $2 million worth, struck into coin for use in the bank. He charged the bullion to his personal account—much of it belonged to outsiders—and thus saved a probable run on the bank by going $2 million in debt, without authorization, to the assay company that he controlled. He borrowed every cent he could on his Spring Valley Water stock, though as yet he did not really own it. When those sums failed to suffice, he over-issued 13,180 shares of Bank of California stock and on that spurious paper managed to raise $1,319,277.25. The lender did not receive the actual stock certificates (Ralston dared not issue them because they would not have borne the necessary counter-

This picture of William C. Ralston, taken during the last years of his life, suggests the strain under which he labored.

signatures by other bank officials) but simply a note saying that they were on deposit at the bank. When even this did not suffice, he abstracted from his vaults Southern Pacific bonds that had been left with him in trust and borrowed another $300,000 on them.[21]

The state of his nerves is suggested by an overwrought letter he sent on August 14, 1875, to his daughter Emelita's private tutor. (The emphasis in the letter is Ralston's.) "You know I am *so* anxious Emelita shall be so educated & instructed as to be a *noble* high-minded honorable *woman*—ready to take *every one by the hand,* no matter if they err or make blunders thats *just the* reason why she should take hold and *help*. Save me from pretenders & would-be Puritans . . . "[22] What was it he wanted this friendly woman to think and to tell his daughter, namesake of his dead sweetheart's mother, when the damning revelations began to pile up and up?

While Ralston was borrowing, he was also selling his unencumbered assets at sacrificial prices. Sixteen thousand acres of prime agricultural land in Kern County went to his father-in-law, John D. Fry, for $90,000. Mills paid $900,000 for his stock in the Virginia & Truckee Railroad. The big wrench was parting with his half interest in the Palace Hotel. From the outside the giant building looked finished. As soon as the last touches were completed inside—target date was October 2—the entryway could be thrown open for the sort of grand inaugural ball in which Billy Ralston, the premier party giver of the West, reveled most. Already guided tours were trooping through the hostelry on weekends and emerging wide-eyed. A palace indeed! Yet it had to go—to Sharon for $1.75 million cash.[23]

That money melted, too. On August 22 he appealed to Sharon and Mills to save him from personal ruin. Sharon, who had strained his credit producing cash for the Palace, said he could not help. Mills, however, loaned $750,000, which Ralston used for retrieving some of the over-issued bank stock held in escrow for lenders who, growing suspicious, had begun putting on pressure.*[24] On August 23, he persuaded Thomas Bell, in whom Charles Stuart of The Oriental Bank had confidence, to wire London requesting additional credit for The Bank of California. Stuart, who had denied an appeal from Ralston himself on July 1, did not even reply to Bell's wire.[25]

On August 25 the jittery San Francisco stock market, which had rallied earlier in the month, gave way to the general malaise. During the day stock in the Consolidated Virginia dropped 45 points, even though the

---

*Later rumors, impossible of verification, said that Sharon was plotting Ralston's downfall—that he was unnecessarily slow about producing the cash he had promised for the Palace and equally slow, a little later, about carrying Mills's loan, which had been entrusted to him, on to Billy.

mine was then paying out $1 million a month in dividends. Ophir, in which Ralston and Sharon were both heavily interested, fell 17 points. Other shares suffered comparably.

The next day, Thursday, August 26, was worse. Sharon ordered his brokers to sell all his Ophir stock and much of the rest of his portfolio of mining shares for whatever they would bring. Perhaps he panicked and was trying to grab what he could while he could. Perhaps he was shorting the market, as he had done the preceding January. Or perhaps, some whispers said, he wanted to guarantee Ralston's downfall before the September elections opened the doors to possible escape through a sale of Spring Valley to the city. In any event, the impact of his tens of thousands of shares was disastrous. Ophir fell 7 points in 7 minutes.

The floor of the exchange became pandemonium. One broker, watching the turmoil, wondered aloud to another whether Sharon was trying to raise cash to save The Bank of California. The question turned into a statement and skittered like a dry, hot wind along the edges of the crowd. Here and there brokers began to edge out of the room toward the bank, intending to withdraw their deposits.

In those gold-short days it was the very sort of assault the bank could not withstand. Stockbrokers depended heavily on The Bank of California. Because of the rapid turnover of money in their business, between $6 million and $9 million in gold coin moved across the bank's counters during a normal day.[26] Because disbursements and receipts almost balanced, it was not necessary to have reserves of $6 million or so on hand. A third of that would suffice unless withdrawals significantly outpaced deposits.

Throughout the summer Ralston had let reserves dwindle below the danger point. He had disguised the fact from the other bank officials by various stratagems. In July he had borrowed, for twenty-four hours only, $2 million in gold coin and had somehow gotten it into the vaults as part of the bank's normal transactions. It had been counted dutifully by the tellers and entered as part of the reserves. Surreptitiously, then, Billy had returned the money to the lenders.

When appreciable amounts of coin became impossible to borrow, he wrote checks in the bank's favor against his personal account. He put what were called "cash tags" on the checks and let them be counted as part of the normal reserves, even though his account had no coin in it[27] —and was generally overdrawn anyway.* On the evening of August 25, when the directors at last faced up to the precariousness of his position, they had sought to obtain help from Flood and O'Brien of the yet-

---

*It is worth noting that in 1872 and again in 1874 the California legislature rejected bills that would have created a bank commission armed with the power to investigate private commercial banks.

FRANK LESLIE'S ILLUSTRATED NEWSPAPER, 1875

In 1875 a severe break in the stock market, followed by a wild run,
forced The Bank of California to close its doors.

unopened Nevada Bank, but were rejected.[28] Thus the vaults of The
Bank of California held only $1.4 million in coin when the stockbrokers
began their run.

About 1:00 P.M. the men in the bank noticed that withdrawals, many
of large sums, were accelerating. By two o'clock lines of customers
reached from the counters outside the doors. Police had to be summoned
to keep the people moving in and out. Pale tellers called again and again
for fresh trays of coin and, using little scoops to move it, paid it out as
fast as they could verify the checks that were thrust at them.

The panic fed on itself. Clots of excited people jammed both streets
outside the bank, Sansome and California. Some were morbidly hopeful
of disaster; some were merely curious. Struggling angrily to get through
them were depositors who had taken fright too late. At 2:35, twenty-five

minutes short of closing time, a distraught teller informed Ralston that the vaults were empty. Billy replied with an order to close the doors.[29]

By then the excitement had drawn most of the directors to the beleaguered institution. After a little discussion they prepared a news release. "The Trustees are under the painful necessity of stating to the creditors of The Bank of California and to the public that the bank has been compelled to suspend business. At this moment of excitement . . . they are not prepared to make a statement as to the situation of the bank. But they are now examining into it critically, and will at the earliest possible moment make a definite report."

The curt announcement was too evasive for the city's newspapers. Reporters cornered Ralston in his office. He answered their questions calmly, showing anger only when he denied an innuendo that Flood and O'Brien of the Nevada Bank had brought about the collapse by withdrawing their deposits a few days earlier. A shortage of coin, Ralston admitted, had indeed forced the suspension, but it was a statewide shortage and not attributable to the malice or machinations of anyone. He insisted that "there is no question whatsoever as to the ability of the bank to meet all its obligations, with considerable surplus besides." But he confessed to a doubt—probably he was speaking out of his own deep weariness—about the bank's ever opening for business again.[30]

He had dinner at his normal time with Lizzie at their Pine Street home. Still showing no emotion, he told her of the collapse and said that they would have to close both the town house and Belmont and live with her foster father until he had brought order back to his affairs. Her response is unknown. Whatever it was, it did not calm his restlessness. A little after dark he ordered a horse saddled and rode back down the ten steep blocks to the bank. Most of the employees were still there, rustling dazedly through their papers. He called them together; at least one, John Goddard Clark, had worked for him since his arrival from Panama. For the first time his voice broke as he talked about the crash and about the hounding he had received from "certain newspapers of this city" and then he promised what he could not fulfill: "I this night enter into a contract to provide each and everyone of you with a first-class position."

Somberly then he rode through the darkness back to his home. A friend, Alfred Cohen, was waiting there, and they sat up until long after midnight, talking. His great desires, Cohen remembered two days later, were to pay the bank's depositors in full, distribute a large dividend to the stockholders, and leave his children a good name.[31]

The next day crowds still milled around California Street, staring at the shuttered bank as if waiting for some sign. Inside the board room the directors were studying balance sheets hastily prepared during the night. Ralston was $9,565,907 in debt. Of that sum he owed the bank $4,655,973. He owed Sharon nearly $2 million. The remainder was due various in-

dividuals and several of the city's savings banks. Somewhere between
$3.5 million and $5.6 million of the total debt was not backed by adequate
security. As for the bank, its liabilities exceeded its available assets by
roughly $4.5 million. It would be solvent again only if the directors col-
lected what Ralston owed it.[32]

Ralston said vehemently that if he were granted time, he could pay.
A successful election and the sale of the Spring Valley Water Company
to the city would assure him the leverage he needed.

The directors, all of whom had known for some time that the bank was
in danger yet had failed to face up to that knowledge, were not persuaded.
After acrimonious discussion they forced Ralston to revoke the will he
had drawn up a month earlier in Lizzie's favor and to execute a deed of
trust conveying to Sharon all his property, real and personal, "in trust
to collect and receive the rents, issues, incomes, and profits thereof . . .
to have and to hold . . . forever."

The idea was that Sharon, as one of Ralston's principal creditors,
would be keenly interested in straightening out the shambles so that he
could pay off both the bank and himself.

The signing of the document did not still the bitterness, and Ralston
was asked to leave the room. Sharon then offered resolutions that Ral-

HARPER'S WEEKLY, 1875

*Ralston died in San Francisco Bay while swimming from the Neptune
Bath-House (foreground) out past the steamer* **Bullion** *(left).*

ston be asked to resign as president and that the request be carried to him by Darius Mills. Ralston complied with complete calm and then, with no indication of his feelings, went outside.[33] At the door he encountered Dr. John Pitman and suggested that they go for a swim, a normal procedure for one who sought that sort of relaxation, as Ralston often did.

Pitman was not free and so Ralston continued alone to North Beach, nearly two miles away across the hilly town. Customarily he rode horseback on these excursions, but that afternoon, as if to emphasize that he had surrendered everything he owned to Sharon, he either walked or (accounts vary) took an omnibus for part of the distance. It was an unusually hot day, and the exercise made him perspire freely.

His destination was the Neptune Beach House at the end of Larkin Street, a wooden building scaly from the ravage of salt winds. It stood at the foot of a precipitous clay bluff, and swimmers could, if they wished, dive into the icy waters of the bay from the end of a short pier. A few hundred yards away a much longer pier reached out into the water from Thomas Selby's lead smelter, whose tall brick chimneys were dragging a black smear across the sky. The *Bullion*, a small sternwheel steamer belonging to the smelting company, was anchored about 200 yards off the end of the long pier.

Billy showered, rubbed down briskly, and walked out onto the beach house pier. He had not been there since Monday. According to testimony given later by Michael Reese, Ralston had been patronizing the establishment for less than a month and was not familiar with the local currents, which were treacherous and had caused recent fatalities.[34] He seemed to feel no hesitation, however, but dove vigorously from the end of the pier.

Though fleshy, he was a strong swimmer and had soon gone past the *Bullion* in the general direction of Alcatraz Island. Suddenly the watchers at the beach house saw, even at that distance, that he was in trouble. Before they could do anything, a small boat put out from the *Bullion*. The men in it pulled Ralston aboard and rowed hard to the strip of sand between the beach house and the smelter. The group that met them there worked hard over Billy for nearly an hour, chafing his limbs and applying artificial respiration. Then a doctor came along with a wagon, and they took the body home.

EPILOGUE:

What Was Left

The funeral had to be postponed. Gossip said that the stunned widow refused certain pallbearers who were suggested and that the resultant embarrassment required delicate handling. A more cogent reason was a charge that the *Bulletin* picked up somewhere and spread throughout the city like wildfire. Ralston, it was said, had committed suicide by drinking a vial of poison just before diving into the bay.

The accusation needed airing. So disgraceful an end would plunge the shaken city deeper into gloom and increase the difficulties of re-opening the bank, if the directors decided on that course. Moreover, un-less Billy was exonerated, Lizzie would not be able to collect the $68,000 life insurance policy her husband had left unencumbered. That policy just might end up being her principal resource.

The new strain fell hardest on a jury that the city coroner, Benjamin Swan, had appointed shortly after Ralston's death. Each of the eight members was an intimate friend of Billy's. One was Alfred Cohen; another was the deceased's lawyer, W. H. L. Barnes; a third was broker J. R. Keene, who had handled much of his investment business; a fourth was Robert F. Morrow, a director of several of the Comstock mines controlled by Union Mill and Mining. These men, their four fellow jurors, and a dozen others had rushed to Ralston's home on hearing of his drown-ing and had been there when the coroner arrived. Supposing that the ex-amination into the cause of death would be routine, they had acceded without protest to his request that they serve on the jury. Now suddenly the case was not routine.

The body was taken to the city morgue for an autopsy. The next morning, Saturday—the funeral had been tentatively scheduled for that afternoon but, as noted, had been postponed—Dr. John T. Cook examined the lungs, which contained only a small amount of water, and the brain, which showed marked congestion. He removed the stomach, which held very little material—Ralston had eaten no lunch the day before—and sent it for testing to chemist Louis Falkenau, an expert on poisons. The corpse was then turned over to undertakers, who repaired the damage and placed the remains in a casket. The casket in turn, reported the *Alta California,* "was packed into a rosewood ice-box with a plate-glass top so as to fully expose him to view." On Sunday, casket and container were delivered not to Billy's Pine Street house, but to the home of John D. Fry, where Lizzie was staying.[1]

Throughout the day and into the night friends of the family and even strangers, many obviously poor, trooped through the house to peer into the casket and leave tokens of respect. The air grew cloyed with the scent of floral offerings shaped into crosses, wreathes, anchors. In the churches ministers eulogized the departed. After the sermons and outside Fry's home, people talked and talked and talked—talk whose tenor swept through the city as rapidly as had the rumors of suicide.

As yet no report had come from the coroner's jury and would not until the chemist testified on Tuesday. In the absence of definite word, most people were inclined to concede that Ralston may have taken his own life. After such calamities as he had endured! And what had caused those calamities? Surely a man like Billy Ralston could not have been dragged down except by evil design.

A small paper known as *Thistleton's Jolly Giant* caught the mood and on Monday, August 30, froze it into words. "Ralston was murdered. We baldly and fearlessly assert before God and the world that to a certain extent the 'Bulletin' and 'Call' have been accessory to the man's death. The bank over which he presided was the victim of a foul conspiracy to 'cripple it' as the saying goes. Pickering and Fitch [editors of the offending papers] were unquestionably paid to assist in the dirty work of crying down, or rather 'hounding down' Ralston and his ring." After accusing Flood and O'Brien of locking up money that might have saved The Bank of California, the *Jolly Giant* finished, "This, together with the continual hounding of the two papers, led to the Board of Directors demanding the resignation of William Ralston, which act drove him to commit suicide."

As popular resentment at the *Call* and *Bulletin* deepened, praise for Ralston's virtues soared. His efforts, it was repeated over and over, had not been devoted to his own advancement—though he had advanced —but to bringing employment, prosperity, convenience, beauty, and culture to San Francisco. His faith in the West Coast had been boundless. Now that depression was hurting the nation, now that the confidence which had brought half a million people to the edge of the Pacific was being shaken, now was the time to remember that boundless faith.

Spontaneously they poured from their homes to express those feelings as best they could at his funeral—a solemnly treading procession at least three miles long. Afterwards came the efforts to find adequate ways of saying what so many felt. In columns bordered by heavy black *The California Farmer* demanded on September 2, "What will a man give in exchange for his life? What would our citizens repay to recall William C. Ralston? Amid every trial, even with a mind tortured by the deepest anxiety, he stood like a Granite Pillar amid the storms; and had his counsel and entreaties been accepted, when he said, *leave it to me*, I WILL CARRY THE BANK THROUGH SAFELY, W. C. Ralston would have been alive today, the Bank sound and solvent and that noble soul *Respected*, LOVED, and HONORED as its PRESIDENT still."

The verdict of the coroner's jury, delivered the day after the funeral, completed the martyrdom. Ralston had not been fleeing in disgrace. Chemist Falkenau had not found poison in his stomach. The testimony of those who had seen him last had not revealed the least indication of suicidal desires. Before diving into the cold water, said this jury of his friends, he had used reasonable precautions to reduce his overheated condition. Unfamiliar with the area, he had ventured out too far. Flood tides caught him and carried him beyond his power to return. His struggles to regain control of his course had brought on a congestion of the brain and vital organs—today the condition might have been called a stroke—and that, coupled with drowning, had ended his life.[2]

The directors of the bank were quick to take advantage of the outpouring of sympathy. Fearful in part of the California law that made stockholders responsible in proportion to their holdings for a company's liabilities, they had decided on the Sunday preceding the funeral to avoid bankruptcy and try to rehabilitate the institution. The first step was the formation of a fund out of which all of the bank's debts could be paid. Sixty-four individuals and corporations, the stock exchange being among the latter, pledged a total of $7.9 million to the reserve. Sharon, Mills, and Lucky Baldwin each subscribed $1 million. Keene, of the coroner's jury, pledged $225,000; Morrow, also of the jury, promised $200,000; Cohen, another juror, $150,000, a sum matched by such longtime friends of Ralston's as Thomas Bell, Peter Donahue, and Maurice Dore.

Since the labors of the committee on reorganization, which was headed by Sharon, would be easier if supported by popular goodwill, the city's emotional jag was deliberately kept alive. For five consecutive days heavily bordered advertisements appeared in most of the city's newspapers stating that friends of the late William C. Ralston were requested to attend a meeting at Union Hall on the evening of September 8, 1875.

When the eighth came, 8,000 people pushed their way inside the hall. Another 7,000 gathered around a speaker's stand outside. An overflow

The Bank of California was heavily draped in black crepe
for days following Ralston's sudden death.

crowd of 5,000 more was pulled together a short distance away at the corner of Third and Howard streets. Close by all these meeting places rose the massive walls of the Palace Hotel.

California's most dramatic orators stirred the crowds with their rhetoric. Cried Dr. J. C. Shorb to the 7,000 outside the hall: "When the intelligence of his sudden death flew wildly and madly through the paralyzed city, women wrung their hands, strong men grew pale and shuddered in the streets, and through their ashy lips struggled the half articulated question—'can this be true? Almighty God! can this be true that RALSTON is dead?'"

Inside, Tom Fitch shouted, "Unnumbered deeds of private generosity attest his secret charity. . . . Despair has been lifted into hope by his bounty. . . . Heaven kissing spires chronicle his devotion to the cause of religion. Schools claim him as their patron. Hospitals own him their benefactor. Art has found in him a supporter. Science has leaned on him while its vision swept the infinite. The feet of progress have been sandaled with his silver. . . . Of all her public possessions the commonwealth of California never owned any more valuable than this man's life; of all her public disasters she has never had one greater than his death."

Praise alone was not enough. Those gathered at the meetings, Fitch declaimed, must also "express here and now . . . our general and unanimous contempt and abhorrence of the cold-blooded, cowardly, treacherous, malignant scoundrels who hounded William C. Ralston to death!" He then read a resolution condemning "the savage brutality and cruelty of certain of the daily newspapers in this city. . . . '' A crash of sound declared the motion passed.[3]

Against the background the reorganization committee worked swiftly. Ralston, it will be recalled, owed the bank $4.5 million. Apprehensive that liquidating his debts would take a long time and perhaps yield less than anticipated, the committee sold the claim to Sharon (who was head of the committee) for $1.5 million plus a promise of another $500,000 if he recovered that much more from the dead man's estate, of which he was trustee.[4]

He never paid the $500,000. How much he actually recovered from the estate cannot be determined. He settled with Ralston's creditors on whatever basis he could. Because trustees are supposed to deal equally with all creditors, his differing scales of settlement left him open to suits, which rained upon him without producing anything definite in the way of figures. Lizzie Ralston, who two years after Billy's death began spending such funds as she had on a dazzling but already married suitor, also sued him for an accounting. Though Sharon denied owing her anything, he settled out of court for $250,000. Meantime he moved into Belmont; and of course the Palace Hotel was entirely his, as were several other of Ralston's erstwhile possessions.[5]

People who claimed to have seen Sharon's books during the various legal actions were frequently quoted as saying that Ralston's assets were worth more than his liabilities and that he could have saved himself, and the bank, too, if his supposed friends had given him a chance.[6] In view of his reckless past, one wonders. As for his future, he had been pinning his hope on electing a city administration that would buy his Spring Valley Water Company. The emotional backlash that followed his death buried the Dolly Varden slate supported by the *Bulletin*. There was no carry-over of support to Ralston's candidates, however. They were resoundingly defeated, and the Democratic slate, lightly regarded before the election, swept into power. Since Ralston's martyrdom did not help his candidates, it seems unlikely that they would have won with him alive. When the Democrats were offered Spring Valley, they turned it down. Ralston's last hope, it appears, was not very good after all.

As for the bank, the reorganization went smoothly under Sharon's able direction. Mills was reelected president, and the doors were re-opened to a cheering crowd at 10:00 A.M. Saturday, October 2. Artillery boomed from Telegraph Hill; flags went up on the adjoining buildings. Deposits that day totalled $1,020,000. Withdrawals were $254,000.[7] Stability assured, The Bank of California regained its former prosperity, grew to be one of the major banks of the United States, and became unique in being the only financial institution of its sort to cover all three Pacific Coast states.

From the bank a festive crowd swarmed on across Market Street to

The reorganized Bank of California opened October 2, 1875. The Palace Hotel, its "Grand Entrance" shown above, followed shortly.

the Palace Hotel. They filled the central court and swirled on through the public rooms, mingling with the workers. The formal opening would not come until October 14, but the management made no attempt to turn out the celebrants or put the laborers back on their jobs. A band appeared, struck up a lively tune in the court, and after a while Senator Sharon appeared on the second-story balcony. When quiet came he made a little speech.

"In this crowning hour of victory, in the presence of this grand witness to your skill in the mechanic arts, in this glorious temple of hospitality, in all this flood of light and music, I experience a sense of almost overwhelming sadness. I miss, as you do, the proud and manly spirit of him who devised this magnificent structure, and under whose direction and tireless energy it has been mainly reared. I mourn, as you do, that he is not with us to enjoy this scene of beauty, and I offer here, with you, the incense of respect and affection to his memory."[8]

For a little while, as he talked, he may have thought that he actually meant what he said.

Notes

CHAPTER 1. MISSISSIPPI SEEDBED

1. Sparse details on Ralston's youth are provided by the introductory pages of Andrew Jackson Ralston's manuscript biography of his brother William in the Bancroft Library, University of California, Berkeley (hereafter cited as "Ralston"); and by Cecil G. Tilton, *William Chapman Ralston, Courageous Builder* (Boston 1935), pp. 15–24.
2. J. C. Ainsworth, "Statement," Ms. P-A 72, Bancroft Library, University of California, Berkeley.
3. H. W. Phillipps, Wheeling, West Virginia to Ralston, April 18, 1875 (Bank of California collection). See also George D. Lyman, *Ralston's Ring* (New York, 1937), p. 325.
4. For Garrison: Julian Dana, *The Man Who Built San Francisco* (New York, 1936), pp. 14, 22; Frank Soulé, John H. Gihon, James Nesbitt, the *Annals of San Francisco* (reprint, Palo Alto, Calif., 1960), pp. 744–747.
5. Clifford M. Drury, *William Anderson Scott, No Ordinary Man* (Glendale, California, 1965), pp. 152–158, 191. Charles Wendte, *The Wider Fellowship* (Boston, 1927), pp. 140ff. Tilton, *Ralston,* p. 415.
6. Ray A. Billington, *Westward Expansion,* (New York, 1963), pp. 332, 398.
7. In an interview with a reporter from the *Annals of San Francisco,* loc. cit., p. 744 (which also tells of the burning of Garrison's ship) Garrison states that he went directly to Panama from New Orleans to open a bank. Most biographers follow this. However, Tilton, *Ralston,* pp. 37–38, following James Cox, *Old and New St. Louis* (St. Louis, 1894) p. 137, shows that Garrison went first to California and Oregon to check on steamboating, a conclusion accepted by James Hunter, *Partners in Progress* (San Francisco, 1950), p. 13. Howard M. Corning, *Dictionary of Oregon History* (Portland, Oregon, 1956), p. 130, and Hamilton Boner, "The Bank of California," *The Pony Express,* July, 1954, add details about Kamm and the machinery.
8. Lyman, *Ralston's Ring,* p. 326; Tilton, *Ralston,* pp. 303–305; Warrick Martin to W. C. Ralston, August 10, 1869 (Bank of California collection).

CHAPTER 2. THE PANAMA MORASS

1. This chapter relies primarily on eyewitness accounts of the Panama crossing left by the following: H. H. Bancroft, *California Inter Pocula* (San Francisco, 1888); J. D. Borthwick, *Three Years in California* (Edinburgh, 1857); E.S. Capron, *History of California* (Boston, 1854); Jessie Benton Fremont, *A Year of American Travel* (New York, 1878); Joseph W. Gregory, *Gregory's Guide for California Travelers via the Isthmus of Panama* (New York, 1850); Frank Marryat, *Mountains and Molehills* (London, 1855); Bayard Taylor, *Eldorado* (New York, 1850); Robert Thomes, *Panama in 1855* (New York, 1855).

   The standard secondary account is John Haskell Kemble, *The Panama Route, 1848–1869* (Berkeley and Los Angeles, 1943). See also Oscar Lewis, *Sea Routes to the Gold Fields* (New York, 1949); David Howarth, *Panama* (New York, 1966); Sally L. Barieau, "Migration to California by Way of the Isthmus of Panama," MA thesis, University of California, Berkeley, 1937.
2. For Vanderbilt and the genesis of his Nicaragua project: Wheaton J. Lane, *Commodore Vanderbilt* (New York, 1942) pp. 1–94.

CHAPTER 3. SLIPPERY FOOTHOLDS

1. Soulé et al. *The Annals of San Francisco,* p. 744.
2. Isaac Wister Jones. *Autobiography* (Philadelphia, 1914), pp. 162, 300–301.
3. Ernest Wiltsee, *Gold Rush Steamers* (San Francisco, 1938), p. 114, quoting the San Francisco *Alta California* of Feb. 8, 1850.
4. "I have made *a number* of trips back and forth [Ralston's emphasis] and I assure you, I think no more of going to New York, than you would do, to go on a Packet Boat to New Orleans." (Ralston to "Miss Annette," June 3, 1859; letter in possession of Ralston's granddaughter, Dorothy Page Buckingham.) Since Ralston made few journeys to New York while living in San Francisco, he must have made those numerous trips between the coasts during the years when his headquarters were in Panama.
5. J. C. Ainsworth, "Statement," Bancroft Library.
6. For an account of one such episode and the rage it elicited among the stranded, see Benjamin B. Richards, ed., *California Gold Rush Merchant: The Journal of Stephen Chapin Davis* (San Marino, Calif. 1956), p. 63.
7. A. J. Ralston, "Ralston," ms., Bancroft Library. Wiltsee, *Gold Rush Steamers,* pp. 33ff. Kemble, *Panama Route,* pp. 47–48. Sorting out the different owners, agents, lien

holders, and silent partners in the competing steamship lines—to say nothing of determining who controlled which vessels when—is next to impossible in many cases.
8. Panama *Star,* Feb. 6, 1853.
9. Lane, *Commodore Vanderbilt,* pp. 85ff. A description of the Nicaragua crossing by one early traveler is in E. S. Capron, *History of California,* pp. 270–306.
10. Wiltsee, *Gold Rush Steamers,* pp. 42–44, 68. Kemble, *Panama Route,* pp. 49–55.
11. Wiltsee, *Gold Rush Steamers,* pp. 44–45. Kemble, *Panama Route,* p. 49.
12. Wiltsee, *Gold Rush Steamers,* p. 73.
13. As in note 11 above.
14. Kemble, *Panama Route,* p. 221.
15. The Bank of California collection contains a letter from Ralston to a Judge McHenry, which bears the abbreviated date New York, Friday, 30th. This letter refers to the ship *Warren* on the Columbia River. The *General Warren* reached the West Coast in December, 1850, and sank in January, 1852. The only Friday the 30th during that period is in May, 1851. Ergo, Ralston was in New York at least on May 30, 1851.
16. An assumption. Still, Sam Ralston did arrive in Panama in 1851. (A. J. Ralston, "Ralston") and though he may have traveled alone, it seems reasonable to link his journey with Billy's.

CHAPTER 4. SCRAMBLING HIGH

1. Panama *Star,* July 15, 1851.
2. Ibid.
3. Wiltsee, *Gold Rush Steamers,* p. 49. Kemble, *Panama Route,* p. 250.
4. For the Stockton troubles: Kemble, *Panama Route,* pp. 49, 221.
5. Daniel W. Coit, *Digging For Gold—Without a Shovel* (Denver, Colo., 1967), pp. 104–105.
6. Rodman W. Paul, *California Gold* (Cambridge, Mass., 1947), p. 118.
7. Different writers have given varying accounts of the *New Orleans* episode: Lyman, *Ralston's Ring,* pp. 27–28; Tilton, *Ralston,* p. 41; Dana, *The Man Who Built San Francisco,* pp. 27–31. These accounts follow A. J. Ralston, "Ralston," in stating that as a reward for his successful journey William Ralston was made a partner of Garrison and Fretz. The firm's advertisements in the Panama *Star* show, however, that A. J.'s memory was faulty; William's elevation did not occur for another year and a half.
8. Edgar W. Wright, *Marine History of the Pacific Northwest* (Portland, Ore., 1895), pp. 188–190.
9. Dana, *The Man Who Built San Francisco,* pp. 40–44, 47–48. Gilbert Kneiss, *Bonanza Railroad* (Stanford University, 1941), pp. 31ff. H. H. Bancroft, *History of California,* (San Francisco, 1888), vol. VI, pp. 137–138.
10. It would have been one of the few times that Ralston could have made a continuous journey from San Francisco to New York, a trip he later insisted he had made on several occasions. See chapter 3, note 4 above.
11. Benjamin B. Richards, ed., *California Gold Rush Merchant,* p. 65.
12. Wiltsee, *Gold Rush Steamers,* p. 79. Apparently disgruntled by developments, Howard and Sons started a new steamer, *City of Pittsburgh,* around the Horn. She burned at Valparaíso, Chile, October 24, 1852. Ticket holders waiting in Panama were carried to San Francisco aboard the *New Orleans,* which by then had been returned to Garrison & Fretz. (Panama *Star,* Nov. 20, 1852.)
13. Kemble, *Panama Route,* p. 221. William Nelson to William Ralston, July 27, 1869 (Bank of California collection) says that he owned a one-quarter interest in the *Stockton;* Fretz and Ralston owned three-quarters.
14. Kemble, *Panama Route,* pp. 52, 64.
15. The tale of the ball first surfaced publicly in the San Francisco *Chronicle* on Dec. 8, 1877, two years after Ralston's death. It served as an introduction for a gossipy disclosure of his widow's romantic embroilments in Europe. Except for the patness (doesn't a tragic romance demand Viennese waltzes?) there is no particular reason for either believing or disbelieving the account of the grand ball.
16. Robert Thomes, *Panama in 1855,* pp. 143–144. David Howarth, *Panama,* pp. 175ff.
17. Hunter, *Partners in Progress,* p, 13, suggests that Ralston settled in Aspinwall on first arriving on the Isthmus in 1849. Aspinwall did not exist until the end of 1851, however, and Ralston's other activities would have prevented his doing much there before the middle of 1852.
18. Panama *Daily Star,* March 3, 1854.
19. Garrison & Fretz advertisements in the Panama *Star* during the fall and winter of 1852. See especially issue of Dec. 18, 1852.
20. Panama *Star,* Feb. 2, 1853.

21. Panama *Star*, Feb. 18, 1851, Nov. 11, 1851; Barieau, "Migration," pp. 74–75.
22. As in note 19 above.
23. J. W. Raymond to W. C. Ralston, January 14, 1853 (Bank of California collection). Wiltsee, *Gold Rush Steamers*.
24. Panama *Star*, Dec. 14, 1852.
25. Wiltsee, *Gold Rush Steamers*, pp. 118–119.

CHAPTER 5. DESOLATION
1. I assume the messenger and hypothesize the contents of his message from the following. Garrison reached Panama City at 11 P.M. on March 3, 1853. (Panama *Star*, March 4, 1853.) His connection with Vanderbilt was publicly announced the next day. But the *Sierra Nevada* had been halted several days before. (The *Star* of Feb. 25 describes a Washington's Birthday ball held aboard her in the roadstead at Taboga Island.) Garrison & Fretz began advertising themselves as agents for both the *Sierra Nevada* and the *Cortes* on February 26. So messages about halting and advertising the ship, and hence about Garrison's activities, must have reached them ahead of Garrison himself.
   There is some evidence that although Vanderbilt's company used the *Sierra Nevada*, she was owned in part by Garrison. (Wiltsee, *Gold Rush Steamers*, p. 341.)
2. The complexities of Vanderbilt's dealings with Accessory Transit Co. are revealed in depositions connected with the case of *Charles J. Macdonald v. Cornelius Garrison and Charles Morgan*, New York Court of Common Pleas, 1859—Bancroft Library, University of California, Berkeley. See also Lane, *Commodore Vanderbilt*, pp. 79, 99–104.
3. Soulé et al., *The Annals of San Francisco*, p. 747.
4. Ralston's ledger account for 1853, preserved among the Garrison, Fretz & Co. papers in the archives of The Bank of California, dates his New York trip from March, 1853, through May, 1853. The same ledger gives his salary as $4,000.
5. There is no reason to assume, as the writer of the San Francisco *Chronicle* story of Dec. 8, 1877, did (chapter 4, note 15 above) and as Ralston's biographers since then have assumed, that the Thornes objected to the marriage and hurried Louisa aboard the *North Star* to get her away from her suitor. The European trip had been in the making for a year, and the girl's parents did not wish her to miss it. Ralston, no mere shipping clerk then (as the *Chronicle* stated), was well liked by Commodore Vanderbilt, as will appear. So why should the Thornes object? Finally, as we shall also see, Ralston's relations with the Thornes always remained cordial.
6. Wiltsee, *Gold Rush Steamers*, p. 128. Kemble, *Panama Route*, p. 65.
7. Wiltsee, op. cit., pp. 107–108. San Francisco *Alta California*, March 24, 1853.
8. Oscar Lewis, *Sea Routes*, pp. 253–254, says 125 lives. Lane, *Vanderbilt*, pp. 103–104, says 176.
9. Lewis, *Sea Routes*, pp. 250–252. The beaching of the leaky *Pioneer* has been omitted from the present account.
10. "To the Stockholders of the Accessory Transit Company of Nicaragua, Dec. 31, 1853," reprinted in Wiltsee, op. cit., pp. 340–346.
11. Lane, *Vanderbilt*, pp. 105–109. Kemble, *Panama Route*, pp. 66–68.
12. The 15,000–mile trip is unctuously described by the minister whom Vanderbilt carried along as private chaplain for his touring family: John O. Choules, *The Cruise of the Steam Yacht North Star* (Boston, 1854).
13. Lane, *Vanderbilt*, p. 109.
14. San Francisco *Chronicle*, Dec. 8, 1877.
15. Lane, *Vanderbilt*, p. 111. Wiltsee, *Gold Rush Steamers*, pp. 128, 137. See also Panama *Daily Star*, March 4, 1854.
16. Wiltsee, *Gold Rush Steamers*, pp. 128–129. See also "Report to Stockholders," ibid, pp. 340–346.
17. Details of the trip are in the Panama *Daily Star*, March 3, 1854.
18. Wiltsee, *Gold Rush Steamers*, p. 132. Fretz and Ralston's first office was not on Sacramento St. "next to Duncan's Chinese Salesroom," as is generally said. As contemporary pictures clearly show, that building housed the offices of Garrison's Nicaragua Steamship Company agency and the insurance companies that Garrison represented.
19. San Francisco *Alta California*, July 8, 1854.
20. Dana, *The Man Who Built San Francisco*, p. 79.
21. Clifford M. Drury, *William Anderson Scott*, p. 157.
22. The report in the Panama *Daily Star* of Dec. 25, 1854, valued the service at $12,000; the San Francisco *Alta California*, $10,000. A retrospective story of Garrison's accomplishments as mayor appeared in the *Alta California* for July 9, 1869.

23. Charges against Garrison: the *Alta California,* Feb. 3, 1855; Dorothy Huggins, *Continuation of the Annals of San Francisco* (reprint, Palo Alto, Calif., 1966) pp. 12–13: the San Francisco *Daily Bulletin,* August 30, 1875. William T. Sherman, a banker in San Francisco during the 1850s, also doubted Garrison's honesty in handling the waterfront property. Dwight L. Clarke, *William Tecumseh Sherman, Gold Rush Banker* (San Francisco, 1969), pp. 131–132. For Garrison's expenditures on elections, Richard Reinhardt, "Tapeworm Tickets and Shoulder Strikers," *American West,* vol. III, no. 4, Fall, 1966.

24. Tilton, *Ralston,* p. 50.

25. Oscar Lewis, *Sea Routes,* pp. 242–243.

26. Kemble, *Panama Route,* p. 68.

27. Wiltsee, *Gold Rush Steamers,* pp. 131–132.

28. In describing the wreck of the *Yankee Blade* I have relied principally on the stories in the *Panama Weekly Star and Herald,* Nov. 6, 1854, and in the San Francisco *Alta California,* Oct. 10 and Oct. 16, 1854. See in addition Huggins, *Continuation of Annals,* pp. 16–17; Wiltsee, *Gold Rush Steamers,* pp. 147–148; Oscar Lewis, *Sea Routes,* pp. 248–250.

29. Dwight L. Clarke, *William Tecumseh Sherman: Gold Rush Banker* (San Francisco, 1969) pp. 57–141 passim; Theodore H. Hittell, *History of California,* San Francisco, 1898, vol. III, pp. 415ff; David Lavender, *California, Land of New Beginnings,* (New York, 1972), pp. 236ff.

30. Josiah Royce, *California* (reprint, New York, 1948), p. 340; Walton Bean, *California* (New York, 1968), pp. 158–159; William N. Ellison, *A Self-Governing Dominion,* (Berkeley, 1950), pp. 284–286.

31. Clarke, *Sherman,* pp. 50, 85, 132.

CHAPTER 6. LESSONS IN ELASTICITY

1. Clarke, *Sherman,* p. 132. The head office of Lucas, Turner & Company was in St. Louis.

2. Ibid., p. 86. More evidence concerning Garrison's movements during the period comes from the testimony of Theodore A. Wakeman, given in the suit of *Charles J. Macdonald* v. *Cornelius Garrison and Charles Morgan,* heard in the New York Court of Common Pleas, 1859. (2 Hilton 510). Many of the affidavits, depositions, letters, etc., offered as testimony during this suit are at the Bancroft Library, University of California, Berkeley. Hereafter cited as "Macdonald case."

3. Wakeman testimony, Macdonald case. Also Panama *Star,* Dec. 25, 1854.

4. Details concerning the bank did not emerge in San Francisco until November, 1855. (Clarke, *Sherman,* p. 167.) They could hardly have taken shape, however, without face-to-face discussion between Morgan and Garrison. This contact could have occurred only in the winter of 1854–55. I assume, therefore, that the plan had matured enough by February, 1855, for Garrison to present it to Fretz and Ralston as described in the text.

5. My account of the panic leans primarily on Clarke's *Sherman,* pp. 107–118. See also Ira B. Cross, *Financing An Empire: History of Banking in California* (San Francisco, 1927), vol. I, pp. 181–199.

6. A summary of the debate over banking in the constitutional convention is in Cross, *Financing,* I, pp. 95–110. See also Walton Bean, *California* (New York, 1968), pp. 199–201.

7. W. Turrentine Jackson, "Wells Fargo: Symbol of the Wild West," *Western Historical Quarterly,* vol. III, no. 2, April, 1972.

8. Clarke, *Sherman,* p. 132. At this late date there seems no way to evaluate the merits of the cases.

9. Louis R. Miller, "The History of the San Francisco & San Jose Railroad Company," MA thesis, University of California, Berkeley, 1948.

10. Clarke, *Sherman,* p. 132.

11. Robert O. Briggs, "The Sacramento Valley Railroad, 1853–1865." MA thesis, Sacramento State College, 1950.

12. Clarke, *Sherman,* p. 131.

13. Briggs, op. cit., pp. 40–45.

14. For Walker, Albert Z. Carr, *The World and William Walker* (New York, 1963); Lawrence Greene, *The Filibuster* (Indianapolis and New York, 1937); William O. Scroggs, *Filibusters and Financiers* (New York, 1916), and Walker's own account, *The War in Nicaragua,* (Mobile, Alabama, 1860).

15. Walker, *War in Nicaragua,* pp. 86–87. William V. Wells, *Walker's Expedition to Nicaragua* (New York, 1856) passim.

16. Cholera: Lewis, *Sea Routes,* p. 244. Ralston's bet, "The California Recollections of

Caspar T. Hopkins,'' *California Historical Society Quarterly,* June, 1947, p. 176. Hopkins was a passenger on the same ship as Ralston.

17. Hopkins, p. 177.
18. J. P. Baughman, *Charles Morgan and the Development of Southern Transportation* (Nashville, Tenn. 1968), pp. 76, 78.
19. The rate adjustment is in Baugham, *Morgan,* pp. 75–76.
20. Fitzgerald to Thomas Lord, Nov. 17, 1855. Macdonald case, (see note 2 above).
21. Walker deposition, Macdonald case.
22. Wells, *Walker's Expedition,* pp. 70–83. Greene, *The Filibuster,* pp. 121–181. Scroggs, *Filibusters,* pp. 116–120. Also Fitzgerald to Lord, as in note 20 above.
23. Depositions collected in the Macdonald case offer sharply conflicting evidence on the point.
24. Baughman, *Morgan,* pp. 77–78.
25. Fitzgerald to Lord, as in note 20 above.
26. Deposition of Alexander Crittenden, who says he heard Garrison dress Macdonald down. See also separate letters from Garrison and B. F. Voorhees to Thomas Lord of the Transit Company, both written on Nov. 20, 1855.
27. Baughman, *Morgan,* pp. 80–83.
28. Carr, *Walker,* p. 169.
29. In May, 1856, W. T. Sherman characterized Ralston as one of San Francisco's rich men. (Clarke, *Sherman,* p. 210.) It is hard to account for the wealth without assuming that some came from the bilking of Vanderbilt, once his prospective grandfather-in-law. This is pure guesswork, however.

CHAPTER 7. THE CLEANSING

1. "The very nature of the country," observed W. T. Sherman in 1856 (Clarke, p. 305) "begets speculation, extravagance, failures, and rascality." Few residents were equally ready to place blame where it belonged.
2. An earnest but to me not wholly convincing defense of Broderick's basic integrity is David A. Williams, *David C. Broderick, a Political Portrait* (San Marino, Calif. 1969).
3. Williams, *Broderick,* pp. 96–98, 103–104; Kevin Starr, *Americans and the California Dream* (New York, 1973), pp. 94–95.
4. Although the executive committee of the vigilantes worked in secrecy and later destroyed part of its records, literature about the insurrection is plentiful. In addition to the other works cited in this chapter, I relied on the second volume of H. H. Bancroft, *Popular Tribunals* (San Francisco, 1887); William Ellison, *A Self-Governing Dominion: California, 1849–1860* (Berkeley, Calif., 1950), pp. 232–267; T. H. Hittell, *History of California* (San Francisco, 1898), vol. III, pp. 460–649; Josiah Royce, *California from the Conquest in 1846 to the Second Vigilance in San Francisco* (New York, 1949), pp. 341–366; Roger Olmstead, "San Francisco and the Vigilante Style," *The American West,* January and March, 1970; and an anonymous account, *Judges and Criminals, Shadows of the Past—History of the Vigilance Committee of San Francisco, Calif.* (San Francisco, 1858).
5. Clarke, *Sherman,* p. 210.
6. Their reminiscences and those by a contemporary newspaperman, James O'Meara, can be read together in Doyce Nunis (ed.), *The San Francisco Vigilance Committee of 1856* (Los Angeles, 1971). See also Clarke, *Sherman,* pp. 210–211.
7. Julian Dana, *The Man Who Built San Francisco,* p. 193.
8. Clifford M. Drury, *William Anderson Scott* (Glendale, Calif., 1967), pp. 186–188.
9. As in note 7 above.
10. Hittell, *History of California,* vol. III, p. 626.
11. Clarke, *Sherman,* p. 235.
12. Drury, *Scott,* pp. 190–192.
13. Clarke, *Sherman,* pp. 248–256.
14. Charles Macdonald to Morgan and Garrison, Sept. 27, 1856. Macdonald case (see note 2, chapter 6).
15. Details can be found in the works by Carr, Lane, Scroggs, and Walker, cited in chapter 6.
16. Clarke, *Sherman,* pp. 274–298, passim. Rodman Paul, *California Gold* (Cambridge, Mass., 1947), p. 118.
17. Clarke, *Sherman,* pp. 296–311, passim.

CHAPTER 8. ON THE MOVE

1. Ira B. Cross, *Financing an Empire* (San Francisco, 1927), p. 81.
2. W. Storrs Lee, *The Sierra* (New York, 1962), pp. 325–327.
3. Clarke, *Sherman,* pp. 228–232.

4. Ibid., pp. 232–233.
5. Gertrude Atherton, *Adventures of a Novelist* (New York, 1932), pp. 4–8.
6. Cross, *Financing an Empire,* pp. 229–230.
7. Clarke, *Sherman,* p. 237
8. A. J. Ralston, "William Chapman Ralston," Bancroft Library, University of California.
9. W. C. Ralston to Morrison, Jan. 1, 1857. (Copy in possession of Dorothy P. Buckingham, Ralston's granddaughter.)
10. James Rolph in Leroy Armstrong and J. O. Denny, *Financial California* (San Francisco, 1916), p. 118. See also Charles Wendte's estimate in *The Wider Fellowship* (Boston, 1927), vol. I, pp. 132–134, and the manuscript reminiscences of Thomas Bell, Andrew Forbes, and Stephen Franklin in the Bancroft Library.
11. *California Historical Society Quarterly.* II (1923) p. 207.
12. This story first appeared in print in the San Francisco *Chronicle* of Dec. 8, 1877, two years after Ralston's death. The account was designed to explain Liz Ralston's carryings-on as a widow and is as suspect as any newspaper gossip. Ralston's descendants accept the tale, however, and so perhaps he really did qualify his proposal in this odd way. (Author's interview with Ralston's granddaughter, Dorothy Page Buckingham, April 15, 1973.)
13. Francis P. Farquahar (ed.), *The Ralston–Fry Wedding, From the Diary of Miss Sarah Haight* (Berkeley, Calif. 1961).
14. Lane, *Vanderbilt,* pp. 133–134. Kemble, *Panama Route,* pp. 77–79.
15. Albert Shumate, *A Visit to Rincon Hill and South Park* (San Francisco, 1963), pp. 2–7.
16. Ibid.
17. W. C. Ralston to Andrew Jackson Ralston, August 27 and Sept. 1, 1859. Bancroft Library, University of California.
18. Lane, *Vanderbilt,* pp. 166–167.
19. John S. Hittell, *The Commerce and Industries of the Pacific Coast of North America* (San Francisco, 1882), p. 127.
20. Clarke, *Sherman,* pp. 134–136. Charles Wendte, *The Wider Fellowship,* I, pp. 134–136. Wendte's reminiscences deal with The Bank of California immediately after its opening in 1864. As Sherman's letters show, however, conditions during the latter part of the 1850s were the same.
21. San Francisco Chamber of Commerce, miscellaneous papers, Box 2, reports of the Committee of Appeals, December, 1858. (California Historical Society).
22. Robert O. Briggs, "The Sacramento Valley Railroad," (MA thesis, Sacramento State College, 1954), p. 271.
23. Ira B. Cross, *Financing an Empire.* Fretz, Ralston, and other bankers to Milton Latham, December, 1859. (Latham papers, California Historical Society.)
24. Wilkins, James H., Reminiscences published as "When 'Society' Did the Honors on Rincon Hill." San Francisco *Bulletin,* March 15, 1913.
25. W. C. and Elizabeth Ralston to "Miss Annette," June 3 and 4, 1859. Dr. William R. Clark (Miss Annette's son) to Mrs. A. Page, Nov. 4, 1942. Copies of these letters are in the possession of Ralston's granddaughter, Dorothy Page Buckingham.
26. W. F. Thompson, "The Political Career of Milton Slocum Latham of California," MA thesis, Stanford University, 1952. Royce Delmatier et al. (eds.), *The Rumble of California Politics, 1848–1970* (New York, 1970), pp. 20–24. See also miscellaneous letters from Ralston to Latham in the Latham papers at the California Historical Society.

CHAPTER 9. REACHING OUT
1. This summary of the early strikes rests on Dan de Quille (William Wright), *History of the Big Bonanza*; Eliot Lord, *Comstock Mining and Miners*, both available in various editions; and, especially, on Grant H. Smith, *History of the Comstock Lode* (Reno Nevada, 1943). The accounts disagree on some points.
2. Lord, *Comstock* (reprint, Berkeley, Calif., 1959), p. 62.
3. Ibid.
4. Smith, *Comstock,* pp. 18–19.
5. Background information on the harbor from Margarette L. Voget, "The Waterfront of San Francisco," PhD dissertation, University of California (Berkeley, 1943), pp. 1–12. See also Gerald D. Nash, *State Government and Economic Development* (Berkeley, 1964), pp. 106–110.
6. Two of the pamphlets, available in the Bancroft Library, are "Tax-payers' Review and Objections to the Parson's Bulkhead Bill" (San Francisco, 1859) and "The Antidote to the Poison . . . " Published by the Citizens' Anti-Bulkhead Committee of San Francisco (San Francisco, 1860). "The Majority and Minority Report of the Special Committee on the Bulkhead" can be found in the *Appendix to the Journals of*

the Senate of the Eleventh Session of the Legislature (Sacramento, 1860). See also C. E. Kunze, "How the Chamber of Commerce Guarded the Port as a Public Trust," *San Francisco Business,* Oct. 7. 1925.

7. George Wallace to Latham, April 19, 1860; Eugene Casserly to Latham, same date, both among the Latham papers, California Historical Society. See also H. H. Bancroft, *Chronicles of the Builders* (San Francisco, 1892), vol. II, p. 137.

8. San Francisco *Evening Bulletin,* August 30, 1875.

9. The *Alta California* of Sept. 8, 1875, in rebutting the *Bulletin*'s charges pointed out the necessarily limited nature of Ralston's involvement. The *Alta*'s documentation, however, is as skimpy and inconclusive as the *Bulletin*'s.

10. Quoted in Voget, "Waterfront," p. 14.

11. Profits rose from $92,946 in 1859 to $105,265 in 1860—"Sacramento Valley Railroad Company, Report of the President . . . " December 31, 1860 (San Francisco, 1861). Pamphlet at the Huntington Library, San Marino, Calif.

12. Ibid.

13. David Lavender, *The Great Persuader* (New York, 1970), pp. 85, 97.

CHAPTER 10. NO TIME FOR CAUTION

1. For early mining and milling procedures, see Lord, *Comstock,* pp. 80–85 and Smith, ·*Comstock,* pp. 23–25.

2. Rodman Paul, *Mining Frontiers of the Far West* (New York 1963), pp. 63–68.

3. For the Ophir mill, see Smith, *Comstock,* p. 80; Lord, *Comstock,* p. 123.

4. For early Gould & Curry, Smith, *Comstock,* p. 84.

5. This tale, like the one about Ralston's qualified proposal to Elizabeth Fry, first saw print in the San Francisco *Chronicle* for December 8, 1877, and since then has been accepted as accurate by Ralston's descendants. See note 12, chapter 8.

6. For the telegraph maneuvers (which do not mention Ralston by name although he was almost surely involved), see Frank Zornow, "Jeptha H. Wade in California," *California Historical Society Quarterly,* December, 1950, pp. 345–356; Gerald Nash, *State Government,* pp. 53–54; H. H. Bancroft, *Chronicles,* vol. V, pp. 215–217.

7. Ira B. Cross, *Financing an Empire,* vol. I, pp. 215–217.

8. Data on Civil War sentiment in California is drawn from vol. IV of Theodore Hittel, *History of California;* Milton Shutes, *Lincoln and California* (Stanford, 1945); and Oscar Lewis, *The War in the Far West* (New York, 1961). See also John J. Earl, "The Sentiment of the People of California with Respect to the Civil War," American Historical Association *Annual Report,* vol. I (Washington, D.C., 1907) and Benjamin F. Gilbert, "Confederate Activity and Propaganda in California," MA Thesis, University of California (Berkeley, 1940).

9. William F. Thompson, "The Political Career of Milton Slocum Latham of California," MA thesis, Stanford University (Stanford, Calif.) pp. 101–107.

CHAPTER 11. SPUME FROM THE WAR

1. Ralston gave the Union Club as his address when enrolling in the home guard on August 30, 1861. (Muster Roll 5, Andrew J. Kellogg, Bancroft Library.) See also Dana, *The Man Who Built San Francisco,* pp. 150, 156.

2. Dana, pp. 146–147.

3. Muster Roll 5 as in note 1 above. Horace Davis, "The Home Guard of 1861," in H. Morse Stephens and Herbert E. Bolton, eds., *The Pacific Ocean in History* (New York, 1917, pp. 363–373).

4. Quoted by Dana, p. 384.

5. *Daily Alta California,* September 15 and 19, 1862. Kevin Starr, *Americans and the California Dream* (New York, 1973), pp. 97–104. Russell M. Posner, "Thomas Starr King and the Mercy Million," *California Historical Society Quarterly,* December 1964, pp. 292–302.

6. Benjamin F. Gilbert, "Confederate Activity," p. 99. Oscar Lewis, *War in the Far West,* pp. 173–177.

7. Latham papers, California Historical Society, San Francisco, Calif.

8. King to Randolph Ryers, September 10, 1862. King papers, Bancroft Library, University of California.

9. Asbury Harpending, *The Great Diamond Hoax and Other Stirring Incidents in the Life of Asbury Harpending,* reprint edition, (Norman, Oklahoma, 1958) pp. 5–60. Benjamin F. Gilbert, "Kentucky Privateers in California," *Register of the Kentucky Historical Society,* July, 1940, pp. 256–266.

10. Benjamin F. Gilbert and Edward H. Hoves, "Land and Labor in Kentucky in 1865." *Register of the Kentucky Historical Society,* January, 1950, p. 26.

11. Benjamin F. Gilbert, "San Francisco Harbor Defense During the Civil War," *California Historical Society Quarterly*, September, 1954, pp. 234–235.
12. John Haskel Kemble, *The Camanche, Defender of the Golden Gate*, Los Angeles, 1964. Robert R. Miller, "The Camanche, First Monitor of the Pacific," *California Historical Society Quarterly*, June, 1966. Oscar Lewis, *War in the Far West*, pp. 218–228.
13. In addition to the *Bulletin* story of August 30, 1875, see Nash, *State Government*, p. 113, and Lamberta Margaretta Voget, "The Waterfront of San Francisco," pp. 17–18. Voget states that improper influence was used in passing the bill but does not cite Ralston by name.
14. Voget, p. 29.
15. See, in addition to the *Bulletin*, Nash, *State Government*, pp. 115–116, an account that does not name Ralston specifically but otherwise supports most of the *Bulletin*'s statements.
16. Harpending, *Diamond Hoax*, pp. 61–73.
17. Dana, pp. 190, 194–195.
18. Interview, April 15, 1973, with Emelita's daughter, Dorothy Page Buckingham of Los Angeles.

CHAPTER 12. THE BANK OF CALIFORNIA

1. Eliot Lord, *Comstock Mines and Miners*, pp. 122–123. Grant Smith, *History of the Comstock*, p. 34.
2. Smith, *Comstock*, pp. 34–85 passim.
3. Rodman Paul, *Mining Frontiers*, p. 72.
4. Lord, *Comstock Mines*, pp. 124–129.
5. Smith, *Comstock*, p. 86.
6. Cross, *Financing an Empire*, pp. 238–239; Paul, *Mining Frontiers*, p. 75.
7. Elliott, *History of Nevada*, p. 96.
8. Rodman Paul, *California Gold* (Cambridge, Mass., 1947), p. 241.
9. Lord, *Comstock Mines*, pp. 125–126. King is quoted by Grant Smith, *Comstock*, p. 29.
10. B. E. Lloyd, *Lights and Shades in San Francisco*, (San Francisco, 1876); Dana, *Man Who Built San Francisco*, p. 160.
11. Quoted in Cross, *Financing an Empire*, p. 349. My account of paper money in Civil War California follows Cross, *Financing*, pp. 289–361 and the same author's "Californians and Hard Money," *California Folklore Quarterly*, January, 1946.
12. Dana, p. 153.
13. Cross, *Financing*, p. 350.
14. Ibid., p. 356.
15. San Francisco *Chronicle*, March 12, 1872.
16. For Buena Vista, Paul Frederickson, "The Authentic Haraszthy Story," *Wines and Vines*, 1947; Joan Marie Donohoe, "Agoston Haraszthy, A Study in Creativity," *California Historical Society Quarterly*, June, 1969.
17. For Pacific Insurance, Gerald D. Nash, *State Government and Economic Development*, pp. 92–98; "The California Recollections of Caspar T. Hopkins," *California Historical Society Quarterly*, Dec. 1947, pp. 357–358. (Hopkins' recollection of dates is not always precise.)
18. P. W. Gillette, "A Brief History of the Oregon Steam Navigation Company," *The Quarterly of the Oregon Historical Society*, June, 1904; Irene Popleton, "Oregon's First Monopoly—the O.S.N. Co.," *The Quarterly of the Oregon Historical Society*, September, 1908; Dorothy O. Johansen, "Capitalism on the Far-Western Frontier: The Oregon Steam Navigation Company," PhD dissertation, University of Washington, 1941: Henry H. and Lucetta A. Clifford, eds., "Steamboating on the Columbia River" [Ainsworth's reminiscences], *The Westerners Brand Book*, LX, Los Angeles Corral, 1961.
19. Ainsworth, in H. and L. Clifford, "Steamboating," p. 141.
20. Ainsworth, "Statement," Oct. 27, 1883. Bancroft Library, University of California, Berkeley, pp. 3–4.
21. Cross, *Financing an Empire*, p. 219.
22. A. J. Ralston, "William Chapman Ralston" ms. Bancroft Library.
23. Nash, State Government, pp. 87–88.
24. LeRoy Armstrong and J. O. Denny, *Financial California* (San Francisco, 1916) pp. 20–21. 191.
25. The bank's articles of incorporation were signed by twenty-three men, including Ralston and Ralph Fretz. (Photo, Neill C. Wilson, *400 California Street*, San Francisco, 1969, p. 12.) Within a few months six more men were listed as stockholders (ibid., p. 23).

26. A routine document, dated June 25, 1854, and involving Lees and Waller is in the Garrison & Fretz Collection, Bank of California archives.
27. Zoeth Eldredge (himself a banker), *History of California* (New York, 1915) vol. V, pp. 433–434.
28. Harry M. Gorham, *My Memories of the Comstock,* (Los Angeles, 1939) p. 23.
29. Armstrong and Denny, *Financial California,* p. 20.
30. Dana. p. 175.
31. Neill Wilson, *400 California Street,* pp. 21–22.
32. Garrison & Fretz folder. Bank of California archives.

CHAPTER 13.   THE FIRST STORMS

1. Milton H. Shutes, *Lincoln and California* (Stanford, 1943) pp. 195–197. Senator Eugene Casserly to Ralston, Dec. 10, 1870. Bank of California Archives.
2. Cecil G. Tilton, *William Ralston, Courageous Builder* (Boston, 1935), pp. 135–141.
3. Charles Wendte, *The Wider Fellowship* (Boston, 1927), vol. I, p. 140.
4. Rodman Paul, *Mining Frontiers,* p. 77; Russell R. Elliott, *History of Nevada,* p. 126; Eliot Lord, *Comstock Mines and Miners,* p. 246.
5. Grant Smith, *History of the Comstock Lode,* p. 91. But cf. ibid., p. 59. For Sharon's version of his early days in Virginia City, see H. H. Bancroft, *Chronicles of the Builders,* vol. IV, pp. 51–53.
6. Judah's career is summarized in Carl Wheat, "A Sketch of the Life of Theodore D. Judah," *California Historical Society Quarterly,* September, 1925. A less eulogistic account is in David Lavender, *The Great Persuader* (New York, 1970), pp. 50–140 passim.
7. Judah's proposal to the board of directors is in a pamphlet, "The Central Pacific Railroad of California," dated San Francisco, November 1, 1860.
8. Judah, "Report of the Chief Engineer to the Board of Directors and President of the Central Pacific Railroad," (Sacramento, July 1, 1863).
9. Lavender, *Persuader,* pp. 131–132.
10. W. Turrentine Jackson, "Wells Fargo Staging over the Sierra," *California Historical Society Quarterly,* June, 1970, pp. 103–113 passim. The San Francisco alignment against the Central Pacific is outlined in a pamphlet, "The Pacific Railroad: A Defense against its Enemies," and in N. W. Winton's speech, "The Pacific Railroad," to the Nevada Senate, February 27, 1865. Both pamphlets are in vol. V of the collection, *Central Pacific Railroad Pamphlets,* Huntington Library, San Marino, Calif.
11. Marcus Boruck, testimony before the United States Pacific Railways Commission, 50 Cong., 1 sess., Senate Executive Document 51, p. 3421. Charles Crocker, ms. reminiscences Bancroft Library, University of California. Winton, "Speech," as in note 6. Hubert H. Bancroft. *Chronicles of the Builders,* vol. VI, p. 226.
12. Lavender, *Persuader,* pp. 151–157.
13. *Central Pacific Railroad Pamphlets,* vol. V, no. 2, p. 42, and no. 3, p. 9.
14. Sacramento *Daily Union,* March 4, 1865.
15. Lavender, *Persuader,* pp. 162–163.

CHAPTER 14.   IN FULL COMMAND

1. Books that resulted from the trip include Samuel Bowles, *Across the Continent* (Hartford, Conn., 1868) and a revised, updated second edition, *Our New West* (Hartford, 1869) and Albert Richardson's *Beyond the Mississippi* (Hartford, 1867).
2. Several letters and telegrams, some of the latter in code, James Lees (who handled the negotiations) to William Ralston, December, 1864, through April, 1865, indicate the course of the arrangements with The Oriental Bank and the considerations raised by the early shipments of bullion. (Lees and Waller Collection, Bank of California archives.)
3. Samuel Bowles, *Across the Continent,* pp. 298–300; J. S. Hittell, *Commerce and Industry of the Pacific Coast* (San Francisco, 1862), pp. 440–441.
4. Neill Wilson, *400 California Street* (San Francisco, 1969), p. 26.
5. Ms. statements of Stephen Franklin, A. J. Ralston, Thomas Bell, and A. J. Forbes in the Bancroft Library, University of California. The letter to Latham, October 28, 1861, is among the Latham papers at the California Historical Society. Cf. Daniel Boorstin's analysis of three midwestern boosters in *The Americans: The National Experience* (New York, 1965), pp. 115–123.
6. *Our New West,* pp. 407–413. *Daily Alta California,* August 18, 1865.
7. *Our New West,* p. 335.
8. My summary of Bowles's observations is an amalgamation from *Across the Continent,* pp. 325ff, and *Our New West,* pp. 336ff.

9. *Our New West*, pp. 371–372.
10. Ibid. pp. 340–341.
11. *Across the Continent*, pp. 360–361.
12. *Daily Alta California*, Sept. 2, 1865.
13. *Across the Continent*, p. 439.
14. "Address of the Honorable William Bross, Lieutenant Governor of Illinois on the Resources of the Far West . . . Before the Chamber of Commerce of the State of New York, January 25, 1866." Central Pacific Railroad Pamphlets, vol. VI, no. 5. Huntington Library, San Marino, Calif.
15. For early bank data, including the effect of the move on real estate values and also descriptions of the building: John Martyn Bowden, "The Dynamics of City Growth," PhD dissertation, University of California (Berkeley, 1967), p. 195; Julian Dana, *The Man Who Built San Francisco*, pp. 195–223 passim; Ira Cross, *Financing an Empire*, vol. I, p. 263; Zoeth Eldredge, *History of California*, vol. V, pp. 435ff; Hunter, *Partners in Progress*, pp. 24–27.
16. *Daily Alta California*, June 6 and June 20, 1867.
17. Parrott to Donohoe, June 28, 1867, in Barbara Donohoe Jostes, *John Parrott, Consul* (San Francisco, 1972).

CHAPTER 15.   TO THE SEAS AGAIN

1. Holladay deserves a judicious biography. Of the two offerings so far, Ellis Lucia's *The Saga of Ben Holladay* (New York, 1959) is racy but superficial, while J. V. Frederick's more scholarly (and plodding) *Ben Holladay: The Stagecoach King* (Glendale, Calif., 1940) concentrates on a single phase of his varied career.
2. Raymond W. and Mary L. Settle, *War Drums and Wagon Wheels* (Lincoln, Neb., 1966), pp. 103–106, 249–250.
3. John H. Kemble, *The Panama Route* (Berkeley and Los Angeles, 1943), p. 98; *Sacramento Daily Union*, March 4, 1861. These accounts differ from Lucia, *Holladay*, p. 230, who says that during 1860–61, Ben spent $600,000 for eight ships. Though details are murky, Holladay may have acquired the *Sierra Nevada* in a separate transaction. Kemble, p. 247.
4. The receipt for the stock, dated March 28, 18–1, is in the Garrison and Fretz Collection, Bank of California archives. The missing figure has to be a 6. There was no Fretz & Ralston after June, 1861 and no Ophir before 1860.
5. A thorough survey of the OSN's development is Dorothy O. Johansen's PhD dissertation, "Capitalism on the Far-Western Frontier: The Oregon Steam Navigation Company." (University of Washington, 1941.)
6. Details about the different routes and the costs and miles involved are in Oscar O. Winther, *The Old Oregon Country* (Stanford, California, 1950), pp. 216–225.
7. John C. Ainsworth of the Oregon Steam Navigation Company wrote his fellow director Simeon G. Reed on May 11, 1866, "I find the Csn Co. in connection with the Pacific Railroad are offering inducement to parties who will ship for Idaho via the Sacramento River." The letter is in Frank B. Gill and Dorothy O. Johansen, "A Chapter in the History of the Oregon Steam Navigation Company," Oregon Historical Society *Quarterly*, vol. 38 (1937), p. 315. This "Chapter," as it will be cited, appeared in four instalments of the *Quarterly*, three in vol. 38 and one in vol. 39.
8. D. F. Bradford to John Ainsworth, Sept. 29, 1866, in Gill and Johansen, "Chapter," OHS *Quarterly*, vol. 38, p. 406. See also vol. 38, pp. 15–18, 25.
9. Ainsworth quoted Ralston's letter to him when analyzing the situation for J. W. Ladd and D. F. Bradford, May 11, 1866. "Chapter," OHS *Quarterly*, vol. 38, pp. 315–316.
10. Ibid., p. 400.
11. Arthur Throckmorton, *Oregon Argonauts* (Portland, Ore. 1961), pp. 301–302.
12. Gill and Johansen, "Chapter," OHS *Quarterly*, vol. 39 (March, 1938), pp. 50–64; J. C. Ainsworth's reminiscences, "Steamboating on the Columbia River," in the Westerners' *Brand Book*, LX, Los Angeles, 1961.
13. Johansen dissertation, "Capitalism on the Far-Western Frontier," pp. 93–95, 173–182. See the same author's "The Oregon Steam Navigation Company," in *Pacific Historical Review*, vol. X (1941), pp. 185–188.
14. Simeon G. Reed to J. W. Ladd, March 27, 1867, in Gill and Johansen, "Chapter," OHS *Quarterly*, vol. 39, pp. 50–51.
15. John Parrott to Joseph A. Donohoe, April 30, 1867, in Barbara Donohoe Jostes, *John Parrott, Consul* (San Francisco, 1972), p. 177.
16. Lees and Waller, telegrams to W. C. Ralston, April 9 and 10, 1867. Lees and Waller Collection, Bank of California archives.
17. As in note 15.

18. Gill and Johansen, "Chapter," OHS *Quarterly*, vol. 39, pp. 57–62.
19. Friedlander's operations are described in two articles by Rodman Paul: "The Wheat Trade between California and the United Kingdom," *Mississippi Valley Historical Review*, December, 1958, and "The Great California Grain War: The Grangers' Challenge to the Wheat King," *Pacific Historical Review*, November 1958. The 1868 figures are from Samuel Bowles, *Our New West*, pp. 357–358.

CHAPTER 16. RAINBOWS EVERYWHERE
1. George Gordon to J. T. Doyle, July 22, 1866, California State Library, Sacramento. I am indebted to Dr. Albert Shumate of San Francisco for calling my attention to this letter.
2. Edward McCook to W. C. Ralston, May 1, 1869, Bank of California archives.
3. Robert E. Kelley, *Gold vs. Grain* (Glendale, Calif., 1959), pp. 37–50.
4. Ibid., p. 51. At the time of Ralston's death his holdings in the North Bloomfield Company were valued at $228,000. Cecil G. Tilton, *Ralston*, p. 417.
5. "The California Recollections of Caspar T. Hopkins," *California Historical Society Quarterly*, June, 1948, p. 167. Hopkins, the head of a rival insurance company, despised Hunt, whom he called "a born gopher, always burrowing underground and appearing under somebody's orange tree or potato patch . . . where his mischief was done before he was discovered." (Same *Quarterly*, December. 1947.)
6. Hopkins, *California Historical Society Quarterly*, June, 1948, pp. 165–168. Gerald D. Nash, *State Government and Economic Development* (Berkeley, 1964), pp. 92–98.
7. San Francisco *Daily Evening Bulletin*, June 5, 1867. Harold F. Taggart, "Sealing on St. George Island, 1868," *Pacific Historical Review*, November, 1959, p. 352.
8. The progress of the leases is described in John S. Galbraith, *The Hudson's Bay Company as an Imperial Factor* (Berkeley and Los Angeles, 1957), pp. 166–174.
9. In addition to the sources cited above, see Victor J. Farrar, "The Background of the Purchase of Alaska," *Washington Historical Quarterly*, April, 1922, and the same author's "Senator Cole and the Purchase of Alaska," in the same *Quarterly*, October, 1923. Archie E. Shiels, *The Purchase of Alaska* (Alaska, U. S. A. [sic], 1967), pp. 1–16. Cornelius Cole, *Memoirs*, (New York, 1908), pp. 281–285. "The Cession of Alaska," The San Francisco *Argonaut*, May 3, 1884, p. 11. Cecil G. Tilton, *Ralston*, pp. 110–114. These accounts are discrepant in several instances.
10. Taggart as in note 7.
11. Meade to Ralston from Sitka, Feb. 5, 1869. Bank of California archives. Donald Orth, U.S. Board of Geographic Names, to author, Feb. 7, 1974.
12. McCook correspondence. Bank of California archives.
13. Taggart, op. cit., pp. 358–359.
14. J. F. Miller to Ralston, Feb. 27, 1870. Bank of California archives.
15. Ernest Gruening, *The State of Alaska* (New York, 1968), p. 67. See also M. B. Sherwood, *Exploration of Alaska* (New Haven, 1965), p. 44.
16. Rodman Paul, *California Gold*, pp. 272–275.
17. Some details can be found in Leonard Asher's "Lincoln's Administration and the New Almaden Scandal," *Pacific Historical Review*, vol. V, 1936, and Milton H. Shutes, "Abraham Lincoln and the New Almaden Mine," *California Historical Quarterly*, vol. XV, 1936. Lincoln was involved through bad advice. An adverse court ruling returned the Castillero (New Almaden) claim to the public domain. Squatters occupied it. Lincoln was prevailed on to order them removed by a federal posse, after which he planned to lease the area to Butterfield's New York Quicksilver Mining Company. Miners who feared that the precedent would subject them all to removal from public lands protested vigorously, and Lincoln cancelled the order.
18. A sketchy review of the mine's history is in Robert J. Parker, "William McGarrahan's Panoche Grande Claim," *Pacific Historical Review*, vol. V, 1936, pp. 212–220.
19. Ibid., pp. 218–219. See also *Congressional Globe*, 41 Cong., 3 sess., pp. 1402–1407, and appendix, pp. 132–134.
20. *Congressional Globe*, 41 Cong., 3 sess., pp. 143–145.
21. Paul, *California Gold*, pp. 275–277.
22. Letters from Axtell, Casserly, Hutchinson, and Smith about the case are in the archives of The Bank of California.
23. A former steamboat captain, E. W. Gould, in *Fifty Years on the Mississippi*, (St. Louis, 1889), p. 309, states that Ralston hearing somehow that his old friend "Herrick" Martin had fallen on hard times sent him $10,000 out of pure kindness. Ralston's biographers have repeated the story, but Martin's own correspondence, preserved in The Bank of California archives, puts a different light on the matter.

24. *Congressional Globe*, 41 Cong., 3 sess., appendix, p. 1408.
25. Congressman Samuel Axtell to Ralston, April 10, 1869. Bank of California archives.
26. Worries among Ralston's acquaintances in the East about the effect of these attacks, which reached a crescendo in 1870, are reflected in letters to him by newspaperman Samuel Bowles (Jan. 15, 1870), Senator Eugene Casserly (Dec. 10, 1870), New York banker James Lees (Dec. 1, 1870), John F. Miller of the Alaska Commercial Company (Jan. 26, 1879), lobbyist Francis Smith (Jan. 26, 1870), and D. J. Williamson (Feb. 12, 1870). These letters are in the archives of The Bank of California.
27. Ralston to D. J. Williamson, March 12, 1870. Bank of California archives.
28. Claude Bowers, *The Tragic Era* (Cambridge, Mass., 1929), pp. 327–328.
29. Sutro's career is covered in Robert E. Stewart, Jr., and Mary Francis Stewart, *Adolph Sutro, a Biography* (Berkeley, 1962).
30. W. C. Ralston to Adolph Sutro, March 1, 1865. California Historical Society. Russell Elliott, *History of Nevada*, pp. 129–130.
31. W. C. Ralston to Oriental Bank, May 4, 1866. California Historical Society.
32. Ralston to Sutro, who was then in New York, Sept. 15, 1866. Sutro papers, Bancroft Library, University of California.
33. Stewart and Stewart, *Sutro*, p. 59.
34. Eliot Lord, *Comstock Mining and Miners*, pp. 239–242, 297.
35. Stewart and Stewart, *Sutro*, pp. 60–61.
36. John S. Hittell, *A History of the City of San Francisco* (San Francisco, 1878), p. 365. Grant Smith, *A History of the Comstock Lode*, p. 205.
37. Lord, *Comstock Mining and Miners*, pp. 302–303.
38. Paul, *Mining Frontiers*, pp. 84–85.

CHAPTER 17. THE CITY SHAPERS
1. Alvin Averback, "San Francisco South of Market District, 1850–1950," *California Historical Quarterly*, Fall, 1973, pp. 198–199.
2. Cecil Tilton, *Ralston*, pp. 366–367, drawing on charges appearing in the San Francisco *Evening Bulletin*, August 30, 1875.
3. Tilton, op. cit., pp. 157–158.
4. *San Francisco Municipal Reports, 1866–1867.*
5. Ibid., pp. 484–488. Also John Martyn Bowden, "The Dynamics of City Growth: An Historical Geography of San Francisco's Central District." PhD dissertation (University of California, Berkeley, 1967), pp. 276–282; and Gunter Barth, "Metropolitism and Urban Elites in the Far West," in F. C. Jaher (ed.), *The Age of Industrialism in America* (New York, 1968), pp. 158–171.
6. *Charles D. Carter's Real Estate Circular*, issues of May, 1868, through July, 1868.
7. Asbury Harpending, *The Great Diamond Hoax* (reprint edition, University of Oklahoma Press, Norman, Okla., 1958) pp. 86–87.
8. Barth, as in note 5 above.
9. Harpending, *Diamond Hoax*, p. 84. Bowden, as in note 5 above, pp. 290, 293.
10. John S. Hittell, *A History of the City of San Francisco* (San Francisco, 1878), pp. 372ff.
11. Ibid., p. 311. Harpending, *Diamond Hoax*, pp. 81–82. *Carter's Real Estate Circular*, Dec., 1868. Carter says Harpending paid only $100,000 for Woodworth's lot. He does not say what Woodworth had been asking originally.
12. Barth, as in note 5 above. Harpending, *Diamond Hoax*, pp. 103—104.
13. Harpending, *Diamond Hoax*, pp. 104–111.
14. *Carter's Real Estate Circular*, Oct. 1868.
15. Stuart Daggett, *Chapters on the History of the Southern Pacific Railroad* (New York, 1922), pp. 98–99.
16. Bowden, as in note 5 above, pp. 288–290.
17. Data from Dr. Albert Shumate of San Francisco, who is preparing a biography of Gordon.

CHAPTER 18. EXTRAVAGANCES
1. A. A. Cohen, "Reminiscences," Bancroft Library, reprinted in Dana, *The Man Who Built San Francisco*, pp. 381–382. Harpending, *Diamond Hoax*, p. 87.
2. Constance Estella Smith, "The Design and Furnishings of Belmont . . ." MA thesis (San Jose State College, 1965), pp. 26–30.
3. Dana, *The Man Who Built San Francisco*, p. 222.
4. Alan Gowans, *Images of American Living* (Philadelphia and New York, 1964), p. 14. See also Harold Kirker, *California's Architectural Frontier* (San Marino, California, 1960), pp. 53–69.

5. The descriptions of the house are drawn primarily from Smith, note 2 above. See also Dana, pp. 213–215, and Marian Goodman, "Ralston's Magnificent Mansion," *Peninsula Midweek*, April 15, 1967.
6. Clifford Drury, "Anson Burlingame," *Pacific Historian*, summer 1971, pp. 35–37. Dana, pp. 247–249.
7. Ralston to James Macdonald, Feb. 3, 1869. Bank of California archives.
8. Gertrude Atherton, *Golden Gate Country* (New York, 1945), p. 218.
9. Ralston's granddaughter, Dorothy Page Buckingham, told the story to the writer during an interview on April 15, 1973.
10. Descriptions of the theater are drawn primarily from Edmond M. Gagey, *The San Francisco Stage* (New York, 1950), pp. 103–114 passim and Lois F. Rodecape, "Tom Maguire, Napoleon of the Stage," *California Historical Quarterly*, June, 1942, pp. 161–166.
11. Constance Rourke, *Troupers of the Gold Coast* (New York, 1928), pp. 208–213. *Charles D. Carter's Real Estate Circular*, Sept. 1969.
12. She was in Paris by April, 1869. Mrs. F. Henschell to Ralston, April 5, 1869.
13. Dana, pp. 245, 288–290.
14. T. Scott Stewart to Ralston, May 25, 1869, and March 18, 1870. Bank of California archives.
15. San Francisco *Chronicle*, Dec. 8, 1877.
16. Senator Eugene Casserly to Ralston, Sept. 22, 1869. Bank of California archives.
17. Frederick Macondray to an unidentified correspondent, Sept. 21, 1869. Huntington letters, vol. I, Huntington Library, San Marino, Calif.

CHAPTER 19. THE RAILROAD MORASS
1. Eliot Lord, *Comstock Mining and Miners*, pp. 268–277, says 34 died. Grant Smith, *History of the Comstock*, pp. 122–123, says 37. George D. Lyman, *Ralston's Ring*, pp. 135–137, says 45, as does Russell Elliott, *History of Nevada*, p. 131.
2. Lord, *Comstock*, p. 278.
3. Rodman Paul, *Mining Frontiers of the Far West*, p. 74.
4. Lord, *Comstock*, pp. 302–305. Smith, *Comstock*, pp. 93ff.
5. The document is dated simply May 10—no year. However, it is typical enough of the grim mood of 1869 that I include it here.
6. Elliott, *History of Nevada*, p. 126.
7. Minute book of the Virginia & Truckee Railroad, Special Collections Dept., Getchell Library, University of Nevada, pp. 1–4, 8. I have also drawn on Cecil G. Tilton, *William Ralston*, pp. 149–153, and Gilbert H. Kneiss, *Bonanza Railroads* (Stanford, California, 1941), pp. 53–61.
8. Quoted in Kneiss, pp. 55–56.
9. Minute Book, Virginia & Truckee Railroad, pp. 9–24.
10. Ibid., pp. 58–59.
11. Convenient summaries of the complex struggles between the railroads are in O. O. Winther, *The Old Oregon Country* (Stanford, California, 1950), pp. 294–297, and David Lavender, *Land of Giants* (New York, 1958), pp. 356–360.
12. S. A. Clarke, "The Oregon Central Railroad," *Quarterly of the Oregon Historical Society*, June 1906, p. 134. David M. Ellis, "The Oregon California Railroad Land Grants," *Pacific Northwest Quarterly*, October, 1948, pp. 253–255.
13. Holladay to C. Temple Emmett, Sept. 24, 1869, letterbook 5, pp. 114–116, Holladay Collection, Oregon Historical Society, Portland.
14. Huntington to Mark Hopkins, Oct. 26, 1867, in vol. I of *Letters from Collis P. Huntington to Mark Hopkins et al., August 20, 1867, to August 5, 1869* (New York, 1892). A copy of this very rare book is at the Huntington Library. See also George T. Clark, *Leland Stanford* (Stanford, Cal., 1931), pp. 224–225. Julian Dana, *The Man Who Built San Francisco*, p. 229.
15. Lavender, *The Great Persuader*, pp. 247, 258; Clark, *Stanford*, pp. 235–236.
16. Huntington to Hopkins, March 7 and April 21, 1870, and to C. Crocker, June 9, 1870, in vol. II of *Letters from Collis P. Huntington . . . August 5, 1869 to March 26, 1873*. (See note 14 above.) Other references to the bond issues, showing Ralston's awareness of what was going on, are W. S. Halsey, Holladay's New York agent, to J. B. Dickenson, Sept.—1869; Holladay to William Norris, Oct. 27, 1869, and May 4, 1870, all in letterbook 5, Holladay Collection, Oregon Historical Society, Portland.
17. Ralston's participation in the purchase emerged during a lawsuit, *The Central Pacific Railroad Company* v. *Alfred A. Cohen*. Transcripts of documents concerning the case are in the Huntington Library, San Marino, Calif.
18. Data on the Central Pacific's acquisitions are in Lavender, *The Great Persuader*, pp. 212–224 passim. For Modesto: Tilton, *Ralston*, p. 177.

19. Kneiss, *Bonanza Railroads*, p. 47.
20. John H. White, Jr., "The Railroad Reaches California," *California Historical Quarterly*, Summer 1973, pp. 138–139.
21. Thomas Brown to Mark Hopkins, May 8, 1869. Hopkins Correspondence, vol. X, Stanford University Ms. Collections. Although the letter is signed by Brown, most of it is in Ralston's handwriting. See also Tilton, *Ralston*, pp. 108–110.
22. C. P. Huntington to Mark Hopkins, Nov. 18, Dec. 3, Dec. 7, 1868, and to Leland Stanford, Nov. 2, 1868, loc. cit., note 14 above.
23. Brown to Hopkins as in note 21 above.

CHAPTER 20. *NOT ENOUGH GOLD*
 1. Stanford interview, San Francisco *Chronicle*, Sept. 8, 1875.
 2. James B. Fry to Ralston, Oct. 10, 1869. Bank archives. Ezra Clark Carr, quoted in Dana, *The Man Who Built San Francisco*, p. 299.
 3. Grace Greenwood, *New Life in New Lands* (New York, 1873), pp. 189–194. Olive Risby, Seward's adopted daughter, to Ralston, Sept. 6, 1870. Bank archives.
 4. James Lees to Ralston, June 23, 1870. Bank archives.
 5. *Alta California*, July 8, 1869. See also Sargent's "card" in the San Francisco *Bulletin*, July 20, 1869.
 6. Donohoe, Kelly & Co., et al., (a total of six bankers and three assay companies) to Congress's Committee on Coinage, Jan. 20, 1869. Eugene Kelly to Congressman G. G. Cox, July 13, 1870. Copies of both documents are in The Bank of California archives.
 7. Rodman Paul, *California Gold*, pp. 346–347. Paul's figures are derived from Louis A. Garnett, manager of the controversial San Francisco Assaying and Refining Company.
 8. San Francisco *Evening Bulletin*, April 23, 1869.
 9. Ralston to Lees and Waller, coded telegram, April 4, 1869. Bank archives.
 10. The July date is Harpending's in the *Great Diamond Hoax* (Norman, Okla., 1958), p. 92.
 11. Ibid., pp. 92–95.
 12. Bank of California to Lees and Waller, telegram in code, Aug. 10, 1869. Bank archives.
 13. Ibid., plus Ralston to Lees and Waller, Aug. 13, 1869, and H. R. Linderman to Lees and Waller, Aug. 18, 1869. Bank archives.
 14. C. P. Huntington to Stanford, Aug. 5, 1869. Huntington, *Letters to Mark Hopkins et al*. (New York, 1892).
 15. Lees and Waller to Bank of California, coded telegrams, Sept. 3 and 6, 1869, and letter to D. O. Mills and Ralston, Sept. 11, 1869. Bank archives.
 16. John S. Hittell, *History of San Francisco*, pp. 365ff.
 17. Lees and Waller, coded telegram, to Bank of California, May 12, 1869. The impact of the grain harvest is noted in Charles J. F. Stuart of The Oriental Bank to D. O. Mills, July 6, 1869. Both documents are in the Bank archives.
 18. Stuart to Mills, as in note 17 above. Also to Lees and Waller, July 7, 1869. Bank archives.
 19. W. W. Cargill to Ralston, Oct. 21, 1869. Bank archives.
 20. Charles F. J. Stuart to Ralston, Oct. 21, 1869. Thomas Bell to C. F. J. Stuart and Ralston, Nov. 11, 1869. Bank archives.
 21. James Lees to D. O. Mills and Ralston, Sept. 11, 1869. George Bradbury to Ralston, Sept. 30, 1869. Bank archives.
 22. Francis H. Smith, in Washington, to Ralston, Jan. 26, 1870. Congressman A. A. Sargent to Ralston, May 10, 1870. Bank archives.
 23. James Lees to Ralston, Feb. 17, 1870. Bank archives.
 24. Ibid.
 25. Charles F. J. Stuart to Ralston, June 2, 1870. Lees to Ralston, June 23, 1870. Bank archives.
 26. Lord, *Comstock Mining and Miners*, p. 283. Grant Smith, *Comstock*, p. 122.

CHAPTER 21. *WHY NOT DIAMONDS?*
 1. Background material on Arnold from Bruce A. Woodard, *Diamonds in the Salt* (Boulder, Colorado, 1967) pp. 1–5.
 2. Ibid., p. 7. George D. Roberts to Harpending, March 13 [1871] and a letter from Pechy's lawyers to Harpending, Jan. 23, 1871, Box 1, Folder 4, Harpending papers, California Historical Society. See also Roberts to the editors on the London *Times*, March 2, 1871, printed in the paper on March 24, 1871.
 3. Russell Elliott, *History of Nevada* (Lincoln, Neb., 1973), pp. 103–104.

4. James Lees to D. O. Mills, Dec. 19, 1872.
5. Roberts to Harpending, March 13 and March 20, 1871. Harpending papers, loc. cit.
6. Woodard, *Diamonds*, pp. 11–12, and Rita and Janaloo Hill, "Alias Shakespeare, The Town Nobody Knew," *New Mexico Historical Review*, July 1963, pp. 213–214. The Hills' information, based on items in the Tucson *Weekly Arizonan*, suggests that some other Brown than W. D. may have been the prospector involved. I stick with the more conventional version, meanwhile acknowledging my obligation to the Hills for pointing out the items to me.
7. Woodard, *Diamonds*, p. 14.
8. Hill and Hill, p. 215.
9. Ibid., pp. 215, 217.
10. Woodard, *Diamonds*, p. 13. Hill and Hill, p. 217.
11. Woodard, p. 13.
12. Harpending, *Diamond Hoax*, p. 125.
13. Dana, *The Man Who Built San Francisco*, pp. 291, 296.
14. Roberts to Harpending, March 20, 1871. Box 1, Folder 4, Harpending papers, California Historical Society.
15. Hill and Hill, p. 216, drawing on the Tucson *Weekly Arizonan* for Nov. 11 and Nov. 19, 1870.
16. J. H. Beadle, *The Undeveloped West* (Philadelphia, 1873), pp. 541–542.
17. Roberts to Harpending, Jan. 8, 1871. Harpending papers.
18. Roberts to Harpending, Jan. 20, 1871. Harpending papers.
19. Ralston to S. L. M. Barlow, Oct. 24, 1871. By some strange feat of transference, Ralston's letterpress copy of this communication found its way into the Harpending papers now at the California Historical Society. The document is next to illegible. There is a partial transcript at the Huntington Library, San Marino.
20. As in note 18 above.
21. Roberts to Harpending, Jan. 20 and Feb. 5, 1871, Harpending papers. In his *Diamond Hoax*, pp. 137–139, Harpending suggests that he launched the *Stock Exchange Review* in 1872. However, Clark C. Spence, *British Investments and the American Mining Frontier* (Ithaca, N.Y., 1958), pp. 17, 57 dates it as Jan., 1871.
22. Roberts to Harpending, Feb. 5, 1871. Harpending papers. This letter gives the value of $3,000 to one of the cut diamonds.
23. Ralston's early lack of interest is attested to by his own summary of events to S. L. M. Barlow, Oct. 24, 1871. Loc. cit. note 19 above.
24. Roberts to Harpending, Feb. 5 and March 13, 1871. Harpending papers.
25. S. L. M. Barlow, letterbook 33, p. 417. Barlow papers, Huntington Library.
26. Woodard, *Diamonds*, p. 23.
27. London *Times*, Jan. 30, 1871.
28. Spence, *British Investments*, p. 57.
29. William Cargill to Ralston, Jan. 28, 30, 1871. Oriental Bank Collection, archives of Bank of California.
30. Roberts to Harpending, March 20, 1871. Harpending's tale in *The Great Diamond Hoax*, p. 142, that Ralston sent him a $1,100 cablegram about the diamond mines is implicitly contradicted by Ralston's letter to Barlow, Oct. 24, 1871, note 23 above.
31. Evidence given in a suit by Alfred Rubery against Baron Grant and reported in the London *Times* of Dec. 18, 1874.

CHAPTER 22. BEDAZZLED

1. Details on the seduction of Lent and Dodge come primarily from an unidentified newspaper clipping, "The Diamond Swindle" in the Harpending papers, California Historical Society. The date is probably Dec. 1873. At that time a commission was taking evidence in San Francisco in connection with Alfred Rubery's libel suit against the London *Times* for linking him with the swindlers. Dodge's testimony was summarized in the clipping. See also Woodard, *Diamonds*, pp. 23–24.
2. London *Times*, Aug. 28 and 29, 1872, and Dec. 24, 1874. Woodard, *Diamonds*, p. 24.
3. The proportions appear in contracts drawn up in New York on October 31, 1871. Harpending papers.
4. Asbury Harpending, *Diamond Hoax*, pp. 146–147, states that before he arrived in San Francisco, Ralston sent two investigators—"my impression is that David Colton was one"—to the fields (the men were taken in blindfolded) and that their report "set Ralston and his associates wild." Harpending dates the trip as occurring while he was still in London, i. e., March. He forgot his geography. Because of winter conditions no trip into that area would have been possible.
   More modern accounts (for instance, A. J. Liebling, "Annals of Crime, the Amer-

ican Golconda," *The New Yorker*, Nov. 16, 1940) say that *after* Arnold and Slack had returned with their first big sack of stones, Ralston prevailed on the pair to take Colton to the fields. The timing of the trip is better in this version, but that's all. If Ralston ever received a report that packed any kind of weight, he surely would have mentioned it to S. L. M. Barlow when trying to convince that shrewd lawyer of the field's authenticity. His letters to Barlow (Barlow papers, Huntington Library, San Marino, Calif.) are devoid of such references. In my opinion the fields had not yet been salted and no outsider saw them until Arnold led in the Janin party in June, 1872.

5. Albert V. House, "The Samuel Latham Mitchill Barlow Papers," *Huntington Library Quarterly*, August, 1965.
6. Barlow to Lees and Waller, Oct. 16, 1871, and a retrospective letter, Barlow to Samuel Butterworth, May 2, 1873. Barlow papers, Huntington Library.
7. As in note 19, chapter 21.
8. Woodard, *Diamonds*, pp. 26–28.
9. The agreements, dated Oct. 31, 1871, are among the Harpending papers at the California Historical Society. See also Woodard, *Diamonds*, pp. 28–29.
10. Woodard, *Diamonds*, pp. 29–30.
11. Ibid., p. 31. London *Times*, August 30, 1872; Jan. 13, 1875.
12. Barlow to Ralston, Jan. 10 and 24, 1872. Barlow letterbook, Huntington Library.
13. Butler to Barlow, Dec. 8, 1871. Box 73, Barlow papers.
14. The search can be followed in Barlow letterbook 21, pp. 737, 783, 785. Huntington Library.
15. Roberts to Harpending, March 18, 1872. Harpending papers, California Historical Society.
16. Barlow to Harpending, April 13, 1872; Slack to Harpending, April 26, 1872. Folder 5, Box 1, Harpending papers. Rubery testimony, London *Times*, Dec. 19, 1874, p. 11, col. 4.
17. Barlow letterbook 22, pp. 580, 594, 885.
18. Ralston to A. Harpending and George Dodge in New York, April 29, 1872. Harpending papers.
19. Rubery testimony, London *Times*, Dec. 19, 1874.
20. Woodard, *Diamonds*, p. 36.
21. Rubery's account of the trip is in the London *Times*, Dec. 19, p. 11. See also the *Mining and Scientific Press*, Dec. 14, 1872; Harpending, *Diamond Hoax*, pp. 155–159; Woodard, *Diamonds*, pp. 37–41.
22. On July 20, 1872, Arnold gave Harpending a power of attorney to collect Lent's $75,000 draft and Roberts' $150,000 note. He also authorized Harpending to handle his remaining 3,750 shares of Golconda Mining Company stock. Harpending papers. See also Woodard, *Diamonds*, p. 43, and Harpending, *Diamond Hoax*, p. 165.
23. Harpending, *Diamond Hoax*, p. 187, says that Slack disappeared after the summer trip to Colorado and intimates that he may have been slain by Arnold. Actually Slack stayed in Kentucky for a period (an unsigned letter from Elizabethtown, Ky., March 23, 1873, Harpending papers). He then moved to St. Louis and bought a firm that manufactured coffins, went broke, and joined a mining rush to White Oaks, N.M., where he died in 1896. Woodard, *Diamonds*, pp. 169–172.
24. Ibid., pp. 45–46.
25. Ibid., pp. 45, 91.
26. Ibid., p. 58.
27. Frank Hall, *History of Colorado* (Chicago, 1890), vol. II, pp. 126–146, is devoted to the frenzy in that state alone. See also Woodard, *Diamonds*, pp. 85–96.
28. Arnold, in Laramie, Wyo., to Harpending, Aug. 18, 1872. Harpending papers. Henry Janin, "A Brief Statement of My Part in the Unfortunate Diamond Affair." (Pamphlet, privately printed, no place or date.)
29. London *Times*, Aug. 27, 28, 29, 30, 1872.
30. Barlow to Ralston, Aug. 30, 1872. Barlow letterbook 23.
31. Woodard, *Diamonds*, pp. 73–83.
32. Barlow to illegible, Oct. 7, 1872. Barlow papers.
33. Firsthand accounts of the exposure include Clarence King to Brig. Gen. A. A. Humphreys, Chief of Engineers, U.S. Army, Nov. 27, 1872, Record Group 77, National Archives. S. F. Emmons, "Records of the Geological Survey, Geological Notebook 1113," Record Group 57, National Archives. Allen D. Wilson, "The Great California Diamond Mines," *Overland Monthly*, NS, vol. 43, April, 1904.
34. Barlow to Wm. Lent, March 26 and May 2, 1873. Barlow papers.
35. Barlow to Ralston, Dec. 11, 1872. Janin to Barlow, Jan. 24, 1873. Barlow papers.
36. Roberts to Harpending, June 18, 1873. Harpending papers, Harpending, *Diamond Hoax*, p. 193.

37. Roberts to Harpending, July 4, and Dec. 11 [1873], Box 1, Folder 6, Harpending papers, California Historical Society.

CHAPTER 23. COIN OF TWO REALMS

1. Russell Elliott, *History of Nevada*, pp. 128–129; Grant Smith, *The History of the Comstock Lode*, pp. 130–131; Lord, *Comstock*, pp. 283–285.
2. "The California Recollections of Caspar T. Hopkins," *California Historical Quarterly*, Sept., 1948, p. 270.
3. W. C. Ralston to R. G. Dun, Dec. 27, 1871. Bank of California archives.
4. P. Campbell in London to W. C. Ralston, Oct. 12, 1871. Bank archives.
5. Tilton, *Ralston*, pp. 202–207. A copy of the invitation is in the Bancroft Library, C–B 814:3.
6. T. Ellard Bean, president of the Bank of San Jose, to W. C. Ralston, Jan. 22, 1872, enclosing a clipping from the San Jose newspaper. Bank archives.
7. James McDonell, in Hong Kong, to W. C. Ralston, intermittently April 12, 1872, through July 26, 1872. William Cargill, in Yokohama, to Ralston, March 26, 1872. Bank archives.
8. Lina Fergusson Browne, *J. Ross Browne, His Letters, Journals & Writings* (University of New Mexico Press, 1969). Browne was the promoter of the expedition. When it failed he repaid the $5,000 advanced by Richthofen's backers, simply because "I persuaded them into it and they lost . . . I care less about money and can bear it better."
9. William Cargill to W. C. Ralston, Oct. 12 and Nov. 3, 1871. Bank archives.
10. William Alvord to Benjamin Alvord, quoted by George D. Lyman, *Ralston's Ring*, p. 210. Ralston to Mark Hopkins, Jan. 23, 1872. Vol. II, Hopkins Correspondence, Stanford University Library.
11. T. F. M. Adams and Awao Hoshii, *A Financial History of Modern Japan* (Tokyo, 1964), p. 5.
12. The original contract is in the archives of The Bank of California.
13. Ralston to Jay Cook (sic) May 3, 1872. Bank archives.
14. E. Herbert Norman, *Japan's Emergence as a Modern State* (New York, 1940), p. 115.
15. Ibid., p. 114. For examples of foreign pressure, see Edwin Reischauer, *Japan: The Story of a Nation* (New York, 1970), pp. 130ff. For Japan's preference for Americans, Ralston to Secretary of State Hamilton Fish, May 3, 1872. Bank archives.
16. John Robertson to Ralston, March 26 and Aug. 22, 1872. Charles F. J. Stuart to Ralston, April 26 and May 18, 1872; William Anderson to Ralston, May 16, 1872. Bank archives.
17. Ralston to Cook[e] and Fish as in notes 13 and 15 above. Ralston to James Lees, May 3, 1872. Bank archives.
18. Elliott, *History of Nevada*, p. 135. Smith, *Comstock*, pp. 137–138.
19. James B. Fry to Ralston, Oct. 24, 1869. Bank archives.
20. Newspaper accounts concerning the matter are the San Francisco *Chronicle*, May 8, 9, and 11, 1872, and the *Virginia City Enterprise*, May 9 and 10, 1872. Summaries are in Lyman, *Ralston's Ring*, pp. 212–218, and Tilton, *Ralston*, p. 276.
21. James Lees to Ralston, June 10, 1872. Bank archives.
22. "Memorandum," Ralston to Mills, Sept. 8, 1872. Bank archives.
23. Elliott, *History of Nevada*, p. 162. Kneiss, *Bonanza Railroads*, p. 68. Minute Book, Virginia and Truckee Railroad; a condensed copy is in the archives of The Bank of California.
24. John J. Knox to W. C. Ralston, Nov. 1, 1869. Bank archives. John M. Willem, Jr., *The United States Trade Dollar* (New York, 1959), pp. 61–62.
25. The lobbyists included Washington banker W. S. Huntington and ex-congressman Robert J. Stevens. Huntington to W. C. Ralston, Dec. 29, 1870; Jan. 11 and 25, 1871. Stevens to Ralston, Dec. 11, 1870. For the payments to Linderman, Linderman to Ralston, March 26, 1871, and Ralston's reply, April 5, 1871, all in the archives of The Bank of California. For general data on the bill: Walter Nugent, *Money and American Society*, (New York, 1968) pp. 59–161 passim; Allen Weinstein, *Prelude to Populism* (New Haven, 1970) pp. 8–32; Don Taxay, *The United States Mint and Coinage* (New York, 1966), pp. 249–260.
26. Linderman to W. C. Ralston, May 19, 1872; Ralston to George B. Williams, June 7, 1872. Bank archives.
27. Linderman to W. C. Ralston, March 9, 1873. Bank archives.
28. Letters in the bank archives from William Cargill, John Robertson, and James McDonell, to W. C. Ralston, intermittently from May 10, 1873, through 1874 indicated the activities involved in having the trade dollars accepted.
29. George B. Williams to W. C. Ralston, Aug. 31, 1873, and Nov. 3, 1874. Archives of The Bank of California. Theo Dierks of Fairfax to California, various communications, 1973–74, to the author concerning the cabinet that supposedly came from the Emperor.

CHAPTER 24. SOFT SPOTS
1. Statistics from J. S. Hittell, *History of San Francisco* (San Francisco, 1878); pp. 360–390 passim; Ira B. Cross, *Financing an Empire* (Chicago, 1927) pp. 367–370; Oscar Lewis and Carroll D. Hall, *Bonanza Inn* (New York, 1939), pp. 5–7; Edgar M. Kahn, *Cable Car Days in San Francisco* (Stanford, Calif, 1940), chapters I and II.
2. Brother Cornelius, *William Keith, Old Master of California* (New York, 1942), pp. 84–85; membership files of the Bohemian Club, San Francisco; Charles Nordhoff to W. C. Ralston, Dec. 19, 1872; and Ralston to C. P. Huntington, n.d. Bank archives.
3. Matthew Deady, diary, Aug. 5, 1874. Oregon Historical Society, Portland, Ore.
4. Julian Dana, *The Man Who Built San Francisco*, pp. 330–331.
5. David Lavender, *California, Land of New Beginnings* (New York, 1972), p. 296.
6. Robert Kelley, *Gold vs. Grain* (Glendale, Calif., 1959), pp. 47–50.
7. Cecil Tilton, *William Ralston*, p. 417.
8. Kelley, *Gold vs. Grain*, traces the controversy from its beginning to the final victory for the farmers.
9. Rodman Paul, "The Great California Grain War: The Grangers Challenge the Wheat King." *Pacific Historical Review*, Nov., 1958. Cross, *Financing an Empire*, p. 395.
10. The quotation is from Edgar Kahn, "Andrew S. Hallidie as Writer and Speaker," *California Historical Quarterly*, March, 1964, p. 12. Other data on the young university are from the 1872 report of the Board of Regents, printed in the Sacramento *Daily Union*, Feb. 8, 1872; Patrick J. Foley, "The Antecedents and Early Development of the University of California, 1849–1875." (PhD dissertation, University of California, Berkeley, 1970); Verne A. Stadtman, *The University of California, 1868–1968* (New York, 1970) pp. 8–50.
11. Quotation from Foley, note 10 above. Foley gives the number of female students finishing the year as 17. I draw my figures from the Regents' report of 1872, which was printed before the conclusion of the academic year.
12. *Appendix to the Journals of the Senate and Assembly of the Twentieth Session of the Legislature of the State of California* (Sacramento, 1874), vol. IV, p. 74.
13. Daniel Coit Gilman to W. C. Ralston, Sept. 13, 1872. Bank archives.
14. Foley, op. cit., p. 104.
15. Ibid., pp. 124–129. Appendix, as in note 12 above, pp. 233–237, 351–356.

CHAPTER 25. PATHS TO DISASTER
1. Data on the talks appear intermittently in *Letters from Collis P. Huntington to Mark Hopkins et al.* (New York, 1892), vol. II. See, for example, Huntington to Hopkins, Nov. 4, 1871, April 18 and 20, 1872, May 2, 1872, Jan. 23 and March 7 (but misdated Feb. 7) 1873; to Stanford, Nov. 20, 1871, Sept. 2, 1872.
2. Ralston, memo to Mills, Sept. 8, 1872. Bank of California archives.
3. J. S. Hittell, *History of San Francisco*, pp. 390–391. H. H. Bancroft, *Chronicles of the Builders* (San Francisco, 1891), vol. VI, pp. 301–302.
4. Ralston, memo to Mills, Sept. 9, 1872. Bank archives.
5. Ibid.
6. "The California Recollections of Caspar T. Hopkins," *California Historical Quarterly*, Sept., 1948, pp. 271–274; and Dec. 1948, pp. 339ff.
7. Lavender, *The Great Persuader*, pp. 213–289 passim. As matters developed, the SP built from Gilroy only as far as the hamlet of Tres Pinos. It then hopped over into the valley, where another subsidiary of the Central Pacific, the San Joaquin Railroad, was building southward through spreading wheat lands. At Goshen, the Southern Pacific took over the work of the San Joaquin—the San Joaquin was not entitled to any land grants—and pushed rails south to Los Angeles, east to the river.
8. Hittell, as in note 3 above. Tilton, *Ralston*, pp. 175–176.
9. Hopkins, "Recollections," *California Historical Quarterly* Dec., 1948, p. 339. Bancroft as in note 3 above.
10. Huntington, *Letters*, vol. II. To Hopkins, May 8, Aug. 23, Sept. 4, Sept. 28, 1872.
11. Memo to Mills, as in note 4 above.
12. Memo to Mills, as in note 2 above.
13. Hopkins, as in note 9 above.
14. H. H. Bancroft, *Chronicles of the Builders*, vol. III, pp. 205–206.
15. William D. Lawrence, "Henry Miller and the San Joaquin Valley," MA thesis (University of California, Berkeley, 1933), p. 103. "Report of the Board of Commissioners on the Irrigation of the San Joaquin, Tulare, and Sacramento Valleys . . . " (Washington, D.C., 1874), pp. 14–15.
16. C. J. F. Stuart to W. C. Ralston, Aug. 15, 1872. R. M. Brereton to Ralston, July 18, 1872. Bank of California archives.

17. "Report," as in note 15 above. Senator Cole to W. C. Ralston, Feb. 2, 1873. George Gorham, Secretary of the U.S. Senate, to W. C. Ralston, Jan. 30 and Feb. 16, 1873.
18. James Lees to W. C. Ralston, Aug. 20, Sept. 18, Nov. 7, 1872. Charles J. F. Stuart to Ralston, Oct. 4, Nov. 16, 1872. Bank archives.
19. Ralston to C. J. F. Stuart, Oct. 26, Dec. 11, 1872. Tilton, *Ralston*, pp. 301–303.
20. James Lees to W. C. Ralston, Dec. 6, 7, 9, 19, 1872; Ralston, Mills, and Bell to James Lees, Dec. 6, 1872.
21. Charles DeLong to W. C. Ralston, Feb. 16, 1873; John Hagar to Ralston, Jan. 30, 1873. Bank archives.
22. Tilton, *Ralston*, pp. 385–386.
23. Grant Smith, *History of the Comstock Lode* (Reno, Nev., 1943), pp. 131, 138.
24. "Life of Mr. Mills." New York *Daily Tribune*, Jan. 5, 1910. Tilton, *Ralston*, pp. 385–386.
25. Ralston to Asa T. Lawton, May 5, 1873. Bank archives.
26. Russell Elliott, *History of Nevada*, pp. 139ff.
27. Dana, *The Man Who Built San Francisco*, pp. 343–345.
28. J. M. Bowden, "The Dynamics of City Growth" (PhD dissertation, University of California, Berkeley, 1967), p. 297.

CHAPTER 26. COLLAPSE

1. Except where otherwise noted, data on the Palace are drawn from Oscar Lewis and Carroll D. Hall, *Bonanza Inn*, (New York, 1939), pp. 19–27.
2. George Seward, Shanghai, to W. C. Ralston, Aug. 4, 1874. John Robertson, Yokohama, to Ralston, Aug. 13 and Sept. 12, 1874. Bank archives. J. H. Hittell, *Commerce and Industries of the Pacific Coast* (San Francisco, 1882), pp. 464, 602, 673. Lewis and Hall, *Bonanza Inn*, p. 27.
3. W. F. Coolbaugh, Chicago, to W. C. Ralston, Aug. 28, 1874. Bank archives. Lewis and Hall, *Bonanza Inn*, p. 75.
4. John Martyn Bowden, "Dynamics of City Growth," pp. 301–302.
5. Hittell, *Commerce*, pp. 285, 699. W. G. Hume to W. C. Ralston, April 17, 1874. Bland Ballard to Ralston, April 25, 1873. H. S. Lansing to Ralston, Dec. 6, 1873 and Jan. 6, 1874. John Harlan to Ralston, May 2, 1874. Bank archives.
6. Eliot Lord, *Comstock Mining and Miners*, p. 308, gives $50,000 as the cost. Grant Smith, *The History of the Comstock Lode*, pp. 145–146, suggests $100,000.
7. The charge was made openly by the *San Francisco Chronicle* on May 20, 1875, and privately by Charles DeLong, ex-minister to Japan in a letter to his wife, Jan. 31, 1875. (Tilton, *Ralston*, p. 332.) Russell Elliott repeats the tale in his *History of Nevada*, p. 135. The gaudy history of the Big Bonanza can be best followed in Grant Smith, *History*, pp. 145–190.
8. *Virginia City Evening Chronicle*, October 20, 1874.
9. Sam Davis (ed.), *History of Nevada* (Reno, 1913), p. 421.
10. Dana, *Man Who Built San Francisco*, p. 340.
11. San Francisco *Bulletin*, Aug. 30, 1875.
12. Elliott, *History of Nevada*, p. 136.
13. Quoted in Tilton, *Ralston*, p. 332.
14. San Francisco *Bulletin*, Aug. 30, 1875.
15. Andrew T. Hall to W. C. Ralston, Feb. 17, 1874.
16. Yoshida to W. C. Ralston, Dec. 27, 1874. (Yoshida does not identify the daughter; I assume it was Emelita.) James B. Fry to Ralston, Feb. 8, 1875. Bank archives.
17. Mrs. Orville Pratt to W. C. Ralston, Jan. 17, 1875. Bank archives.
18. Data on Spring Valley are drawn from the president of the company's report, June, 1875; Mayor Hewston's final speech, reported in the *Alta California*, Dec. 7, 1875; William J. McAlpine, *A Memoir on the Water Supply of the City of San Francisco* (San Francisco, 1870); T. W. W. Espey, "Calaveras Reservoir," in *San Francisco Water*, Jan. 1924; Ray W. Taylor, *Hetch Hetchy* (San Francisco, 1926), pp. 1–21 and the biased account in the San Francisco *Bulletin*, Aug. 30, 1875. Tilton, *Ralston*, pp. 370–372, and Dana, *Man Who Built San Francisco*, follow Hittell, *History of San Francisco*, p. 405, in setting Ralston's offer to the city at $10 million. I lean toward Mayor Hewston, who puts it at $14.5 million and Taylor, *Hetch Hetchy*, who says $15.5 million.
19. Cross, *Financing an Empire*, p. 398. Hunter, *Partners in Progress*.
20. Tilton, *Ralston*, p. 345.
21. Ibid., pp. 388–390. Statement by Thomas Bell, Ms C–D 346, Bancroft Library, University of California, Berkeley.
22. Letter in possession of Ralston's granddaughter, Mrs. Charles Buckingham.

23. Tilton, *Ralston*, pp. 351–353. Dana, *Man Who Built San Francisco*, p. 347.
24. "Life of Mr. Mills," *New York Daily Tribune*, Jan. 5, 1910.
25. Zoeth Eldredge, *History of California*, vol. V., pp. 437–438. Charles Stuart to Ralston, July 1, 1875. Bank archives.
26. Thomas Bell, statement, loc. cit., note 21 above.
27. Ibid.
28. Cross, *Financing an Empire*, pp. 403–404.
29. San Francisco newspapers for Aug. 27 and 28 were filled with accounts of the panic. The most satisfactory are the *Chronicle*, both days, and the *San Francisco Daily Stock Report*, Aug. 27.
30. *San Francisco Chronicle*, Aug. 27, 1875.
31. *Alta California*, interview with A. A. Cohen, Aug. 29, 1875; *San Francisco Chronicle*, Aug. 30, 1875.
32. Stephen Franklin, ms. biography of Ralston, Bancroft Library. Zoeth Eldredge, himself a banker, *History of California*, vol. V, pp. 439ff.
33. Tilton, *Ralston*, p. 414. "Life of Mr. Mills," loc. cit.
34. The layout is described with sketch in *Harper's Weekly*, Sept. 25, 1875. Reese's testimony is in the *Bulletin* for Aug. 31, 1875.

EPILOGUE: WHAT WAS LEFT

1. The *Bulletin*, despite its unfriendliness toward Ralston, on Aug. 3, 1875, printed a full account of the inquest. Other data are from the *Alta California*, Aug. 30. Dana, *Man Who Built San Francisco*, pp. 362–363.
2. *Bulletin*, Aug. 31, 1875.
3. Descriptions of the meetings and transcripts of the speeches are in a memorial edition published by the *Alta California*, Sept. 9, 1875.
4. Tilton, *Ralston*, p. 414.
5. Ibid., pp. 415–416. Lizzie's "affair" is recounted by the *San Francisco Argonaut*, April 22, May 5, June 23, 1877, and the *San Francisco Chronicle*, Dec. 8, 1877.
6. Dana, pp. 386–387, quoting C. L. Tilden, who said he saw Sharon's accounts. Also Harpending, *Diamond Hoax*, pp. 202–204.
7. Hunter, *Partners in Progress,* p. 42.
8. Quoted in Lewis and Hall, *Bonanza Inn*, pp. 40–41.

Bibliography

Unpublished Material, Including Theses

The chief manuscript source for this biography is a collection of several hundred letters in the archives of The Bank of California. Most are addressed to William C. Ralston; in addition there are a few dozen written by him. Other collections that proved useful are the Milton S. Latham and Asbury Harpending papers in the California Historical Society, San Francisco; the Samuel Barlow letterbooks at the Huntington Library, San Marino, California; the Ben Holladay letterbooks at the Oregon Historical Society, Portland; and statements given by men who knew Ralston to interviewers employed by historian H. H. Bancroft; the last are on file at the Bancroft Library, University of California, Berkeley.

Individual citations, especially to theses for advanced degrees, follow.

Ainsworth, John C., "Statement." MS P-A 72, Bancroft Library.

Barieau, Sally L., "Migration to California by Way of the Isthmus of Panama." MA thesis, University of California, Berkeley, 1937.

Bell, Thomas, "Statement." MS C-D 346:1 Bancroft Library.

Bowden, Martyn J., "The Dynamics of City Growth." PhD dissertation, University of California, Berkeley, 1967.

Briggs, Robert O., "The Sacramento Valley Railroad, 1853–1865." MA thesis, Sacramento State College, 1950.

Carter, John D., "The San Francisco Bulletin, 1855–1865." PhD dissertation, University of California, Berkeley, 1941.

"The Central Pacific Railroad v. *Alfred A. Cohen."* Transcripts of documents relating to the case are at the Huntington Library.

Cohen, A. A., "Reminiscences." Bancroft Library.

Crotty, Homer. "The Great Diamond Swindle." Ms. in possession of Mrs. Crotty.

Foley, Patrick J., "The Antecedents and Early Development of the University of California, 1849–1875." PhD dissertation, University of California, Berkeley, 1970.

Forbes, Andrew J., "Statement." MS C-D 346:2 Bancroft Library.

Franklin, Stephen, "Statement." Bancroft Library.

Gilbert, Benjamin F., "Confederate Activity and Propaganda in California." MA thesis, University of California, Berkeley, 1940.

Johansen, Dorothy O., "Capitalism on the Far-Western Frontier: The Oregon Steam Navigation Company." PhD dissertation, University of Washington, 1941.

Johnson, W. D., "Inland Steam Navigation in California." MA thesis, Stanford University, 1952.

Lawrence, William D., "Henry Miller and the San Joaquin Valley." MA thesis, University of California, Berkeley, 1933.

Macdonald, Charles J. v. *Cornelius Garrison and Charles Morgan*, heard in the New York Court of Common Pleas, 1859 (2 Hilton 510). Many papers connected with this case are in the Bancroft Library.

Miller, Louis R., "The History of the San Francisco & San Jose Railroad Company." MA thesis, University of California, 1948.

"Minute Book of the Virginia & Truckee Railroad." Getchell Library, University of Nevada.

Ralston, Andrew Jackson, "William Chapman Ralston." Bancroft Library.

San Francisco Chamber of Commerce, Miscellaneous papers, Box 2, California Historical Society.

Smith, Constance E., "The Design and Furnishings of Belmont . . . " MA thesis, San Jose State College, 1965.

Thompson, William F., "The Political Career of Milton Slocum Latham of California." MA thesis, Stanford University, 1952.

Voget, Margarette L., "The Waterfront of San Francisco." PhD dissertation, University of California, Berkeley, 1943.

Books

Adams, T. F. M. and Awao Hoshii, *A Financial History of Modern Japan* (Tokyo, 1964).

Armstrong, Leroy and J. O. Denny, *Financial California* (San Francisco, 1916).

Ashbaugh, Don, *Nevada's Turbulent Yesterdays* (Los Angeles, 1963).

Atherton, Gertrude, *Adventures of a Novelist* (New York, 1932).

———, *California, an Intimate History* (New York, 1914).

———, *Golden Gate Country* (New York, 1945).

Bancroft, Hubert H., *California Inter Pocula* (San Francisco, 1888).
——, *Chronicles of the Builders* (San Francisco, 1891–92).
——, *History of California*, vols. V-VII (San Francisco, 1884–90).
——, *Popular Tribunals* (San Francisco, 1887).
Baugham, J. P., *Charles Morgan and the Development of Southern Transportation* (Nashville, Tenn., 1968).
Bean, Walton, *California, An Interpretive History* (New York, 1968).
Billington, Ray A., *Westward Expansion* (New York, 1963).
Borthwick, J. D., *Three Years in California* (Edinburgh, 1857).
Bowers, Claude, *The Tragic Era* (Cambridge, Mass., 1929).
Bowles, Samuel, *Across the Continent* (Hartford, Conn., 1868).
——, *Our New West* (Hartford, Conn., 1869).
Browne, Lina F., *J. Ross Browne, His Letters, Journals and Writings* (Albuquerque, New Mexico, 1969).
Capron, E. S., *History of California* (Boston, 1854).
Carr, Albert Z., *The World and William Walker* (New York, 1963).
Carr, Clark Ezra, *My Day and Generation* (Chicago, 1908).
Choules, John O., *The Cruise of the Steam Yacht North Star* (Boston, 1854).
Clark, George T., *Leland Stanford* (Stanford, Calif., 1931).
Clarke, Dwight, *William Tecumseh Sherman, Gold Rush Banker* (San Francisco, 1969).
Coit, Daniel W., *Digging for Gold—Without a Shovel* (Denver, 1967).
Cole, Cornelius, *Memoirs* (New York, 1908).
Corning, Howard M., *Dictionary of Oregon History* (Portland, 1956).
Cox, James, *Old and New St. Louis* (St. Louis, 1894).
Cronise, Titus F., *The Natural Wealth of California* (San Francisco, 1868).
Cross, Ira B., *Financing an Empire: History of Banking in California* (San Francisco, 1927).
Daggett, Stuart, *Chapters on the History of the Southern Pacific Railroad* (New York, 1922).
Dana, Julian, *The Man Who Built San Francisco* (New York, 1936).
Davis, Horace, "The Home Guard of 1861," in H. Morse Stephens and Herbert Bolton, eds., *The Pacific Ocean in History* (New York, 1917).
Delmatier, Royce, Clarence F. McIntosh, and Earl G. Waters, eds. *The Rumble of California Politics, 1848–1892* (New York, 1970).
Drury, Clifford M., *William Anderson Scott, No Ordinary Man* (Glendale, Calif., 1965).
Eldredge, Zoeth, *History of California* vols. IV–V (New York, 1915).
Elliott, Russell, *History of Nevada* (Lincoln, Neb., 1973).
Ellison, William M., *A Self-Governing Dominion: California, 1849–1860* (Berkeley and Los Angeles, 1950).
Farquahar, Francis P., ed., *The Ralston-Fry Wedding, from the Diary of Miss Sarah Haight* (Berkeley, Calif., 1961).
Frederick, J. V., *Ben Holladay: The Stagecoach King* (Glendale, Calif. 1940).
Fremont, Jessie Benton, *A Year of American Travel* (New York, 1878).
Gagey, Edmond M., *The San Francisco Stage* (New York, 1950).
Galbraith, John S., *The Hudson's Bay Company as an Imperial Factor* (Berkeley and Los Angeles, 1957).
Gorham, Harry M., *My Memories of the Comstock* (Los Angeles, 1939).
Gould, E. W., *Fifty Years on the Mississippi* (St. Louis, 1889).
Greene, Lawrence, *The Filibuster* (Indianapolis and New York, 1937).
Greenwood, Grace, *New Life in New Lands* (New York, 1873).
Gregory, Joseph N., *Gregory's Guide for California Travelers via the Isthmus of Panama* (New York, 1850).
Gruening, Ernest, *The State of Alaska* (New York, 1968).
Harpending, Asbury, *The Great Diamond Hoax* . . . (reprint edition, Norman, Okla., 1958).
Hittell, John S., *The Commerce and Industries of the Pacific Coast of North America* (San Francisco, 1882).
——, *A History of the City of San Francisco* (San Francisco, 1878).
——, *The Resources of California* (San Francisco, 1875).
Hittell, Theodore H., *History of California*, vols III–IV (San Francisco, 1898).
Howarth, David, *Panama* (New York, 1966).
Huggins, Dorothy, *Continuation of the Annals of San Francisco* (reprint edition, Palo Alto, Calif., 1966).
Hunter, James, *Partners in Progress* (San Francisco, 1950).
Huntington, Collis P., *Letters to Mark Hopkins and others*, vols I–II (New York, 1891–92).

Jones, Isaac Wistar, *Autobiography* (Philadelphia, 1914).
Jostes, Barbara Donohoe, *John Parrott, Consul* (San Francisco, 1972).
Judges and Criminal, Shadows of the Past—History of the Vigilance Committee of San Francisco, anonymous (San Francisco, 1858).
Kahn, Edgar M., *Cable Car Days in San Francisco* (Stanford, Cal., 1940).
Kelley, Robert E., *Gold vs. Grain* (Glendale, Calif., 1959).
Kemble, John H., *The Panama Route, 1848–1869* (Berkeley and Los Angeles, 1943).
————, *The Camanche, Defender of the Golden Gate* (Los Angeles, 1964).
Kirker, Harold, *California's Architectural Frontier* (San Marino, Calif., 1960).
Kneiss, Gilbert, *Bonanza Railroads* (Stanford, Calif., 1941).
Lane, Wheaton J., *Commodore Vanderbilt* (New York, 1942).
Lavender, David, *California, Land of New Beginnings* (New York, 1972).
————, *The Great Persuader* (New York, 1969).
Lewis, Oscar, *Sea Routes to the Gold Fields* (New York, 1949).
————, *The War in the Far West* (New York, 1961)
————, and Carroll D. Hall, *Bonanza Inn* (New York, 1939).
Lloyd, B. E., *Lights and Shades in San Francisco* (San Francisco, 1876).
Lucia, Ellis, *The Saga of Ben Holladay* (New York, 1959).
Lyman, George D., *Ralston's Ring* (New York, 1937).

McAlpine, William J., *A Memoir of the Water Supply of the City of San Francisco* (San Francisco, 1870).
Marryat, Frank, *Mountains and Molehills* (London, 1855).
Nash, Gerald D., *State Government and Economic Development* (Berkeley, 1964).
Norman, E. Herbert, *Japan's Emergence as a Modern State* (New York, 1940).
Nugent, Walter, *Money and American Society* (New York, 1968).
Nunis, Doyce, ed., *The San Francisco Vigilance Committee of 1856* (Los Angeles, 1971).
Outcalt, John, *History of Merced County, California* (Los Angeles, 1925).
Paul, Rodman, *California Gold* (Cambridge, Mass., 1947).
————, *Mining Frontiers of the Far West* (New York, 1963).
Radcliff, Corwin, *History of Merced County* (Merced, Calif. 1940).
Reischauer, Edwin, *Japan: The Story of a Nation* (New York, 1970).
Richards, Benjamin B., ed., *California Gold Rush Merchant: The Journals of Stephen Chapin Davis* (San Marino, Calif., 1956).
Richardson, Albert, *Beyond the Mississippi* (Hartford, Conn., 1867).
Rourke, Constance, *Troupers of the Gold Coast* (New York, 1928).
Royce, Josiah, *California from the Conquest in 1846 to the Second Vigilance Committee in San Francisco* (reprint edition, New York, 1949).
Russell, Carl P., *One Hundred Years in Yosemite* (Stanford, Calif., 1931).
San Francisco Municipal Reports, 1860–1875.
Scroggs, William O., *Filibusters and Financiers* (New York, 1916).
Settle, Raymond and Mary L. Settle, *War Drums and Wagon Wheels* (Lincoln, Nebraska, 1966).
Shiels, Archie E., *The Purchase of Alaska* (Alaska, U.S.A. [sic], 1967).
Shumate, Albert, *A Visit to Rincon Hill and South Park* (San Francisco, 1963).
Shutes, Milton, *Lincoln and California* (Stanford, 1945).
Smith, Grant H., *History of the Comstock Lode* (Reno, Nev., 1943).
Soulé, Frank, John H. Gihon, and James Nesbitt, *The Annals of San Francisco* (reprint edition, Palo Alto, 1966).
Spence, Clarke C., *British Investments and the American Mining Frontier* (Ithaca, N.Y., 1958).
Stadtman, Verne A., *The University of California, 1868–1968* (New York, 1970).
Starr, Kevin, *Americans and the California Dream* (New York, 1973).
Stewart, Robert E. and Mary Francis Stewart, *Adolph Sutro, a Biography* (Berkeley, 1962).
Taxay, Don, *The United States Mint and Coinage* (New York, 1966).
Taylor, Bayard, *Eldorado* (reprint edition, New York, 1950).
Thomes, Robert, *Panama in 1855* (New York, 1855).
Throckmorton, Arthur, *Oregon Argonauts* (Portland, 1961).
Tilton, Cecil G., *William Chapman Ralston, Courageous Builder* (Boston, 1935).
Tutorow, Norman, *Leland Stanford: Man of Many Careers* (Menlo Park, Calif., 1971).
Walker, William, *The War in Nicaragua* (Mobile, Ala., 1860).
Weinstein, Allen, *Prelude to Populism* (New Haven, Conn., 1970).
Wells, William V., *Walker's Expedition to Nicaragua* (New York, 1856).
Wendte, Charles, *The Wider Fellowship* (Boston, 1927).
Williams, David A., *David C. Broderick, a Political Portrait* (San Marino, Calif., 1969).

Willem, John M., Jr., *The United States Trade Dollar* (New York, 1959).
Wilson, Neill C., *400 California Street* (San Francisco, 1969).
Wiltsee, Ernest, *Gold Rush Steamers* (San Francisco, 1938).
Winther, Oscar O., *The Old Oregon Country* (Stanford, Calif., 1950).
Woodard, Bruce A., *Diamonds in the Salt* (Boulder, Colo., 1967).
Wright, Edgar, *Marine History of the Pacific Northwest* (Portland, Ore., 1895).
Wright, William (Dan de Quille), *History of the Big Bonanza*, various editions.

Articles and Pamphlets
  (Key to Abbreviations: CHQ is the *California Historical Quarterly*; OHQ is both the
  Quarterly of the Oregon Historical Society and its successor, the *Oregon Historical
  Quarterly*; PHR is the *Pacific Historical Review*.)

Asher, Leonard, "Lincoln's Administration and the New Almaden Scandal," PHR, 1936.
Averbach, Alvin, "San Francisco South of Market District, 1850–1950," CHQ, Fall, 1973.
Barth, Gunter, "Metropolitanism and Urban Elites in the Far West" in F. C. Jaher, ed.,
  The Age of Industrialism in America (New York, 1968).
Boner, Hamilton, "The Bank of California," *The Pony Express*, July, 1954.
Bross, William, "Address . . . on the Resources of the Far West," (Jan. 25, 1866), Central
  Pacific Railroad Pamphlets, vol. VI, Huntington Library, San Marino, Calif.
Bulkhead Bill—several pamphlets are in the Bancroft Library. See also *Appendix to the
  Journal of the Senate of the Eleventh Session of the Legislature* (Sacramento, 1860).
Central Pacific Railroad Pamphlets. A large collection is at the Huntington Library.
  Vols. V–VI were particularly useful for this work.
"The Cession of Alaska." San Francisco *Argonaut*, May 3, 1884.
Charles D. Carter's Real Estate Circular, issues May, 1868, through Sept., 1869.
Clarke, S. A., "The Oregon Central Railroad." OHQ, June, 1906.
Clifford, Henry H. and Lucetta Clifford, eds., "Steamboating on the Columbia River"
  [Reminiscences of John C. Ainsworth]. *The Westerners' Brand Book* LX (Los Angeles,
  1961).
Cross, Ira B., "Californians and Hard Money." *California Folklore Quarterly*, Jan., 1946.
Donohoe, Joan Marie, "Agoston Haraszthy, A Study in Creativity," CHQ, June, 1969.
Earl, John J., "The Sentiment of the People of California with Respect to the Civil War."
  American Historical Association Annual Report, Washington, D.C., 1907.
Ellis, David M., "The Oregon and California Railroad Land Grants," *Pacific Northwest
  Quarterly*, Oct., 1948.
Espey, T. W. W., "Calaveras Reservoir," *San Francisco Water*, Jan., 1924.
Farrar, Victor J., "The Background of the Purchase of Alaska," *Washington Historical
  Quarterly*, April, 1922.
———, "Senator Cole and the Purchase of Alaska," *Washington Historical Quarterly*,
  Oct., 1921.
Frederickson, Paul, "The Authentic Haraszthy Story," *Wines and Vines*, 1947.
Ganoe, John T., "The History of the Oregon & California Railroad," OHQ, Sept., 1924.
Gilbert, Benjamin F., "Kentucky Privateers in California," *Register of the Kentucky
  Historical Society*, July, 1949.
——— and Edward H. Hoves, "Land and Labor in Kentucky," *Register of the Kentucky
  Historical Society*, Jan., 1950.
Gill, Frank and Dorothy O. Johansen, "A Chapter in the History of the Oregon Steam
  Navigation Company," OHQ, vols. 38–39 (1937–38).
Gillette, P. W., "A Brief History of the Oregon Steam Navigation Company," OHQ,
  June, 1904.
Hill, Rita and Janaloo Hill, "Alias Shakespeare, the Town Nobody Knew," *New Mexico
  Historical Review*, July, 1963.
Hopkins, Caspar T., "Recollections," CHQ, June, 1947 through Dec., 1948.
Jackson, W. Turrentine, "Wells Fargo: Symbol of the Wild West," *Western Historical
  Quarterly*, April, 1972.
———, "Wells Fargo Staging over the Sierra," CHQ, June, 1970.
Janin, Henry, "A Brief Statement of My Part in the Unfortunate Diamond Affair,"
  Pamphlet, privately printed.
Johansen, Dorothy O., "The Oregon Steam Navigation Company," PHR, 1941.
Judah, Theodore D., "The Central Pacific Railroad of California" (San Francisco, Nov. 1,
  1860).
———, "Report of the Chief Engineer . . ." (Sacramento, July 1, 1963).
Kahn, Edgar, "Andrew S. Hallidie as Writer and Speaker," CHQ, March, 1946.
Klose, Nelson, "Louis Provost and the Silk Industry of San Jose," CHQ, Dec., 1961.

Kunze, C. E., "How the Chamber of Commerce Guarded the Port as a Public Trust," *San Francisco Business*, Oct. 7, 1925.

Liebling, A. J., "Annals of Crime, The American Golconda," *The New Yorker*, Nov. 16, 1940.

"Life of Mr. Mills," New York *Daily Tribune*, Jan. 5., 1910.

"Memorial of William C. Ralston." A collection of journalistic reports about Ralston's death, funeral, and eulogies, published by the *Alta California*, San Francisco, Sept., 1875.

Miller, Robert R., "The Camanche, First Monitor of the Pacific," CHQ, June, 1966.

Olmstead, Roger, "San Francisco and the Vigilante Style," *The American West*, January and March, 1970.

Parker, Robert J., "William McGarrahan's Panoche Grande Claim," PHR, 1936.

Paul, Rodman, "The Great California Grain War: The Grangers' Challenge to the Wheat King," PHR, Nov., 1958.

———, "The Wheat Trade Between California and the United Kingdom," *Mississippi Valley Historical Review*, Dec., 1958.

Popleton, Irene, "Oregon's First Monopoly—the O.S.N. Co.," OHQ, Sept., 1908.

Reinhardt, Richard, "Tapeworm Tickets and Shoulder Strikers," *The American West*, Fall, 1966.

"Report of the Board of Commissioners on the Irrigation of the San Joaquin, Tulare, and Sacramento Valleys," Washington, D.C., 1874.

Rodecape, Lois F., "Tom Maguire, Napoleon of the Stage," CHQ, June, 1942.

"Sacramento Valley Railroad Company, Report of the President . . ." Dec. 31, 1860 (San Francisco, 1861).

Shutes, Milton H., "Abraham Lincoln and the New Almaden Mine," CHQ, 1936.

Taggart, Harold F., "Sealing on St. George Island, 1868," PHR, Nov., 1959.

Wheat, Carl, "A Sketch of the Life of Theodore Judah," CHQ, Sept., 1925.

White, John H., Jr., "The Railroad Reaches California," CHQ, Summer, 1973.

Wilson, Allen D., "The Great California Diamond Mines," *Overland Monthly,* n.s., April, 1904.

Winton, N. W., "The Pacific Railroad: A Defense Against Its Enemies," Pamphlet, n.p., 1865.

Zurnow, Frank, "Jeptha H. Wade in California," CHQ, Dec., 1950.

Newspapers

The following journals were consulted for contemporary views on specific events. The chapter notes provide exact citations.

The *Alta California* (San Francisco)
The *Congressional Globe*
The London *Times*
The Panama *Star*
The Sacramento *Daily Union*
The San Francisco *Chronicle*
The San Francisco *Daily* (later *Evening*) *Bulletin*

Index

Body type: Times Roman by CBM Type, Mountain View, California.
Display type: Kalligraphia by Letraset. Printing and binding by
Kingsport Press, Kingsport, Tennessee.

Design by Dannelle Lazarus Pfeiffer
and
Cathy Drees